D0860590

Selling Ourselves Short

Selling Ourselves Short

Why We Struggle to Earn a Living ***and*** *Have a Life*

Catherine M. Wallace

Published by Brazos Press
a division of Baker Book House Company
P.O. Box 6287, Grand Rapids, MI 49516-6287
www.brazospress.com

Printed in the United States of America

Library of Congress Cataloging-in-Publication Data is on file at the Library of Congress, Washington, D. C.

Grateful acknowledgment is made to Henry Holt and Company for permission to reprint lines from Robert Frost, "The Death of the Hired Man" from *The Poetry of Robert Frost: The Collected Poems, Complete and Unabridged,* edited by Edward Connery Latham (New York: Holt, Rinehart and Winston), copyright© 1969. Reprinted by permission of Henry Holt and Company.

An index for this book can be found at www.brazospress.com\resources.

Contents

Acknowledgments

One cannot "earn a living" writing books like this one: serious writers need day jobs or institutional support of some kind. With a grateful heart I acknowledge that most of this book was written with the support of a grant from the Lilly Endowment. I am also grateful to Seabury-Western Theological Seminary, its Trustees, and its Dean and President, the Reverend James Lemler, for hospitality provided in conjunction with this grant. At various points Professors Paula Barker, J. Robert Barth, S.J., L. William Countryman, Stanley Hauerwas, and Warren Wallace offered kindly criticism and helpful explanations. I am grateful for expertise so generously shared; I hope they are satisfied by the revisions!

This book has also been shaped by long conversations with ordinary parents who seek, as Thoreau advised, to live deliberately. At a difficult, messy, midway point, I was blessed by the patience and regard of my friends at The Women's Exchange, a civic organization in Winnetka, Illinois, where I have taught noncredit classes for several years (www.womens-exchange.org). In particular, three women read the whole rough manuscript and met with me one evening a week for eight weeks: Donna Doberstein, an independent entrepreneur endlessly vigilant for stringy sentences and foggy language; Judy Luken-Johnson, human resources pro and yoga teacher, alert to wider social ramifications; and Fiona Wilcher, an engineer whose quiet, careful logic kept all of us on our toes. Those were wonderful evenings: every writer dreams of such readers. I hope they hardly recognize the book that eventually emerged.

I'm also grateful for the generosity and the intelligence of various friends, some of whom I need to acknowledge by name. I enjoyed arguing rational-actor theory with Beth Roche, an MBA and at-home parent; I debated child-care issues with Betsy Kocsis and through her with other readers she solicited on her own. Betsy also put me in touch with Betty Walters, who helped me to find my way around census data. I was blessed by long thoughtful lunches with Nan Murnian, attorney and storyteller, with Tom McGrath, writer and one-time editor of *U.S. Catholic*, and with Deborah Williams, editor and gardener extraordinaire. Each of them helped me to clarify key issues at important moments.

Rodney Clapp and the staff at Brazos have been a pleasure to work with every step of the way. Brazos says of itself that publishing books is a labor of love: in this market-driven business, that's uncommon—and for an author, uncommonly wonderful. Particular thanks go to Rebecca Cooper, managing editor, and to Paula Gibson, art director. Interior page design is by Dan Malda; cover design is by Chris Gilbert of UDG/Design Works, with art by Eric Giriat. As we all spend more time reading on-screen, I think we are becoming even more aware of the physical pleasure of holding and reading a well-designed book: the artistry of these people needs to be acknowledged more often than it is. And thanks to my sister, Mary Anne Vydra, for the picture of me, taken at a Murphy family reunion.

Thanks above all are due to my husband, Warren Wallace, with whom I have shared thirty years of this struggle to earn a living and to have a good life together. His quiet warmth and his steadfast, pragmatic support have sustained me. So have the loyalty and kindness of our three children—Mark, Carolyn, and Timothy. One of Judith Viorst's children said once, "My Mommy is a typewriter; I think my Daddy is too." Our three have gone from that stage to bringing me sandwiches and cups of tea. At one point Carolyn copyedited my book proposal and designed a cover for it as well. Parenthood is clearly moving into yet another stage in this household.

Life is good. Hard times are real, but so are moments like these.

Skokie, Illinois
March 17, 2003

Part One

What Does It Profit?

Wanting More from Life Than a Paycheck

Autobiographical Prelude: Of Kids, Careers, and Craziness

In my first twenty years of motherhood, I tried every trick in the book. I worked full-time as an English professor. I was home full-time as the flummoxed mother of twin newborns and a child barely two years old—all three of them dangerously prone to pneumonia, bronchitis, and asthma attacks. Later, as a freelance editor and writer, I tried every arrangement from part-time to overtime. I worked from a home office; I worked from a "real" office; I worked on a lapboard in the car at the sidelines of soccer practice. There were good times, and there were bad times; but there was never any time I'd label "happily ever after." As far as I can see, there is no one best way to balance earning a living with having a life.

Furthermore, every option I tried succeeded or failed in its own way. The success of what succeeded—the failure of what failed—were visibly rooted in the quirky variables of my own household. What worked and what didn't reflected our mix of personalities. It reflected the kinds of stress I can cope with and the kinds of stress that drive me crazy, what we could do without as a family and what proved essential.

Worse yet, even good solutions did not last. Like all kids, ours were on a relentless, helter-skelter developmental path: they kept *changing*. What they needed kept *changing*. And so did my husband and I. Growth and change are part of what it means to be human. (That's a polite way to say that as fast as we figured out one stage, we found ourselves lost inside the next one.) Even if *we* could stand still developmentally—impossible though that would be—work and school present a fluid, evolving set of challenges. As the novelist Anne Tyler laments in her hilarious essay "Still Just Writing," a cousin has a baby, somebody dies, the dog gets sick, a kid comes down with appendicitis, spring break happens, and afterwards the garage erupts into disorder that has to be put to rights. Something or other is always going on in our lives, something exceptional, some crisis large or small.[1]

Bit by bit, I realized that such exceptions to the ordinary week are themselves the rule. The "ordinary week" is a rare and no doubt endangered creature, as elusive as the Loch Ness Monster or the Abominable Snowman. People glimpse one from time to time, but only through fog or after too much to drink. There's a "Calvin and Hobbes" cartoon that I dearly love: the father, sitting up in bed at night, thinking aloud to his wife, observes that if he had known that adults were simply ad-libbing their parts, he would not have been in such a hurry to grow up.

Adulthood is an ad-lib routine, an endless improv exercise. We are not exactly faking it, but neither is life a settled script with an unchanging cast of characters and a single well-unified plot. Still, when screwball week followed screwball week, I felt at times that I was just faking it. I'm a highly trained rationalist sort: I wanted my life to make sense. At the core of my struggles was some black hole of incoherence. Something just didn't add up, but I was too busy coping to figure out what it was. In the middle of the night, however, I would sometimes awaken. I'd lie awake awhile, listening to the furnace cycle on and off, listening to my husband breathing. I would wonder why ordinary life sometimes felt like more than I could manage. I work hard; by all accounts I'm reasonably capable. "Kids plus careers is craziness," I thought to myself. I felt trapped inside a formula whose only outcome was insanity. Would my "room of one's own" turn into a padded cell?

The more I tried to do it all—to keep my career moving, to pay attention to the kids, to enjoy my friends and extended family, to take time for the new neighbors or the elderly couple next door—the harder I tried simply to be a decent human being in all of life's activities and relationships, the more I found myself at odds with myself. On bad days or dark nights, life felt like a zero-sum game whose final outcome was failure.

But I was not failing. I was facing reality, up close and firsthand. When I was a child, I thought it was possible to do what I ought to do. I thought the world was an essentially reasonable place in which ability, responsibility, resources, and power all comported themselves in harmonious ways. If I was supposed to make my bed and practice my spelling list and set the table for dinner, that's because it was possible for me not only to do each of these things but also to do all of them—every day. Alas, adult life is more complicated than that. Adults are endlessly handed responsibilities without commensurate power, authority, or insight. Becoming an adult and a mother would have been a whole lot easier if, at the same time, I had become a god. But that's not how it works.

Parenthood often felt a lot like juggling cinder blocks. Life was good in the intervals between eruptions of ordinary chaos, but if I dropped anything, if I was distracted and lost rhythm even for a minute, cinder blocks kept falling on my head. Then I had to dodge with the reflexes of a Zen Master; and with the resolute patience of a Benedictine monk, I had to pick up and begin anew. The first time I read the famous Rule of Benedict, outlining the pattern of life in sixth-century monasteries, my overwhelming impression was that St. Benedict was trying to create for monks the endless disruptions that parents face. Monks haul themselves out of warm beds to pray and chant psalms together at three a.m.—when other people are up feeding infants, consoling toddlers, or arguing with teenagers. One way or the other, on mountaintop monasteries or here in the suburbs with three kids and a rusty minivan, the good life seemed to demand an uncommonly high measure of moral fortitude.

Oh. Something in me muttered quietly. *Hmmm.*

"What!?" I answered, annoyed. "What?" But it was just a muttering, nothing more, a muttering silence that settled into some remote corner of my mind and commenced building a nest, like mice in the attic. I caught sounds of it, rustling and scurrying about, as I did some historical background research for a book I wrote about how parents might explain and defend the idea of sexual fidelity to their kids. So when that book was finished, when the interviews and travel and book-signings died down, I got myself something like a ladder, and something like a flashlight, and I went searching for that nest and its scurrying, muttering inhabitants. I went back to the historical issues around which the muttering seemed to be centered. And that was the origin of this book: I needed to get a clear look at questions that had been loose in my head for years.

What I was up against, lying awake in the dark in the middle of the night, was that virtues such as compassion, commitment, and fidelity have been marginalized by a combination of historical and cultural developments in the last five hundred years. Our inherited beliefs and patterns of learned behavior have shifted in response to historical events such as the growth of cities, the rise of industrial capitalism, and the development of liberal democracy.

These changes wrought a paradigm shift in Western social ethics: competitive self-seeking has displaced generous compassion as the ostensible norm of ordinary adult behavior. That's the story that this book tells. This book describes both the cultural history and the ethical complexity of earning a living *and* having a life. Everybody knows that cultural context matters. Everybody knows that what we feel and how we think are deeply influenced by the historical past and the cultural present. But understanding *that* we are shaped by history does not explain *how* history comes to bear when we try to think through a complicated issue. As I will show, historical pressures come to bear upon us through buried metaphors that interlock in ways that can leave us feeling trapped, tired, and too often frustrated.

And so, this is a book for people who want to think through the big questions for themselves. This is a book for people who wonder why work-life problems set everyone's teeth on edge. Why is it that anger, frustration, and guilt all glitter in people's eyes whenever the issue comes up? Over the years of work behind a book like this one, people have often asked me what I'm writing about. When I say "the conflict between earning a living and having a life," they react immediately. For one brief, vulnerable moment, their faces sag. Shoulders droop with exhaustion. I've been astounded by how universal that response is: obviously I am not the only person who sometimes lies awake at night, listening to the furnace hum. This is a book for people who have had their fill of feeling haunted and guilty about too many demands, too little time, and not much that counts as genuine satisfaction or true peace of mind.

I have no magic wand. I don't have a stunning new policy proposal, complete with painless financing. But I certainly can shine a good light upon the nests of unexamined assumptions and hidden metaphors that drive most of us crazy. What you do from there is up to your own good conscience, your own courage, and the practical constraints of your own situation.

But at least you will understand what you are up against, and why, and what's at stake. That's the first step toward individual integrity and away from the bleak depths of feeling haunted and guilty.

1

How Competition Has Replaced Compassion in American Culture

The conflict between life and work is a spiritual predicament, perhaps *the* spiritual predicament of our times for anyone who wants more from life than a paycheck. Coping with that predicament brings us face to face with life's big questions. These are the kinds of questions that define the core of anyone's spiritual orientation. These are the questions that haunt us when tragedy strikes, when problems overwhelm us, when we find ourselves hopelessly wide awake in the middle of the night. What does it mean *to be human*? Does life—*your* life, *my* life—have purpose and meaning? Or are we merely the by-products of DNA seeking molecular immortality? When push comes to shove, what matters most in life? And why? Whom do you trust, for whom do you care, for what will you sacrifice? To whom or what, if anything, are you accountable for the decisions that you make?

Work-life conflicts corrode our souls, I propose, because our cultural moment is shaped by utterly inhuman answers to our ultimate questions. The "spirituality" of the 24/7 global marketplace goes like this:

> He who dies with the most toys wins.
> Look out for #1.

Nobody gives a damn: remember that!
Get the most, give the least.
The bottom line is the top priority.

No wonder work-life questions drive us crazy. There is no other sane response. As one theologian puts it, "market ideology has become our way of life, almost our religion, telling us who we are (consumers) and what is the goal of life (making money)."[2]

In what follows I offer a close look at the spiritual poverty and the sociocultural contradictions of these distorted, commonplace, often unconscious assumptions about what it means *to be human.* These assumptions have evolved rapidly under the combined pressures of capitalism, modernity, and postindustrial urban design. We need to take notice, because if we notice we are apt to disagree. And if we understand why we disagree, then surely it will be easier to disregard the ongoing pressure that these invisible presuppositions and hidden persuaders generate in our lives. Ultimately, we are up against cultural pressures unrelentingly focused upon free-market competition and consumption, as if the meaning of life is *Compete, Consume, and Die.*

Although we struggle to lead lives based on rich, generous, compassionate human relationships, we live in a culture shaped by a radical individualism that is inimical to relationships. We struggle to lead lives based on responsibility and mature self-sacrifice in a culture shaped by ruthless ambition and consumerist self-gratification. Above all, we struggle to survive as people in a world in which employees are too often regarded as commodities. We need to protect our own essential humanity if we are to meet the needs and respect the humanity of those who depend upon us, but we live in a culture that structurally ignores or denies the full scope of what it means to be human.

We are at stake. Our sanity and the meanings of our lives are at stake. Also at stake is the rich but fragile cultural heritage that understands how there is more to life than earning a living and greater pleasures than those available for purchase. Compassion—once celebrated both East and West as the principal virtue of the holy or the enlightened soul—has been reconfigured in practical terms as sentimentality, exploitation, victimhood, and a failure to achieve autonomous self-realization.

To some extent, of course, this has always been the case: to the fool, wisdom seems folly; and popular culture has seldom been shaped by the wise. But our loss of wisdom—our loss of a proper understanding of compassion—has led to the widespread anxiety, frustration, and spiritual emptiness which afflict so many people in our day. We have come up against the edge of William Blake's acerbic aphorism: *if the fool would persist in his folly, he would become wise.*[3] We are situated *to become wise,* perhaps, because we have become so miserable. What makes us miserable is the idea that most people are out mostly for themselves and for themselves alone. That makes us miserable because reasonable trust is crucial for ordinary human social life, and especially for sophisticated or complicated forms of cooperation. So when compassion is reduced to sentimentality, when trust becomes naïveté, we are in trouble. All around us, social structures that should support trust and nurture our humanity are instead breaking down and grinding slowly to a halt. Our material prosperity is being hollowed out by a spiritual poverty that leaves us starving.

The Tinker Man's Endeavor

When I was a child, we jumped rope to a rhyme that went like this:

> Tinker, tinker, tinker man
> Sitting on a fence,
> Trying to make a dollar
> Out of fifteen cents.
> He missed! He missed!
> He missed like this!

In many ways, parenthood involves a set of propositions only slightly less impossible than the tinker man's endeavor. No matter how adeptly we manage, for most households with small children there's no escape from the hard truth that providing for children financially conflicts with nurturing them personally. Both duties, in equal measure, are an expression of the basic parental instinct and moral obligation to care for one's children.[4] But cutting back on work to see more of our kids is at odds with saving for college. Depending upon circumstances, it may also conflict with living in a good school district. For households headed by single adults, it interferes with buying groceries; and the percentage of single-parent families has increased 190.2 percent since 1970.[5]

Furthermore, according to government statistics, in 1970 the cost of rearing a child to age 18 was 3.6 times the median annual family income. By 1999 (and despite more mothers in the workforce), rearing a child to age 18 costs 5.1 times the median annual family income.[6] Childrearing has not become that much more expensive. But the purchasing power of the median income has declined, and so has the relative value of the IRS standard deduction for dependents. That's a huge double whammy: median income households are endlessly struggling to make a dollar out of fifteen cents, and so of course there are enormous pressures to work longer hours or to take a second job. Keep in mind, if you will, that the "costs of child-rearing to age 18" does not include college tuition, which for many years has been rising exponentially faster than the cost of living. For instance, one of my three undergraduate children has seen tuition increases of 42 percent over three years; another faces increases of 18 percent next year alone. In January of 2003, the board of the State University of New York recommended tuition increases of 41 percent in a single year.

But longer working hours to cope with rising costs is not a simple solution. Long working hours generate sociocultural problems of many kinds. Psychologists and pediatricians argue that an insufficient measure of lively, loving, consistent, secure personal attention wreaks havoc with the developmental path of a young child. Laurence Steinberg and his colleagues argue that teenagers are also dependent upon generous measure of strong, consistent parental attention.[7] Both parents can be employed full-time and stay richly engaged with their older children and teenagers, but that remains quite an achievement. Unless the parents have either very high income or heroic levels of energy and devotion, long working hours are going to collide with the demands of active parenthood. As sociologist Arlie Hochschild documents, many households suffer deeply when parents prove to be mere mortals, exhausted and frazzled and coping endlessly with chaos.[8]

But part-time work pays poorly and never offers benefits. Furthermore, as plenty of us have discovered firsthand, most professional careers are all-or-nothing deals. "Sequencing" is great in theory: parents should cut back their hours or one partner should take a few years off altogether so as to provide children with the personal attention they need. But it can wreak havoc with one's career. Economist Lester Thurow explains this quite adeptly: "The decade between age 25 and 35 is when all lawyers become partners in the good firms, when business managers make it onto the 'fast track,' when academics get tenure at good universities, and when blue collar workers find the training opportunities and the skills that will generate high earnings. . . . [This is also] precisely the decade when women are most apt to leave the labor force or become part-time workers to have children. When they do, the current system of promotion and skill acquisition will extract an enormous lifetime price."[9] As Kathleen Hall Jamieson argues in *Beyond the Double Bind: Women and Leadership,* "Sequencing carries a cost to one's career. Unless women can translate time spent rearing children into an asset in the public sphere, sequencing means that women of a given age will have less professional experience than men of the same age."[10]

The differential in professional experience and work hours is usually cited as one central reason for persistent differentials in income between men and women. For instance, median income for women with a bachelor's degree is $28,594; for men, it's $47,325. For women with a doctorate, median income is $46,499; for men, it's $70,452.[11] That is, women with a Ph.D. earn less than men with a B.A. In *The Price of Motherhood,* journalist Ann Crittenden argues that, for a college-educated woman who seriously compromises her career for the sake of her children, the lifetime cost of motherhood can easily add up to $1 million dollars.[12] She summarizes work by economist Jane Waldfogel: "By 1991, thirty-year-old women without children were making 90 percent of men's wages, while comparable women with children were making only 70 percent."[13] Such grim numbers testify vividly to the burdens families carry because there is inadequate public-policy support for the needs of children.[14]

In short, parents face very bitter choices everywhere they look. So does anyone else who accepts responsibilities for the well-being of other people. Furthermore, our personal responsibilities to our families, friends, and neighbors can be at odds with our professional responsibilities to clients, colleagues, customers, students, patients, etc. We are all actively responsible for the common good in a world that needs the full measure of talent and hard work from every single one of us. Even after the kids are grown and gone, these conflicting responsibilities continue unabated. The conflicts parents encounter as parents everyone else encounters in other ways and for other reasons. Taking time off to "have a life" is penalized, no matter what the reason.

Work-life conflict is part of the human predicament: fifteen cents will never make a dollar, and no measure of managerial skill can add two minutes to the span of twenty-four hours. We are finite creatures living within the constraints of culture, material reality, and personal mortality. Adept, aggressive management will never rescue anyone from pain, sacrifice, and suffering, nor will consumerist self-indulgence console us. The good life is grounded in good conscience and practical wisdom, both of which require hard-nosed, honest insight into the hidden persuaders of our own cultural moment.

Who Cares?

The 24/7 demands of the postindustrial, postmodern global economy have escalated the human predicament into a crisis. Robert Reich, former Secretary of Commerce under President Clinton, argues that the tremendous competitive pressures of our economy necessarily generate longer hours, higher productivity demands, and what have come to be called "pre-emptive" layoffs. As Joanna Ciulla explores in *The Working*

Life: The Promise and Betrayal of Modern Work, this situation has led to a generalized decay in the implicit social contract between employers and employees.[15] As a result, the threat of unemployment enforces the demand for longer hours and greater productivity. Work consumes ever more of our physical and psychological energy. It is a struggle to balance *earning a living* with *having a life* in responsible and soul-satisfying ways, because employers are not held accountable for the social-capital costs of their demands upon us.

A century or more ago, companies were not held accountable for the pollution they produced. In the nineteenth century, it was commonly assumed that the natural environment had an unlimited capacity to absorb and to neutralize dangerous industrial toxins. For most of the twentieth century, it was thought that the social and cultural environment had a similarly limitless carrying capacity. The waters of care, so to speak, were thought deep enough and wide enough to "dilute" the impact of any particular set of individuals who work such long hours under such pressure that their caring relationships are cut short. But like small towns poisoned by chemical plants, we are helpless in the face of unregulated socioeconomic power. That power now has global scope.

These economic pressures have led to a systemic collapse in our national capacity to provide the care that is vitally important both to the national interest and to the common good.[16] This collapse has had devastating consequences. As so many experts in so many different fields have argued, our society is increasingly inimical to its own children[17]—and, I would add, to anyone else who cannot survive or flourish in utterly self-sufficient isolation, and to those who cannot afford the economic consequences of their own willingness to care about people in need.

Economist Nancy Folbre puts it well: "Just like people, corporations dream of an island paradise where they can get away from it all. Globalization is increasing the intensity of competition among countries, as well as among firms. Both immigration and capital mobility allow employers to free-ride on the contributions of parents, friends and neighbors. If they're not willing to pay, they should be kicked off the bus."[18]

But "willing to pay" is a slippery concept. As economist Charles Lindblom argues in *The Market System: What It Is, How It Works, and What to Make of It,* the market is "a system of society-wide coordination of human activities not by central command but by mutual interactions in the form of transactions." We can have such "coordination without a coordinator" because influence can be mutual, not top-down. But top-down is how the West has always imagined that order operates, and that presumption certainly informs the kind of sociological analysis that endlessly expects salvation to be announced from inside the Beltway.

As Lindblom explains, "Perhaps the philosophers could not imagine controls exercised in any patterns other than unilateral and hierarchical. Nor, considering their own favored positions in society, would they regard that as an attractive possibility. I suggest that, as a consequence, the study of order or coordination became in large part the study of how elites could unilaterally keep the masses under control, and how they could justify their doing so."[19] Elite policy analysts, like the classic political philosophers, seem to imagine that they could move the world if only they could find a place to wedge their lever. I doubt that's the case.

Good policies will certainly help the current situation, because isolated individuals have so little leverage within these "mutual interactions." But policy alone will not rescue us from the conflict between earning a living and having a life unless we are prepared to face the hard choices and to make the hard decisions about which negative outcomes we are willing to risk. As sociologist Philip Rieff argues, to make these hard choices we probably need the support of a positive community—the support of friends who think as we think, who value what we value, who have seen through the seductive salvation available at the mall.[20]

No matter what, marginalizing compassion so as to maximize profits is cultural suicide acted out in slow motion over several generations. Escalating rates of serious dysfunction among older children and teenagers—suicide, homicide, drug abuse, deteriorating academic achievement—suggest that the process is well under way. We cannot afford to neglect the children who are this nation's future, nor the financial security of the families upon whom these children depend.

Despite the deep anxieties of our day, sooner or later we will realize that the "war on terror," like the "cold war" before it, is a chronic condition. It has no foreseeable conclusion. Security needs and costs must be assessed not in the immediate panic following some crisis, but with sober confidence that we can both protect and nurture this nation—including its children. No matter what battles we may win in this "war on terror," we will lose in the end if we are so obsessed by our fears that we fail to recognize that global markets and international corporations also pose a hidden, systemic threat to the American national interest. Profits, not America's culture and its people, are all that interest them. That's marketplace reality.

Not every toxic threat is chemical, after all. Some toxins are cultural. Cultural pressures are both complex and subtle, as we will see in the chapters ahead. That's because cultural change is also an inexorable process of mutual adjustment and coordination without a coordinator. We must be awake and vigilant to culture-based threats that arise not in distant, exotic lands but right here on the landscape of ordinary Protestant America in its more-or-less secularized contemporary form.

As private individuals, all we can do is cope as well as we can with the toxic environment we face. In a vicious downward spiral, however, the crisis in care puts even greater pressure upon individual households, whose thin resources are thus spread even more thinly. At work we face the demand for more work; at home we face escalating demands for care from all those who depend upon us, not just children. We all know how often people need help after hospitalizations or outpatient surgery. But we also understand what happens in an overworked organization when somebody doesn't show up for work. These are not isolated difficulties: one household in four is caring for a friend or family member who is over age fifty, and two-thirds of the disabled elderly live at home or with relatives.[21] Good people—friends, neighbors, kinfolks—will *want* to do whatever they can to help, but what they *can* do is sharply constrained by what their employers insist they *must* do, no matter what. No wonder divorce rates are up, and the measures of well-being (especially among children and adolescents) have taken such a nosedive.

In *The War Against Parents,* Sylvia Ann Hewlett and Cornel West conclude that "our laws and policies concerning family tell a story that is extraordinarily destructive of the art and practice of parenting."[22] It is no less destructive of the art and the practice of neighborly compassion generally. We are destroying our own social and psychological traditions of sustained, mutual, caring human relationship. After the big auditing scandals, that's a trend even the media are tracking: *Time* magazine's cover for January 28, 2002, announced, "So many choices, and no one to trust. In today's world, You Are On Your Own, Baby." In January 2003, *Atlantic Monthly*'s "The Real State of the Union" issue documented plummeting levels of willingness to trust other people.

Faced with this phalanx of unworkable and interlocked ideologies, popular culture often takes refuge in a vacuous, irresponsible liberalism which insists that every choice every person makes, every opinion every person may hold, is just as good as every other. But some people do make a mess of things, a mess that better judgment could have avoided. Everyone around them suffers. Nonetheless, I contend, each of us remains inescapably responsible for making the choices and resolving the conflicting moral obligations that shape our own lives. Whether or not we are parents, we cannot write off the demands of living in good conscience.

Neither can we insist that someone else sign over his or her conscience to our own imperial authority—or to anyone's Enlightenment pretensions to have absolute certainty about anything. Ned Noddings explains this issue with particular skill: "One of the most objectionable features of liberalism, according to postmodern critiques, is its assumptions on universality. Because rationality—the exercise of reason—is taken as the basic distinguishing feature of persons, the one that confers upon us both agency and an innate right to respect, liberal philosophers often suppose that one mind, used well, can legislate for the whole world. For example, Jeremy Bentham, an early utilitarian, allegedly remarked that he could legislate for all of India, and presumably for the whole world, from the privacy of his study. The insistence on universalizability and the power of rational thought to 'get it right' for everyone is central to the liberal tradition."[23] I think there is a considerable middle ground between the authoritarianism of the rationalist or Enlightenment position and the "well, whatever" relativity of a radical individualist liberalism. That merely reasonable middle ground is the domain of personal integrity and good conscience.

The truth of the matter looks more like this: *In any given household, at any given point in time, some choices will be better or wiser or more successful than other choices.* Surely that's self-evident. So is its corollary: *Especially in the very difficult situations that people now face, the best choices will be made by those who have both good hearts and the widest array of accurate information, including all kinds of data to which only they have full access.*

Consider this: no one can buy sneakers for anyone else. Nonetheless, for any given pair of feet, some sneakers fit properly and some don't. Within the domain of "proper fit," there is scope for personal preferences. These variations reflect the remarkable adaptability and resilience of human societies. Such variations also reflect the stunning complexity of the human mind and brain, which is to say dimensions upon dimensions of continuous variables that remain entirely out of reach for any outside observer. Not only is it the case that nobody else knows what your feet feel like. What you know consciously and thus could defend rationally is only a fraction of what your brain is continuously monitoring about your feet, your knees, your hips and lower back, your gait, and so forth. Your end-stage decision—buy these shoes or those shoes?—reflects a summary judgment of data that is both conscious and unconscious.

Surely our lives are far more complicated than our feet. The consequences of work-life "fit" are massive, both for individual households and for the society as a whole, despite the fact that the array of work-life "sizes" at the moment is insanely limited. As serious runners consult with experts on running shoes and orthotics, so serious human beings consult with sages about the meaning of life and the ways of living wisely. (We will return to that point in part six.) The fact remains that our lives, like our feet, assert and reflect a specific, unique, morally responsible individuality. That's a Christian (and Jewish) teaching, I should point out; but it has been widely assimilated into the secular culture of the West. Part of that assimilation has been blunting the sharp edges of moral accountability into a hopelessly blurry normative nihilism, into a "well, whatever . . ." approach to our responsibility to seek the good and to avoid evil.

Between "well, whatever . . ." and the rigid authoritarianism of both religious and economic fundamentalists there is an enormous middle ground, acknowledging that we are each ultimately accountable to the demands of our own well-formed conscience. All of us have a profound moral responsibility both to parents and to the next generation. Parents in turn have a profound moral responsibility to their own children, even if the part parents play in child development is but a human part. Limited consequences, contingent causes, continuous variables, moral ambiguity, and spiritual mystery are among the defining features of the human condition and the due exercise of human responsibility for one another, whether in the household or in the halls of Congress. As Churchill said of Chamberlain, only good conscience can guide anyone safely and honorably through thickets like these.

We are in this situation, I argue, because the commonplace ideologies of gender roles, "family values," and the marketplace render a false account of our humanity. By "ideology" I refer not to some dark conspiracy advanced by special-interest groups, but rather to the ways in which ideas give rise to political, social, or economic systems. The precept "love your neighbor as yourself" was once the heart of Western social ethics. The ideal was not always observed, of course. But "love your neighbor as yourself" was the official ideal, and behind that ideal stood the cultural and psychological power of the Christian church. In capitalist free markets, however, "love your neighbor as yourself" has been displaced by "get the most for the least." That substitution happens gradually through changes in three densely interwoven ideas that have always shaped Western culture: gender, the family, and the market. In very many ways, I hope to show, these three concepts are among the major "parts of speech" in the spiritual grammar of the West.

Sex, home, and money have always mattered. My Victorian-born grandmothers would have cautioned here that a well-bred person never talks in polite company about sex, money, politics, or religion. Be cautioned, then: this book will talk about all of these things and especially about what happens when you mix them together. In part two of this book, we will take a close look at the history of gender dualism in Western thought. As many historians have explained, this heritage distorts and impoverishes our sense of ourselves as men or as women. More dangerous because more subtle are the ways in which submerged gender-laden metaphors continue to permeate and to distort our critical problem-solving habits.

In part three, we will look at the idea of "Home Sweet Home" through the same mix of historical and psychological lenses. What we cherish as our "private lives" or advocate as "family values" comes under the same relentless, distorting cultural and historical pressure. "Family values" ideology situates the problems of households in one metaphysical category, called "private," and the causes of these problems into a second, radically separate metaphysical category called "public." That's a Catch-22 of catastrophic proportions.

In part four, the focus shifts from the "private" world to the "public" world, to "the marketplace." I hope to unearth the deep, explicitly religious conceptual framework that shapes the way we think about "the market," about our own financial success and security, and about the power of consumerism in contemporary American culture. In the American psyche, "success" has replaced "salvation." As a result, we face enormous but often submerged pressure to decide work-life conflicts in favor of work.

As we will see in part five, the ideologies of gender, "family values," and the marketplace come together to generate the Mommy Wars. Bitter, ongoing debates about daycare are essentially a proxy war for cultural disputes going back centuries. Parents and children alike can be caught in the crossfire.

In most books like this one, the last section offers a set of policy proposals. "The world should be a better place," most books conclude; "and here are some specific suggestions." Most of these suggestions are quite reasonable, but most of them are also quite expensive. Even if we still had the money to pay for such things, all of these proposals run into opposition from policy wonks of different persuasions (see Appendix One). Under any circumstances, change from inside the Beltway won't be implemented in time to make much of a difference for the current crop of babies and parents. In practical terms, all they add up to is "Wait Here for Rescue."

But we can't wait. We have lives to live. We have bills to pay and people who depend upon us. Wait Here for Rescue can be a counsel of despair and passivity for those of us who have very little voice on Capitol Hill. So my concluding section takes a different approach. Part six examines the ancient idea that we are accountable above all to our own good conscience. What, then, does it mean to decide something "in good conscience"? We will take a close look at "discernment," which is an advanced form of spiritual meditation practice in the Christian tradition. Careful discernment does not rescue anyone from the difficulty of adult life, but I think it can contribute quite a bit to (a) sleeping peacefully through the night and (b) not giving way to guilt, frustration, and hostility when cinder blocks keep falling on your head.

The Power of What's Missing

Compassion is so far gone from the center of how we think about our society that it is difficult to see what its absence costs us. It costs us a lot, I argue, because no ideology can displace compassion from its place in the depths of our hearts. We face a structural conflict between what we feel in the silence of our souls and how we think we must behave to compete and to survive. Alas, it is remarkably difficult to tell a story about something that is missing. It is difficult to tell the story about what has been marginalized and what has been misunderstood, and to tell that story well enough to make the absent present and its absence felt. And so in the next chapter I want to offer some reflections on the character and the historical-religious stature of the quality we call *compassion.*

I think it is useful to review the ancient moral and spiritual traditions that offer a different, far older, far more accurate account of what it means *to be human* and to have a life worth living. But if you want to get right to the cultural history of gender identity, feel free to skip ahead.

2

Compassion, Altruism, and the Common Good

Compassion operates on many different levels. On an heroic scale, we see it when someone leaps into harm's way to save another's life. But in far less dramatic ways, all of us are the beneficiaries of small, ordinary moments of compassionate responsibility for the common good. The mechanic who replaced the brakes on your car did so correctly. The mail arrives intact and on time. A bottle of aspirin holds aspirin tablets as promised, manufactured to appropriate standards and then stocked and sold in reasonably competent places. The pages of this book are printed right side up, in the correct order, and securely bound. Human competence in complicated endeavors depends upon a deep-seated ability usually called *altruism*. Some thinkers claim that human competence depends instead upon the profit motive and the fear of reprisals, but that's naïve. For the last fifty years or so, even business-management theorists have acknowledged that financial incentives and disincentives are not enough to sustain the competence that arises from commitment, responsibility, courtesy, and care. Such qualities are all components of compassion; they are all manifestations of altruism.

Altruism means, literally, other-ism. It is the opposite of both egotism and individualism; it is the capacity to foresee and to take practical responsibility through some immediate action for the welfare of others or for the common good. "Generosity" is a reasonable one-word definition. "Altruism" and "compassion" are often used synonymously, and for the most part I will use them interchangeably. But when the terms are distinguished, "altruism" refers more often to the motive for particular acts and "compassion" to the general disposition to identify with those who suffer or those who are in need. But that's a delicate distinction. For the most part, the two terms are synonyms.

Without rudimentary levels of compassion, we would be incapable of the trust and the adaptability that are crucial to social functioning. Daniel Goleman calls those capabilities "emotional intelligence."[24] Although we live and work in a cultural landscape vividly shaped by the energies and achievements of competition, although we all grouse now and then about incompetent service or shabby products, nonetheless our survival depends upon the human capacity to care about the impact of our behavior. An innate disposition toward responsibility and cooperative interaction is characteristic of the reasonably socialized and mature individual.

Genuine compassion differs remarkably from a good win-win business transaction or investment deal. In a pragmatic way, the economy is replete with transactions that benefit both sides and for which benefit exceeds cost for both sides. Benefit to both is not what characterizes compassion. What characterizes compassion is the perception that we exist in such a profound relationship with one another that your well-being matters to me even as my own well-being matters to me. Compassionate people care about others.

Religious Accounts of Compassion

"Compassion" is also as close as one can come to finding a word that names the ethical precept shared by major religions worldwide. "Love your neighbor as yourself," cautions Jewish law; Christian Gospels echo the line. Buddha refused the comforts of Nirvana because he was so moved by his own compassion for the suffering. Many Hindus are vegans because compassion extends to all sentient beings; it is not limited to other humans. The religions of various indigenous peoples sometimes also attain stunning eloquence on this point. At some ultimate moral level, all human beings are interconnected, and from that relationship flows compelling responsibility to one another and to the common good.

This ultimate unity has been described at many levels and from many perspectives over thousands of years of recorded culture. Different religious traditions account in their own ways for the reality that all people are somehow closely interrelated. These are elegant, elaborate, ancient accounts, complete with ethical precepts to guide right action and to develop within believers the capacity for right action. Meeting in Chicago in 1993, the Parliament of the World's Religions agreed upon a core set of moral imperatives that specify the behaviors that most egregiously violate compassion: do not lie, steal, murder, or commit sexual immorality. Religious leaders representing an extraordinary array of different traditions from around the globe signed this document.[25]

But it is not only religious sensibility that perceives this fundamental unity. The reality grasped and articulated in religious language is not created by religion but rather described by religion, and so of course this reality has been variously recognized and described within philosophy and within secular conceptual languages (the environmental movement, for instance). Renaissance humanism, to give another example, demanded our due regard for one another as an expression of the dignity of all human beings. To be human is to share in an essential nobility that all of us possess: at this level, we are all created equal and endowed with inalienable rights. Shakespeare says it well: "What a piece of work is a man! How noble in reason! how infinite in faculty! in form, in moving, how express and admirable! in action how like an angel! in apprehension, how like a god: the beauty of the world, the paragon of animals!"[26]

Throughout American history, an array of immensely popular unchurched spiritualities has variously insisted upon due respect for all other living things, including not only other people but the landscape as well.[27] Social scientists interested in group dynamics provide densely technical accounts of the unity we share with one another. The physical and biological sciences—everything from particle physics to epidemiology, genetics, meteorology, and chaos theory—offer still other sets of concepts and models for exploring the reality of relatedness. Neuropsychologists and neuroendocrinologists argue in some detail that caring human relationships are not only good for our health but also crucial to human survival over evolutionary time. We are wired to be related.

But there is no single answer to the question, "Why is this the case?" or "Why are we related in this way?" Physical and biological sciences are apt to shrug off the question altogether as transparently metaphysical. Social scientists, humanists, and theologians who try their hands at an answer find themselves on hotly contested philosophic grounds. In describing compassion for our purposes in what follows, I will draw upon the conceptual and literary resources of Christianity, because Christianity dominated many relevant dimensions of the development of Western culture. Christianity offers a powerfully relevant conceptual language for the historical issues I want to engage. As we will see, for instance, the conceptual basis of free-market self-seeking depends fairly clearly upon radically secularized ideas derived from the Protestant Reformation.

American culture is profoundly shaped by Christianity, and even within Christian tradition by certain very specific strands that are theologically quite radical. But religious diversity has grown dramatically in the last fifty years, partly through immigration and partly from a resurgence in unchurched spiritualities. Furthermore, the moderately mainline Christian churches have seen considerable declines both in formal church membership and in regular participation. Many Americans are "culturally Christian," but without knowing much about church history or doctrine. As a result, the cultural impact of secularized Christian doctrines can be quite nearly invisible to many people.[28] Begging forgiveness of better-educated Christians, I would like to begin at the beginning in my account of how Christianity explains compassion.

Or at least at the beginning as I understand it. At the disputed, paradoxical, intensely poetic and visionary level of metaphysical explanation, Christianity (as I read it) derives our ultimate connection with and responsibility for one another from the Jewish teaching that we are not merely the creatures but more intimately the children of God and thus siblings of one another. We are made in God's image, the teaching continues, and thereby called upon to love one another as we love ourselves—recognizing and respecting that inextinguishable fiery spark of the Sacred in everyone, in absolutely everyone, no matter what.[29] This creation account gives rise to the two great commandments of both Jewish and, by adoption, Christian tradition: we must love God with our whole heart, our whole mind, and our whole soul, and our neighbors as ourselves. Unlike the deities of many competing religions in the ancient Near East, the God of the ancient Jews cared quite passionately about how people treated one another. The central religious demand was not simply to offer sacrifices, observe liturgical duties, etc., but to attend to the widow and the orphan and to deal honestly with one another.

Most of the Ten Commandments describe our duties to one another. But theologically speaking, our ability to love one another and to lead sane human lives depends upon two things. First, upon the image of God in the core of our own individual identities. Second, upon the primary reality of God's love for us and our response to that love. As Jesus scholar Marcus Borg explains, "Compassion in us echoes and is sustained by the compassion of God, compassion that includes God's grief and God's anger. . . . Hitler and hurricanes can happen. But God grieves, and his love supports our resistance and our recovery."[30] In Christian thought, the psychodynamic and metaphysical foundations of spiritual wholeness are the theological virtues of faith, hope, and love. These three virtues serve in turn as the basis within us for all virtues. As a result, Christian discipleship in its early stages focuses sharply upon understanding and developing faith, hope, and love.

Let me explain how that works and what these terms mean. "Faith" here means *trust,* not "intellectual assent to the abstract concepts and historical doctrines of theology." Love of God and of neighbor is understood to be logically and psychologically inseparable from trust (faith) in God, in our neighbors *and in ourselves.* That mix of love and trust is in turn inseparable from hope. That is, we have to hope that our trust is well-founded and that our love is reciprocated.

All we have is hope. We don't have proof. Love is a gamble; life is a gamble. Nobody can maintain unflagging faith, hope, and love all of the time, of course. But we can certainly try. The effort to try is the spiritual journey. On that journey, our efforts are supported or sustained by spiritual practices. These practices are deeply rooted in networks of relationships with other believers, usually with folks gathered together in some particular place for prayer and joint social action.

In the "fullness of time," hope and trust won't be needed because we will no longer be contingent, limited, mortal beings; but love—the greatest of the three—will always endure. According to this line of thinking, virtue is much deeper than habitual obedience to a given set of moral norms. Virtuous actions are those that both arise from and strengthen a deeply spiritual "gladness and singleness of heart." Such singleness of heart depends in turn upon the inherited disciplines and ancient spiritual practices that sustain our elusive but deeply powerful contact with the presence of God.[31] I'll discuss some of those practices and disciplines in part six.

Ultimately, then, faith is very much like a craft or an art. Faith is not simply intellectual assent to any sort of theory or doctrinal claim. Some Christians, perhaps especially those on the Religious Right, will disagree with me quite sharply on this point, insisting that the core of faith is the assertion "Jesus is Lord" or the confession that Jesus is one's personal lord and savior. The Religious Right is thoroughly modernist in its claim to possess absolute truths and objective certainty. My position is not postmodern or even post-postmodern so much as premodern.

The crucial point for our purposes here is the Jewish and Christian belief that as we develop the capacity to love one another as we should, we outgrow the self-absorption that competitive capitalism presupposes as normative and inescapable. As we escape egotism and learn to love, we develop a characteristic variously called peace of mind, serenity, wisdom, or true happiness. This is the "kingdom of God" that dwells within us; it is the "peace that surpasses human understanding." As art historian John Drury explains, "[Love's] descent into mundane existence is the dynamic of Christ's story, the Christian arch-myth. . . . In Christian doctrine and devotion, dying (metaphorically including any kind of loss) is a gate into new life when love is its motive." Christian doctrine insists that "there is no fulfillment without concomitant loss, no solution without attendant problems. And these can be drastic. . . ."[32] And yet, as Thomas Aquinas (1225–1274) explains, "virtue's true reward is happiness itself. . . . Happiness is another name for God. God is happy by nature: he does not attain happiness or receive it from another. But men become happy by receiving a share in God's happiness, something God creates in them. And this created happiness is a life of human activity in which their human powers are ultimately fulfilled."[33] That fulfillment is real, but it is neither easy nor cheap. Life is always difficult, and the good life demands that we face these difficulties squarely and with courage.

Life in the "kingdom of God" functions within Christian thought more or less as "enlightenment" functions—as far as I can tell—within Buddhism.[34] Both traditions would insist that the "losses" involved are drastic only to the finite, self-centered, insecure, and illusory ego—but that level of egotism is where all of us dwell some of the time, and some of us dwell all of the time. And so, both traditions also generously supply spiritual practices and teachings to help us rustle up the courage to recognize our own petty egocentricity. Both traditions help us to outgrow our own anxious, self-centered illusions. Christianity argues that this new state of mind and soul is dependent upon the sustained loving-kindness of God. The spiritual seeker must discover and learn to depend upon the persistent, personal, trustworthy presence of God, who is the light in our darkness and the solace of our anxiety, our suffering, our losses, and our problems. This is indeed a God who makes a difference about matters that matter.[35]

Although Buddhism understands that the cosmos itself radiates compassion, it does not preach a single, personal deity who is deeply concerned about the well-being and destiny of each person. In his marvelous little book *The Zen Commandments: Ten Suggestions for a Life of Inner Freedom,* Dean Sluyter simply begins from the perfectly reasonable empirical observation that there is this light in us, this fire, this energy in us which Christians insist comes to us from God. Sluyter reformulates ancient ethical precepts as suggestions about how to live rather than as commandments given by God. His accounts work very nicely as far as they go.[36]

On the other hand, the marketplace has its own "theology" which all of us absorb just as medieval peasants absorbed medieval Christianity.[37] Its ethical system is not the Ten Commandments or even the Zen commandments but rational-actor theory. Rational-actor theory offers itself as the perfect inverse of classical ethical teaching about human relationships: according to the rational-actor economists, we seek our own good. Period. End of discussion. The economists argue, furthermore, that the greatest good for the greatest number can be attained by each seeking his own desires, constrained only by others' ability to refuse and to retaliate. On strictly philosophical grounds, that's a dubious claim.[38] Rational-actor theorists assume that we will achieve for ourselves and by ourselves a quality of life that Jewish and Christian traditions insist comes only from depending upon both God and neighbor, who can in turn depend upon us.

If the market system functions culturally as something like a state religion, then competition and consumption are its defining virtues—not compassion and generosity.[39] The governing presumption is that all good things are scarce (or that only scarce things have value), and so we must struggle against one another to acquire them. The governing presumption of classic Christian spirituality, on the other hand, is that the most valuable goods of all are both abundant and free. Yet these goods can be neither grasped nor controlled. We attain them not by bitterly competitive struggle against one another, but through generous sharing.

As I read it, Christian tradition teaches that the key to asserting a reasonable work-life balance is escaping the compulsive consumerism and desperate economic-professional anxieties of our times. The only way to do that is to discover the abiding, effervescent, compelling love that God has for us. "The Way" is described in different ways by different traditions within Christianity, by other religions, by various nonreligious spiritualities, and by an array of nontheological systems of ethical belief and teaching. There are sometimes profound differences among these systems—differences that must not be blurred lest we end up with useless murk and familiar narcissism repackaged in novel vocabulary. But if pursued with care, discipline, and intelligence, each of these Ways delineates a life journey toward an unmistakably gracious and mature humanity. The forms of human grace and maturity are many, and they are often specific to a culture or subculture and to its cosmic vision. But despite these rich and important differences, it's probably fair to say that none of these Ways would be the way of rational-actor self-seeking and ruthless competition with one another in material acquisition. The American spiritual landscape is rich with points of worship and spiritual practice, but none of them are shopping malls.

Which Way one takes is not the point here. My point is that many cultural pressures converge to herd us into the way of radically individualist self-seeking. Cultural pressures enforce the assumption that each of us is out for the self alone and in structural, inescapable conflict with everyone else. That's the mother of all Catch-22s: you have to be a self-absorbed self-promoter to get anywhere, but self-absorbed self-promoters never get anywhere except deeper into anxiety-ridden isolation and spiritual stasis. And the solution to that malaise, we are told, is available at the mall or at least at the pharmacy. Happiness is a consumer good.

A *New Yorker* cartoon: a physician behind a huge desk, a woman, visibly dejected, sitting in a small chair before him. "I want to increase the dose," she explains. "I'm still not as happy as the people in the ads." Then look closely at the faces in the next clothing catalogue that arrives in your mail. In all probability, you are also not as happy as those faces seem to be. But is anyone? What, then, are they selling? Ancient wisdom East and West insists that true happiness is not for sale.

The Altruist and the Rational Actor

The economic rationalizing of Western culture since 1700 calls compassion into question both theoretically and practically. In the chapters that follow, I will describe how these pressures are brought to bear upon each of us as consumers and as competitors in the rat race. I want to begin by explaining how the rational-actor economists understand compassion.

"Compassion," the insistently secular economist might argue, is as much an imaginary entity as "sanctifying grace." The argument continues along these lines: maybe religion argues that we *should be* compassionate—or saintly, or what-have-you—because "God loves us;" but "God" is nothing but a quaintly medieval, psychologically primitive notion. God is "dead" or never existed, and "compassion" is the same sort of pious naïveté. That's just not how we are, the argument continues, and it is unrealistic in the extreme to manage our work-life difficulties on that basis. *Don't be a fool: look out for #1. Everyone is out for himself.*

I think that's an interesting challenge—not because I find it credible, but because we all know it's commonplace. But I'm not going to stop at this point to argue about the reality of God. The nature of the Sacred cannot be demonstrated, and I've already tried my hand at poetic and literary evocations of the Holy One as I have experienced it.[40] Furthermore, 90 percent of Americans say that they believe in God. For my purposes, that's a sufficient reason to set the God question aside for now. I'd like to turn instead to a scholar who has studied compassion using the ordinary and quite secular tools.

With the patience and thoroughness of an academic social scientist, Kristin Renwick Monroe set out to determine whether or not altruism actually exists. "No matter how infrequently it occurs," she points out in *The Heart of Altruism: Perceptions of a Common Humanity,* "the mere existence of altruism represents an important theoretical challenge for economic theory."[41] According to the extended versions of rational-actor theory, she explains, people who contribute to charity do so not from generosity, but because the cost of the donation is less than the cost of defying the social and moral norms of relevant social groups, or less than the cost of the guilt involved in refusing to contribute, or perhaps less than the cost (crime rates, etc.) of unalleviated poverty. More pointedly yet, religious people who appear to give generously are merely seeking their own salvation, which they value more highly than whatever they are giving away.

Monroe looks for evidence that might disprove the key assumption of rational-actor theory that in everything we do, we are seeking our own self-interest. Do we always seek what is best for ourselves, never what's best for someone we love, someone we feel responsible for, or someone whose unmet needs come to our attention? Especially when carelessly formulated, rational-actor theory falls into an obvious logical mistake: all motives are reduced to self-interest, because self-interest is defined as the only possible motive.[42] What you are up against then, I contend, is an ontological or para-religious claim about the nature of the human: we are necessarily and inescapably self-centered and self-seeking. That's the teaching about "innate depravity" found in revolutionary sixteenth-century theologians such as John Calvin and Martin Luther. Unlike Reformed Christianity, however, rational-actor theory offers no hope for redemption and no possibility of grace. We are trapped in our self-centeredness.

More or less submerged within this rational-actor view of radical self-centeredness I perceive a second, equally metaphysical claim: human relationships are locked into a zero-sum, cost-benefit calculation. What I give to you necessarily counts as a loss for me. As an implicit and deeply submerged paradigm for human relationships, the zero-sum model can be quite dangerous. It is also highly dubious: it ignores massive evolutionary pressures to survive by cooperating, pressures that various scientists have documented in various ways.[43] In particular, Shelley E. Taylor describes powerful neuroendocrine systems that elicit "tend and befriend" behavior. As she explains, "We have neurocircuitries for tending as surely as we have biological circuitry for obtaining food and reproducing ourselves."[44] Many of these circuits modulate levels of stress hormones that have a dramatic impact on the immune system.[45]

No reasonable person can doubt that all of us are self-centered some of the time, and some of us are self-centered all of the time. The point at issue is whether any of us are ever truly altruistic. That's the question Monroe sets out to answer. She follows in the footsteps of Diogenes, searching now for a kindly person, not simply an honest one.

Tape recorder in hand, well-equipped with a generous heart, an exceedingly quick mind, and a fascinating set of questions, Monroe listened to the stories and probed the motives of an interesting array of folks. She looks carefully for evidence that what appears to be altruism is actually a complicated or subtle version of ordinary self-interest. When a person's generosity could be understood as serving his or her own needs in any regard, for instance when parents sacrifice for their own children or when believers cite the ethical and moral norms taught by their religion, she defers to those like Gary Becker who insist that such behavior is self-serving at heart because it provides "psychic income."[46]

But even setting the bar that high, she found people whose generosity was transparently disinterested: some of those whom historians call the "Rescuers"—individuals who sheltered Jews from the Holocaust. Such "exemplary altruists," as she calls them, were pure instances of a type that she also found among philanthropists and among ordinary citizens provoked into some exceptional heroism by accident or catastrophe taking place right in front of them.

All of these people, she discovers, feel themselves unequivocally bound to others by the simple fact of shared humanity. Tony, one of the Rescuers, formulates this perception vividly: "I'm not particularly Christian, insofar as men believing in the resurrection of the Lord and stuff like that. But I do believe that one of the most important teachings in Christianity is to learn to love your neighbor as yourself. I was to learn to understand that you're part of a whole, and that just like cells in your own body altogether make up your body, that in our society and in our community, that we are all like cells of a community that is very important. Not America; I mean the human race. And you should always be aware that every other person is basically you. You should always treat people as though it is you, and that goes for evil Nazis as well as for Jewish friends who are in trouble. You should always have a very open mind in dealing with other people and always see yourself in those people, for good or for evil both." Monroe's response to his explanation is succinct: "This captures the essence of altruism."[47] As Monroe sees it, altruists are motivated primarily by their sense of this primal human bond uniting one person with another.[48] As she explains after interviewing another altruist, "her actions were motivated by something even more basic than duty, morality, or empathy: the need of the other person to be helped."[49]

Furthermore, Monroe's altruists consistently describe themselves as having had no sane choice but to act as they have acted. They were reacting to what they saw as real; they were doing what they thought any reasonable person in their situation would do. That's why they reject the label "saint" or "hero." Their altruism constitutes or reflects an entire worldview. As Monroe remarks about one of the philanthropists she interviewed, "she simply sees the world quite differently from the way most rational actors, and probably most economists, see it."[50]

From within the ethical stance of any of the great monotheisms—and from what I can tell Buddhist and Hindu ethical systems as well—rational-actor theory looks not reasonable at all, but rather something like a chronic, low-grade case of paranoia. If you can see that all of us are ultimately interconnected at some unspeakably profound level, then surely the Gestapo were not simply immoral. They were also crazy. They were out of touch with an important level of reality. Genocidal murders of any era are in some sense as deficient as any delusional schizophrenic pushing a stranger in front of a subway train. Those who resisted the Nazis were down-to-earth sane. They were not simply heroic but also psychologically strong enough to resist the cultural pressures exerted upon civilians by the Third Reich.

The predicament of our times is that rational-actor capitalism defines altruism either as an illusion or as a sign of exploitation. Within the conceptual domain of these theories, those who give without prospect of return—without expectation of ultimate profit or enhanced "utility function" of any kind—are victims *by definition*. I do not deny for a moment that some people are victimized and exploited, and furthermore that religious institutions have at times praised the "virtue" of those too powerless to resist "sacrificing" for someone else's benefit. Nonetheless, authentic generosity is not only possible but also upheld by various ancient traditions as a difficult, high-level spiritual achievement. And so, the problem I want to describe is how we have gradually lost the conceptual structures that once portrayed compassion as a virtue deeply rooted in personal strength and unfailing integrity. Understanding that loss can help us to reclaim the best that is in us. That in turn will help us to begin to overcome the frustrated weariness permeating our lives.

Conclusion: Reclaiming the Common Good

What our society fails to provide to children, it fails to provide for all of us. What the dependent among us lack, all of us lack. As social beings, all of us need to be situated within networks of mutual care, within relationships where we are secure, engaged, and valued. Some of us demonstrate the consequences of deficits more vividly than others, of course. The old, the young, and the frail are particularly at risk. But we neglect the common good at our common peril, as Monroe's altruists might explain, because our individual good is inseparable from the larger human whole to which we all belong. When earning a living is too much at odds with having a life, work has become literally inhuman.

"The market" is at odds with the common good when it destroys the social capital upon which businesses—like every other complex form of human interaction—massively depend.

As spiritual beings, we need to create and to sustain social arrangements within which we can hear ourselves called to serve the common good, not simply to succeed in our own economic endeavors. Wisdom insists that "the pursuit of happiness" requires free and generous responsibility, not relentless self-seeking nor desperate consumption. The key to happiness, after all, is love—not money. Lay up treasure "in heaven," as the teaching goes, for where the treasure is, there the heart is also, and "in heaven" there are neither thieves to steal nor fire to burn nor waters to rust away . . . nor stock markets to fall, nor jobs to be lost. Who worships his belly, his end is destruction, according to the sixteenth-century King James translation of the Bible. Who worships his bank account, we might say, his end is not worth counting: such lives are less than fully human.

What takes such a toll upon our souls is the presumption that life at work is purely self-seeking, and life at home is purely self-sacrifice. As we will see in much more detail in the chapters to come, that antithesis is both dangerous and shallow. Our lives and our souls are not a landscape divided between mutually exclusive, relentlessly hostile camps. The calculus that defines work and life as inverse functions of one another is guaranteed to break our hearts.

In the chapters that follow I want to explicate the dominant ideologies shaping the conflict between *earning a living* and *having a life.* Part two looks at the ideology of gender roles; part three, "family values"; and part four, the marketplace. Overall, as I have said, these ideologies render a false account of what it means *to be human* because they combine to insist that "get the most; give the least" is the social and ethical norm around which our society is to be organized. In particular, these ideologies interlock to fund the debate over child care for children less than a year old—a debate conducted almost entirely with flame-throwers. That's part five. In part six I briefly describe the spiritual practice called "discernment," which is the art of making good decisions in bad situations where the way is unclear and the stakes are painfully high.

A couple of lines from Wordsworth's "Lines Written a Few Miles above Tintern Abbey" have haunted this book from its very beginnings. He describes "that best portion of a good man's life;/ His little, nameless, unremembered acts/ Of kindness and of love." I have endeavored above all to write a book that might be an act of kindness. I see those bumper stickers exhorting us to practice "random acts of kindness and senseless beauty," but it seems to me that kindness should not be random, and beauty is never senseless. How have we gotten to the point where kindness itself is portrayed as a furtive act, an occasional, irrational impulse? None of us can control the cultural momentum of the global market, but surely each of us can claim kindness as that best portion of our common humanity. Novelist Marilyn Robinson says it well: "Two things are true," she explains. "Everyone deserves profound respect, and no one deserves it. To understand the claim anyone has on our respect requires compassion and imagination, attentiveness and discipline."[51]

I want to reclaim the claim we make upon one another's respect.

Part Two

The Angel and the Oaf

How the Self Divided against Itself and Everybody Lost

Prelude

What scholars call the "crisis of care" is commonly (albeit implicitly) blamed on women: we have left home and gone to work for pay. What women used to do for families and for communities now either goes undone or gets done on the run, fit around the edges of employers' demands. When that process fails or breaks down, we have to pay someone to do it for us. Few of us can count on that once-enormous network of female neighbors and relations who stepped in promptly to help when help was needed, quietly competent, experienced, gracious, and proud. The tradition certainly endures here and there; but as more of us spend more hours working, caring traditions have come under siege from the implacable demands of earning a living. Economist Mona Harrington adeptly describes the consequences (and her italics are her own): *"Without women's full-time unpaid caretaking labor, families must buy needed care in the private market, and most do not have sufficient resources to buy enough of it. Therefore, the system as a whole is undercapitalized, and the unavoidable result, on the whole, is inadequate care."*[1] There's no denying that, nor the further detail added by yet another economist, Nancy Folbre: "Our modern economy has weakened many forms of patriarchal power that once gave women little choice but to specialize in caring for others. But it has also intensified competitive pressures that penalize women, men, and institutions for engaging in activities that don't improve the bottom line."[2]

No reasonable person could dispute these accounts. But if we see the issue primarily as changes in the socioeconomic position of women, we are seeing only half of what has changed. The second half intrigues me more, as I suspect it intrigues both Harrington and Folbre: compassion itself has a new "socioeconomic role." I propose to delineate that role by tracing relevant changes in how Western thought understands the dicey relationship between "woman" and "virtue."

But before we get started on that, I want to enlarge our working definition of caretaking. Specifically—and as I have argued already—financial support is as legitimate a form of care as personal support. Little kids need laptime; big kids need laptops. Elderly parents need cardiac medications no less than conversation. Communities need tax referendums to pass just as much as they need citizens to volunteer. Everybody all the time needs both warm affection and a warm house at night. Plenty of people work primarily to feed, to shelter, and to provide for those who count on them for financial support. When we delimit "care" to direct interpersonal interactions, we make the care provided through our wage-earning into something morally and culturally invisible—except, perhaps, when "deadbeat dads" refuse to send their monthly checks.

As a measure of what disappears, as a measure of this invisibility and its hidden social costs, consider how much difference it would make both in popular culture and in your own daily life if we saw one another as motivated not by the almighty dollar but by the human need to live responsible lives in caring service to others. What if work were authentically centered not upon success and status, but rather upon proud, well-recognized, meaningful, and caring service both to personal dependents and to professional dependents such as clients, customers, and so forth? Management theorists try to sell that line of thinking to customer service reps (and we will get back to that fact in part four). But on the whole, I suggest, we have lost the cultural frameworks within which such a perception would be natural.

That's a loss easily as significant as the loss of networks of women with time to spare for maintaining communal connections and for taking care of the heartsick, the weary, the wounded, the young, the old, and the newcomer. We will never understand how compassion has been marginalized in our culture if we do not, from the very beginning, understand the full scope of its resonance in our daily lives.

Second, I also want to enlarge what Nancy Folbre means by "our modern economy." The "modern economy" that liberated women from the household is the same "modern economy" that generated the crisis of care in the first place. It did so partly by reconceptualizing work and partly by centralizing economic activity outside the household. The problem is not simply that more women have paying jobs. The problem is that capitalist economic orthodoxy, generalized into a set of cultural norms, presents competitive self-seeking as the norm of adult behavior.

What's at stake here is a fascinating tale indeed. Its key theme is this: gender metaphors and gender-laden divisions in social role permeate the historical process whereby competition displaces compassion as the central social virtue at the core of The Good Life. Gender achieves such prominence or such functional centrality because the major conceptual structures at the heart of Western culture are all dualisms: head vs. heart, mind vs. body, nature vs. nurture, abstract vs. particular, theory vs. practice, objective or impersonal vs. subjective or personal, and so forth. From one point of view, male vs. female is simply part of that series. But more broadly considered, "male" and "female" also serve as metaphors, quite nearly as symbols that carry an enormously complicated conceptual burden as the representative particular instance of one side of each dual pairing. These dualist oppositions are so commonplace, so taken for granted, that they can be invisible. Our task is to learn to see what is hidden in plain sight.

Perhaps a story can best illuminate the point I'm trying to make here. Among ambitious young women in the seventies, when I was in graduate school, *domestic* was quite nearly equivalent to *dim-witted.* Women boasted of their inability to sew on a button as if this were proof of their superior intellects. When a classmate appeared at a lunch gathering of teaching fellows with a big plastic bag of cookies she had made, the cookies disappeared instantly but the disapproving talk didn't die down for a week. Some of the women were outraged by what they took as a treasonous public assault upon our collective effort to be accepted despite our gender.

In my assistant-professor days, such claims about incompetence in practical matters were equally commonplace among both the men and the women who were my academic colleagues. Once again, incompetence in one area (the mundane) was indirect evidence of talents in its opposite (the arcane)—and gender ran through it all. I remember with particular clarity one day when the department photocopier ran out of paper as I was copying a syllabus for that morning's class. The departmental secretaries were busy with a long line of students wanting to add or to drop classes, so I did what I thought any sensible adult should do.

I figured out how to open the front of the machine. Then I got down on my hands and knees, surveyed the array of colored knobs, and set to work installing a new roll of paper. From my position on the floor, I was eye-level with several new rolls back on a shelf below the faculty mailboxes. A senior male professor came into the room with a syllabus of his own just as I was tightening the last knob.

"See here!" he reprimanded, looking down at me and waving his hands in distress. "We have *women* to do this! I would have no idea how to do such a thing!" As I got to my feet and turned to face him, I realized that he was also staring, transfixed, as a considerable length of silky thigh disappeared again under my short wool skirt.

"They are busy with students," I replied, "so take a look." I reopened the front panel of the machine for his edification. "Complete directions—words *and* pictures. Any eight-year-old could do it. I'm not going to stand around helplessly: I have a class to teach!" I turned my back on him, closed the machine again, and tapped the "print" button. The machine hummed and clicked and produced the last few copies that I needed.

My esteemed colleague spluttered at me incoherently, turning violently pink. I scooped my copies out of the tray, smiled with all of my teeth, and bid him good day. With some difficulty, I also resisted the urge to flip the "off" switch as I departed. I headed around the corner and up the stairs to my class, wondering whether that jerk could have figured out the difference between the "print" and the "on/off" buttons without summoning one of the women whose skills were so far beneath his self-importance.

Halfway up the last flight of stairs, however, asthma and common sense brought me to a complete standstill: maybe he couldn't change paper in the photocopier, but he certainly knew how to find my hot buttons! I clung to the railing, dizzy and gasping for breath, laughing and then, of course, late to class after all. Asthmatics should *never* storm up a flight of stairs and then start laughing. But prudence has never been my strong suit, and in those days my hair (now so innocently grey) was dangerously near to red.

Any capable woman of a certain age has a generous supply of such stories. In order to be taken seriously as professionals, some women felt they had to abjure all abilities other than strictly intellectual ones—and in turn many important nonintellectual aspects of their identity were systematically denied by their own social milieu. The tenured women among my colleagues, in fact, had never married (which is to say my husband was the first and only "faculty husband" at faculty gatherings). They reacted to news of my first pregnancy with something close to horror. When I became pregnant a second time, I was accosted quite angrily by a senior man, soon to be chairman of the department, who demanded that I promise never to do this again.

These were perfectly commonplace experiences at the time. The primitive psychodynamics of the whole situation were nicely summarized by yet another tenured male, who told me point-blank, "*I* write books. My *wife* has the babies." I was quite simply violating the orderliness of reality by daring to do both, just as I had so seriously violated gender and gender-laden social-class boundaries with the photocopier. Gender identity is a complicated part of a whole set of either/or rules comprising habitual Western thought.

Despite sociopolitical changes since the middle 1970s, this heritage still lingers in the air. In a variety of subtle ways, it can distort individual perceptions and unduly complicate individual decision-making. In very direct and important ways, these distortions and complications underlie much of the conflict between *earning a living* and *having a life.*

3

How Did We Get into This Mess?

The Spiritual Grammar of the West

In *The Plain Sense of Things: The Fate of Religion in an Age of Normal Nihilism,* James C. Edwards provides a lovely account of the dualism at the core of Western thought:

> These large, deeply embedded, and almost invisible convictions—one might almost call them elements of the spiritual grammar of the West—are the engines driving our most concrete expressions of religious theory and practice. It is important to set them out as clearly as one can. . . . We here in the West have seldom considered reality to be all of a piece. On the contrary, we have typically insisted that reality is divided into two distinct realms, into two different "worlds": "this world" of need and lack and change; and "the other world" . . . of wholeness and haleness and permanence. . . . When one examines the basic religious (and philosophical) texts of our civilization, . . . one finds those books insisting upon a division between (1) some things that are fully real and lack nothing in order to be what they are, things that are resplendent in their completeness, self-sameness, independence, and perfection, and (2) other things that are in some way imperfect and needy, needy in their very being (or Being) in comparison to the first. The omnipresence and familiarity of this distinction should not blind us to its fundamental importance.[3]

An omnipotent, omniscient God is the premier inhabitant of a first, perfect, self-contained, independent realm. For our purposes, and from the wealth provided by Edwards's account and others like it, I want to point out that this realm of the perfectly self-contained and independent is also the cultural domain of masculinity. These two trends intersect, of course, in major Christian creeds professing belief in God "the Father Almighty" or in Jesus' own instruction to pray, "Our Father, who art in heaven . . ."[4] Furthermore, and primarily through the influence of Greco-Roman thought, self-control has often been portrayed as the single most important way in which humans can participate in the perfection that is God. Self-control is the human equivalent of sacred immutability. Hence, it is the key to virtue. At least since Aristotle, virtue in turn has been understood as the crucial foundation of genuine human happiness.

But when virtue depends somehow upon participation in the self-sufficient and the immutable, women are in trouble. Because of menses and because of the whole complex reproductive process generally, women are visibly, dramatically changeable creatures. (In the ancient world, remember, life expectancies were so short and child mortality so high that most women would have spent most of their adult lives either pregnant or nursing a baby.) Women are thus second-rate citizens in the moral universe. Add to that, of course, the "dependence" assigned to women in a warrior society governed—even in its most peaceful periods—by brutal state terror and ruthless imperial policy.

And yet, notice how such an emphasis on self-control presupposes that we are—and should be—in some essential way at odds with ourselves. By this account, which is by no means the only account available within Christian thought, self-discipline is the presumptive ideal. (One major alternative within Christian tradition would describe the ideal not as relentless self-control but as psychological integration or "gladness and singleness of heart."[5]) When the moral norm is self-control, the question inevitably arises, "What aspects of consciousness are to be exerting this control, and what contrary tendencies should be under control?" In a warrior society, in a patriarchal society, men are by definition the ones in control, and so the culturally dominant intellectual and personal characteristics come to be labeled "masculine." That's simply a metaphor, but it's an extremely powerful metaphor that some people will take literally.

In Western tradition, for instance, *male* is strongly associated with intellect and with the work or achievements of culture, including history, science, politics, and the arts. In classical antiquity, the pre-eminently masculine virtues were self-control, restraint, courage, integrity, self-discipline, mathematics, and rigorously objective rationality, such that the word "virtue" itself shares a stem with "virile." Virtue becomes metaphorically engendered, and that engendering is part of what Edwards calls the "nearly invisible convictions" shaping the spiritual grammar of the West. (The character of "virtue" is of course a major topic in theology and in ethics: the interplay between gender metaphor and virtue is one small aspect of a much larger whole.)

The spiritual grammar of the West thus necessarily associates the female—as the male's given opposite—with the qualities opposite to masculine virtue and achievements. Self-indulgence, inconsistency, greed, lust, appetite, cowardice, deceit, and physical weakness were metaphorically so characteristic of "woman" as to justify the ways in which women were to be kept under the dominion of men throughout society. *"La donna è mobile,"* as the song goes: women are fickle, frivolous, impulsive, and unreliable—and that's what drives men wild sexually, to their endless bewilderment. *Female* is also associated with body and with nature or the "natural," including all that is uncultivated, uncivilized, passionate, spontaneous, dangerous, unpredictable, and wild. In contrast to the metaphorically perfect and unchanging domain of the godly male, the metaphorically imperfect (or sinful) female is necessarily linked with all that is needy, defective, and incomplete. A woman needs a baby to "complete" her. A woman needs a man to support and to guide her.

But her deficiencies remain, no matter what. And the deficiency of the female is genuinely dangerous. Women are a profound threat to human social well-being, because women seduce men away from the self-control proper to them. (We elicit erections they cannot control.) According to John Milton, for instance, Adam's sin was "to worth in Woman overtrusting." Eve's sin, on the other hand, "first brought Death on all."[6] Major ancient and medieval theologians went so far as to deny that women are made in the image of God. That's extraordinarily dangerous theological code for claiming that women are not fully human—a claim that historical theologians attribute to the influence of Roman cultural traditions upon early Christianity.[7] Historian and theologian Rosemary Radford Reuther summarizes this cultural tradition quite adeptly: "Women are naturally subordinate, but also naturally insubordinate, and have been put under male domination both to reaffirm their subordinate nature and to punish them for their sinful rebellion against it."[8]

In these ways, sexual identity has always been deeply implicated in the classic Western antitheses of intellect versus passion, theory versus practice, and mind versus body—dualisms whose importance in our culture cannot be exaggerated. When, as we shall see, virtue in general *and compassion in particular* come to be associated primarily with the feminine, that is not (as might seem at first glance) an exaltation of the heretofore inferior woman. It is, on the contrary, evidence that compassion itself is inexorably being shifted off onto the margins, away from the cultural exercise of power. Some also contend that morality becomes "women's work" as religion itself loses ground to advances in science, technology, and historiography. If faith is contrafactual, if religion is silly or psychologically primitive superstition, then of course it is womanly stuff even though men keep control of the churches as rich and powerful institutions. As a general trend at the level of popular culture, that's a reasonable claim. It nicely explains why we find in the nineteenth century trends like "muscular Christianity" and organizations like the YMCA vigorously associating religion and virility, rather as Promise Keepers does more recently.

This is essentially a familiar story, its devastating effect on the lives of women often recounted, its calumny and shabbiness denounced. *Of course* we tend to attribute the crisis in care to changing social roles of women, especially changes that enhance the political and economic power of women. In the Western mind, *disorder* is innately feminine. The changing employment patterns of women are unequivocally real: let there be no dispute about that. Equally real, however, is the fact that men overwhelmingly control policy making by the government, by employers generally, and by the supranational corporations that set the pace of the global economy. Why do we not similarly engender the failure to articulate policies that protect and foster social capital?

That's easy to explain: "masculinity" is metaphorically associated with objectivity, rationality, impersonality, and decisions made on principle, not from personal preference. The men (or male-dominated groups of legislators) who set the minimum wage levels at less than survival levels, the men who vote against paid maternity leave and family-emergency leave, the men who control levels of funding for education and social services—these men are not held personally accountable because they are seen or culturally defined as acting in accord with principle and in response to objective data about real situations. Femininity, however, is just as massively associated metaphorically with the subjective, the personal, and so forth. And so women who work for pay seem to be making "personal" choices that are by definition arbitrary, not substantiated, and for which they are then held "personally" and morally responsible. The men who control policies are being rational and self-disciplined—and therefore, in all probability, free from sin. As literary critics have always insisted, metaphors are powerful, especially when they are taken literally. In many ways, I contend, metaphoric and symbolic language controls the "code" in which "cultural software" is written.

When women's choices are thought to have negative outcomes for society generally, women's choices are portrayed—even by feminist economists—as the most immediate or most obvious "cause" of these negative outcomes. Of course both Nancy Folbre and Mona Harrington go on to probe beneath this surface perception to demonstrate the economic pressures and systematics that both elicit and demand such behavior from women as ordinary rational actors. No doubt some women work primarily because they enjoy the work itself; no doubt others work exclusively for status and for stuff. But no doubt most women work because employment is objectively necessary. Their choices are as culturally invisible as the choices made by men who work primarily to care for those who depend upon them. Both men and women in this compassionate and responsible group are apt to feel more than a little besieged, because their motives and their behavior contravene the ways in which gender metaphors permeate how we think about critical thinking, how we think about the world, and how we think about making decisions.

Virtue and the Good Life

So let's back up quite a ways and consider anew the underlying issue, which is how life's fundamental questions about virtue and the Good Life and so forth have gotten so weirdly entangled with gender in the first place. The story goes back a very long way, and it is hugely complicated. But for our purposes, a quick pencil sketch will do. Imagine, if you will, the floor plan of a house, roughly sketched on the back of an envelope during lunch with a friend. Such sketches are fun and useful, but no one uses them to order carpet or wallpaper. The same sort of common sense is called for here.

In the early centuries of the Common Era, as Christianity developed from a Jewish sect into a "universal" religion, it became deeply enmeshed with the general culture of the Mediterranean basin. Christianity was influenced by the popular culture and the pop psychology of its own times. In particular, its inherited Jewish ideas of virtue began to be assimilated to transparently Greco-Roman norms of *severitas* (self-restraint or self-control)—particularly in the form of Stoicism, a set of philosophical beliefs and practices that functioned socially very much as religions function. This assimilation was well under way in parts of the Jewish community prior to the birth of Jesus of Nazareth.

That much is easy to imagine. The next step is a bit more subtle. The assimilation process in ethical ideas is essentially inseparable from a parallel process in theology itself. That is, one sees something like the assimilation of the Hebrew deity Yahweh Elohim to the cultural norm of *paterfamilias* and emperor. The virtuous Roman (whether the household *paterfamilias* or the emperor himself, the national *paterfamilias*) is a character of strict rationality and absolute self-control. And because authority in the culture generally is understood in these ways, the kind of authority appropriate to the omnipotent Holy One comes to be understood in compatible ways.

Of course there is excellent biblical warrant for this theological shift: despite its prohibition of images of the divine, patriarchal Jewish culture had often imagined its deity as in some ways or at some times a masculine or warrior figure. Nonetheless, the equation between virtue and self-control can reasonably be considered an important change in ethical orientation from Jewish traditions. Yahweh Elohim was originally depicted as a deeply passionate figure, prone to grief, jealousy, compassion, rage, and regret. "He" would not have scored very well on any test of Roman *severitas*. And so, when Christianity began to define virtue itself as self-control, that is something of a collapse of other ethical positions within Christian and Jewish thought, ethical positions that based morality upon spiritual wholeheartedness and psychological integration.

Supporting that claim in full would require a book of its own; let me simply quote an exemplary passage from Psalm 33:

> A king is not saved by his great army;
> a warrior is not delivered by his great strength.
> The war horse is a vain hope for victory,
> and by its great might it cannot save.
> Behold, the eye of the Lord is on those who fear him,
> on those who hope in his steadfast love.[9]

Such texts can be certainly read as invoking a warrior-God's assistance in battle, but they need not be read only that way. If armies and war horses do not save us, then perhaps the "salvation" under discussion is not military victory but something else altogether. Another favorite passage of mine is similar: "Some put their trust in chariots, and some in horses: but we will remember the name of the Lord our God"[10] In such contexts, to "remember the name" of something is to call its essential character to mind. Although at times we are tempted to put our trust in satellite-guided missiles (or at least in the power of a scathing e-mail), at such times we can resolve instead to "remember the name of the Lord our God." We can remember that the essence of the Sacred, an essence in which we share, is loving-kindness, justice, mercy, and compassion.

At issue here is the long biblical argument, fully evident in our own day, whether the phrase "the promised land" or the "kingdom of God" refers to politics and real estate or rather to some inner state, homologous to what Buddhists mean by "enlightenment." This inner state is predicated not upon military triumph but rather upon intentional, spiritually disciplined relationship to the Holy One. Implicit in that argument, all through these millennia, is whether God provides military victory to his Chosen, or whether that expectation is based upon a misunderstanding. In World War I, for instance, German soldiers were issued belts whose buckles were engraved "Gott Mit Uns," God with us.[11] Terrorists claim the same, and so do presidents, and all of them can cite the texts that support them—while accusing each other of blasphemous misrepresentation of the nature of God. I do not deny the presence of these militaristic texts, nor do I wish to question the psalmists' oft repeated lament that if God does not protect the Chosen People then there will be none left to preserve these texts and valuable traditions. I wish simply to observe that these other, more introspective aspects of the Western monotheist tradition were relatively obscured when Christianity became the state religion of the Roman Empire.[12]

In *The Gnostic Gospels,* historian Elaine Pagels explains how monotheism was made to serve as a justification for the strictly hierarchical and centralized control of power. This centralization took place when early Christianity began to develop an institutional form that was transparently modeled upon the Roman political empire. The argument looks something like this: the Lord God is one; the Lord God is utterly transcendent to the created world. In parallel ways, the church in any region needs a single ultimate head; the power of this figure must transcend the power exercised by anyone else. That is, the bishop must be the one single authority within the church to whom all lesser figures necessarily turn. The religious argument—evident still within Roman Catholicism—is that the hierarchical shape or organization of the church must mirror the ways in which God is superior to the created world. Such hierarchy simultaneously mirrors the Roman empire and the virtuous Roman household, in which the *paterfamilias* transcends and controls his own household of subordinates.

In our own day, this heritage of hierarchialism is vividly manifest in ferocious arguments about Roman Catholic church architecture: literalists angrily oppose any movement toward arrangements "in the round" as failing to keep the priest and the sacramental action clearly separate from and "above" the congregation. But the pedophilia crisis demonstrates the hazards of hierarchy as Lord Acton famously described them: power corrupts, and absolute power corrupts absolutely.

As Pagels and others have also argued, this centralizing of authority coincided with the progressive loss of leadership that had been exercised by women within the original Christian communities. When the Edict of Constantine (313 C.E.) established Christianity as the state religion of the empire, the stage was set for an ever-fuller assimilation of Christianity to a Greco-Roman ethical emphasis upon self-control. (Over centuries of institutional evolution, there also arose the idea of the single bishop who presides over all other bishops—the bishop of Rome, the pope.)

This is yet another essentially familiar story, at least to anyone who has studied Western religious history: Christianity comes under massive pressure to assimilate and thereby to mute its traditional norms of compassionate wholeheartedness and radical egalitarianism. In that assimilation, gender appears as a set of metaphors that function in fairly subtle but remarkably powerful ways. As Peter Brown thoroughly documents in *The Body and Society: Sexual Renunciation in Early Christianity,* Christian sexual asceticism and sexual renunciation complemented and extended the *severitas* of the virtuous Roman man into a universal principle of holiness based upon denial of the body and especially the strict control of erotic drives.[13] Patriarchy and misogyny are culturally inevitable parts of any such emphasis upon mind at the expense of body.

As a result of the interwoven cultural pressures exerted by the assimilation of early Christianity to the culture of its times, women were ever-more-firmly associated metaphorically with body and with the seductive powers of sexuality in ways gruesomely tied to death, sin, and decay. Masculinity as a metaphor becomes ever-more-exclusively linked with culture, rationality, and virtue. The ideal male becomes the celibate priest, not the *paterfamilias*; and church leadership is increasingly restricted to those willing to renounce sexuality altogether. Women, who were at least crucial for the acquisition of progeny, lose what status motherhood itself provides when immortality comes to depend upon one's soul, not one's sons.

Emblematic of this shift is the fact that Christians were traditionally enjoined to refrain from sex on Sunday and holy days (hence the movie tune, "Never on Sunday"). Jews, by contrast, are encouraged to have sex on the Sabbath, and to be thus conceived is regarded as a particular blessing. In Tertullian's infamous phrase, Christianity in late antiquity saw women as temples built over sewers—as morally dangerous temptresses. Origen, another of the "Fathers of the Early Church," is equally famous for castrating himself: that's a literal-minded vision of masculine virtue at least as warped as Tertullian's view of women.[14] Ultimately, radical misogyny and radical self-control form a single story or a single complicated development within the larger historical tapestry of Western ethics.

Surviving in a World "Grazed Thin by Death"

In considering the massive power of "male" and "female" as pervasive Western metaphors, one must always bear in mind the equal and opposite pressures asserted by the practical demands of survival. Survival was no easy matter in premodern, preindustrial societies based largely upon subsistence agriculture. Although the tiny cadre of elite and literate men asserted male superiority to justify the concentration of political and ecclesiastical power in the hands of men, such arguments could not and cannot obviate the importance of women's practical contributions to the survival of their families and their communities. Overblown rhetoric about helpless, incompetent, evil women needs to be recognized as thinkers protesting far too much and far too clearly in defiance of everyone's ordinary experience in their own day. We must also remember that women are not directly part of this conversation at all; we are listening in, as it were, on men talking to other men about women. On the whole, women were not part of public discourse at this high level. At least in my experience, single-sex conversations about gender issues tend toward extremes and one-sidedness; and the writings from the ancient world about women are quite emphatically a single-sex conversation.

Meanwhile, however, life had to go on, regardless of what writers had to say about women. And cooperative egalitarianism, no matter how rough-hewn, accords far better with the harsh demands of biological survival. As Peter Brown argues, life in the ancient world was far more constrained than life in the Third World today. What ancient writers denounce, I suspect, is not simply or not merely the female of the species but also the sheer unpredictable agony of mortality and embodiment in the ancient world. Bodily restraint, bodily control, and bodily self-denial make much more psychological sense in a world without general anesthesia and antibiotics, much less bifocals, clean water, central heat, and the means to keep food from spoiling between one harvest and the next. These people lived without effective solace for any of the ills that flesh is heir to. That's very hard to imagine. Consider this mundane fact, from a plethora of bone-chilling details: one of the causes contributing to early mortality was malnutrition secondary to one's teeth rotting away.

And so, as the cultural, psychological, and sexual "other," *woman* carried the projections of a literary and ecclesial elite who were just barely comfortable enough to reflect upon the fact that life is indeed solitary, poor, nasty, brutish, and short. St. Augustine of Hippo—noted for his sexual repressions and anxieties—died in 354 C.E. as his city was falling to invasion by the Huns. During the formative centuries of early Christianity, the Roman Empire was in its long, slow death throes. Mediterranean civilization, as it had been known since the time of Egyptian pharaohs and Greek philosophers, was genuinely coming to an end. One response of the literati was bodily denial, whether Christian, Stoic, Gnostic, or any of the many combinations thereof.[15]

In the Roman Empire even at its height, average life expectancy was no more than twenty-five years, in part because rates of death both in childbirth and in childhood were extremely high. Only four men in a hundred lived to age fifty, and even fewer women did so. Simple maintenance of population demanded that each woman produce an *average* of five children.[16] (By contrast, population maintenance in societies like our own calls for 2.1 births per woman.) A society "grazed thin by death" needs the skills and the labor of all adults.[17] Life was even more lean, survival even more tenuous, during the long "dark ages" after the fall of Rome.

In any such biologically marginal society, the work of women is unequivocally necessary and perforce extends beyond childbearing and child care to include such vital but traditionally feminine tasks as spinning, weaving, needlework, cooking, preserving, baking, brewing, candlemaking, and so forth. The historical lives of ordinary women involved both parenthood and material productivity of various kinds because all adults were needed in both roles—and because there was hardly any "economy" to speak of situated outside the residential household. In a world where all but the highest ranks of nobility worked brutally hard, the division of skilled labor along gender lines is not necessarily oppressive in and of itself. Furthermore, as neuropsychologists and neuroendocrinologists are beginning to demonstrate in some detail, men are hormonally primed to respond to stress with aggression; women are hormonally primed to "tend and befriend" under stress. "Tend and befriend" stress responses assure the survival of offspring and maintain the social bonds that are crucial to human health, cooperation, and survival.[18] Both the aggressive and the bonding responses are vital to the survival of a community under stress.

At issue is the status applicable to various tasks and behaviors, and how that status pragmatically translates into social and political power. When "male vs. female" participates metaphorically in a whole array of dualisms, one term of which always dominates the other, the biologically mediated social division of skills will always carry with it unequal divisions of power and status. That division has persisted despite all the ways in which our greater physical security has allowed greater expression of innate human adaptability and thus a loosening of gender-role restrictions. Relatively few men are warriors these days, for instance; and many of those who are work with computer systems, not spears. As social skills and the executive ability to manage complex cooperative endeavors have come to matter more than muscle mass and upper-body strength, women's social roles have naturally enlarged.

But that has been a slow process, because the ideology of gender is so deeply embedded. As Rosemary Radford Reuther explains in *Christian-*

ity and the Making of the Modern Family, with the rise of a more stable and prosperous high medieval society, women began to be marginalized from material productivity.[19] That happened because the recovery of Aristotle at this point in time gave renewed credibility to gender-based hierarchies: if Eve's sin was disobeying God, Adam's sin was listening to his wife.[20] High medieval society could afford to begin to set aside the skills of women, which in a prosperous time mattered less than the ideological and metaphorical meaning of "the female." Later, as the Middle Ages gave way to Renaissance and Reformation, Protestant reformers closed self-governing convents, excluded women from guilds, closed women's guilds, and so forth. As we will see in more detail later on, the Protestant Reformation also involved the recovery of self-control and self-denial as the foundation of virtue.

As we have seen, the ancient world lived with spectacular contradictions between the practical importance of women and the ideologically weighted denunciation of women. As we approach modernity, these contradictions continue but in new, ever-more convoluted forms.

4

Can We Blame the Victorians?

The Challenge of Industrial Capitalism

The rise of industrialization in the eighteenth and early nineteenth century adds a most peculiar twist to this odd tale of how gender and virtue are entangled in the spiritual grammar of the West. In the first half of this chapter, I want to sketch three cultural aspects of the Industrial Revolution: the way work moved out of households, the way capitalism began to re-imagine human society, and the way "virtue" was redefined as an emotional response, not a rational standard. Then we will take a look at what impact all this had on the cultural meaning of gender roles, including the status of femininity.

Prior to the Industrial Revolution, economic productivity meshed with parental roles and responsibilities because the household was the locus of both work and family. In general, everyone worked at home. As Witold Rybczynski attests in *Home: A Short History of an Idea,* "home" was not the private, exclusively domestic territory it is today. As industrialism, commercial banking, and the various locales and structures of capitalism gained strength throughout the course of the eighteenth century, "work" increasingly named a place and not simply an activity that engaged all adults, regardless of gender. "Work" happened in factories and in banks, in commercial districts and in warehouse districts that were increasingly separated from residences.

The rise of industrialism in the eighteenth century also involved the rise of capitalism, which proved to be a significant cultural development and not simply an innovation in finance, investment, and banking. Capitalist visions of a competitive marketplace increasingly replaced the feudal vision of reciprocal obligation, such that "work" became a domain separate from the household both physically and morally. Medieval feudalism imagined a society knit together by countless strands of responsibility to one another. These reciprocal responsibilities were grounded in moral imperatives that had great seriousness and resonance. The worker was morally obligated to work well and honestly; the employer was morally obligated to reward such honest labor with honest recompense. To pay less than a "living wage" would have been judged intrinsically evil.[21] Although peasants were often exploited, sometimes brutally so, this abuse was regarded as inescapably wrong—not as a morally neutral or insignificant part of how markets function. Capitalism replaces such mutual moral obligations with bare-fisted mutual exploitation. Exploitation is something close to a socioeconomic norm, not a sin: workers do the least work they can get away with doing; employers pay as little as they can get away with paying. Decent people who resist—whether as workers or as managers—are deemed "irrational" in strict market terms.

As Stanley Hauerwas recounts in his commentary on William Law's "A Serious Call to a Devout and Holy Life" (1728), moral responsibility cannot be put in abeyance as one walks into the marketplace.[22] By 1728, that moral principle needed specific assertion because it was beginning to unravel. A century later, its unraveling was substantial: the geographical division between workplace and household had become a moral divide of increasing importance. As Christopher Lasch explains in both *Haven in a Heartless World* and *Women and the Common Life,* the nineteenth-century household supposedly remained a place shaped by traditional moral obligations and personal responsibility. Bare-fisted exploitation had no theoretical legitimacy in the home. But the rise of capitalism devastates the conceptual and practical foundations of the social order upon which the household depends. As a result, the family household progressively loses both its practical autonomy and its coherent function as a moral alternative or locus of resistance to the cultural authority of socioeconomics.

The mutual exploitation characteristic of capitalism was not understood as morally preferable to feudalism or even as a matter of deliberate personal or cultural choice. The operations of the free market were more or less construed as an impersonal natural law operating as independently of human volition as Newton's. Nonetheless, by draining work relationships of their moral foundation in reciprocal duty and social obligation, capitalism moved economic productivity into the same category as hunting or warfare: work becomes ruthlessly competitive, amoral at best, a more or less stylized violence exercised now not against marauding enemies, threatening predators, or animals needed for meat but rather against other members of one's own community. Capitalist economic theory imagines a society in which all are at war with all, an idea for which Darwin later provided stunning credibility. When the "world of work" is defined in these ways, that makes work metaphorically masculine, and so the "nonwork" domain of the household begins to seem metaphorically feminine.

The Changing Vocabulary of Virtue

As capitalism develops in the West, it becomes progressively more difficult to make reasonable sense of compassion or altruism as centrally important human virtues. As sociologist Stephanie Coontz explains in *The Way We Never Were: American Families and the Nostalgia Trap,*

> [After the Enlightenment,] a growing preoccupation with personal equality, individual self-reliance, and objective contractual rights made it very hard for theorists to incorporate positive notions of interdependence or neediness into their ideal models of socioeconomic and political arrangements. Instead, liberal theory projected all dependence onto women and children. . . . Political and economic relationships came to be organized around the contractual rights of equal, independent individuals; only gender and family relationships remained organized around personal needs, individual differences, and dependence. This led to a growing divergence between politics, law, and economics—the site of competition and objective laws, [which are] men's arenas—and interpersonal relations [which are] the site of altruism and subjectivity, [and hence] women's arenas. It also created a polarization between public rights and private needs that eventually hampered people's ability to develop a reasonable approach to either. . . . [T]he Western tradition gradually came to view independence and concern for others as mutually exclusive traits. Caring for others was confined to women, and personal autonomy was denied them; personal autonomy was reserved for men, and caring for others was either denied them or penalized.[23]

The ancient world thought that women lack the self-discipline and intellectual resources that are necessary for moral selfhood. The gender ideology of the Enlightenment (circa 1600) was quite similar, although over time the vocabulary for saying so had changed a little. Enlightenment thinkers continued in classic Western ways to portray women as morally deficient, but the crucial disabilities came to be called a lack of "competitiveness" or "personal autonomy."[24] In capitalist terms, compassion is irrational (which is to say "sinful"), and in the West anything that is irrational and sinful is necessarily associated with metaphors of the feminine. Enlightenment gender ideology projects onto the very idea of femininity everything that absolute modernist rationality tries to deny and to repress about what it means *to be human*. This is devastating not only for women but also for children and for anyone who needs the help of other people: compassion has been redefined as a symptom of deficiency. Those who care for others do so from a lack of autonomy, intellectual prowess, or social power. As a friend of mine said about the Haitian nanny caring for her weeks-old infant, "This woman is great. She is smart enough to be responsible and dumb enough to want the job."

Compassion is nonetheless vital for our collective survival, no less than attentive and skillful mothering is necessary for society's biological continuity and flourishing over time. As a result, the ways in which capitalism redefined what it means *to be human* were resisted by wise and thoughtful people from the beginning. (Even Adam Smith, for instance, insisted that human benevolence naturally and inevitably constrained the invisible hand of the market.[25]) That resistance involved a temporary, somewhat marginal revaluation of the "feminine" traits of responsive care.

Over the course of the eighteenth century, classic Enlightenment thinking was increasingly challenged in a variety of ways. One of these ways was a tendency to redefine or to relocate ethics: morality was often portrayed as a variety of sentiment and as rooted in the subjective. This development is sometimes called the "cult of sensibility."[26] Virtue, so long associated with severe rationalist self-control, becomes associated instead with nonrational emotional impulse. (To the orthodox or rationalist capitalist, of course, anything other than absolute self-seeking will be seen as irrational.) As the eighteenth century slowly spins out, virtue becomes increasingly associated with the natural rather than the cultured or "civilized," with the spontaneous rather than the rational and self-controlled, with warm reactive sensibility rather than careful, critical, "good sense" and intelligent rationality (hence Jane Austen's novel, *Sense and Sensibility*).

The eighteenth-century cult of sensibility also drew upon the status of the Virgin in the late Middle Ages (roughly from the twelfth to the fourteenth centuries). Medieval devotion to the Blessed Virgin Mary established a link between the divine and the feminine—something like a goddess figure—that had been more or less submerged in Western religious culture ever since Christianity became the state religion of the Roman Empire. Medieval worship of Mary was part of a broader, ongoing effort to reclaim the humanity of Jesus and to reclaim *chesed*—usually translated "loving-kindness"—as the defining characteristic of Christianity's God. Through this new attention to Mary, there arose also an awareness of or an attention to the Holy Family (Mary, Joseph, and Jesus) that eventually provided a submerged cultural archetype for the Victorian family in which the mother-and-child unit is the ethical center and the father—like Joseph—is essentially a moral bystander despite his public social status and economic power.

The cult of sensibility also derives in part from the late-medieval courtly love tradition. The beloved of the courtly lover was not the ultimately inaccessible Virgin Mary herself, but rather a human virgin or at least a sexually inaccessible woman. Petrarch's Laura, Dante's Beatrice, and a thousand lesser women real or imagined served as some combination of muse, goddess, and platonic ideal. *Woman* as a metaphor (and a psychological projection)—she who let pain and suffering into the world—is briefly transformed into the highest possible ideal of the human in direct converse with the Holy. In Christian thought, no human being has come closer to God than the Virgin who carried him in her womb. In the mindset of the courtly love tradition, any ordinary virginal woman—one who is as-yet free of the moral taint of sexual experience—can be imagined as participating metaphorically in the moral stature of the Blessed Virgin.

These late-medieval traditions may feel remote, but the cultural currents they set off are very much alive if you know where to look. At breakfast this morning I was looking idly through a *Signals* catalogue, where I spotted a plaque. On it were lines that women have been forwarding to one another on e-mail for many years. This is what it said:

Three Wise Women would have
Asked directions,
Arrived on time,
Helped deliver the Baby,
Cleaned the stable,
Made a casserole,
Brought practical gifts and
There would be
Peace on Earth.

Such attitudes are the cultural descendents of the cult of Mary. Implicitly, the plaque claims that what Mary began was ruined when men got involved. But if women ruled the world, we would have the kingdom of

God on earth: women are—like Mary herself—uniquely God-bearers. Protestant reformers, who closed women's guilds and women's self-governing convents, also denounced devotion to Mary as superstition and idolatry. (Nonetheless, centuries later Protestants also began to ordain women. Roman Catholics still do not ordain women, despite their continued devotion to the Virgin. History is an attic full of odd wonders.)

One way or another, the cult of sensibility held up passionate feeling and human relationships—not Roman *severitas*—as the most noble aspect of our humanity. This vision permeates the literature of the era, especially fiction. The eighteenth- and nineteenth-century novel resituates the beloved of the sonnet tradition into the middle-class family: a daughter's courtship and betrothal or marriage forms the core plot of a remarkably high percentage of these novels. As Rachel Brownstein demonstrates in *Becoming a Heroine: Reading About Women in Novels,* these novels astutely critique the cultural and metaphorical projections upon women, while also portraying how women struggle with the contest between enjoying interpersonal intimacy and maintaining healthy personal autonomy. That contest lies at the psychic core of life in a capitalist system.

We also see the low-key persistence of the cult of sensibility in the ongoing association of goodness with the "natural" or the "organic." There seems to be something morally superior about the handmade, the minimally processed, the 100% cotton, and all things herbal. Any dietary supplement labeled "natural" is taken by some people to be completely safe and beneficent, as if the "natural world" has no natural poisons or naturally hazardous substances. I finally understood this movement when I spotted "100% organic" dental floss in a friend's bathroom: what we have here is a contemporary form of ancient bodily and dietary orthodoxy found in many ancient religions. If "get the most for the least" is the rationalist economic premise of modern life, then of course morality must be located outside of "civilization," which is to say in a domain—a "natural" and "organic" separate sphere—that is already replete with profoundly feminine associations and metaphors. "Mother Nature" would never hurt us. The logic here is dangerously flawed, but it sells a lot of "natural" supplements nonetheless.

The Rise of Victorian "Separate Spheres"

We have been looking at three late-eighteenth-century developments: the industrialist separation of work from households, the capitalist collapse of mutual accountability into mutual exploitation as the preeminent foundation of the social order, and the relocation of moral instinct into the domain of the "natural," the "spontaneous," and the "emotional." These three historical developments had an enormous impact upon Victorian popular psychology and popular culture. At the most rudimentary level, these developments intersect to provide the conceptual foundation for the Victorian doctrine of "separate spheres." According to this infamous model, men work "at work." "Work" names the location of male economic activity—an office, a factory, a mine, a store. When men are "at work," they are outside the familial household. Women, on the other hand, do remain in the household, running its affairs and caring for children. "Work" and "home" name separate spheres, one for men and the other for women.

Women's separation from the world of "work"—from the ruthless competition of early industrial capitalism—generated around women an aura of moral purity that in a Christian culture is necessarily asexual. The Victorian Angel in the House echoes Rome's Vestal Virgins, young women who served the shrine of Hestia, goddess of the hearth. The cultural archetype *woman* becomes not the moral sewer, not she by whom came death into this world, but rather the gracious loving guardian of ethics and morality in a society otherwise dominated by ruthless competition. The woman at home, caring for her family in compassionate opposition to the new requirements of industrial capitalism, functioned as the protectress of all that is true, honorable, just, pure, lovely, and gracious.[27]

Woman (as metaphor and cultural archetype) could assume this responsibility in part because the relationship between mother and infant is clearly at the opposite pole from the interpersonal dynamics of capitalism. More importantly, I think, *woman* assumed this responsibility primarily because in Western thought *woman* had always functioned as a metaphor associated with the spontaneous, the emotional, and the "natural." The cultural or metaphorical meaning of femininity had not changed. All that had changed is the ethical significance of the elements with which femininity is metaphorically associated: the spontaneous, the emotional, and the "natural" become (at least temporarily) the loci of virtue rather than, as traditionally, the loci of depravity. As historian John Gillis observes, "To the challenge of sustaining the material basis of family life was now added the awesome task of providing for its spiritual requirements."[28] As he explains in detail, this task involved—and still involves—creating the "family rituals" that are somehow to compensate for the loss of those public and religious rituals which once provided moral coherence to the complexity of our lives.

More dangerously yet, the Victorian Angel in the House is god and priest rolled into one. Rather than all adults helping and supporting one another in the effort to be decent people leading decent lives, we project all of our moral responsibilities upon the mother—who of course, *ex officio*, should love us no matter what. If she doesn't, we have wounded inner children, and that excuses whatever we mess up in our lives as adults. What a setup! And when this essentially narcissist radical individualism goes awry, as of course it must, women are at fault. In the 1950s, the fault was called "smother love" producing "mother's boys." Now the blame is more likely laid at the door of "working mothers" or "two-career households." One way or another, women are at fault, at least metaphorically. If we are not the omnipotent Mother Almighty, Daughter of the Virgin, then we are simply the daughters of Eve, the source of all cultural and moral disorder.

The Victorian separate-spheres doctrine is so bent by its own interior contradictions that it would not roll downhill, but oddly enough those contradictions may also account for its persistence as popular psychology and social construct. It both renews and undercuts the ways in which gender participates in and symbolizes all the dualist oppositions funding Western culture at its deepest levels. On the one hand, women belong at home because *woman* is metaphorically inferior to *man* in competitiveness, hardheadedness, rationality, executive ability, and self-discipline. *Woman* lacks the virtuous Roman *severitas*. *Woman* is metaphorically a soft, sentimental, frivolous, irrational, impulsive creature who would never survive in the bare-fisted, mutually exploitative capitalist market. When the radical faction of the Southern Baptists insisted just a few years ago that wives should be subject to their husbands, this was the historical model or heritage that supported their claim.

On the other hand, *woman* should remain home with children because she is morally pure. *Woman* is innately generous and spontaneously self-sacrificing. *Woman* is noble, pure, honorable, and wise. As a result, *woman* both embodies and transmits to children all the virtues so deeply undermined by industrial capitalism. Women belong at home because the culture as a whole is projecting upon *woman* all sorts of powerful ambivalence about its own movement toward exclusively competitive models of human interaction. There is something profoundly wrong about the strict capitalist claim that all of us are systematically and intentionally out for ourselves and for ourselves alone. Uneasy with this capitalist and rational-actor vision of human nature, we projectively "locate" our essential compassion in this motherly Angel, who stays home—clean and clear of moral pollution by the ruthless marketplace.

Kathleen Hall Jamieson brilliantly summarizes this situation as a set of double binds that women face. As she explains,

- Women can exercise their wombs or their brains, but not both.
- Women who speak out are immodest and will be shamed, while women who are silent will be ignored or dismissed.

- Women are subordinate whether they claim to be different from men or the same.
- Women who are considered feminine will be judged incompetent, and women who are competent, unfeminine.
- As men age, they gain wisdom and power; as women age, they wrinkle and become superfluous.[29]

Borrowing from novelist Joseph Heller, we recognize these false oppositions as varieties of Catch-22. Jamieson argues that they all originate in persistent Western habits of dualist thinking, and she goes on to recount the ways in which women have deconstructed these double binds in the last fifty years.

That progress has very long roots. Women were swift to seize upon the incoherence of separate-spheres doctrine, combining both the cult of sensibility and Angel in the House metaphors into a lever by which to move the society as a whole toward far more egalitarian distribution of power, education, and social rights. As early as 1792, Mary Wollstonecraft was insisting in *A Vindication of the Rights of Women* that women had to be provided with access to education if they were to fulfill these dramatic cultural and moral responsibilities.[30] Powerful nineteenth-century reformers made the quite obvious argument that she who rules the household should by the very same logic have a hand in the ruling of the nation, whether by attaining suffrage or by implementing various social reforms such as temperance, abolition, expanded education of children, and care for the poor. Victorian women organized themselves and exercised public and political influence to such an extent and with such shrewd skill that they set the stage for yet-broader social equality between men and women. As Christopher Lasch argues in *Women and the Common Life,* it is only by crudely equating "work" with "paychecks" that activist Victorian women can be portrayed as trapped within the domestic sphere.

In very many ways, nineteenth-century reformers demonstrated that women have tough-minded intelligence and ambitious leadership equal to those of men and thus deserve an equal share in political power and powerful professions. All of that is perfectly true. But as a successful strategy it also tended to enforce all the ways in which aggressive moxie and nose-to-nose competition have always been exalted over caring. On the whole, it seldom directly challenged the psychological division into strong superior "male" traits and weak inferior "female" traits that fueled gender metaphors in the first place. "As capable as any man" leaves intact the ancient Greco-Roman and rationalist suspicion that compassion is an irrational weakness or a failure of shrewdness, not a spiritual achievement.

On the other hand, at the practical level, separate-spheres doctrine reflects the simple reality that *somebody* has to stay home to take care of the children, the elderly, the needy, etc., because these "nonproductive" individuals are no longer a perfectly natural part of the social space in which work happens. The workplace—often a dangerously primitive factory—becomes a domain radically separated from the many complex activities of the sprawling medieval household. The separate-spheres doctrine is not simply an evil conspiracy by misogynist brutes. It is more reasonably understood as a *post hoc* effort to understand and to make the best of technological changes that were mirrored in urban design. The changing landscape of cities generated confusing and difficult problems in social organization, particularly for nonmarket human endeavors such as maintenance of communal bonds and care for the young, the old, the needy, and the ailing.

Both Angel in the House metaphors and the deep-rooted "cult of sensibility" failed to triumph over the older, more powerful Greco-Roman ethical and cultural traditions. Their strategic emphasis on the natural, the organic, and the emotional never stood a chance against the cultural forces culminating in railroads, factories, urbanization, modern technology, and so forth. When a culture that is shaped by science and technology comes to view science and technology as normatively "masculine," women and the archetype *woman* will occupy a most peculiar niche—a niche defined overwhelmingly by its deficits from this norm. Women who want to get ahead in such a culture will have to adopt the skills and the mannerisms of those already in power.

So despite the arguments and the achievements of the Victorian reformers both in Britain and in the United States, the rapid development of industrial technology and modern science assured the unquestioned priority of traits that were traditionally associated with metaphors of masculinity: logic, mathematical precision, self-discipline, control, dominance, ambition, drive, aggression, courage, etc.

Compassion, like organic produce or unbleached 100% cotton bed linens, hovers culturally on the verge of being little more than a lifestyle option.

5

Why Gender Dualism Leaves Us All Half-Crazy

Distortions and Deteriorations of Gender Identity

Gender ideology and the Victorian doctrine of separate spheres quietly undermine our efforts to construct a life we can live with a firm, clear sense of personal integrity and moral coherence. As we struggle to find a life we can live with, we come up against the obscure and submerged pressure this heritage exerts. In particular, murky notions of gender identity come into play when we try to think critically about both personal choices and policy decisions. We can minimize the distortions our heritage entails if we bring these notions out into the open light of conscious understanding.

Let me explain what I mean by that, because this will come up repeatedly. A friend of mine married into a large family that expected her to house and to feed various brothers-in-law who would appear at her doorstep for the holidays. The first Christmas, one of these fellows objected, rather more imperiously than seemed appropriate, that "It's just not Christmas without creamed onions!" She invited him to make creamed onions himself. To his credit he did—and has continued to do so every Christmas for many years amidst much good-natured teasing.

Something of the same discernment is called for with our cultural heritage as well. We need to reconsider minimally conscious assumptions such as "It's just not Christmas without creamed onions." Maybe we can do without them. Maybe we can take responsibility for getting them ourselves rather than blithely expecting that creamed onions will simply appear as part of the midwinter metaphysical order. Maybe we can say, "I don't think that creamed onions are crucial, but by all means make some if you like." At its best, wise self-awareness in such matters can generate good family stories, told with a laugh for years, where instead there might have been abiding conflict—particularly when what's at stake is much more serious than Christmas dinner.

For instance, it seems to me that the separate-spheres doctrine wreaks havoc upon our concept of masculinity just as it does (as we have seen) with our understanding of femininity. When women become uniquely responsible for the entire care and upbringing of children, not merely for the breast-fed infant, men lose the major roles they once played in the education and socializing of their children—and especially their major responsibility for the acculturation of their sons beginning by age six or seven at the very latest. Men become increasingly marginal to family life and to the familial circle of affection, respect, intimacy, and moral influence. Over time, men have become as widely excluded from care as women once were excluded from power. And of course there are many who still argue that these exclusions reflect the natural desires and true character of those who are excluded.

Men are not simply cut off from children. They are transformed into overgrown kids themselves. As Gillis trenchantly observes, "Over the course of the [nineteenth] century, middle-class men became ever-more incapable of making a home for themselves. Undomesticated as children, they tended to turn their wives into mother figures and their children into playmates, with the result that the Victorian father figure became a curious combination of contradictory images: the stranger, the intruder, the clown, and the biggest child in the family."[31] (Homer Simpson, I am told, plays this role.) Men are supposedly incapable of rudimentary adult judgment and skill in the basic biological tasks of cooking, cleaning, or washing clothes. They cannot manage the alert attention, fast judgment, and sensitive understanding needed to guide and to protect five-year-olds. Dishwashers and washing machines are over their heads, just as adding more paper to the photocopier was beyond my colleague, despite his Ph.D. from Yale. Men may be sharply observant scientists, economists, or engineers, but around the house or in the presence of children they supposedly become oblivious. They may understand (and control) an array of relevant theories, but they are dangerously inept and unreliable at practice. Or so the story goes.

Above all, men are seen as emotionally and psychologically so underdeveloped that—despite masculine dominance in a variety of relevant professions—they are at most marginal members of the family psychological system. They "belong" at work because working is all they are capable of doing: the household needs their paychecks but not their personal presence, not their souls. If to some ways of thinking the woman home caring for her children is but an oppressed servant, the corollary of her exaltation as Angel in the House is that the man becomes an oppressed servant, working brutally long hours but excluded from the magic circle of pure love, spiritual development, and psychological intimacy that the woman weaves. The dark partner of the Angel in the House is the Oaf in the Office. Angelic Mommy is paired with Dimwit Daddy—insensitive, inept, hovering always on the edge of violence. And then people wonder why divorce rates skyrocketed once women had the legal rights and educational opportunities necessary to become self-supporting.

William Julius Wilson attributes the decline in marriage rates to the fact that many women now earn enough to survive without men's incomes, at which point men's failure to contribute to the work of child care and household render men a net drain upon the family system. In the inimitable manner of social scientists, Wilson devised a numerical "marriageability index" for potential husbands, quantifying a man's value as a mate as a complex balance of earning power relative to the potential wife and willingness to do housework. If any sociologist of Wilson's eminence took to scoring women as wives, the popular press would screech for weeks; the newsweeklies would make it a cover story. As far as I can tell, that didn't happen to Wilson.[32] Nor would any advertiser long survive producing commercials that depict women in the ways that so many commercials depict men.

Nonetheless, evidence is mounting up on all sides that fathers play a vitally important role in the well-being of their children. When men are either physically or psychologically absent from the household, children across the socioeconomic spectrum suffer a wide range of what sociologists blandly call "negative outcomes" that are demonstrably independent of lost income from "deadbeat dads." Sons are more likely to be violent; daughters are more likely to become pregnant out of wedlock. No one does as well in school as other indicators would predict. When divorce or career pressures prevent men from being active participants in their own households, children suffer enormously.[33]

Fathers are crucial, not incompetent. Men are not "worse than the kids" but spectacularly important to them from the very first days of life—an importance that, according to census data, many fathers actively claim.[34] The overwhelming evidence for the negative impact of father absence absolutely dwarfs what small evidence we have for the deleterious effects of daycare. Furthermore, fathers who regularly provide for children's ordinary daily physical care (bathtimes, bedtimes, trips to the orthodontist, help with homework, fixing and eating a meal together) have children who are the most compassionate as adults.[35]

But men who want to reclaim the full scope of their paternal masculinity come up against historical traditions no less daunting than those faced by ambitious, capable women. For instance, Victorian women were told that too much time reading books would ruin their sexual fertility and perhaps turn them into lesbians. That antithesis between femininity and intellectual achievements persisted well beyond the Victorians: twenty-some years ago, a senior colleague of mine called when she heard that I was pregnant to ask if I would have an abortion—and it was clearly her expectation that I would (or should). The very same gender-laden ideology is now undercutting men who want to be fathers in more than a biological sense.

Consider, for instance, a *Newsweek* account of why "banking honcho Jimmy Lee" cut back on his hours and corporate responsibilities in order to have more time with his children:

> In the macho arena where Lee thrived, he knew that talk about family values could brand him at best a wimp and at worst a liar. "In the power alleys of Wall Street and the East Coast, it's not manly to admit that work/family is an issue," Lee shrugs. "In fact, the manly thing is to say, *I don't have a life and I'm proud of it.*" And true to form, rumors have raced through Chase that Lee is being pushed out.[36]

Lee's fate or his motives are not the point here: what matters is how confidently both he and the magazine lay out the conventional wisdom that it's not "manly" for a man to care about his family. Because men dominate both the highest levels of management and the most powerful political roles, such conventional wisdom about masculinity in our culture probably contributes to inaction at the level of national policy.

Another Victorian heritage complicates both policy debates and our personal decision-making: division among feminists. Plenty of nineteenth-century women disagreed quite significantly with the full-equity agenda of their sisters. The so-called traditional women were not opposed to women having power and authority. They simply located this power and authority in dramatically different arguments and skills, which is to say in opposition to the new capitalist ethos and the radically individualist social order within which men (and the "new women") competed in all these ruthless ways. These so-called conservative or traditional women believed that the full political and economic equality of the sexes would destroy the new moral legitimacy and authority that the separate-spheres model provided to women, whereas the more aggressively egalitarian women saw themselves as deconstructing the fraudulent hierarchical assumption that women belong at home with children primarily because women are incapable of any other role in the world.

In complexly evolved form, this division among women persists. It is all the more powerful for having such complicated origins in the whole Western crisis of how to reconcile personal intimacy and interpersonal morality with a culture based on capitalist markets. Elite women don't mend, scrub, cook, sew, weed, paint, etc. in the same ways as working-class women, partly as a matter of their own social-class identity and partly as a matter of their psychosocial identification with "masculine" social and economic roles. In a myriad of ways, elite women seem to me far less likely than working-class women to respect the work and the skill involved in such ordinary household tasks. Working-class and lower-middle-class women are rightly offended when feminists who are highly educated professionals disparage traditional "women's work" as dull or meaningless, and when they castigate women home with their children for being passive, stupid, without ambition, without a sense of self, or oppressed by their husbands. Even with two salaries, only the most elite households can afford to delegate the majority of routine housework to servants or servant substitutes such as cleaning services, landscaping services, consultants, decorators, nannies, cooks, and restaurants. Women who either cannot afford or refuse to commodify and then "outsource" all household-based work and care of children suffer both the contempt of the elite and what Ann Crittendon calls a "Mommy Tax" of lost wages, substantially diminished career trajectories, and much lower lifetime earnings.[37]

National child-care policies won't stand a chance if the premise of socially elite policymakers is that women home caring for their children are wasting their lives in demeaning triviality, irresponsible self-indulgence, or oppressed boredom. Working-class and median-income parents will think that upper-class, highly educated parents simply want—at taxpayer expense—to avoid caring for their own children just as they avoid scrubbing their own floors, repairing their own faucets, or cutting their own grass. As Joan Williams acknowledges in *Unbending Gender: When Family and Work Conflict and What To Do About It,* many lower-class women regard caring for their own children at home as a yearned-for privilege of the wealthy and as a crucial opportunity to transmit their moral ideals and stabilizing cultural traditions to their own children.[38] Their priorities differ sharply—and legitimately—from those of women who prefer to work outside the household but who can't find affordable quality child care. As a result, we have what neither group wants, neither substantial paid maternity leave and very high deductions for preschool-age dependents nor high-quality federally funded child care.

Perhaps the most intimate, most elusive damage wrought by the metaphoric associations of "male" and "female" is a sorting of the virtues into gender-specific lists. According to these categories, when a woman is courageous and resilient she is being masculine or "calling upon her masculine side." When a man is being gentle or self-aware he is being feminine. The moral ideal is an androgyny that is biologically impossible and thus symbolically bankrupt. For me to be resolute or, when necessary, aggressive has never felt to me like any compromise of my essential femininity. (Perhaps my working-class upbringing and Irish origins play a role in my feelings here; there's no way for me to tell.) Nor do I see tenderness or skill with a youngster as diminishing a man's masculinity. But if we buy into a shabby, shallow androgyny, and we live and work in a ruthlessly competitive global economy, then a man's generous compassion threatens both his job and his masculine sexual identity. For women, success and feminine sexual identity are wildly at odds from the beginning. That's what I ran into during graduate school in the early 1970s: buried deep within "androgyny" as a norm is the long-enduring Roman norm of *severitas,* according to which the ideal human is a male who would never, ever make cookies for a lunch meeting. No wonder social capital is plummeting, men and women are having increasing trouble staying married, and the well-being of children and other dependents has deteriorated so badly.

Gender Metaphors and the Loss of Compassion

Victorian women and their generations of daughters have certainly demonstrated that logic, mathematical precision, self-discipline, ambition, courage, etc. are not gender-specific traits, but women's assimilation to and deconstruction of the supposed "masculinity" of these abilities leave a host of other valuable characteristics languishing in the cultural margins. Compassion is the pre-eminent virtue on that list, but compassion generates a host of other socially crucial moral capabilities: generosity, kindness, care, patience, forbearance, tolerance, hope, and genuine humility. "Random acts of kindness and senseless beauty" are now advocated as an occasional subversive gesture, as a sort of individualist guerrilla action, rather than informing a vision of how we all should live, all of the time—a vision that once had broad cultural validity supported by major, publicly credible institutions such as the Christian churches.

The exalted Angel in the House was not only a cheap, sentimental, ultimately degrading vision of women. It was also based upon a wildly inadequate understanding of virtue and of the relationship between virtue and intelligence or tough-minded, resilient decision-making. Gender metaphors dangerously separate thinking from caring. Autonomy becomes the opposite of altruism. These literal-minded oppositions destroy or at least misunderstand compassion by confusing it with weakness.

As a consequence of this gender ideology, compassion is implicitly characterized as both a lack of resolute strength and as an "easy" or "natural" characteristic of the weak-willed and irrational. That is, of course, how the wise and the compassionate have always appeared to the fool—as the Victorian "conventional" or "traditional" feminists understood. Wisdom traditions delight in that paradox, enshrining it in koan, aphorism, and parable. One should not be surprised to see foolishness (embodied within gender ideologies) driving certain aspects of socioeconomic organization.

Yet neither should one be deceived. Developing genuine compassion requires the difficult "inner work" of getting beyond the self-centered grasping and incessant anxiety of mere egotism. It requires sustained, disciplined spiritual practice to achieve a new configuration of the relationship between "self" and "other." Compassion is not the mere capitulation of one naïve, unconscious egotist to another, stronger one. Genuine compassion demands the highest levels of self-integration: it is not merely the triumph of sentimental passivity among those too ditzy and too deficient in willpower to put up any resistance to the aggrandizement of rationalized patriarchy.

Gender ideology also generates a devastating separation of critical thinking from intelligent caring. If women don't think and men don't care, if women are irrational and men are oblivious, then we are as a species incapable of wise decisions because all of us are either men or women. Marketplace models don't work here, because thinking and feeling are not naturally or essentially opposed as buying and selling are opposed. Thought without care and care without thought are both severely deficient. If we have not yet found our way to wise policies about how to provide the care upon which social capital depends, that is in part because policy making is hamstrung by the mistaken idea that critical thought and compassionate responsibility are opposites.

Consider this as an angle on the question: the Christian doctrine of the Incarnation embodies the hope and the vision of healing these culturally enforced divisions within the soul. The doctrine tries to explain who Jesus was, and it's a fabulously thorny teaching: almost any explanation will elicit charges of heresy from one side or another. At the risk of that, however, I'd suggest that the doctrine of the Incarnation serves systematically or structurally to overcome classic Western dualism by asserting or imagining the possibility of the absolute in relative form. The Incarnation imagines that the transcendent can be made immanent, the immutable and immortal made developmental and mortal, the rigorously abstract made vulnerably human, and so forth. The doctrine is a vision of wholeness both cosmic and personal. It is visionary poetry of the first rank, not metaphysics. And it is powerfully opposed to the duality-making habits of the Western mind. Is Jesus human? Or is he God? The doctrinal answer goes far beyond "all of the above" to a radical, deeply symbolic revision of human nature. Part of revising the human necessarily includes a revised vision of the human relationship to the Divine, for whom the Incarnation revealed hitherto unexpected complexities. Closed or logically systematic systems of thought can neither express nor encompass genuine symbolic thinking at this level.

Finally, gender ideology obscures or destroys the ways in which altruism and autonomy exist in a dynamic relationship whereby each comprises the boundaries of the other. Marketplace ideology aside, self and other cannot be fundamental antagonists if we are to survive. On the one hand, sacrifice for others or my generosity is limited by the primary integrity of one's sense of self. By sheltering Jews in defiance of the Nazis, for instance, the Rescuers demonstrated extraordinary autonomy and a ferociously independent sense of themselves as human beings. On the other hand, the boundary of anyone's self-expression or self-realization has to be responsibility for the common good, or else the "self" will darken into the demonic and the self-destructive.

As Erik and Joan Erikson have explained in so many ways, in so many places, and with such simple, direct eloquence, the reciprocity of altruism and autonomy is the quandary of intimacy. Self-realization depends upon intimate relationship to an other, but that intimacy depends in turn upon a clarity about difference. Intimacy demands a clarity about boundaries. Intimacy requires that the self and the other remain two entities, related but not submerged into a single, doomed, and shapeless conglomerate.

Carol Gilligan aside, moral maturity demands equal and nuanced attention both to rights and to responsibilities, both to autonomy and to altruism. They cannot be separated from one another and assigned to a gender identity.[39] The long and complicated heritage of gender ideology muddles our efforts to find and to exert that moral maturity when it comes to meeting our duty both to provide for children and to nurture them, to cuddle them and buy them carrots, to sing songs and to provide insurance. When the crisis of care reaches even to the relationships between parents and children, compassionate responsibility among adults is in more trouble yet. *What we are up against* here is the pressure to divide our souls in two, which is a form of moral and cultural suicide. Success radically separated from kindness becomes ruthless acquisition; generosity radically isolated from a strong sense of self rots into sentiment and emotional extortion. One way or the other, for men *and* for women, the cultural and psychological foundations of mature compassion are eroded as we lose sight of the wholehearted moral and spiritual singleness at the core of our humanity.

Gender Metaphor and Contemporary Motherhood Polemics

Publishers release a small but steady stream of books about motherhood, often quite passionate books written by women whose first children are still very young. Such books recount, more or less naïvely, not only the persistence of gender ideology but also the array of conceptual and moral problems that arise from taking engendered metaphors literally. Susan Chira, for instance, a *New York Times* journalist, seems to have written *A Mother's Place: Taking the Debate About Working Mothers Beyond Guilt and Blame* largely to refute what she takes to be the usual moral norm for motherhood: "self-immolation" or "self-annihilation."[40] Chira argues that according to this norm a "good mother" necessarily must lose all sense of self as a separate entity because her own needs no longer count for anything. She calls the persistence of this oppressive social norm "a kind of June Cleaver vampire: No matter how many times you kill her, she never dies."[41]

Such a primary loss of psychological boundaries would of course be devastating both for the mother and for the child. The fear of such dissolution will inevitably generate an incapacitating fear of intimacy, a fear which perforce curtails anyone's abilities to function successfully as a parent, a spouse, or a loyal friend. But Chira argues that the operant cultural expectations for mothers involve just this kind of devastating dissolution, and so of course she resists. She does not seem to recognize the history of what she is up against, nor the considerable history of resistance to it by shrewd and self-possessed women. As a result, she feels terribly isolated, alienated, and uncertain:

> As a mother, I have often felt like an outlaw, my love for my children suspect, because I did not fit that ideal of the good mother. . . . I often found staying at home with an infant frustrating and lonely. . . . I still battle a sense of shame, a belief in a secret corner of my heart that my emotions brand me as a bad mother, alone amid a tide of rapture. That is why the drumbeat of criticism still rings so loudly in my ears and those of so many

> mothers I know—it echoes the reproaches we level at ourselves. . . . [But] A mother who has lost all sense of herself, whose sacrifices make her feel unhappy and ineffectual, is someone whose self-denial has become poisonous to herself and may well poison others around her.[42]

As a result of her beleaguered isolation, she bridles angrily at mainstream accounts of children's developmental need for attentive nurture. She reacts so strongly because she sees all such accounts as attacks upon her own primary psychic autonomy.

She insists that we must "force children to confront the fact that their mothers are separate persons with equally legitimate needs, not extensions of themselves who are there only to wait on them."[43] Ultimately, every one of us needs to realize that our parents are separate persons in this way, but how and when is that lesson learned? Chira cites approvingly a role-play experiment with toddlers that sought to elicit their understanding of the claim (vis-à-vis their employed mothers) that "I know you could wish to have your own life as I wish to have mine."[44]

But no matter how often and how clearly parents demonstrate the sane boundaries of their own sense of self, a recognition that parents are fully separate persons at best glimmers intermittently for teenagers. For toddlers, it is simply impossible: they do not have the fully formed sense of self that the recognition requires. We elicit that sense of self and we teach our children to love by loving them.[45] We help our children to develop the capacity for solid autonomy and mature intimacy by meeting their dependency needs, not by limiting our relationships with them in this rationalist, contractual way. All those toddlers really learned, I suspect, was to feel guilty about wanting their mothers.

What we are seeing here is that the radically individualist self is the necessary opposite of the literally selfless Angel in the House. What's lost in that transaction is any solid perception of how we can give of ourselves without literally giving ourselves away—how we can achieve generous, intimate compassion without the loss of healthy psychological boundaries. Toddlers will of course make grandiose demands, which parents will gently but firmly refuse. Children need such repeated encounters with firm but loving limits, not role-playing exercises in the tenets of radical individualism.

Chira's difficulty is how her normative definition of "healthy self" depends upon access to the sort of immediate individualist gratification which makes for what she calls a sense of "effectiveness." For Chira, as for so many in our culture, the principle source of such "effectiveness" is employment. In part, we see the assumption that the skills exercised at work are one's only skills or the only outlets for one's talents. More to the point, I suspect, is the fact that the paycheck is power. It is public status. To surrender or even to diminish one's paycheck is thus to lose one's crucial weapon in the ruthless capitalist struggle of each against all. One who does so risks becoming—or becoming seen as—nothing at all, invisible, without autonomous social status.

No wonder, then, that some women writing in defense of "working mothers" glorify work (and despise women home with children). The attitude toward work in these books is flatly contradicted by everyone else writing about work these days. Other books about the role of work in our lives and in our culture recite such a litany of complaints that a good excuse to take a year off from work would seem like deliverance indeed.

Joan Peters makes the connection between employment and self-definition or social status exquisitely clear. In *When Mothers Work,* she cautions sternly that women who care for their children in ways that allow them to become financially dependent upon their husbands take terrible psychological risks: "The danger of this choice is that dependence upon a husband rarely remains solely financial. Eventually it weakens the active self, fostering a further confusion of boundaries by moving the center of identity from oneself to another, from her to him."[46] The core sense of self, it seems, is defended primarily by an armor of paychecks. By this reading, one's self is defined by one's earnings and, even more powerfully, by the trajectory of one's career: ". . . people [who] parent according to the flawed ideal of self-sacrificing motherhood . . . may often look perfect but be emotionally tense with resentments. How could it not be so if women violate their training, their ambitions, and themselves when they become mothers? Mothering has proved a disaster for most career women, who compromise, veer off track, cut back, and scale down, ending up far below the level their credentials suggest they could have achieved."[47] As business theorist Al Gini puts it, what we see here is an implicit equation between *my job* and *my self.*[48]

The only exception Peters makes is for men who stay home with their children. She interviews one such man, a freelance writer, attributing his obvious satisfaction with this arrangement to "the advantage of male confidence. He parents in a way that's comfortable for him, not according to some maternal ideal."[49] Once again, the fundamental Western "spiritual grammar" is evident: men are strong, immutable, autonomous, confident; women are weak, subject to pressures, dependent, and uncertain. "I used to think that having a child would feel like a vacuum cleaner sucking me out of the world," Peters explains, "and I was not entirely wrong."[50] But the man she interviews can resist these pressures. Women who are freelance writers—as both she is and I am—could not resist these pressures as successfully as he does. Why not?

Like Chira, Peters remains trapped within the narrow constraints of gender ideology. The sacrificial Angel is defined by self-immolating deference to everyone else's desires; the self-authenticating, self-actualizing individualist is defined by prowess at satisfying his own desires. Once again, however, employment is crucial. "If we did not pressure women to withdraw from their work lives to mother," she objects, "they would not imagine that a child could fulfill their high expectations of self-gratification."[51] Such expectations are wildly inappropriate to begin with.[52] Furthermore, over the long haul most jobs are not gratifying to that extent either. As Christopher Lasch astutely observes, "Professional careers are not more liberating for women than for men if those careers are governed by the requirements of the corporate economy. . . . [Such jobs] will be unable to satisfy the desire to become not just self-supporting but useful and self-respecting."[53]

At the hands of thinkers like Chira and Peters, generous compassion is logically—even if inadvertently—configured as a character flaw. Self-assertion takes its place as the central or generative concept underlying our moral norms for what it means to be most fully human. Chira and Peters are both fighting fire with fire, and in the end both are badly burned: rather than recognizing the mirages elicited by gender ideology, they merely swap positions from female to male within its dehumanizing system. As a result, children are implicitly redefined as a source of gratification to us as adults. Unfortunately, children will regularly fail in that role, such that rational people will meet their need for significance, recognition, etc., in the separate sphere of public life.

In that arrangement, the beautiful child, like the good-looking spouse, is a natural and lovely concomitant to the good life. As Peters puts it, "when mothers work—at least, when they work under humane conditions—not only do they help themselves and their families to live more balanced lives, but they more fully experience how much children can enrich life."[54] Children can indeed enrich life. Parenthood certainly has its wonderfully rewarding moments. But children also impose a stunning array of moral, physical, and financial obligations that, like any set of complicated obligations, will often prove exhausting, frustrating, and not much fun at all. Shabby, sentimental projections upon *woman* as a cultural archetype are but shabby, sentimental projections. Simply recognizing that the projections are insane doesn't get us where we need to get, whether as individual households with small children or as a society concerned about its own future.

Chira admiringly describes the devotion of a friend of hers, who does her best during the workweek to get home in time to spend half an hour or so with her children after they are tucked into bed but before they fall asleep. She observes that this woman feels warmly connected to her children. That may well be the case: adults have such abilities. I feel very close to any number of people I see a lot less often than once a day. But what about the child? Parents who work that kind of schedule define themselves as largely irrelevant to their children's daily life and thus to their children's development across the board. Such parents are, perforce and regardless of gender, the remote Victorian father, droning away in the workplace and dependent upon employment and earnings for a sense of self.

As both Chira and Peters discover, their children become as passionately attached to their nannies as any young child to its mother.[55] When the nannies leave, the children are inconsolably grief-stricken. The parents are stunned, although developmental psychologists have long recognized that mother-loss is devastating for a child.[56] The nurturant, psychologically crucial parental bond between adult and child is established by countless small daily interactions, not a half-hour of *paterfamilias* "quality time" before bed. Young children do not distinguish between quantity time and quality time.

The problem here, as we will see in more detail in part four, is that the paycheck functions poorly as the generative core of one's sense of self. In a variety of quite manipulative ways, employees—perhaps especially at the higher levels of education and earnings—are being maneuvered into giving to the corporation the kind of energy and attention that might instead be devoted to personal relationships both within and beyond the household. Daily life with young children is extraordinarily demanding at times, especially in the isolated contemporary household; but daily life on the professional fast track is not the solution that Chira, Peters, and others seem to imagine it is. As decades click by, as the work (no matter how varied) slowly becomes routine, status begins to get stale, and all the glitzy stuff we have purchased slowly begins to feel like clutter. Imperial Roman *severitas,* refurbished for the 24/7 global economy, threatens the souls of adults and children alike.

Some put their trust in chariots, some in the stock markets, some in luxury cars or dynamite careers. Some seek wisdom—and the means to pay the mortgage too.

Conclusion: Reclaiming Our Humanity

Bram Dykstra's *Idols of Perversity* is a spine-chilling exercise in art history. He looks closely at nineteenth-century portraits of women who are artistically idealized and yet simultaneously presented as dead, dying, or mortally ill—or else surrounded by morbid images of death, decay, and lassitude unto death. Self-evident within the tradition is the artistic recognition of how moribund and corrupt were the moral norms funding the portrait of women as Angels in the House, and how culturally hopeless were the moral tasks such women were supposed to accomplish. The carnage that was the First World War, the unspeakable brutality of the Second, and the blind rage of both genocide and terrorism testify no less eloquently to the equal and opposite morbidity of the Angel's gender opposite: neither the abolition nor the utter indulgence of ego solves the predicament of what it means to be human in our times, despite the constraints of a postindustrial social organization.

Let us turn, then, and examine the problem from a slightly different perspective: the ideology of "family values." "Family values" offer no solution either, alas, because it echoes at the level of social organization all the shabby and self-defeating antitheses of dualist gender metaphors. Once again, as we will see, altruism is marginalized and compassion is deconstructed in favor of a brutally ascetic and rationalist devotion to earning money.

PART THREE

Home Sweet Home

How "Family Values" Fail Us

Prelude

Imagine for a moment a world utterly without conflicts between men and women. Imagine that no more tension exists between men and women than currently exists between people born in even-numbered months and people born in odd-numbered months. Such equanimity may be difficult to imagine, but for five seconds give it a try.

Then consider this: even if we could magically resolve both all the classic sexual tensions between men and women and all the metaphoric engenderings of Western dualisms, there would still be many questions about how any given household relates to the wider society. How does our *private* identity as members of a given household relate to our *public* identity as members of the society generally?

Cultural arguments about gender can be distinguished in this way from cultural arguments about individual households—even though in practical terms all of us have to cope with all of it. In the chapters ahead we will examine how "family values" ideology relocates the moral life of our society from its traditional anchor in powerful public religious institutions into a new psychosocial locus within the private family and its symbolic domicile, Home Sweet Home. As we will see, the supposed moral autonomy of the household is inescapably undermined and trivialized by the far greater power of the surrounding culture. We will look at that process from several different angles. The result, I argue, is that "family values" ideology disrupts our practical sense of what it means *to be human.* It is as if we can be fully human, fully ourselves, neither at home nor at work: like the Victorian Oaf, we are to be heartless (at work); like the Victorian Angel, we are to be brainless (at home). For those of us who have both heads and hearts no matter where we are, coping with "family values" ideologies is like living atop a geological fault whose dynamics rattle our souls in the night.

6

Making It Official

Why Morality and Compassion Don't Belong in Public

Family Values and the "Public" World

The concept "family values" rests upon the division of reality into the dualist pairing *public* and *private*. The *public* realm of politics, business, and power is shaped by rationality and by conflict. The *private* realm of family household is shaped by (benevolent) emotion and by harmony. "Family values" thus refers to all of the behaviors that facilitate social harmony and express benevolent feelings. "Family values" are called "family" values because they are held to originate in the *private* realm. There is no correlative set of values originating in the *public* realm, because—as the story goes—the *public* realm deals in objective facts, not values (which are by definition "personal," "private," and "subjective"). At most, one can say that the *public* realm is shaped by logical or rationalist principles such as the profit motive or the individualist will-to-power. The *public* realm is formally or systematically amoral, just as the *private* realm is systematically nonrational.

This distinction between *public* and *private* derives from two different historical developments. The first is the geographical centralizing of market activity that also underlies the gender ideology of separate spheres. That is, *work* has become not only an activity but also a locale. We work *at work*, by definition. What, then, do we do *at home*? As *home* became the opposite of *work* as a mythic and psychic locale, then by illogical but inexorable extension the activity of the household was reconfigured as rest or as leisure rather than as labor.

As a result, the work of running a household begins to disappear from the psychic map of the culture. A whole array of vital social and physical tasks becomes relatively invisible and painfully without status: raising the children, caring for ill or dependent adults, attending to the needs and networks that sustain community life and social capital, and doing the physical work of keeping the house clean, the people properly nourished, and everything in good order at many different levels. Such important duties "disappear" because *public* socioeconomic doctrine defines "significance" in terms of the economic exchanges of buying and selling. Unpaid work done within the household, *because it is unpaid,* is not included in economists' calculations of the Gross National Product, nor does it "count" toward one's eventual Social Security payments.

The issue goes much deeper than the socioeconomic status of washing clothes and running errands. For instance, I spent an unexpected hour recently consoling a distraught friend whose eight-year-old daughter was sexually assaulted in the school bathroom. I sat clutching the phone, perched on a stool in my kitchen, listening to her struggle to think clearly, to evaluate her options, and to manage her gut-level responses constructively. None of that "counts" in the domain of *public* socioeconomic doctrine unless she pays me and I report it on my IRS Schedule C. I do not mean to deny that she also may have needed a lawyer and a therapist. That's not the point here. The point is whether first she needed a friend. How, as a society, are we to think about our own need for this depth of friendship? Do we honor and recognize it? Or do such conversations fail to "count" for anything because nothing "countable" happened?

As we have seen, the Victorian exaltation of the motherly Angel in the House was an attempt both to assert the significance of nonmarket care and to persuade women to take solo responsibility for this invisible work, but the conceptual foundation of that effort was morally and intellectually incoherent. It rapidly decayed into patronizing sentimentality and manipulative oppression. As John Gillis trenchantly observed, "the desire to honor the idea of motherhood has too often been accompanied by a neglect of the plight of actual mothers."[1] Separate spheres as a cultural experiment was doomed, its doom was knelled by Mary Wollstonecraft in the 1790s, but here we are in the twenty-first century, still struggling to imagine anew outside the unworkable categories of early industrial capitalism. "Family values" doctrine is hardly more than a new, less gender-laden label for separate-spheres doctrine. Like its predecessor, it is corrupt, corrupting, and doomed to failure.

The fact remains that interpersonal care and social networks demand time and energy that must perforce be taken from *public* market activities that confer social status and generate income. Yet, as intensely social creatures, we are inevitably, perhaps unconsciously, attuned to doing what confers social status. Ignoring the allure of income and prestige will never come easily. Doing so is much more feasible, of course, if we have friends who think as we think and who value what we value. These friendships generate a countercultural status all their own. Phillip Rieff calls such friendships a "positive community," which is a group that confers prestige and offers meaning according to its own norms.[2] These communities can be as elaborate as formal religious organizations with budgets and buildings. They can be as simple as book groups or pickup volleyball games every Thursday at the local gym.

Small towns once functioned as communities of meaning and of affirmation in this way. But as Robert Bellah wryly observes, small-town life has mostly died out because people found small towns small-minded and confining.[3] In my experience, closely knit ethnic neighborhoods (urban or suburban) once functioned in the same way as small towns: everyone was known, and nothing much was missed by vigilant observers. Neighborhood churches functioned as mainframe computers do in maintaining the Web. Religious congregations are or were yet another major cultural instance of the positive community. But according to Freud, these positive communities are or were held together by their ability to inflict guilt, a claim that shelves full of memoirs certainly support. Rieff argues that the therapeutic turn of modern culture has discredited such guilt, which is to say that countercultural communities are simply doomed.

Maybe. Maybe not. Rieff's dim view of positive communities is challenged by burgeoning attention to spiritualities, to traditional religious practices, and to both books and websites offering help in finding varieties of countercultural communities. Humans are deeply social creatures, and religion is apparently innate to the human psyche. The question here, I suppose, is whether positive communities have to be as powerful and as widespread as, say, "Christendom" once was. Do countercultural positive communities have to have national officers, audited budgets, and nonprofit organization tax ID numbers? Do they have to be major, culturewide phenomena? Or can your book club count? Your softball team?

The issue, of course, is whether or not people in these relatively informal social groups hold one another accountable to moral standards. Some do; some don't. My point is that if we do not belong to what functions as a successful normative community one way or another, then all we have left is the marketplace. To stand against consumerist standards enforced by commercial after commercial after commercial demands both strength of character and relentless intentionality. It's hard to sustain that entirely on your own.

Furthermore, the paycheck serves as the principle *public* measure of meaning in our lives and as the major *public* arbiter of social status. That fact distinguishes the contemporary United States from traditional societies in which the meaning of one's life and one's standing in the community are configured on much more complex grounds than one's annual income. Plenty of people find the marketplace measures demeaning. Wise folks will always shrug and think, *Yah, but we know better than this.* Furthermore, the notion that both circles of friends and religious congregations necessarily trade only in guilt strikes me as psychologically naïve and historically shallow. No matter how corrupt churches have been at times, or how treacherous small towns, the fact remains that wisdom traditions and human relationships nurture the best that is in us.

Where the Golden Rule Has Gone—and Why

The second major historical development funding the distinctive contemporary ideology of "family values" antedates the separate-spheres argument by several centuries. Western culture was originally divided into these two rhetorical domains—the *public* and the *private*—in response to religious wars that swept through Europe after the sixteenth-century Protestant Reformation.

In the aftermath of the Reformation, religious beliefs and doctrines came to be regarded as exclusively *private* matters, not as grounds for calling out the troops or blockading a city whose clergy advocated heretical theological positions. Watching genocidal murder along supposedly "religious" lines in the Balkans, or after terrorist attacks supposedly motivated by radical Islamic jihad against infidels, I find it easy to sympathize with seventeenth-century thinkers who wanted to banish religion from *public* life once and for all. But in the seventeenth century, banishing religious belief to the *private* life was never intended nor imagined to include any challenge to the centrality or the universality of a wide range of Judeo-Christian moral obligations. These moral standards were so deeply embedded in Western culture as to seem logically self-evident—and therefore independent of religious doctrines and beliefs. At the political level, in the *public* realm, society was still to be governed by such precepts as the "Golden Rule," which reformulates not only Jesus' teaching that "As you wish that men would do to you, do so to them" (Luke 6:31 RSV) but also the ancient Jewish injunctions to love your neighbor as yourself and to be gracious to the stranger. All that was to be "banished," generally speaking, was a set of internecine disputes about certain details of Christian doctrine and a correlative set of disputes about church organization.

What we are up against these days, however, is how capitalism does challenge traditional Western social ethics. At the level of theory, the triumph of market-based economies replaces the Golden Rule with "get the most for the least." One's behavior toward another is constrained not by transcendently grounded reciprocal moral obligation, but by the other's ability to refuse, to retaliate, and to resist. When religion is consigned to *private* life, to the domains of family and household—not the economy and the nation—moral obligation in *public* life is reduced to law and order as calculated on a narrow cost-benefit basis. "Right and wrong" become no more than "legal or illegal": if a lawyer has found a loophole, one is free to claim that one has done "nothing wrong." Arthur Levitt, former chairman of the Security and Exchange Commission, put it this way: "The business community tends to look at these things [i.e., accounting rules of the kind violated by Enron] in terms of what we can get away with rather than what's right. Optics has replaced ethics."[4] What matters is how things look—how the light might be bent to create a favorable illusion for Wall Street. When the alternative to that seems to be violent, repressive regimes managed by religious extremists, we shrug and try to live with the consequences of keeping morality merely *private*. But the consequences are bitter.

The division between *public* and *private* is an ideological strategy whereby the whole cultural weight of Western moral and ethical tradition is to be relocated from church and synagogue as authoritative public institutions to the family household. The individual family, not religious teachers, traditions, and practices, is now the principal advocate and guardian of such virtues as kindness, generosity, patience, humility, forbearance, respect, industry, sobriety, social justice, and honesty in all things. For parents struggling simply to keep their children fed and reasonably well-behaved, it's a breathtaking prospect to imagine. Religious tolerance is necessary in a multicultural society, but the individual nuclear family is inadequate to the cultural burdens placed upon it by the radical division of reality into *public* and *private* realms. Economic systems exert tremendous pressure upon culture, pressure that individual households are on the whole powerless to countermand. As Christopher Lasch contends, "From the beginning, the glorification of domestic life simultaneously condemned the social order of which the family allegedly served as the foundation. In urging a retreat to private satisfactions, the custodians of domestic virtue implicitly acknowledged capitalism's devastation of all forms of collective life, while at the same time they discouraged attempts to repair the damage by depicting it as the price that had to be paid for material and moral improvement."[5] In short, "family values" are as doomed as the Angel in the House.

How "Family Values" Undermine the Common Good

Although relocating ethical foundations from churches to households predates "Angel in the House" gender ideology by at least a century, it suffers from the same tendency to divide our souls into unworkably opposing parts. It falsely divides critical intelligence from self-possessed virtue; it treats thinking and caring as formal opposites. When heart and mind are divided each from the other, the soul starves. Wisdom is silenced and set aside. As "Angel in the House" gender ideology wreaked havoc in the primary psychodynamics of the household, turning both men and women into dysfunctional caricatures, so "family values" wreaks havoc in the household of the nation as a whole. This radical separation of our *public* lives or *public* identities from our *private* selves trivializes our moral capacity for decent human relationships with colleagues, neighbors, and fellow citizens, even while it unleashes all of our ordinary hostile and aggressive tendencies. Home is sentimentalized; both employment and politics are set free from moral restraints and ethical commitments—as if what is legal and what is morally right are always equivalent. We resist, of course. Kind, decent, ordinary people commonly resist, but we feel inescapably besieged.

Such a division is also stunningly naïve sociologically. John R. Gillis argues at length that prior to the Industrial Revolution, the community as a whole regulated and supported the individual household by means of institutions grounded in ethical norms that had transcendent warrant. Furthermore, individuals had a variety of public family-substitutes upon which they could rely to make up for any deficiency in their own households: guilds, clubs, teams, study groups, sewing circles, book groups, garden exchanges, debating societies, service clubs, community-based political organizations, and church-centered groups of many different kinds.[6] But as Robert Putnam documents in considerable detail in *Bowling Alone: The Collapse and Revival of American Community,* we are rapidly losing the infrastructure that supported the networks of friendships whereby individuals and individual households sustained these noneconomic, cooperative, and supportive contacts with one another.[7] Nonetheless, according to "family values" ideology, these isolated and beleaguered individual households are supposed to make up for the deficits of the larger society and to do so despite the fact that these moral deficits have massive economic warrant. Worse yet, the family is supposed to teach and to support virtue despite the fact that the marketplace not only rewards greed, selfishness, and exploitation but also represents these as economically normative behaviors.

As Stephanie Coontz insists, very few people can sustain personal values inside the household that are wildly at odds with the values or behaviors demanded in their public and economic lives.[8] Some people can. Some people certainly do. But as a society we would be wiser not to depend upon everyone's ability to resist the *public* cultural norms based upon competitive, ruthless self-seeking and the profit motive. As she argues, we need public norms and public institutions that support the best that is in us. We need social structures that elicit and affirm not only the depth of our ordinary human decency but also the depth of our common yearning to live honorably and with compassion for one another.

This systematic opposition between individual and society ultimately marginalizes the common good. With the loss of a credible public locus for morality, we lose the credible public grounds upon which to formulate and to debate the common good and to persuade one another to joint action in its service. In its place all we have is the sum of private goods and private interests, which too often translates into policies determined not by wise assessment of the common good but rather by pollsters and by consultation with special-interest groups. It is a toxic mix of Adam Smith and Jeremy Bentham: the greatest good for the greatest number is determined by the sum of campaign contributions arranged by lobbyists. Capitalist self-seeking may suffice to produce breakfast cereals with the trendiest nutritional supplements or computers that become obsolete as fast as a normal mortal can learn their updated software. But the common good is much more than the sum of immediate personal interests.[9]

A Plague of Experts

As Christopher Lasch passionately argued in several books written over a span of decades, the cultural pressures that families are supposed to resist have in fact invaded the family itself in the guise of social-service experts of many different kinds: parenting educators, marriage counselors, life-adjustment teachers in the schools, sex education teachers, therapists and counselors of every possible kind.[10] Wardrobes can be managed by fashion consultants, and personal shoppers can buy presents for friends and family. A personal coach can be hired to nag us into maintaining the orderliness of the closets our closet consultant designed and installed. A personal trainer can design and supervise our exercise program, while a spiritual director can oversee our spiritual development. A psychological therapist can help us cope with our past, and an investment counselor can help us cope with the future. Although we are supposedly a society of radically autonomous individuals, in fact we are surrounded by experts—by strangers—eager to supervise every detail of our "private" lives.

This is radical expressive individualism? It seems to me more like radically isolated and uncertain individuals reaching out to other people. A lot of money can be made trading on the fact that as social creatures we have not only respect for one another's ideas but also an innate desire for community and for cordial help with life's ordinary challenges. Those plain and decent human needs have been systematically exploited by a thousand transient commercial exchanges and transparently manipulative psychological ploys that do not meet our need for responsive, helpful, compassionate relationships. Too many people no longer belong to diverse, vibrant, intimate "positive communities" where they can find—for free—the casual advice that common sense reasonably desires.

But the foundation of that old-fashioned arrangement was the ordinary assumption that our abilities ultimately belong not to us as individuals but to the common good. If I can coach your kid for his SATs or proofread your new résumé, if you can explain to me the home-office deduction or help me transplant a big old rose, well, among friends such help might be both offered and received as a matter of course. Once we shared what now we buy. Even this little sketch of such communal give-and-take now sounds hopelessly sentimental, even in my ears—although I remember growing up in such a neighborhood. At times I have seen communities like that bloom again briefly, like wildflowers in the woods or like a pair of cardinals who nested in my yard for a few years and then disappeared. Such neighborliness is neither nostalgia nor illusion, but it depends upon the intentionality generated and sustained by vibrant positive communities of one sort or another.

All of this happens, however, only against the more general cultural pressure to leave all such help and advice to paid consultants. Consider, for instance, how broadly the schools have taken over teaching children about sex, diet and healthcare, driving, self-esteem, conflict resolution, and social skills. The obvious presumption is that parents are doing a terrible job in all these tasks, that parents lack the expertise of experts, that families are so universally dysfunctional that our kids will probably be better off if we keep our mouths shut on a lot of these topics no matter what. What's worse, any sensible person knows that many parents are indeed failing in all of these regards, for a whole array of reasons beginning with how many hours people spend at jobs that they are apt to lose in the next round of "pre-emptive downsizing." Furthermore, much in the popular culture suggests that the quality of a person's life ultimately depends not upon parents—those wretches responsible for so many wounded inner children—but upon a good therapist and a solid effort at therapeutic work at some point on down the line.

But if caring for children effectively is beyond the scope of most parents no matter what, why worry about it? Especially why take time to worry about it when that's apt to shortchange everyone's economic security? Rosalind C. Barnett and Caryl Rivers are typical of many Mommy Wars writers when they insist that money, not personal attention, is what kids need most from their parents. "Women's incomes are keeping millions of families from sliding into poverty, homelessness, and despair," they explain. "Even in middle-class families where the husband has a decent job, without the mother's income there would be no money for college or for the educational enrichment that will help children to compete in what is becoming a savagely competitive society. . . . Many mothers think their kids will be better served by the funds for a college education than by any number of home-baked cookies."[11]

Barnett and Rivers are right when they contend that a mother's paycheck keeps many households out of poverty. That's beyond question, as is the brutal cost of college education. Last year we spent close to $55,000 on college tuition, a miniscule dorm room, and cafeteria food for our three children—never mind at least $500 per semester per child in books, plus pocket money and the cost of travel. That may sound like a lot, but most parents my age will be astounded by how little that is for top-ranked universities. Now all three are talking about graduate school, and the minimum annual tuition increase has been at least five times the rate of inflation. These realities are undeniable; fear of them haunted me for decades.

Discounting Ourselves

The cost of education is beyond question. But can we understand these realities and nonetheless find the chutzpah to value the personal attentive care that a parent can offer to a child? Barnett and Rivers call into question the value of the personal attentive care that any one person can offer to another, regardless of the biological relationship between them. "Home-made cookies" or "milk and cookies after school" is a common trope in the Mommy Wars. It's a synecdoche for commonplace, low-key parental availability—not highly intentional, carefully planned and scheduled "quality time" episodes on weekends, but rather adults letting kids set the agenda both pragmatically and psychologically. What matters—the key to the figure of speech—is that she who has time to bake cookies surely has time to listen, and she makes that willingness visible to the child in such regular, commonplace rituals as sitting together nonchalantly for an after-school snack.

I think that Barnett and Rivers are being deliberately literal-minded when they suggest that mothers involved only (or primarily) in nonmarket work don't have the brains and the moral fiber to recognize the value of a B.A. They are reverting to the classic image of *woman* as intellectually and personally deficient—unless, of course, a paycheck redeem her, a paycheck demonstrate her objective rationality and fully adult (i.e., in the grammar of the West, "masculine") status. For all those many households that are not struggling to stay above "poverty, homelessness, and despair," finding the appropriate balance between engaging kids personally and providing for them financially can't be settled as easily as such writers would settle it. It's the kind of core conflict that awakens mature, thoughtful, weary parents at three in the morning.

Money in a college savings account I could see. I could measure its accumulation, year by year, and feel thereby assured that I was meeting some measure of my duties as a responsible parent. I have no equally "objective" measure of countless hours I spent listening to a kid who came in after school and flung himself into the armchair in my home office. I listened and I certainly enjoyed doing so, but running minimized in the background of my mind were Mommy Wars voices insisting that what this child really needs is a mother who will stay on task with her paid work. *Your education was in literature and philosophy,* something muttered, *not psychology and adolescent development. What do you know? If there's something wrong, call a therapist; otherwise, send the kid back downstairs and get back to work.*

So what did it cost me to listen, and what would it have cost them if I had not done so? Life offers no answers to questions like that, none at all. Of course I knew the value of a B.A.! But I had also taught undergraduates at elite institutions, almost always in small classes where they did a lot of writing and I had a chance to get to know each student fairly well. I was thoroughly unnerved by how many of them arrived on campus well prepared and smart as blazes but quietly melancholy and utterly starved for personal attention. And I knew the research demonstrating that optimism predicts undergraduate grade-point averages better than SAT scores.[12] I'd seen that for myself as well: the solidly secure, emotionally brighter students always out-performed their classmates—even those who were intellectually brighter or better prepared.

So my kids and I ate a lot of cookies, and we drank a lot of milk: I know full well when I'm being needled by pop-culture voices in my head.

Everyone does. Most of us, most of the time, resist quite successfully. But over time, such needling, such nasty remarks by the likes of Rivers and Barnett, take a genuine toll. I saw that one day sitting on the back porch of a friend of mine, who was taking an extended maternity leave when her children were small. Tears in her eyes, she insisted to me that she had won a First Amendment case argued before the Supreme Court of the United States: if she wanted to stay home with her boys she had earned the right. But what about the women who don't have a J.D. from the University of Chicago and a career like that? Or a Ph.D. and a list of publications like mine? Do we have to "earn" the right to stay home with our own children, "buy" it on the open market of *public* professional success? But the alternative—which I have also seen firsthand among my friends—can be feeling utterly defenseless before the contempt of those who think that such generosity is both irrational and irresponsible. I think it is asking a lot to expect that every young parent home with small children will be either particularly gutsy or else historically sophisticated enough to see through the presuppositions altogether.

Furthermore, this is merely the parent-specific version of a pressure faced by any decent, compassionate adult. What is the value, what is the meaning of time spent listening to our friends, who perhaps should talk to therapists instead of us, or kibitzing with elderly neighbors who, if they are lonely, should perhaps join a discussion group at the senior center. It's no wonder, in Robert Putnam's wonderful image, that now we go bowling alone.[13] The commonplace compassion people offer to one another, the commonsense wisdom we share in reflecting generously on one another's problems or important experiences—all of that is now available for purchase, the expensive service of an expert. As somebody said once, we are the first culture in human history to pay someone just to listen to us. That's a stunning devaluation of ourselves as wise, compassionate listeners, and it testifies to a dangerous loss of social capital.

In short, Coontz's complaint needs to be taken one step further. It's not only unrealistic to expect that most people will cling to personal values in defiance of social norms generally. It is probably also unrealistic to expect that beleaguered parents will effectively and steadily resist the ways in which their own wisdom and beneficence are deconstructed by various experts convinced that parents are at best insignificant and at worst hazardous to the development of their children. As Juliet Harris argues explicitly in *The Nurture Assumption,* parents contribute the most by earning the most so as to pay for the best sorts of schools, orthodontists, dermatologists, fashion consultants, and so forth—perhaps even plastic surgeons. Both Mommy and Daddy are reduced to Victorian drones, outsourcing the emotional and moral core of the household to a fleet of hired angels. As Penelope Leach astutely observes, we have discredited the roles that parents necessarily play. "What is needed now," she explains, "is . . . a reappraisal of the importance of parenting and fresh approaches to the continuing care and education of children in, and for, changing societies."[14] If, as Harris contends, parents have so little to offer even to their own children, of course it is mere sentimentality to suppose that adults have anything significant to offer to one another as friends or as neighbors.

And then, of course, what free time we do have with our families has been targeted by the leisure-time industry of computer games, amusement parks, after-school activities, vacation-resort programs, television and movies, the Internet, and bitterly competitive organized sports for kids. The array of such stuff makes the separatist instincts of the Amish look far less quaint, far more wise. The upshot of the public/private division has been, on the whole, something close to the annihilation of the *private* as a powerful, effective locus of care, compassion, and moral responsibility for one another. As Lasch observes, "A retreat into 'privatism' no longer serves to shore up values elsewhere threatened with extinction."[15] What we face, in short, is the ethical equivalent of Catch-22: the sole remaining domain in which commitment and care are honored is the family household, but the solitary *private* household is so terribly besieged by the power of the *public* domain that its ethical and socializing role has to be taken over by *public* experts and expensive consultants even for such mundane tasks as buying a sofa, planning a wedding, or applying to college. Resistance to this trend is not rare, but it is always exhausting.

7

What Counts Is What Counts—and Nothing Else Does

The Rise of Quantification

Family values fail not only because the *public* domain overpowers the *private* domain, but also because the *public* domain is increasingly characterized by complex, proficient habits of quantification. Rational-actor theory, for instance, testifies vividly to the triumph of quantification in the public realm: these theorists offer elaborate mathematical formulae quantifying our most intimate and nuanced moral decisions.[16] But quantification was underway long before the rise of rational-actor formulae in the 1950s. As we shall see, the rise of quantification began in the late Middle Ages. Quantification echoed through medieval culture in at least a couple of ways that are still relevant. First, quantification validates the commonplace Western dualisms we have been examining all along. Second, it amplifies the competitive spirit inherent within capitalism.

In *The Measure of Reality: Quantification and Western Society 1250–1600,* Alfred W. Crosby traces the evolution of mathematical habits of mind in the development of Western culture, a development that he sees as complicated from the first by the "nagging insufficiency of [the West's] traditional explanations for the mysteries of reality." The insufficiency to which he refers is the Western heritage of unworkable dualisms.[17] *Public* and *private,* nature and nurture, mind and body, the scientific rationalist *male* and the subjective emotional *female,* the systematic rational Greek and the transcendently religious Jew—using many different labels, we have struggled for thousands of years both to divide our experience of the world into two mutually incompatible dimensions and then to cope with the disastrous consequences of this division. Crosby describes quantification as one of our many attempts to cope with this heritage, one of many conceptual adjudications, adjustments, tinkerings, and improvisations. "The West," Crosby explains, ". . . had a chronic need for explainers, adjusters, resynthesizers" of its peculiarly cantankerous habits of conceptual dualism.

Quantification, he explains, is a "shot-gun marriage" between measurement and mathematics. The West makes "a flying leap of faith" that reality is radically uniform both temporally and spatially. Despite some glaring inadequacies, that daring assumption nonetheless paid off brilliantly in the West's dominance over the rest of the globe.[18]

But such quantification only works by resolutely ignoring what it chooses to ignore. And if we forget the reality of what we are choosing to ignore, we trap ourselves in a deliberate, dangerous blindness. Globe-spanning empires and mind-boggling technologies have trapped us into this habitual blindness: we too quickly, too shallowly assume that what is quantifiable is somehow more real than what cannot be quantified. In particular, the quantifiable has seemed distinctly more substantial and more significant than the paradoxical, symbolic, psychological, interpersonal, aesthetic, and spiritual realities that elude numeric tally.

As we struggle to think about the moral difficulties of our blindly obsessive faith in numbers, it helps to remember that belief in the priority of the quantifiable has massively theological origins. The Western mind inherits a sturdy belief that nature has a rational, orderly, coherent, comprehensible structure because it is the product of the mind of God, who is presumed to be supremely rational, consistent, and intellectually coherent. But with the rise of modern physics, Western tradition tended to read its astounding discovery of the mathematical orderliness of the physical world back onto the nature of God. That's why Blake's famous image of God shows God bending down with a geometer's compass in his hand, not (as in the Sistine Chapel) extending his own hand to touch the upraised hand of Adam. Given the brilliant achievements of Brahe, Kepler, Copernicus, Galileo, and Newton, the rational coherence of the mind of God takes on a specifically mathematical color.

This development in Western thought yields the theological position called "Deism." Deism believes that a watchmaker God set the universe ticking according to fixed mechanical and mathematical rules—and then he sat back or went off to other things, leaving the priestly caste to enforce a set of absolute rules upon the rest of us. Deism thus lends a murky religious authority to our deliberate blindness to the nonquantifiable. As we tend too easily to reduce religion to rules (which conservatives follow scrupulously and liberals adeptly deconstruct), we also too easily forget the moral significance of realities that elude numeric tally. We are too easily blind to whatever is paradoxical, symbolic, psychological, interpersonal, aesthetic, and spiritual. We too easily assume that what can't be counted doesn't count for much—and that is a cultural loss of the first order.

But prior to the rise of quantification in the thirteenth century, numbers were used to name *both* quantities *and* qualities. Furthermore, qualities were by far the more important of the two. Numbers were used more to designate qualitative impact or human significance than as morally neutral, impersonal, quantitative markers. The "old Europeans . . . were as poetic about numbers as about words. . . . [T]he balance scale, the yardstick, and the hour glass were devices of little more than immediate practical convenience. The old Europeans' universe was one of qualities, not quantities."[19] And so we find reports of battles replete with utterly improbable numbers or estimates of distance or physical size that boggle the imagination.

For instance, prior to publishing *A Distant Mirror: The Calamitous Fourteenth Century,* Barbara Tuchman wrote about her complicated difficulties trying to determine how many people died in a particular small area of France as a result of warfare and plague during the fourteenth century. Her modern, commonsense yearning for disciplined quantification was baffled time and time again by numbers far more poetic and illustrative than quantitatively precise.[20]

How many did the fourteenth-century Black Plague kill? The best way to answer that question may well depend upon one's motives for asking the question in the first place. Metaphorical mathematics, to coin a phrase, may provide a more accurate picture of what the ravages of the fourteenth century were like for those who lived through it, or what the Black Plague meant to the people who witnessed it. In some situations, that is what some of us want to know. What did this mean to those people? What was it like for them? What can we learn from them about how a culture survives epidemiological disaster? From AIDS to SARS to biochemical warfare, that threat is still present.

The quantitative demographics of modern epidemiology may be more precise in certain limited ways, but such numbers are intentionally drained of immediate, passionate, embodied interpretation of what the enumerated event means in human terms. But the "old Europeans" wanted their numbers to have red-blooded meaning in that way. Using numbers merely to count would have been like using a trained Lipizzaner to plow a field, or perhaps a Porsche to deliver wet, moldy lawn clippings to the recycling center. Maybe in some situations that might be a transient practical necessity, but for the most part numbers were magnificent creatures that served profound and morally important cultural needs.

Quantification forces an astounding reversal in this understanding of what numbers are "for." That reversal depended in all sorts of wonderful, quirky ways upon the European acquisition of Hindu-Arabic numbers (rather than Roman numerals), symbols for the basic arithmetic functions (+, –, =, etc.), and above all the "number" zero, the counterintuitive mathematical signifier for the presence of absence. In the high Middle Ages, numbers begin to function with modern precision:

> Beginning in the miraculous decades around the turn of the fourteenth century (decades unmatched in their radical changes in perception until the era of Einstein and Picasso) and continuing on for generations, sometimes swiftly, sometimes sluggishly . . . Western Europeans evolved a new way, more purely visual and quantitative than the old, of perceiving time, space, and material environment. . . . In practical terms, the new approach was simply this: reduce what you are trying to think about to the minimum required by its definition; visualize it on paper, or at least in your mind . . . and then divide it, either in fact or in imagination, into equal quanta. Then you can measure it, that is, count the quanta. Then you possess a quantitative representation of your subject that is, however simplified, even in its errors and omissions, precise.[21]

Quantification brilliantly serves our efforts to master the physical environment, to develop useful technologies, and to convey or share information across distances and between strangers who have no reliable cultural context for interpreting one another's metaphorical math. It plays a leading role in the drama whereby the West rapidly extended its power in mighty colonial and commercial empires stretching around the globe. Yoking mathematics to the purposes of accounting and engineering has transformed both the physical and the cultural landscape.

But this progress comes at a cost. It comes at the cost of ignoring what cannot be quantified. It comes at the cost of ignoring qualities; it demands that we develop the capacity resolutely to set aside vitally important dimensions of human experience. The nonquantifiable, like the *female,* encompasses a domain that is soft, subordinate, unreliable, inconsistent, emotional, mystical, and unpredictable—and therefore insignificant. *La donna é mobile,* but the quantifiable is solid, objective, "hard," and "real." In the spiritual grammar of the West, quantification is metaphorically male. Quantification also demands the assumption that the realities that come under its purview are all perfectly uniform.

If the task at hand is counting bricks or bolts of wool, that works. But our souls and our lives are not so uniform, particularly when we face subtle and massively complex moral questions about how best to manage conflicting responsibilities.

Finally, quantification does not help us to develop analytical procedures adequate to solving problems that do not involve enumeration. The ancient spiritual practice of personal moral discernment rapidly cedes ground to social sciences and policy studies, whose statistical bases can generate the illusion that there is a numerically most probable ideal solution to the human condition. Professionals in these fields know better, but popular culture pays remarkably little attention to the limited range of inference understood by people highly trained in statistics. As we will see later on, the child-care debate comes to grief repeatedly upon the fact that morally and psychologically vital aspects of childhood development cannot be easily quantified and thus cannot be defined or measured with "scientific" accuracy. There are more things in heaven and on earth than such yardsticks can measure.

Double-Entry Bookkeeping: The Either/Or Cosmology of Spreadsheets

The most immediate utility of quantification was not, as one might expect, in science or in engineering. The overwhelmingly important application was in bookkeeping, particularly in the development of double-entry bookkeeping. Anyone who has ever kept a household budget, no matter how primitive, has done double-entry bookkeeping. If a double-entry bookkeeper were to buy a book, for instance, he or she would subtract $25 from cash-on-hand, and then also add $25 to an appropriate budget category (research expenses? leisure/recreation? gifts?). By tradition, debits, like the goats and the damned, go on the left; credits, like the sheep and the saved, go on the right—a habit preserved in the design of checkbook registers.

If you do this for every transaction all month, at the end the two columns should add up to exactly the same number. One will be a positive number, of course, and one a negative number; if you add these two numbers together, you get an answer famously known as the zero sum. That's not just any zero: it's zero as the result of adding together a positive number and a negative number that are numerically the same. By metaphoric extension, whenever two things cancel each other out exactly, one can speak of the result as a "zero sum."

Our imaginary household accounts could be further balanced by adding up the amounts spent in each budget category, then adding these totals and comparing that figure to the debits-in-general. Money-management software now helps the utterly compulsive to track every last dime in these ways. It can also help the merely prudent to ask whether too much is being spent on books, or what lifestyle compromises will be necessary to save thus many thousands of dollars over the eighteen years between birth and college matriculation. Life is full of questions for which any sensible person turns to double-entry bookkeeping.

Today this feels like rudimentary common sense: keeping track of where the money goes helps anyone to reach long-term goals and to plan for major expenditures wisely. But once it was a brilliant innovation that made it possible for traders precisely to attribute both their profits and their expenses to particular items purchased for trade. There were spectacular economies to be achieved when merchants for the very first time started keeping detailed track of inventory, demand, shipping costs, profit margin, and so forth. Such information made possible, made reasonable, the huge capital investments in sailing vessels, port development, warehouses, etc., that significant international trade requires. Colonial empires followed in the wake of these capital expenditures.

Because of its stunning impact on trade, the simple technique of double-entry bookkeeping reverberated through the culture at many levels, perhaps as cheap microchips have reverberated through our own—desktop and laptop computers, ATMs, PDAs, cell phones, the Web, voicemail, etc. In particular, double-entry bookkeeping added tremendous credibility and a powerful new technique to enforce pre-existent habits of dividing everything into one or another formally opposite categories:

> [It] . . . encouraged in us our often useful and sometimes pernicious practice of dividing everything into black or white, good or evil, useful or useless, part of the solution or part of the problem—either this or that. When Western historians look for the founts of our enduring Manichaeism, they point to the Persian prophet Manes himself and to Aristotle and his concept of the "excluded middle." Let me suggest that the influence of these men has been less than that of money, which speaks to us so eloquently in balance sheets. Money is never middle-ish. Every time an accountant has divided everything within his or her purview into plus or minus, our inclination to categorize all experience into this or that has gained validation. In the past seven centuries, bookkeeping has done more to shape the perceptions of more bright minds than any single innovation in philosophy or science.[22]

The conceptual or cultural pressure exerted by double-entry bookkeeping can perhaps be illustrated by a very small example. At one point I tried keeping detailed track of household expenditures, as one of my endless schemes to manage my life. In no time at all, I realized how very blurry the line is between books I buy as research expenses and books I buy for leisure/recreation. Although sometimes that distinction is quite clear, the most creative domain of my research has always been the "middle-ish," the "both-and" not the "either-or," whether that's in books or in conversations that are in equal measure playful and serious.

The domain of the excluded middle is also the domain of the twice-blessed, the serendipitous, the fruitful quirk, the inspired impulse. In the broadest possible way, spreadsheets encourage—they may demand—that we divide our lives into pre-existing categories and set these categories into zero-sum relationships with one another. But I'm convinced that all such categories are an imposition upon reality. They are primarily habits of thinking, not objective features of the landscape itself. Sometimes they are good and useful, but sometimes they are quite misleading—the teeth on the conceptual traps that hold us, making us feel frustrated and hostile and bewildered.

If Crosby is right—and as an historian he makes a very persuasive case indeed—then the cultural influence of credit and debit ultimately funds the whole early-modern or Enlightenment resurgence of mind/body, male/female, public/private dualisms that we have been examining. Sometimes that resurgence is attributed to Descartes or at least traced from Descartes. But perhaps both Cartesian graphs and Cartesian philosophical dualism had such a cultural impact in part as creative extensions of the utilitarian zero-sum spreadsheet. Like the spreadsheet, the Cartesian graph has negatives on the left (and below the horizontal axis); positives go on the right and above, metaphorically speaking closer to heaven. Such graphs also allow the spatial visualization of many kinds of spreadsheet data, thereby combining the quantification of space with the quantification of marketing. What Crosby calls the "Old European" mind certainly did not disappear overnight. The tendency to think of mathematics metaphorically could easily have seized the Cartesian graph as visual metaphor for double-entry bookkeeping and modern quantification generally. Perhaps that is part of why Cartesian philosophical dualism proved so influential in Western culture, despite the ways in which it was criticized immediately by professional philosophers. Cultural changes that combine "something old and something new" in this way are particularly powerful.

"Price quantified everything," Crosby explains.[23] And we all know the expression, "everything has a price." Historian Joel Kaye contends, in fact, that the development of money triggered the rise of quantification in the first place.[24] Thus, double-entry spreadsheets served as a way to keep track of everything: one can assign cash value to everything and then put the cash value into either/or categories. But not everything actually can be parsed out into one or another paired opposites, at least not without serious distortions. As a conceptual habit carried outside of its own proper domain of accounting, what we might call "spreadsheet thinking" can be hazardous. It is especially hazardous when the "opposites" are handled as literally and as mechanically as zero-sum thinking handles them.

In particular, it is dangerously misleading to imagine that thinking and feeling, mind and heart, intelligence and compassion, or self and other are opposed as debits and credits are opposed. When we give honestly, when we give in maturity and from strength, we do not give our souls away. Time is more than an asset that we debit from or credit to competing accounts when we decide to "spend" some time doing one thing rather than another. *What we are up against* in the work-life conflict is this false and shabby idea that life itself is a zero-sum game in which he who dies with the most toys wins. We are selling ourselves short if we allow our lives to be framed and managed as if our moral choices were as simple as buying and selling, debit and credit.

The good life is a lot more complicated than a balanced bottom line showing appropriate levels of return upon "investment," or perhaps a gorgeous rational-actor formula according to which we can calculate our private gain in "utility function" as a result of some decision or choice. Those formulae have their place in the larger scheme of things, I suppose; but ultimately we need to remember that meaning and moral value cannot be calculated as plainly as profit, nor can the costs of virtue and the benefits of virtue be set against one another in any simple calculation. Philosophic and poetic traditions alike testify unequivocally that meaning is made up of paradox, paradoxes such as "he that would gain his life must lose it" or that what we give from the heart returns to us multiplied and transformed. Such paradoxes cannot be formulated, taught, understood, or sustained within the mechanical categories of spreadsheet thinking or strictly logical systematics such as one finds in the formulae of rational-actor theorists. As philosopher Stephen Toulmin explains in detail, our hazardous allegiance to "mathematical" reasoning has nearly obliterated cultural habits or traditions of intelligent, pragmatic reasonableness.[25] Critical thinking needs to be based not simply or exclusively upon rigorous, formal, abstruse theory. Critical thinking also needs deep roots in practical experience and moral virtue.

The cultural danger of zero-sum thinking is how it tempts us to oversimplify our own experience and thereby to distort the delicate fabric of our own lives. As simple utilities, quantification and credit-debit dualism are handy tools. There's no arguing about that. But when they become our massively pre-eminent conceptual paradigms, then an entire range of questions will be mangled, misunderstood, and never successfully answered. As other, more nuanced and ancient paradigms for human experience are shifted into the mere subjectivity of *private* life, our *public* problem solving suffers enormously. One postmodern solution has been to assimilate all "public" discourse to one form or another of the raw will-to-power, the ruthless unbridled drive for self-assertion. The other possibility, as I have been suggesting all along, is to rediscover and to re-employ the moral traditions, practices, and disciplines that have been honed over thousands of years for coping with paradox, with the symbolic, and with spiritual realities.

But what has happened instead is a sentimentalizing of "home" that is parallel to and yet distinct from the sentimentality of Victorian upper-middle-class gender roles. Ultimately, however, the treacle of "family values" proves to be just as ineffective, just as incoherent, and, most dangerously of all, just as easily co-opted as the Angel in the House.

8

Home Sweet Home as Sacred Center

The Mythic Resonance of "Home"

So there is no "Angel in the House," and no Easter Bunny either, and no Tooth Fairy, and not even Santa Claus. That seems to be the rationalist bottom line here, the hard cold facts. Modernity has us surrounded, demanding that we come out with our hands up.

But we don't. Intellectually we can see that "Angel in the House" and "family values" ideologies have failed of their own incoherence, but they sustain enormous cultural resonance anyhow. They carry that resonance because we are absolutely unwilling to give up on the vision—so besieged by economic rationalizing—that *to be human* is to be decent, caring, responsible, and generous. The available ideologies may be shabby and self-defeating, but if they are the best we can find, then we make do with them. And so it behooves us, I think, to take a careful look at the mythology of "Home Sweet Home" as the embodiment of "family values." Doing so can help us both to recognize certain difficulties before they entrap us and ideally (or at least eventually) to find wiser alternatives altogether.

Novelist Marilyn Robinson argues that myths both embody and preserve the ambivalence or the contradictions that shape a culture. The biblical narrative of the Fall, for instance, keeps alive our recognition that the world is both intrinsically good and intrinsically evil.[26] Myths both ancient and contemporary are narratives that help us to cope with and to remember that life is not as simple as double-entry bookkeeping. Myths are narratives that stabilize within memory and within culture all the paradoxes one finds at the core of wisdom traditions; and so, Robinson concludes, we keep coming up with them left and right, large and small, all the time. Myths are not just the adventures of ancient Greek gods. They are narrative accounts acknowledging and recording the elusive complexity of human experience.

Within the ideology of "family values," Home Sweet Home functions as a symbolic locus or as a trope for the ideas of care, compassion, and the common good. It does so despite the logical and sociological difficulties that seem so powerfully arrayed against that association. Robert Frost captures the conflict between mythic function and practical realities in his famous lines, "Home is the place where, when you have to go there,/ They have to take you in."[27] The flat-out contradictory images of *woman* (the Angel and the Ditsy Dame) that fund the separation of women into the household and out of the workplace find immediate echo in our contradictory views of *home* as both the site of "dysfunctional families" (tended by those flocks of hired experts) and as the site of the only enduring and trustworthy relationships that we can hope to have.

Home may not literally be a "haven" guarded by an "angel," but mythically—that is, at the deepest, most powerful levels of culture—it is one of our major points of contact with the sacred. And yet, in our rootless, restless, mobile society, the goal of growing up is to "leave home"; and we are cautioned that "You can't go home again." The myth of "Home Sweet Home" attests to the paradox that the reality we most need and cherish is also a reality in which we cannot remain. What we most treasure about ourselves morally and emotionally is the set of traits that we have to set aside when we leave "home" for "work."

Historians like Stephanie Coontz and John R. Gillis explain in patient detail how inaccurately we understand the actual conditions of generations of families before our own.[28] Their arguments are solidly grounded, but that still doesn't explain why the nostalgic ideal of home persists. It persists, I suggest, because it stabilizes a vitally important, painful, and difficult contradiction at the heart of contemporary experience. Compassion may fund human wisdom, dignity, and virtue; but compassion is disrupted or deconstructed by the rationalist socioeconomic norms of American culture. When we resist that disruption, as of course most of us do most of the time, we expend a lot of courageous energy. At some level we feel the cost of that expenditure, whether or not we have the historical and cultural background necessary to realize why we sometimes feel so tired, so lonely, or so resentful.

The power of "home" as a mythic place in this consummately serious way has its origins not in census data but in psychological development. As child psychiatrist D. W. Winnicot argues in *Home Is Where We Start From,* we all begin life stunningly dependent upon an adult figure, commonly a woman, and much of our later emotional life reflects an unconscious desire to compensate (or overcompensate) for that experience of helpless vulnerability.[29] Our myth of "home" encompasses the paradox that we have deep-set physical memories of solace and safety, and yet the process of maturation relentlessly demands that we learn to cope with a world that is both difficult and dangerous. As relationships among adults have shifted ideologically from mutual obligation to capitalist competition, as the feudal order governed by clan and by church has given way to secular individualism and the postindustrial global economy, we have had ever-fewer public symbols that resonate with or participate metaphorically in the unconscious early experience of care and comfort that so vitally fuels our own capacity to care for and to comfort others.

Psychic energy that might or should be distributed across a variety of "locales" or social experiences is instead concentrated with all the fury of the unconscious upon Home and Home's reigning deity, The Mother Almighty. If we are fully to compensate for our early experiences of helpless dependence, we need to become both maturely autonomous and honestly dependable across the board. We need to express our mature capacity for caregiving in some general way, not exclusively within the family. Otherwise, family relationships continue to bear the unbearable burden of being the solitary objects of absolute needs. Adults need someone to care for and to be responsible for beyond their own biological children. Children need to feel that their parents are not the only trustworthy adults around. Healthy families need to be situated within caring communities.

Yet to function professionally in a contemporary economy, we have to sever the indivisible whole that is both thinking and caring, both well-bounded psychic integrity and generous compassion. And so we are haunted all the more by the image of "home" itself as an icon for the moral coherence of our own adult identity. To understand the situation we are in, I think it helps to take a closer look at what cultural history and comparative religions can tell us about the iconography of human dwelling-places. As we will see, the Home Sweet Home iconography of "family values" marginalizes compassion by shrouding it in patronizing sentimentality and by portraying it as escapist self-indulgence, not classical spiritual challenge.

The Architectural Iconography of "Home"

Contemporary secular life reveals the persistent influence of rich, ancient, psychologically charged religious symbolism. In particular, there are two ways in which habitations acquire their mythic reference or participate in sacred power. First, many early public monuments were situated horizontally along the four points of the cosmic horizon—to solstice or equinox or other astronomical points. So are many of Europe's massive cathedrals. The towns that were built around these monuments harmonized with that cosmic orientation.

Such tendencies to orient architecture persist, albeit unrecognized, because they are rooted not in abstract theological doctrine but somehow deep within the psyche. A suburb near me, for instance, has oddly curled streets and houses oddly placed on their lots because the town's original nineteenth-century designer wanted all houses to face either southeast or northwest. Or consider the recent fascination with feng shui, an Eastern belief that one can direct cosmological energy, called "chi," by properly designing one's house or office and arranging its furniture. The specific rules and regulations of feng shui are instances of this highly charged orientation to what the ancient world understood as the cosmic powers shaping the universe. Even today, the architectural requirements and prohibitions of feng shui are vitally important in some housing markets in the United States. An architectural engineer of my acquaintance discovered that in some parts of Asia even huge commercial buildings must follow the regulations of feng shui.

If something like feng shui were both innate to the West and attuned with contemporary Western science, then we could arrange our living room furniture or orient its doors and windows so as to align with the most elegant equations of astrophysics, particle physics, plate tectonics, etc. By means of that alignment, we could reflect both in our lives and in our homes not only the elegant orderliness of the cosmos but also—and simultaneously—the elegance and power of our own deepest moral capacities and resolves to live harmoniously. If we could do so, who could resist?

Adopting such a scheme from another culture is tempting indeed, as a symbolic gesture even if not a "hard" and "scientific" reality. As Mircea Eliade explains,

> For religious man, space is not homogeneous; he experiences interruptions, breaks in it; some parts are qualitatively different from others. . . . There is, then, a sacred space, and hence a strong, significant space; there are other spaces that are not sacred and so are without structure or consis-

> tency, amorphous. . . . It is not a matter of theoretical speculations, but of a primary religious experience that precedes all reflection on the world.[30]

But the rise of quantification demanded or imagined that both space and time *are* relentlessly homogeneous. Eventually, the enumerable comes to seem more real than the ineffable, the spiritual, or the sacred. Because we have no "hard, objective evidence" for the Holy, there is no holy ground at all. In a strictly quantified cosmology, there are none of what the ancient Celts called "thin places" or times. There are no serious moments when for a brief out-of-focus flicker the world is beautiful and meaningful and one's place in it is both good and utterly clear. None of that. There is—supposedly—no genuine religious experience at all. Every variety of religious experience is essentially subjective if not purely idiosyncratic in its origin: rather than speak of God, we more often speak of Self.

Whether your tastes run to feng shui, to *Better Homes and Gardens,* or to *Architectural Digest,* what's at stake in "family values" ideology is the effort to create and to preserve sacred space as a *private* possession or a *private* reality. The effort may be essentially unconscious or at least deeply inarticulate, but that may only add to its power in ways that marketers can exploit. At the Museum Shop last weekend, for instance, I spotted a $30 trinket: a box, some sand, a few stones, and a rake. It was a do-it-yourself version of a famous Zen shrine in Kyoto that monks have maintained for more than a thousand years. I sat on the steps of that shrine one lovely autumn afternoon in 1985. It was as wonderful a religious experience as I have ever known. I was overwhelmed; it was a time outside of time. I have goosebumps now just remembering. I looked at that little box in a suburban mall, and I wondered angrily whether I'd find peel-and-stick Sistine Chapel decals in the next aisle.

As dream analysts point out time and again, buildings of any sort but especially homes are always images of the self. In parallel ways, our spiritual sense of "home" is always closely allied with our sense of the sacred. And so, the symbolic architecture of "dwelling place" literally embodies our sense of essential *personal* connection to the sacred. Symbolically speaking, "home" is holy ground, home is safe space—safe from all the morally blind predations of profit motives, self-seeking, and the utter indifference of modern economics. And that makes sense: in classic Western religious thought, the love of God and the love of neighbor are two faces of one reality, two mutually necessary or reciprocal expressions of the "pure heart" or the "good heart" or the enlightened soul. "Home" as sacred space orients us appropriately both to God and to nature—and thus to one another.

The second major architectural orientation is not horizontal but vertical, the *axis mundi* linking earth and sky, human and divine. Within the cosmic-oriented town, the individual house is constructed around something that functions symbolically as a moral axis, like the spire on a church. Consider, if you will, how easily our most powerful associations to "home" are centered on the hearth with its vertical chimney or at least to the kitchen, a hearth analogue with a stove rather than a fireplace. Within the home there is a special place that is resonant with the *axis mundi* feeling that here, *here,* is the moral center of my world and my identity.

Notice how upscale homes have gargantuan "family rooms" with massive stone fireplaces. And yet, such houses almost always stand empty during the day, because it almost always takes two incomes to buy them. In every practical way, those families could with much less effort live in tidy city apartments rather than in these looming mansions off in the distant suburbs. But like the "Angel in the House" that is "Haven in a Heartless World," these extraordinary family rooms testify poignantly to moral values and human meanings that are besieged in the culture as a whole. That's why they have to have "cathedral" ceilings and fireplaces big enough to roast an ox.

The size, expense, and sheer impracticality of such rooms endeavor to compensate visually and architecturally for the ways in which "family values" are irrelevant to the economic success that make buying such a house feasible. It is an architectural presence proclaiming an absence and trying to compensate for it. In short, the cosmographic kitchen-family room complex is something like a temple to the persistent cultural archetype of Hestia, the ancient Greek goddess of the hearth, sister of the sky-god Zeus and, both emblematically and literally, the fire that warms and warrants the home as a sacred place. One way or another the contemporary mythology of home, built of course upon the truly ancient mythology of home, testifies to our persistent desire to care despite economic realities insisting that we must compete without any such sentimentality.

No wonder feng shui books sell like mad.

The Mythic Locus and the Shopping Mall

Upscale shopping malls are full of trendy shops like Crate and Barrel, Restoration Hardware, Pottery Barn, and Williams-Sonoma—all of which sell an essentially consistent and predictable image of home as sacred center. The house serves as an essential mythic icon for our terribly threatened sense of ourselves. We try to make our houses fortify our sense of ourselves as carriers of the sacred, as *imago Dei,* as warm human sparks from the vast cosmic fire that is God. In a related level of cultural iconography, The Container Store sells stuff to help keep one's household goods in order; their shopping bags boldly insist, "CONTAIN YOURSELF." *Contain Yourself.* And yet, surely we all know that the older, deeper reaches of our culture provide a far richer, far more subtle and humane set of "containers" for our souls.

On the whole, decorating and equipping the household to the norms of these upscale shops and their glossy catalogues works about as well as planting plastic flowers. It's an effort to ground the meaning of our lives with nothing more than a mix of desperate needs and scattered pieces. People buy stuff and arrange it with feng shui guidebooks in hand, not exactly believing that they are directing genuine cosmic energies but wanting somehow to arrange both their living spaces and their lives to reflect a deep, powerful, inarticulate regard for the sacred, for something profoundly holy deep within themselves and deep within their very best relationships with other living beings.

It's easy enough to see through the marketing ploys. As architectural historian Witold Rybczynski points out in his analysis of Ralph Lauren bedding displays, most of the homes depicted in these stores and their ads might be from rural New England in the mid-nineteenth century.[31] There are no alarm clocks beside the beds, no telephones. Lamps never have cords—if there are lamps at all. Often there are only candles, oil lamps, or sunlight streaming in upon rooms with no evidence of any artificial lighting and certainly no electrical outlets in sight. Televisions may dominate most "family" rooms, but they appear in ads only when the product to be sold is a TV or a stand on which to put a TV. Otherwise they are banished to whatever Valhalla holds alarm clocks. The upscale housewares stores abound with nineteenth-century visual allusions and "retro" trinkets.

Kitchen equipment advertisements may at least implicitly acknowledge that our homes have electricity, but these ads have the same fundamental romanticism about daily life at home. The ideal image conveyed by these gorgeous photos presupposes that we have all the time in the world to cook and to share elegant meals. This is not the real time-constrained family world of meals wolfed on the run, the world where so very much depends upon frozen entrees and carryout, microwave and toaster oven. According to the ads, breakfast is not Cheerios for the kids and black coffee in travel mugs for the parents but rather latte we made in our own espresso machine, along with waffles from the waffle maker and a gorgeous array of fresh fruit served in cute little bowls glazed to look like half a cantaloupe—or maybe juice we have spent an hour or two squeezing for ourselves with the chrome manual juicer. Napkins are cloth, beautifully color-coordinated to everything in sight. *Bon Appétit* goes to the next logical step, which is to dress the dinner-guests in color-coordinated sweaters that complement the dishes and table linen.

The life such ads portray is fantasy pure and simple, even for those of us who cook well and work at home. They are modern equivalents of the eighteenth-century portraits of noblewomen and prosperous merchants' wives dressed as shepherdesses or as Greek goddesses in pastoral settings. We know it's all fake and the merchants know it's all fake: all of us have alarm clocks by our beds, and most of us have low-fat waffles in the freezer. The shelves in our kitchens do not hold a matching set of glass canisters filled with colorful dried beans that must soak overnight and then simmer for six hours.

But we pretend. We go along with such advertisements, pretending that it's just a joke and we are in on the joke. As Freud pointed out, humor is an extremely high-level defense. We are defending ourselves against the recognition that we are trapped on the wrong side of the looking glass. As Arlie Hochschild says so adeptly, we buy stuff we would use if only we had time, thereby equipping ourselves for something like a virtual lifestyle. Here's who I would be, here's the life I would lead, If Only I Had Time. The history of gender ideology and "family values" ideology reveals, over and over again, the psychological and moral power of divisions deep within the self.

No quantity of stuff brought home from the mall, no ferocious dedication to an all-natural 100% cotton pure organic lifestyle or to any possible combination or recombination of either furniture or gender roles can rescue us from the basic predicament posed by our resolutely secular, postmodern, postindustrial culture. Our efforts to orient our lives and our dwelling places toward the profoundly real, toward the most deeply meaningful, can succeed only to the extent that *real* or *meaningful* exist in the first place—no matter how partially, how imperfectly we can define what is "real" or "meaningful." To hope for such meaning in our lives—to hope to have a life worth living—we have to be willing to imagine that moral significance is real. We have to believe that moral significance exists independently or objectively, as an elusive, paradoxical reality that is transcendent to individual human lives, gender identities, or households. And yet, believing in the reality of moral significance and moral accountability is high-stakes stuff. It's a defining choice—a choice that, once freely and honestly made, turns around to define who we are and who we are becoming.

Under any circumstances, Home Sweet Home—with or without an Angel in the House—does not and cannot provide what we most deeply need. What we need is not "family values" but rather strong countercultural warrant for our commitment to teaching and to learning the practice of such virtues as generosity, kindness, integrity, fortitude, patience, foresight, restraint, responsibility, and so forth. Persistent seekers will discover that religious traditions and wisdom traditions have the historical, intellectual, and spiritual resources necessary to provide that warrant. That's the good news. The bad news is that these traditions are always interwoven with human institutions. Alas, human institutions are inescapably fallible, contentious, variously self-serving, and too often devoted to safeguarding the status quo and the self-approval of their members.[32] Joining a church, synagogue, ashram, or New Age meditation center will not guarantee spiritual growth and moral insight, because such things cannot be guaranteed.

Furthermore, waiting around for one of these institutions to develop local programs to support one's moral life is like waiting around for Congress to enact legislation to fix things for us. It's much easier to imagine what *might be done* by somebody else than to consider one's own choices and beliefs in a hard clear light. Whether or not we find our way to an effective countercultural community, then, the first step toward the genuinely good life is laying claim to moral responsibility and to the practice of the virtues in our own lives. We need to realize that we are not for sale, and that what we most fervently dream of having cannot be purchased. From that core assertion, many things become possible. And one of the first things that becomes possible is connecting with others who have similar courage and equal resolve.

9

Having a Soul That's Not for Sale

Has Meaning Any Meaning?

In the absence of positive communities and objective communal consensus, we run the ever-increasing risk that *meaning* will have no meaning beyond either sentimental subjectivity or the will-to-power. *De gustibus non est disputandum*—there's no disputing taste—and so it seems that the best we can do is argue for our personal opinions and our private beliefs as if there is no longer any culturally solid, objective difference between right and wrong. James Edwards calls this state of affairs "normal nihilism": "we are aware of both the existence of radically alternative structures of interpretation and the fact that we ourselves lack any knockdown, noncircular way to demonstrate the self-sufficiency of our own. . . . To be a normal nihilist is just to acknowledge that, however fervent and essential one's commitment to a particular set of values, that's all one ever has: a commitment to some particular set of values."[33] That is—supposedly—one cannot have a commitment to the truth, because there is no way to demonstrate what "truth" is.

I disagree with Edwards's presupposition that such proof is desirable. No God worth having can be the object of the kind of formal demonstration and unequivocal evidence he expects. Spiritual enlightenment, by any of its many different titles, cannot be forced upon a person by "strong" logical demonstration. Neither can I prove that I love my children, or prove that my husband loves me. Much that is valuable is beyond rationalist demonstration altogether. By the nature of things, some morally important knowledge is not based upon hard, objective evidence at all—and the demand for such evidence is simply a roundabout way of denying that such knowledge is possible in the first place. As Stanley Hauerwas argues, if we could have the kind of evidence that some philosophers demand, then we would know for a fact that the God worshiped by Jews and by Christians does not exist.[34]

On the other hand, Edwards's account of our culture is brilliant. We are indeed all too quick to agree that everything is "up to the individual," as if both morality and wisdom are ultimately no more than matters of personal taste. I have challenged friends when they have dropped such phrases casually, and I'm convinced that most of us don't literally mean that *everything* is up to the individual. Reasonable people draw all sorts of lines: child abuse, murder, marital infidelity, fraud, bribery—even littering public beaches, writing in library books, and parking illegally in "handicapped" spots. Nonetheless, the way the phrase is used suggests that, at the very least, we lack a common language for articulating the difference between major moral norms and the ordinary scope allowed both for taste and for life's very tricky judgment calls.

Without cultural consensus about how to articulate moral norms, it is difficult for most people to explain how they distinguish between a person's taste and a person's inescapable moral responsibility for individual actions or personal choices. Sociologist Alan Wolfe has written a couple of books now revealing the mix of warm goodwill, meandering platitudes, and logical incoherence that is the best that most folks can offer when asked to discuss moral issues.[35]

Edwards attributes our "normal nihilism" to our progressive deconstruction of an absolute, transcendent, objective, public ontological ground—whether called "God" or "Higher Power," the "Ground of Being" or "Absolute Self"—that assures the possibility of absolutely true meaning despite the contingency and failures of any particular human consciousness.[36] In the absence of that hard, logical, absolute foundation, he argues, we find ourselves trapped within "our well-documented (and contrary) tendencies both to addictive individualist self-magnification and to (equally addictive) totalitarian fundamentalist rigidity."[37] By "fundamentalism" he refers not to biblical literalism but more broadly to a certain easygoing, comfortable conformity: ". . . one acts as 'anyone' would act. One becomes, thereby, . . . a socially-constructed cipher, wearing the right clothes, working at the right job, seeing the right movies, having the right responses to them, doing what is expected by 'them' of 'anyone.'"[38]

We debate social-policy issues relevant to the crisis of care on the basis of cost-benefit statistics rather than talking to one another about public moral responsibility and the ethics of public and mutual obligation. We don't talk about moral obligation because morality is seen as a densely *private* matter and therefore an unrealistic basis for *public* decisions. *De gustibus non est disputandum.* But the alternative to such quantified and grandiose individualism seems to be reverting to violent theocracy on the model of Wahhabi Muslims or the authoritarian fundamentalists on the Religious Right in our own country. Meanwhile, adults who are struggling both to nurture and to provide financially for those who depend upon them do so in a culture for which the "public" *axis mundi* is the profit motive. We are struggling to lay claim to our own souls. We are struggling to live in a quiet confidence that our souls are not for sale amidst cultural presuppositions that price quantifies everything, and everything has a price.

That's a catastrophe, a catastrophe for which we cannot compensate by decorating our homes from the Pottery Barn catalogue. As Sylvia Ann Hewlett argues,

> Over the long haul, you cannot claw your way up the corporate ladder, work sixty hours a week, *and* be a good parent, spouse, and citizen. . . . The trick is to spread the burden around . . . [to include] husbands and fathers, employers and government. Such sharing of effort is particularly just and fair given the fact that in the modern world the rewards of well-developed children are reaped by society at large, not by individual mothers or fathers. . . . If you are a "good" parent and put together the resources and the energy to ensure that your child succeeds in school and goes on to complete an expensive college education, you will undoubtedly contribute to "human capital formation," enhanced GNP, and helping this nation compete with the Japanese, but in so doing you will deplete rather than enhance your own economic reserves.[39]

Surely that has the ring of truth to it. But notice this: the basis of Hewlett's argument is cost-benefit investment. If we care for children because "the rewards of well-developed children are reaped by the society at large," then the purely rational thing to do, economically, is to invest in children only selectively. Invest primarily in the best and the brightest children, who are most likely to contribute the most to the GNP and international competitiveness. The children of poor parents, especially poor never-married parents, are statistically less likely to "repay" the considerable expense of properly feeding, housing, socializing, nurturing, and educating them for twenty years.

In fact, arguably, this is how the system already works: the arrangements we already have offer the most income to the best educated and brightest parents. Those parents turn around and spend lavishly to provide for the education and development of their children. As a result—some combination of nature and nurture—parental income and education are overwhelmingly the strongest correlates of child outcomes no matter what. To expect the government or the business community to invest in children across the board, from the belief that every human soul is significant and precious beyond all calculating, is to expect such entities to be compassionate rather than rationalist. It seems to me that Hewlett's "investment" argument is naïvely dependent upon the rationalist presumption that children can be seen as something like commodities that will eventually return a profit.

In market terms, compassion and generosity *are* irrational because they are not profitable. Only profitable investments are rational. Rational investments are by definition based upon cost-benefit zero-sum calculations, not upon human rights and moral obligations. At this point, of course, if I were Hewlett then I would shift ground, comparing the cost of running prisons to the cost of proper medical care, decent schools, family services, and standard housing. That data can be very persuasive, although such arguments come down to another form of the familiar "we should be Sweden" argument that business leaders regard as anathema.

Furthermore, in this imaginary debate, another voice appears, arguing that the correlation between crime and poverty disappears altogether if one controls for family structure. That is, if you look only at households in which two parents are rearing their own biological children, or only to adults reared in such households, the crime-poverty nexus disappears.[40] Is the issue poverty? Or family structure? Or is that a chicken-and-egg argument because poverty interferes with forming stable relationships? Yet more voices start to chime in.

So let's sigh quietly and close this door altogether. Maybe one day the policy wonks will figure this out and come back to rescue us. Meanwhile, the closer one looks at what counts as "hard numbers" in social science, the harder it seems to concoct tough-minded cost-benefit arguments for any coherent social policies at all. That may be why we have so very few such policies. Strict quantification does not tell the truth about the social fabric, which is woven of too many threads that cannot be reduced to uniform quanta.

No wonder we so often feel frazzled and weary. No wonder we worry at times that we are either approaching the outer edge of exhaustion or that we are performing marginally in some of our deepest moral obligations. We have defined the *public,* supposedly masculine sphere of work, rationality, objectivity, achievement, and power as a ruthlessly amoral data-based struggle of each against all.

Home Sweet Home doesn't stand a chance.

The Divided Self

When we divide reality into such profoundly different *public* and *private* domains, we divide the self. We are expected to behave according to such very different norms at home and at work that we are in effect forced to develop two competing identities, neither of them whole and thus neither of them adequate or accurate. As a result, the divided self is a diminished self. The divided self is a self under siege, a self some of whose dimensions or "parts" have been marginalized and thereby reduced to an incoherent narcissistic sentimentality. As a culture we are obsessed with self because we are, at heart, profoundly uncertain of self. Anglican theologian Rowan Williams argues that we have suffered the devastating loss of a culturally adequate vocabulary for the genuine nurture of the self; his book is aptly titled *Lost Icons: Reflections on Cultural Bereavement.*[41]

As Dan McAdams argues in *The Stories We Live By: Personal Myths and the Making of the Self,* Freud, Marx, and Darwin each posited new forms of the classically Western dualist accounts of reality.[42] As modernist and secular "theologians," if you will, each of these thinkers argued that what we experience as the ordinary real world is actually controlled by a submerged or essentially invisible force which we can identify only indirectly, only by excavation, inference, and painstaking reconstruction. I would add Adam Smith to McAdams's list, and the hidden hand of market to the list of invisible (nearly transcendent) forces shaping visible reality.

The new version of the old creation myth goes something like this: Although we may think we are compassionate, responsible, decent human beings, or at least we do our best to realize these ideals, in fact our lives are controlled by capitalism's rationalist self-seeking, by Darwinian competition, by Marxist historical dialectics, and by the dark, terror-laden urges of Freudian lust and gratification. The problem, of course, is that somehow our "private" lives, our individual households, are supposed to be pure sacred ground, morally whole, healthy, pure, utterly uncontaminated by all this strife and struggle that otherwise necessarily define reality.

That's unrealistic. That's why we have had an uproar of attention to "dysfunctional families"—even claims that dysfunction is universal, that dysfunction is how we necessarily function. People who make that claim are insisting (and reasonably enough) that families are part of the real world: despite any appearance of surface functioning, at the deep or the real level in any family one always finds innate depravity without the hope of grace or the possibility of redemption.

But to the extent that we struggle not to give in to such depravity, to the extent that we struggle to be compassionate, responsible, and honest, our ordinary commute from work to home must traverse the ontological and psychological ravines that split the Western cultural landscape. The compassion that is real and visible in our private lives becomes invisible, superficial, insubstantial, or deliberate pretense at work. When we get home again at the end of the day, we must reverse that process, transforming a whole array of dark subterranean drives into mere superficialities that are not part of our "real selves."

Such a life demands not changing hats but something much closer to changing heads. No wonder popular narratives of various kinds have adopted the "evil twin" as a standard character. We are all supposed to have or to be such twins, to switch from "Angel in the House" to "Bitch in a Business Suit" and back again, twice a day. On days when we can't find the psychic phone booth in which we can safely swap identities, we can find ourselves feeling fake no matter where we are, feeling dishonest and alienated from any core identity whatsoever. Sociologists refer to this experience as "multiphrenia"—the commonplace, contemporary sense that any single, solid, enduring "self" has been shattered and scattered among too many demands upon our time, attention, energy, and soul.[43]

McAdams argues eloquently for the depth of our compensatory need to forge a single identity, to be one person despite the ways in which the conceptual framework of our culture posits all these radical discontinuities between inner and outer, between depth and surface. We do so, he explains, by struggling to generate one story about who we are. Identity is forged or developed by means of a single complex narrative that accounts for or synthesizes the entire range of our experience.[44] For instance, I might reasonably be seen as both a tender mother and a tough babe, both a well-honed thinker and a quiet introvert, both a serious Christian and a skeptical critic of institutionalized religion.

I am, all of us are, a whole cast of characters, all these and more, for whom McAdams argues we must one day compose a single story with its own solid dramatic unity. In Marilyn Robinson's terms, we need a story or we use a story to stabilize the contradictions we traverse every day. The wider those contradictions, the more powerful our need for a story or the deeper our need for a powerful story to help us resist the pressure to sell ourselves short in the marketplaces of mass culture and glossy four-color ads. The chasm between our public and our private identities, the chasm between our public and our private repertoires of behavior, can grow so large as to challenge our confidence that we are a single self and not merely a mixed bag of reactions that lack a moral core.

Theologian Bonnie J. Miller-McLemore argues that the principal challenge of adulthood in our time is resisting such fragmentation.[45] The Siren song luring us to self-destruction is the wail of the Day-Runner and the Palm Pilot, the call of calendar, voice mail, e-mail, pager, cellphone, and simple unrelenting frenzy. Our days dissolve into slots of time that slice our lives like meats at the deli, thinner and thinner and thinner. If we are to achieve an authentic maturity, she argues, we have to acknowledge our finiteness. We have to realize that we cannot have all of everything, we cannot be everything to everyone, and so we must make the commitments and the attendant sacrifices which define a well-bounded, mature self—a self not for sale at any price. But such choices are incredibly difficult when by definition the self remains profoundly divided into *public* and *private* halves. The "family values" ideology of *public* vs. *private* means that supposedly there is no one place where all of me belongs and finds social recognition, and thus there is nothing—or at least nothing obvious—that elicits what Sylvia Anne Hewlett adeptly calls "a higher loyalty."[46]

One alternative, as many have discovered, is to recognize how all of who we are is both recognized and welcomed by ancient, rigorous spiritual traditions both East and West. Their paradigmatic "meta-narratives" (so-called) anchor and frame our individual narratives of identity. At least in theory or ideally, the worshiping community (whether parish or ashram, mosque or synagogue) both sees and stabilizes or spiritually forms the wholeness of the heart. My practical experience, I must admit, has been mixed. As the three most important facts about a piece of real estate are location, location, and location, the three most important facts about any congregation are leadership, leadership, and leadership. Many other features matter, but none of them creates real "living space" without imaginative, even visionary, leadership.

The Triumph of the Therapeutic

Our efforts to cope with this fragmentation have given rise to what Philip Rieff calls "the triumph of the therapeutic," a triumph wildly at odds with the kinds of commitments that children need from parents and that adults need from one another if we are to be a civilized society and a healthy community.[47] In the thirty years since Rieff's book of that title, "the triumph of the therapeutic" has become a commonplace label for all the ways in which self-actualizing or self-expression can take precedence over duty, obligation, and commitment. Any commitment, any obligation that gets in the way of "being who I am" supposedly loses its legitimacy.

What never loses legitimacy, however, are the nonnegotiable demands of the workplace. These are not seen as moral commitments or moral obligations: these are *public* and objective workplace requirements legitimated by economic threats, not ethical premises. As Christopher Lasch argues in *Haven in a Heartless World,* social science drapes the demands of the marketplace in an aura of "objective reality" that merely disguises an overwhelming demand for conformity and obedience.[48] In the history of Western religion, both the unquestionable status and the particular demands of the marketplace are remarkably parallel to those of traditional nature gods. The nature gods demanded sacrifice of firstfruits and so forth, in return for which they offered guarantee of good harvest. (The monotheist deity Yahweh Elohim had his fertility and harvest festivals, of course; but remarkably strong traditions within the Hebrew Bible argue that the central moral obligation is social justice and compassion for the widow and the orphan—not firstfruit sacrifice and ritual observance. Classic Jewish righteousness and Christian *caritas* are blazingly irrational in market terms.)

Seen in this way, the triumph of the therapeutic looks more like a compensatory rebound, a desperate, ultimately self-destructive effort to refuse to conform to rationalist "business practices" and to claim or to reclaim some fundamental personal integrity. The *private* self, no less than the Angelic housewife or the sacred domain of Home Sweet Home, is subject to a Catch-22: I cannot be myself under the burden of all these *public* absolutist demands, but rejecting whatever demands I can manage to reject simultaneously undermines whatever hope for genuine identity I might have available. That's because the only rejectable or negotiable demands are the authentic moral demands, and authentic moral demands generate the depths of authenticity I am seeking in the first place. The only branch I can saw off is the one I'm sitting on. As Stanley Hauerwas quips, "The appropriately phrased theological question is never 'Does God exist?' but 'Do we exist?'"[49]

I would argue in reply to Rieff that the various classic symbolic languages of moral obligation have lost their cultural power to give meaning to our lives not because they have lost persuasive semiotic or rational content, but because they have been relegated to *private* life, to the *private* domain of mere subjectivity. Their meaning is now subjective and individual rather than objective and authoritative. But without objectivity, *meaning* has no meaning other than taste, other than quirky individual preference.

What has triumphed is not so much psychotherapy as this massive cultural split between *public* and *private*. The cultural role or "triumph" of psychotherapy follows from, rather than causes, the demise of powerful culture-wide systems of symbolic meaning. Symbolic meaning never supplies what James Edwards demands: it does not offer a "knockdown noncircular way to demonstrate the self-sufficiency, solidity, or originality" of one's position.[50] Samuel Taylor Coleridge argues, in fact, that any rich symbolic expression will necessarily remain open to denial by those whose criteria are exclusively rational or formally systematic.[51]

In a store one day I handed the cashier a $10 bill, but she gave me change as if I had handed her a $20. Reflexively, without thinking, I returned to her the extra $10 bill.

"Oh. So you're one of *those* people," she commented sarcastically, with palpable contempt, with a visible subtext: *what a fool!*

Those people. As if honesty, honesty of the most simple and obvious sort, were a minority value, an odd ethnic habit like putting lime in beer or vinegar on baked beans. I don't mind if someone thinks I'm quirky and inexplicable. Perhaps I am: writers spend far too much time alone. But the common life does depend upon the *public* validity of certain virtues, whether or not every person aspires to be virtuous. Some people will always keep extra change: that's not the issue here. What is the issue, what is deeply hazardous, is the loss of *public* cultural consensus about the moral responsibility to be honest.

Conclusion: Caring in Public

Given the cultural history of this ethical split between *public* and *private*, it is tempting to proclaim that what we need here are new or invigorated *public* institutions to reclaim the self-evident truth that our well-being is densely interwoven with everyone else's. This involves no challenge to the pragmatic necessity of separation of church and state in a multicultural society, because integrity, compassion, and generosity are not the exclusive intellectual property of any single region, religion, or people: these virtues are a moral heritage held in common. Given the *public* cultural power of a global economy, the *public* cultural power of free-market capitalism, it seems hardly more than common sense to say that we need equivalently powerful *public* institutions to sustain our wisdom not just our wealth, to foster our integrity not just our income. Robert Bellah and his colleagues argue this point at length in *The Good Society.*[52]

There are three problems with this common sense. The first is that it's no better than waiting around for some policy solution. Maybe it will happen, but what do we do meanwhile? All such proposals come down to "wait here for rescue." We can't wait. We have lives to live, people who depend on us, painful choices to make that we cannot put on hold. Furthermore, *wait here for rescue* suggests that we are absolutely helpless, that we are entirely trapped. That's a counsel of despair. It portrays all of us as helpless victims—as passive consumers of whatever the culture has for sale.

I don't buy that, not for a moment. I can't fix the world, and I can't change the world, but I can certainly rustle up the courage I need to live my own life in good conscience and with all possible integrity. I realize I can't do that entirely and absolutely on my own, John Wayne style. I know I need good company; I need the support of friends who see the world as I do rather than writing me off as absolutely crazy. But finding good company is not the same as waiting around for some public institution to set up shop down the street. What it takes to find such friends is a certain gutsy willingness to say what you believe when you are challenged and to live out your beliefs despite what some people will say.

The second problem is closely related: effective public institutions are not created *ex nihilo* by writers or by readers. The yearning for such an institution is perfectly parallel to the ancient mythic call for a king of greater virtue than the present king. Call it the trickle-down theory of moral authority. The ancient king, like the priest, embodied the *axis mundi,* the point of connection between the sacred and the mundane. The mythography of "kingship" testifies eloquently to how the virtuous "king" possessed the symbolic power to lead the people to virtue. In our day we are much more likely to invent or to wish to reinvent foundations, churches, institutes, public-policy groups, etc. to perform the ancient priestly/kingly function of recentering our humanity upon its deepest, highest moral grounds.

The yearning isn't wrong or defective in some regard, but it can be naïve if we think that funding a foundation is the whole answer. The whole answer must include funding a change of heart—and life—for ourselves. We need not only nonprofit corporations but also a commonplace individual recognition of the countercultural costs and benefits of our struggle to live in good conscience. Otherwise civic organizations can be nothing more than yet another special-interest group, competing in all the ordinary ways with all the other lobbies. A powerful lobby can influence legislation, but influencing culture itself—reaching the human heart, reaching and articulating the ethical core of the culture—is a stunningly more difficult issue. As Pogo warned in that famous cartoon strip, "I have seen the enemy, and he is us."

The third problem is that many of the *public* voices that we need already exist. The ancient and powerful institutions that we need already exist—more or less effectively. They are synagogues and churches, ashrams and temples, mosques and monasteries. On a secular but equally moral basis, the cultural landscape abounds with foundations, institutes, public-policy groups, support groups, and civic organizations worried about families, worried about children, worried about the old, the ill, the poor, and the marginalized. Even before the recent spate of rapacious corporate officers and conniving accountants, plenty of folks were worried about ethics in the marketplace and in a marketplace-dominated culture generally. All of them are doing something about these worries. All of them have list-serves. There is an incredible number of such outfits, all pecking at the grassroots level like grackles in August.

These organizations do a lot of good, I suspect, but they are not as effective as we might wish because they too live in a world they have inherited, not invented. They too grind up against massive global pressures that would consign them to the merely *private,* to the exclusively individualist assertion of personal taste in values and virtues, to functioning as nothing more than a special-interest constituency. Most dangerously of all, if they try to claim *public* voices, then they also contend with the pathological individualism that resists every assertion of cultural authority with zero-sum arguments that to do as anyone else suggests is perforce "inauthentic." Nonetheless, individuals can draw a lot of strength, wisdom, and comfort from membership in such a group.

Ultimately, we face not the triumph of the therapeutic, but the triumph of the marketplace. Competition, reinforced by zero-sum calculations, has become the normative interpersonal relationship. This has left us feeling besieged in our own deepest humanity, in our finest moral capabilities. As a result, many people are adrift in cynicism and a sort of desperate consumerism whose primary manifestation is an empty but radical expressive individualism. Contemporary polemics about gender roles and family values serve only to mask the deeper loss, the more serious loss of the wisdom according to which the key to a good life is compassion and intelligent care for the common good.

Part Four

Secular Salvation and the Divine Right of Markets

He Who Dies with the Most Toys Wins

Prelude

Life and work have always been at odds to some extent. No one can eat, drink, and be merry unless there is someone to make the bread, brew the ale, and play the fiddle—or someone who has earned what it costs to purchase these goods and services. But when moral norms are sequestered into an ever-more-trivialized "private" life, we lose the cultural resources necessary for establishing a rich, coherent, reciprocal relationship between work and life. As Christopher Lasch argues, this is the issue underlying gender-equity arguments in our time: "The problem of women's work and women's equality need to be examined from a perspective more radical than any that has emerged from the feminist movement. It has to be seen as a special case of the general rule that work takes precedence over the family."[1] Work has come to take precedence over everything, not just the family, because competition and the profit motive are no longer effectively framed by compassion and the common good. Without that framework, we have no coherent basis upon which to adjudicate the competing demands of earning a living and having a life.

Over the years, sociologists and historians have delineated the ways in which this situation impoverishes the common life. It also impoverishes our sense of ourselves as morally significant individuals, and that impoverishment goes to the heart of the work-life conflict. As we will see in progressively more detail in the next set of chapters, at the generative core of contemporary consumerism is a desperate, often massively unconscious drive to define and defend our core identity through our ability to earn and spend. What other "public" measure is there? What other objective (which is to say quantifiable) definition? How else can we solace the murky, buried pain of the divided modern self? But the futility of trying to define ourselves by the stuff that we own leaves many people exhausted, lonely, and spiritually frustrated. The interwoven ideologies of gender roles, family values, and the free market obscure our efforts to see how we might lead meaningful lives, honestly contributing to the common good, fully invested not merely in pension plans but also in human relationships.

Of course plenty of people endeavor, quite consciously and successfully, to resist these consumerist pressures. I think that the difficulty and the cost of such resistance has been one of the wellsprings of the contemporary interest in spirituality and in traditional religious practices. Defining social identity through earnings is a spiritual loss and a reductive trap, as many people already realize—but it's a reductive trap with a fascinating history.

One way to begin to deconstruct this trap—or at least to make it far more conscious in usefully liberating ways—is to look carefully at the meanings of "work" in our culture. I want to begin with some basic definitions, and then take a close look at the cultural history and psychosocial pressures shaping the experience of employment in the last fifty years. As we will see, between the manipulative stratagems of management, the blandishments of advertising, and the terror of unemployment, little energy remains for all the dimensions of our humanity that are encompassed by the phrase "having a life."

10

What's Work?

What do we mean by "work"? At some first commonsense level, work is what we get paid to do. But if that's a sufficient definition, what are we to call activities like washing clothes or clearing eighteen inches of snow from the driveway? Neither activity counts as fun as far as I'm concerned. Although plenty of folks do such things for a living, many of us do it for ourselves—and we know full well we are working when we do it. On the other hand, when business managers talk about work-life balance, by "work" often they mean paid employment, and by "life" often they mean everything else—everything from shoveling snow to singing lullabies. From a strict managerial perspective, the point of work-life balance is not the fullness of human spiritual and social development but rather the corporate need to keep the demands of daily life from interfering with an employee's ability to meet the demands of work.

The more formally precise one tries to be, I have discovered, the more elusive the concept "work" can become. Theorists of such things distinguish between romantic and utilitarian concepts of work. Utilitarian theories define "work" as what we have to do to keep food on the table and a roof overhead. That includes both the mortgage and the mopping, both paying for groceries and cooking meals. Romantic theories emphasize all the ways in which the work that we do also functions as a key element in our self-definition, social status, and so forth—quite aside from questions of whether or how much we are paid for it. I want to push this classic distinction just a bit further so as to illuminate what's at stake as we try to reclaim time and energy for *having a life* from the ever-enlarging demands of *earning a living*.

Theologian Miroslav Volf argues that work is activity to meet a need *aside from* the need for the activity as such.[2] Breathing isn't work, for instance, nor sleeping, because these are activities we need as such. Laundry is work, however, because the need is for clean clothes, not for sorting and washing and folding as activities-in-themselves. Enjoying it or not isn't the issue, according to Volf. Nor is inner or outer coercion. The determining characteristic in defining "work" is utility in meeting a need: *work* is a means to an end outside of itself.

Implicit in Volf's definition is the possibility that a given activity may be work or not depending upon whether one seeks that exterior end or depends upon it in some practical way. When Tiger Woods golfs, for instance, he is working. Were I to golf, however, I would not be working. More precisely yet, when I write letters to friends, I'm not working; when I'm writing for publication or even in hope of publication, I am working. I do enjoy my work; and I assume that Tiger Woods enjoys his. But pleasure in the work doesn't really matter one way or the other. I know teachers who enjoy teaching, tax lawyers who enjoy tax law, and salespeople who enjoy selling. What they do counts as *work* nonetheless.

Logically or formally speaking, what matters is whether or not the processes involved serve an end beyond themselves. Publication, like winning tournaments, is an end beyond the process of playing around with words or with little white balls. Furthermore, I could not afford to spend as much time writing, nor (I presume) could Woods afford to spend as much time golfing, if these activities were not in some manner remunerative.

On the other hand, all of us have work we must do for which we are not paid. Most of this work takes place in our "private" lives, and traditionally women have done most of it. As women have claimed access to economic productivity and the status one gains thereby, the status and management of this unpaid household labor has become infamously polemical. When I was newly married, and several of my good friends were newly married, we took to calling this conflict The Housework Wars.

In any given marriage many things are at stake, but from all that complexity I'd like to point out one interesting historical fact. Housework is unpaid labor, and in our culture what is not paid for tends to be not counted. Given our modernist presumption, first, that price quantifies everything, and, second, that everything real is quantifiable, then work which is without price becomes oddly unreal—until the kitchen turns into a health hazard and the bottom of the bathtub turns black. Gender-role disputes add layer upon layer of acrimony to the issue.

In *Unbending Gender: Why Family and Work Conflict and What To Do About It,* legal theorist Joan Williams proposes to distinguish between *market work*—for which one earns money—and *family work,* which is unpaid but no less essential.[3] I see three major drawbacks to that label. First, although *family work* seems to include child care in a rhetorically more central way than the older label *housework,* it thereby obscures all the necessary work within the household that has nothing to do with children, spouses, or partners. There is a huge category of adult responsibilities that have nothing whatever to do with marital or parental status. There's nothing particularly familial about changing bed linens, filing insurance claims, cleaning the kitchen, or scrubbing the bathtub.

"Family work" also obscures characteristics of housework that we cannot afford to obscure. Housework is often repetitive and physical. Housework is often closely linked to maintaining cleanliness and to meeting bodily needs. Aristotle regarded such tasks as fit only for slaves—or women, of course. The status of work closely follows the ways in which intellect has been traditionally higher in status than body. When Williams reaches for a phrase like "family work," she is proposing a category label that sounds like much higher-status stuff than "housework." "Family work" as a label tries to reach back to the moral privilege accruing to Home Sweet Home and the Haven in a Heartless World, and to the moral superiority credited to women by "difference" feminists such as Carol Gilligan.

By contrast, "housework" sounds like something that the cognoscenti either hire someone else to do or ignore as the neurotic preoccupation of bored suburban housewives. "Housework" conjures up washing dishes, sweeping the floor, and taking out the trash after dinner, not reading to an eager toddler or taking a ten-year-old to the pediatrician. "Family work" is a label much more acceptable to the corps of elite women and academic feminists for whom Williams writes.[4] Of course there's nothing *a priori* wrong with wanting or coming up with a higher-status label. There is a legitimate rhetorical problem in properly naming important work that has been relegated to invisibility or denigrated as the insignificant preoccupation of people marginalized by gender and by socioeconomic status (and often by race as well).[5] There is no easy answer.

Nonetheless, "family work" is clearly an inadequate answer, because it suggests that the family is a locus of labor. But the locus of labor in our "private" lives is the house, not the family. "Family work" rather than "housework" implies that being a family, having a family, is a job like any other job. We do commonly talk about "working at" relationships, but that's the careless formulation of common language. Intimate relationships—family, friends, and so forth—exist for their own sake. Nurturing these relationships is not work because it is not an instrumental activity serving a need distinct from the activity as such. One might cultivate relationships with clients on that basis, I suppose—hoping for a sale, for instance. But intimate relationships are not conducted on an instrumental, profit-oriented, cost-benefit basis—unless, of course, you are a rational-actor economist for whom absolutely all human endeavors are based upon cost-benefit calculations.[6]

Intimate relationships—genuine or substantial friendships, broadly defined—are part of life, not work, and furthermore they are part of everyone's life, not simply the lives of those living with legally-defined kinfolk. Maintaining a healthy intimate relationship with a child demands more time, energy, attention, and insight than maintaining a healthy intimate relationship with another adult, because the child is still developing the capacity for such relationships. That's why children need so much individual attention from the adults who love them: children become capable of intimacy only to the extent that loving adults gradually elicit in them the capacity for such connection. Nonetheless, loving and being loved are part of *life* not *work*. We can't hope to find a way to balance work and life appropriately until we find a way to recognize that not all humanly necessary work is market work.

Above all, I argue, it is both morally wrong and culturally dangerous to conceptualize the parental version of the work-life conflict in language that obscures the ways in which the parents of small children face problems that are an acute instance of needs that every employee has. That's not simply a matter of equity between workers who are parents of dependent youngsters and those who are not. It is, more profoundly, a matter of recognizing that a healthy society is a finely woven network of friendships. Job demands that systematically impede the sustenance of enduring friendships will come, in the end, to destroy the social capital upon which the economy itself depends. Subsuming our needs for friendships under the label "family work" is grounded in the "family values" ideology which attributes all moral authority and substantive ethics to the "private" sphere.

This much seems reasonably clear and straightforward, or so I hope, because the issues involved suddenly get complicated. What is the opposite of work? At first glance, the opposite of work—not working—is lying around, doing nothing, snoozing on the sofa on a Sunday afternoon. To the extent that work takes energy, to the extent that doing something for the sake of something else obviously demands energy, not working should be not demanding. Or so it seems. But such casual logic leads us astray. "Having a life" does take energy.

Having a Life and Finding "Flow"

Mihaly Csikszentmihalyi has spent decades studying the human experience that he calls "autotelic" activity. As he defines it, such activity is the logical opposite of "work" as defined by Volf. A purely autotelic activity is one that we find intrinsically satisfying. The experience of doing it is the main goal.[7]

For instance, I tend a few perennials on either side of my front door simply because I enjoy doing so. It's not an investment in real estate values, nor an attempt to fit into the neighborhood. My neighbors clearly think that I'm nuts. They are polite about it, of course; a couple of times in fifteen years I've even had someone comment that it looks nice. I doubt that they have ever heard of Csikszentmihalyi, but they clearly understand that I'm doing this simply because I want to. In a quiet and friendly way, they find that desire mildly amusing because they see how much effort is involved.

Csikszentmihalyi discovers that launching ourselves into an activity done for its own sake always demands such an initial outlay of physical and emotional energy. It also requires that the task at hand must be genuinely challenging to our skills—but not so much so as to overwhelm us with frustration and failure. When we are fully engaged with such a task, we enter a state of mind he calls "flow." We lose track of time and we lose self-absorption. Our brain waves become more regular and harmonic. When we emerge, we might be muddy and tired, but at some level we are also relaxed and emotionally satisfied—not strung out and frazzled. "If only I could weed all winter," a friend of mine lamented, "I'd be a lot less crazy by March."

Although "autotelic activity" and "work" are formal or theoretically defined opposites, in practice there are places of overlap. Csikszentmihalyi explains that the happiest, most satisfied people among those he studied were those who could find an autotelic, flow-inducing challenge within almost any task they had to undertake. That was true even when the task itself was unquestionably work (as that term was defined by Volf: something done not for its own sake but for the sake of something else). For instance, when the snow is dry, the sky is clear, and wind is calm, I can enjoy shoveling snow. Before I read Csikszentmihalyi, it had always puzzled me that I find myself doing an unnecessarily precise, even elegant job of it when sloppy would be sufficient. Who looks at the little lines of snow left between shovel strokes or at the neatness of the edge between sidewalk and lawn??? My "problem" was that I just couldn't enjoy sloppy-looking work. And if I didn't enjoy the work at least in some regard, then having to do it left me feeling hostile and oppressed.

Marlane van Hall, in her marvelous little essay "The Zen of Housework," makes the same point: the "enlightened soul," she contends, can achieve what Csikszentmihalyi calls "flow" by centering "on the great mystery of the fact of our actually living our lives." She goes on, "This 'way' is no escape but instead a total response to all the aspects of our life, in our home and in the world. It makes no distinction between the ordinary and the extraordinary, between spiritual practice or nonpractice."[8] At least in my experience, it can take tremendous energy and mindfulness to silence my opinions about tedious chores. Sometimes I can do it; sometimes I can't. I know I am a lot more sane when I find the energy to transcend the tedium of utilitarian work, focusing instead upon doing whatever needs to be done with some sustained, mindful grace. But it takes a lot of energy.

There is a further paradox here that needs careful consideration. Pure autotelic activity always demands highly focused energy. We need to understand, Csikszentmihalyi argues, that intimate relationships are a particularly demanding autotelic activity. If we don't protect the time and the energy it takes to love and to be loved, then our intimate relationships will suffer. Although he is talking here specifically about families, what he says also applies to mature friendships of any kind:

> . . . it takes more than food in the fridge and two cars in the garage to keep a family going. A group of people is kept together by two kinds of energy: material energy provided by food, warmth, physical care, and money; and the psychic energy of people investing in each other's goals. Unless parents and children share ideas, emotions, activities, memories, and dreams, their relationship will survive only because it satisfies material needs. As a psychic energy, it will exist only at the most primitive level. Amazingly enough, many people refuse to see this point. . . . Businessmen know . . . [that] entropy is a constant factor, and if it is not attended to, the company will dissolve. Yet many of them assume that families are somehow different—entropy cannot touch them and so they are immune to change. . . . When parents come home exhausted from their jobs, they hope that being with the family will be an effortless, relaxing, invigorating experience. But to find flow in family relations requires as much skill as any other complex activity. . . . Parenting is supposed to be one of the most rewarding experiences in life; but it isn't, unless one approaches it with the same attention as one would a sport or an artistic performance.[9]

When we all work long hours then come home exhausted to face life's inescapable array of nonmarket work, love suffers. Children, who need a lot of love, suffer acutely. But all of us suffer. Friendships suffer, and as I have argued elsewhere, marriage is best understood as a variety of friendship.[10] Community suffers as well, because community depends upon both a network of nonfamilial friendships and upon the wide array of nonmarket work necessary to run civic organizations such as garden clubs or bowling leagues, to attend local government meetings and hearings, or to maintain churches, synagogues, and other religious organizations. Few of us can take time for nonmarket work outside the household until after the nonmarket work of our own household is under reasonable control. As Csikszentmihalyi argues, when we hardly have the energy genuinely to engage our spouses and children, then we are unlikely to have time for our friends either. As he says, friendships—with spouses, with other adults generally, or with children—are remarkably creative and high-energy endeavors. As Robert Putnam laments in *Bowling Alone: The Collapse and Revival of American Community,* the social fabric itself is frayed when none or few of us have the time we need to do the communal nonmarket work that sustains communal friendships. Nonmarket work is the material substratum of community life just as it is the material substratum of family life.[11]

In *Luxury Fever: Money and Happiness in an Era of Excess,* economist Robert H. Frank pushes these insights one step further. He has tested the levels of enduring life satisfaction that people derive from conspicuous consumption—luxury cars, colossal homes, and so forth. He found the same pattern that others have found in studying the lasting impact of windfalls such as winning the lottery: after a while, the thrill wears off. No matter how thrilled a person was initially with a $100,000 car, eventually it's just "the car." The mansion becomes merely "the house." More dangerous still is the parallel situation in which I increase the likelihood of my promotion by working longer hours than everyone else—until everyone else starts working longer hours as well. Then we once again share a similar probability of promotion, but now we are all working longer hours (longer hours that can be enforced by greater indebtedness for bigger houses, fancier cars, etc.).

The conclusion Frank draws demands careful thought: "Yet no family, acting alone," he concludes, "can solve this problem, just as no nation can unilaterally stop a military arms race."[12] That's competition run amuck, he contends, and in our day competition had gotten wildly out of hand in just this way. Frank compares our predicament to that of deer growing ever-larger antlers, which confer evolutionary advantage in the competition for mates. Antlers get larger and larger until the bucks become vulnerable to predators who chase them into the woods, where their large racks get tangled in low-hanging branches. They would all be better off with smaller antlers, but only if they could all change together.[13] Bucks can't. Neither can people, generally speaking. But the ingenuity and diversity of human culture does create options for individuals sharp enough to realize what is going on—and bold enough to seek alternatives.

Frank contrasts such competition run amuck and conspicuous consumption with what he calls "inconspicuous consumption." Economic and psychological resources can be "invested" not in conspicuous luxury goods but in human relationships, healthy communities, environmental protection, shorter commutes, and so forth. Like Csikszentmihalyi, he realizes that having a life demands complex and sometimes difficult moral choices, because we do not live in a world of infinite time and limitless resources. But life-satisfaction studies have revealed that our "investment" in nonconspicuous consumption yields levels of life satisfaction that rise over time.[14]

For instance, I had lunch yesterday with a friend I've had since 1977. We had not seen or heard from one another in many years. It was a glorious reunion. In 1977, when we first met, I also bought my very first car. One's first car is a thrill too—there's no denying that. But twenty-five years later, the car is worthless; the friendship is priceless. And no matter what one pays for a car, there's less thrill in driving an old car than there is in seeing an old friend. That's the difference between conspicuous and inconspicuous consumption. But devoting resources to inconspicuous consumption, like finding flow in family life, demands clarity and courage about one's own priorities. Once again we see that *having a life* demands energy just as *earning a living* does.

"Something More" than Work

In *The Feminine Mystique,* Betty Friedan famously argued that women were suffering from a nameless urge for "something more" than husband, children, and home. These days, Joanne B. Ciulla argues, both men and women suffer from a similarly obscure desire for "something more" to their lives than the endless round of paid work.[15] It is as if the Angel in the House has joined the Oaf in his Office—where both of them have recognized themselves as exhausted drones. Both men and women can find themselves trapped in marginal lives, just as medieval peasants were trapped, even though contemporary workers are incomparably better nourished and better housed than these ancestors were. We need to understand the cultural pressures we are up against as we struggle to reclaim the time and the energy required for autotelic endeavors across the board—and especially for vital intimate relationships with family and friends—or those pressures can trap us into selling ourselves short.

Since World War II, Ciulla explains, management theorists such as Peter Drucker have endeavored "to find a cause, a mission, or a set of ideals that would give work a social meaning and create the kind of commitment that they had seen in the war effort."[16] In a major, widely influential study published in 1971, the Department of Health, Education, and Welfare documented a widespread hunger for the quality of social meaning that these management theorists had been talking about for decades. Soon thereafter, Studs Terkel published the best-seller *Working*—later made into a musical—in which he interviewed people who gave human voices to the dissatisfactions that the report described.[17] In one often-quoted interview, a worker complains that his job is too much smaller than his soul, and he insists that many people yearn for jobs that provide scope for their souls.

In some ways, of course, it seems that this fellow is yearning for a job that provides more of what Csikszentmihalyi calls "flow"—a job that offers both an engaging challenge and something worth doing for its own sake. But his explicitly religious language suggests that there's much more at stake than simple boredom. What's at stake here is a dimension of "flow" that as far as I can tell Csikszentmihalyi does not discuss. Behind the unsatisfied quest for "social meaning" and for soul-worthy work, I'd contend, is the deep human need to contribute to the common good.

I think that compassion is the deepest wellspring of "flow," because compassion both arises from and strengthens that fiery spark of the Holy One dwelling in each of us. Love of neighbor strengthens love of God and—paradoxically—a spiritually mature self-love as well. It does so because the love which is God (which is God's) is pure grace. Such love is not earned, and so we don't have to worry about earning it. We are freed at last from anxious self-absorption and the fear that our best efforts will prove inadequate in the end. When we do the best we can at a challenging task and yet we do so without anxiety about our performance, our actions are at some deep level effortless. They are not constrained by ego. The absence of such constraint is part of what we mean by "graceful." God simply calls us to be our deepest, truest selves. God does so without threat and without coercion. At the very depths of our deepest selves, there is the indelible image of God. The *imago Dei* can be obscured by pain, by history, by fear, by failure, by the blind demands of human egotism. But it is indelible, and the love of God calls us to find it again and to live in the light of what we have found.

Our jobs starve our souls when—for whatever reason—the work involves selling *ourselves* short—this deepest self, the truest self, the self made in the image of God and intended for transformative or enlightening friendship with God. I suspect that work would probably have to be inherently exploitative to have no potential whatsoever for flow (running a brothel, for instance, or one of those slave-labor factories). Far more common are working situations where corporate culture tends to obscure the deep-seated spiritual need to feel that one's work honestly and visibly serves the common good. And behind any local corporate culture is the larger sociocultural matrix of meaning—what I'm calling the ideology of the marketplace, according to which the bottom line is the measure of all that matters, and all of us are nothing more than rational actors out for ourselves alone.

There's no denying that all of us are self-centered some of the time, and some of us all of the time—but compassion, generosity, honor, responsibility, and self-respect are no less central to who we are as human beings. The problem here is not the jobs themselves, but the cultural definitions and cultural contexts shaping how we think about the work that we do for pay. The ideology of "the marketplace" simply, programmatically insists that employment is a cost-benefit contract in which both employers and employees set their own needs first.

From traditional religious perspectives, that's a wildly false (or at least hopelessly degraded) understanding of what it means *to be human*. No wonder, then, that many good, decent, ordinary people spend a lot of psychic energy consciously or unconsciously resisting the ways in which marketplace ideology defines the cultural terms of their employment. Many people want to take honest pride and deep-seated pleasure in doing a good job—and hence finding flow—at whatever it is they do to earn a living. There is real pleasure to be found in working with other good people who also care deeply about doing the job right—not simply about collecting a paycheck. But it takes both energy and insight to maintain that quality of cooperation in the face of marketplace ideology insisting that the bottom line is the top priority and that all of us are out for ourselves alone.

As Ciulla explains, under pressure from management theorists such as Peter Drucker, "personnel departments took the place of the Protestant work ethic, and morale replaced morality as the motivation to work."[18] But it hasn't worked. Employees are increasingly alienated, and the list of reasons why gets longer all the time. Long hours disrupt personal life; job transfers disconnect people from communities and kinfolk in ways that dilute the common life, dissolve supportive friendships, and diminish trust. As Robert Reich argues at length, mergers, globalization, e-commerce, etc. have so severely rationalized the marketplace that layoffs and downsizing have become ever-more common, ever-more severe, and ever-more disconnected from both job performance and the profitability of the company itself.[19]

You can do an outstanding job for a company that is securely profitable and still find yourself out of work without warning if management decides that a round of pre-emptive layoffs will raise quarterly earnings or at least impress financial analysts that the company's management is utterly ruthless—which is what "professional" has come to mean.[20] As a result, many people have quite reasonably withdrawn their commitment to employers whose commitment to them has proven no more than a pretense, no more than shabby hype from the folks down in personnel. In such an unpredictable environment, as Ciulla shrewdly observes, the Protestant work ethic has been replaced by the fear ethic. Unlike its progenitor, "the work ethic of fear does not hold out hope of salvation, but only offers the opportunity to work more."[21]

No wonder we want more to our lives than what employment alone can provide: often it's not clear what, beyond this week's paycheck, we can count on jobs to offer. But that doesn't stop some employers from trying to elicit an allegiance they do not or cannot reciprocate. From her perspective as a professor in a school of business management, Ciulla offers a detailed, witty, and well-documented history of management fads. It's a story in equal measures appalling and intriguing: management theories closely track developments in popular culture as they seek the available means of persuasion. It's no surprise, then, that "spirituality" is the very latest fad, offering "a combination of religion 'lite' and therapy 'lite.' This approach attempts to satisfy what some want from religion without the work of faith and what some want from therapy without the work of changing."[22]

Like all the fads before it, this new approach encourages us to turn to work itself—or to continue to seek in work—some satisfaction for our humanly profound, morally important need to live in accord with what it truly means *to be human*. Underneath all our ordinary quirks and failings, beyond our deepest fears and darkest scars, there glimmers the image of God and with it the burning capacity to be compassionate. The "something more" that is missing in our lives cannot be found if all we do is alternate between office and exhaustion in a cultural context that systematically obscures and distorts our sense of ourselves and our lives. But it's no easy task to keep in focus for ourselves all the ways in which our paid work can indeed be understood as a morally significant, soul-satisfying, flow-eliciting contribution to the common good.

Many good people do keep this focus, of course, and when they are managers or owners they are good news for everyone who reports to them. Culture itself is fabulously dynamic because there are always countercultural pressures from such people. In every time, in every place, there are always natural leaders pushing against all the default settings and all the commonplace assumptions of their own era. But it's hard. And it's especially hard if you don't have the cultural-historical background to recognize what you are up against. As a result, many good people, especially those who are without countercultural community support, find themselves frustrated and unhappy without exactly understanding why—or what to do about it.

Offering pseudospirituality to such frustrated, unhappy employees is like offering yet another brand of floor wax to Friedan's frustrated housewives. Such management practices, Ciulla angrily concludes, "amount to psychological manipulation or empty propaganda."[23] They generate not commitment but cynicism, especially among younger workers raised on Dilbert cartoons, pop psychology, and sophisticated attention to canny advertising ploys. They add to the alienation they are intended to combat. But that doesn't discredit how legitimately we need to contribute to the common good and to express the compassion that glows in the depths of us—whether in "public" at work or in "private" at home.

In *When Work Doesn't Work Anymore: Women, Work, and Identity,* Elizabeth McKenna describes her own midlife discovery that despite how much she enjoyed her job, the identity on her business card came to feel insufficient.[24] Under the obvious influence of thinkers such as Carol Gilligan and Mary Field Belenkey, she attributes the problem with jobs to gender difference. Women are unhappy; men, she argues, are happy as clams at high tide because the workplace was designed around the masculine psyche, which she believes is perfectly content to be the amoral workplace drone imagined by separate-spheres doctrines. Women who carry most of the burden of what Arlie Hochschild calls "the second shift" certainly have plenty of reason to be unhappy, but it's vitally important to realize that the widespread yearning for something more than a paycheck is not a gender-specific complaint. The overwhelming demands that employment can make upon our lives is a cultural problem, a human problem, not merely a problem for women alone.

The real problem is not that—despite management hype—many jobs are, or become, mostly tedious routine in which it can be hard to find the quality of challenge necessary to finding flow. The problem is that marketplace ideology has deep—and deeply disguised—religious roots. As we will see, marketplace ideology is inextricably entangled with classic Protestant teachings about innate depravity. This buried connection generates the murky but unmistakable sense that we have an essential, nearly transcendent obligation to make the most money possible, as if the success of one's career is the measure of one's soul. That's a trap.

But escaping that trap is only part of what I'm after here. Disentangling the religious roots of marketplace ideology will also help us to claim—and to reclaim—our honest pleasure and moral pride in a job well done. Good work serves the common good in part by honestly contributing to the particular good of colleagues, customers, students, clients, etc. Good work is a variety of honest, generous compassion; it is not simply the egocentric and ruthlessly amoral struggle of each against all. Reclaiming the moral significance of good work provides a solid basis upon which to rebalance the relationship between earning a living and having a life by recentering both domains upon the sacred human capacity for compassion.

How does that happen? If we understand our need to serve both our clients (for instance) and our friends or family, how does that help when our duties to one conflict with our duties to another? For those of us who work from home and sometimes on very tight deadlines, this is an exceedingly immediate problem: children always want 150 percent of parents' attention, and clients always want everything by yesterday morning. What then?

Serious, unmet needs take a toll. They are costly; they are painful. Faced with too many needs and too little time, we have to compare the human pain we cause or fail to avert on either hand. That's never easy, but it's seldom impossible. If my client doesn't get the speech I've been writing in time to give it, that's a bigger failure of responsibility than refusing (for now) to listen to a he-said-she-said account of a squabble at school. On the other hand, there are and have to be moments when the demands of a personal relationship trump the demands of a professional relationship, times when the needs of a child, a friend morally exceed the wishes of a customer—or, more difficult yet, the personal ambitious drive for success and the status it brings.

It is inevitably painful to compare the moral importance of competing needs we face, but it is worse yet to imagine that the demands of "work" are always absolute and the demands of "life" are always adaptable. As we will see in the chapters ahead, in our day that's a commonplace—and commonly invisible—assumption.

11

The History of Our Dilemma

Downsizing and Damnation

The deep question here, I propose, is "Why has work become so important? Why does work dominate our lives?" In particular, why does it dominate our lives in ways that leave so many people feeling overextended, frazzled, and frustrated? The answer to such questions leads us back once again to the history of culture, this time to the Protestant Reformation and its two principal theologians, John Calvin (1509–1564) and Martin Luther (1483–1546).

In *The Protestant Ethic and the Spirit of Capitalism,* sociologist Max Weber argues that the Protestant Reformation appropriated religious energies for economic purposes by representing work itself as sacred duty (not merely practical necessity) and by making prosperity an indirect marker of God's favor.[25] Through the Puritans, this complex of ideas exerted tremendous and lasting influence on American culture, in part because its basic ideas are secularized without much difficulty—as Benjamin Franklin demonstrated in works like *Poor Richard's Almanac.* As Ciulla points out, it's a very small step from hoping that prosperity will prove we are saved to hoping that prosperity will make us happy or give our lives meaning.[26] And meanwhile, as Weber shrewdly observes, we will work very hard indeed because "idle hands are the devil's workshop" and because leisure has been redefined as an immoral waste of time and money rather than—as Aristotle believed—the foundation of a good life.

In the hands of the Reformers, Weber recounts, the asceticism and self-discipline characteristic of vowed religious elites such as monks and nuns become general cultural norms: we work and sleep and work again, with cell phones and e-mail rather than church bells to summon us over and over again to one or another relentless and inescapable obligation. *Of course* there is little time for anything but work: that's how the system is designed. And as long as women remained in their separate sphere of housework and child care, monastic capitalism—so to speak[27]—generated extraordinary economic development without necessarily disrupting the flow of social capital, the development of children, or the mundane, crucially important nonmarket work of household and community. When that social arrangement collapses, then the demands of work make what Arlie Hochschild calls "emotional ascetics" of us all: we deny the depth or extent of our need both to care for others and to be cared for by them in return. (We will get back to Hochschild in chapter twelve.)

As both historians and storytellers have explained, modern Western economic development came at the cost of the tremendous personal anxiety provoked by Reformation doctrines. This deep-rooted anxiety still haunts our nightmares about downsizing and career paths and "making it." Like many other obscure terrors, however, this one may lose some measure of its power when it is excavated and examined in broad daylight.

Reformed or Protestant theology is a richly nuanced body of thought; for our purposes, however, two doctrines matter most. One is Martin Luther's understanding of the nature or meaning of work; the other is John Calvin's understanding of the nature or meaning of prosperity. Let's begin with Martin Luther and the meaning of work.

In its millennium-and-a-half of existence, Christianity had evolved a hierarchical social organization that mirrored the social order of its times. Bishops, priests, and vowed religious (nuns, monks, etc.) were as spiritually superior to laypeople as nobility were socially superior to commoners. Furthermore, many church leaders were drawn from the ranks of the hereditary nobility. They were second sons, excess daughters, and so forth. Within the church, however, their social authority formally rested not simply upon their noble birth but rather upon the idea that the "Princes of the Church" had been called by God to a distinctly religious life that rendered them morally superior to ordinary laypeople.

Martin Luther disputes that authority by arguing that God calls each person to his or her place and task in society: all work is sacred calling, not only work within church hierarchy.[28] Work thus becomes a central moral obligation. Work itself becomes holy. Prior to the Reformation, work had no particular religious significance. It was mere practical necessity. Religious and moral significance accrued only to *how* the work was done, to the interpersonal or social virtues such as honesty, justice, nonviolence, and appropriate respect for others. Excessive attention to work, in fact, was morally suspect. Working too hard, accumulating too much wealth, might be a sign of greed, lust, envy, or idolatry. Luther's claim reflected not only the growing cultural authority of the hard-working, prosperous, urban and entrepreneurial middle class, but also the Renaissance humanist emphasis upon the dignity of the individual. Every individual is called by God, not just the clergy.

The connection between attitudes toward work and more specifically ecclesial and theological issues is a bit more complicated, but no less important. The Reformers also objected that church hierarchy had abrogated a power that belongs to God alone—the power to save and to damn—by presuming to answer the ancient question, "What then must I do to be saved?" or "How do I know if I am saved?" Theologically speaking, that's a moot question: God is utterly transcendent and thus ultimately inscrutable. All we know is what God has revealed to us in Scripture: God is just and loving, full of compassion, quick to forgive and abounding in mercy. That should be enough: there is a sort of literal-mindedness involved in excessively systematic or excessively logical arguments about what is, at heart, a profound spiritual mystery. Spiritual maturity, whether it is called "salvation" or "enlightenment," cannot be reduced to checklists or calculated like a bottom line.

On the other hand, when everlasting torment was thought to be the consequence of failure to be included among "the saved," church leaders possessed a spectacular psychological and cultural authority. Some churchmen did, at times, claim to know who is among the damned, and such men at times proclaimed the damnation of their enemies for their own political purposes.[29] They could be quick to specify required religious practices and pious observances, especially when these added to their own social prestige, political power, or income. Morally responsible leadership was endlessly seduced by political and social expedience: the church may be holy, but its leaders are merely men. As Barbara Tuchman elegantly recounts in *A Distant Mirror,* the history of religious institutions is an endlessly repeated cycle of decadence and reform.[30]

Church reformers like Martin Luther and John Calvin responded to such abuse of power in their own day by taking up an equal and opposite position, radically asserting that God's opinion in the matter is utterly unknowable and, above all, immutable. God's opinion is immutable because a perfect, unchanging, omnipotent, omniscient God knows everything ahead of time, never changes his mind, and cannot make mistakes. Crudely put, Reformed theology tends to imagine God as some combination of absolute monarch and the personification of a radical philosophic idealism: perfect knowledge on the one hand, and, on the other, the power to assure that what is known and what *is* are necessarily and inescapably identical.

As a counterstrategy to how the "Princes of the Church" were acting like any other absolute monarch in Europe, it's a fairly ingenious gambit with legitimate foundations in certain aspects of Christian theological tradition. As a "reading" of the passionately loyal and yearning Holy One of Israel, however, and especially in far less skillful hands than Calvin's or Luther's, the position deteriorates into all sorts of complicated and culturally powerful difficulties. (There are complexly theological work-arounds for all these difficulties, especially in the dense, nuanced, multi-volume scholarly writings of Luther and Calvin themselves—but that's another story altogether.)

For our purposes, what matters is this: the Reformers argued ferociously that one does not attain salvation by observing the ritual and liturgical duties of traditional ("Catholic") Christianity nor by practical charity and good works. One does not *attain* salvation at all. That's not how it works. Whether one is saved or not is determined by God's choice, period. And God's choice was made before time began, without regard to any supposed worthiness we might strive for during our lifetimes. We cannot "work our way to heaven" by acts of compassion, generosity, and personal integrity, because we cannot obligate God to reward us with eternal life.

On the one hand, I think this is a perfectly legitimate spiritual insight: there is no celestial spreadsheet on which our virtues are balanced against our vices; the good life simply grows out from our recognition of the *imago Dei* within us. Theologically speaking, the good life arises from the good heart grounded in faith, which at the cosmic level is purely a gift. We can cultivate the good heart—we can attend in spiritually disciplined ways to the *imago Dei* within us—but nonetheless we must remember that the good heart is not an achievement of the ambitious, aggressive, determined ego.[31] The good heart is a surrender of the grasping, controlling ego that might otherwise set its sights upon "managing" God or "managing" the cosmos itself. Spiritual traditions across the board are usually quite clear on this point: "enlightenment," by whatever particular name it is known, cannot be reduced to a list carefully entered into one's PDA.

And yet cultivating the good heart is no easy task. It is an art, and like any art it has its master practitioners and its apprentices at various levels. This is why many spiritual traditions provide guiding practices such as the study of sacred writings, regular schedules of communal prayer or meditation practice, etc., plus such public moral norms as the Ten Commandments and famously paradoxical teachings such as koans, parables, and narratives. The Reformers rightly challenged what they saw as a decadent, exploitative collapse of these public and communal spiritual practices into the hollow formulae of magic.

The Reformers believed, generally speaking, that allowing for any human spiritual initiative at all impinged upon the absolute omnipotence of God. They were convinced, in short, that "we cannot be good without God." What appears to be human virtue is merely the manifestation of God's grace, not human maturity, courage, resolve, etc. But to the extent that the Reformers (or their more radical followers) denied the salvific efficacy of all spiritual practices, they soon found themselves trapped within literal-minded positions that had massive cultural consequences. Pre-eminent among these consequences is the "Calvinist" doctrine of predestination.[32]

Predestination: How Do I Know If I'm "Saved"?

To trace the consequences of "predestination," I need a small detour here into the history of arguments within Christian thought about what it means *to be human*. In the very early tradition, humanity was seen as innately capable of virtue because we are made in the image of God, who is good. As I've said before: the *imago Dei* in us is wounded or imprisoned by suffering, fear, and human egotism; but the *imago Dei* is still there and still powerful if we can just get back in touch with it. Spiritual practices serve that end: mindfulness, by whatever name, liberates the *imago Dei* from its psychic obscurity.

This belief persists within Eastern Orthodoxy. It persisted among the Celts. But after the fifth century it was—generally speaking—replaced in the Western or Latin church by a dramatically more pessimistic view of what it means to be human. This pessimistic view held that the *imago Dei* was obliterated by the Original Sin of Adam and Eve in the Garden of Eden.

What happened in the fifth century was a definitive conflict between Augustine, bishop of Hippo in northern Africa, and one Pelagius, a monk, reportedly Irish or at least revered among the Irish, who thought that people are innately capable of recognizing and effectively seeking the good. Little is known about him beyond what his theological opponents had to say; few of his own writings survive.[33] In contrast to Pelagius, Augustine had a very bleak view of what it means *to be human*, probably through the influence upon his thinking of Manicheanism, a syncretic, neo-Platonic blend of religious and philososphical thought that competed with Christianity for quite a while. Augustine trounced Pelagius, to be short about it. Augustine was also prolific, persuasive, and brilliant. His influence was massive: "Pelagianism" is officially considered the heresy according to which humans have no need of God at all. (That's almost undoubtedly *not* what the real Pelagius believed.)

Of course, more than a thousand years separate Augustine from Luther and Calvin; a lot happened in theology during that interval. Optimistic voices were of course heard now and then. Pre-eminent among them was Thomas Aquinas (1225–1274), who believed, in the words of one historian, that "Even if we have achieved all that one can reasonably desire, we want more because there is this fascinating, annoying, compelling hunger in us for the divine. . . . [T]he *imago* can never be totally lost, despite the most blinding ignorance and the most debilitating sin."[34] Various late-medieval mystics—such figures as Julian of Norwich (1342–1416?), for instance—also had a warmer or "higher" construction of what it means *to be human.*

The Reformers, however, reached back over these later developments to reclaim Augustine of Hippo. Drawing upon Augustine and other sources, the Reformers argued that we are all innately and utterly depraved because of Adam's sin, and so we all deserve eternal damnation. We have no grounds upon which to accuse God of injustice in refusing to "save" us—to grant us eternal life rather than eternal suffering for all our failures. But through the obedient and sacrificial death of the "second Adam," Jesus Christ, God arbitrarily chooses to redeem from their otherwise inevitable damnation a small group called the "Elect" who alone are destined—*predestined*—for eternal life.

The elect are chosen not through any particular or distinctive merit of their own—all human beings are totally depraved, including the Elect. The Elect are simply *chosen* for God's own inscrutable reasons to be the beneficiaries of Jesus' sacrifice. They are, thereby, made capable of virtuous behavior—not on their own, mind you, but by and through God's transmission through Jesus of the grace to be virtuous. According to the Westminster Confession of 1647, if you are not among the Elect, then even your greatest efforts at leading a virtuous life are both pointless and doomed. It's important to keep in mind that no less a Puritan than John Milton was revolted by that claim: "Though I may be sent to Hell for it, such a God will never command my respect."[35] There was a range of opinion within Reformed tradition to which my short summary gives short shrift.

When I have complained to my Reformed-tradition friends that the Reformed tradition portrays God as both arbitrary and astoundingly vindictive, they reply quite seriously that they know they are saved—and so am I—and above all one shouldn't worry about being "saved." Only Catholics worry about being saved, they tease me. I should trust in the graciousness of God and give up this scrupulous anxiety, this existential angst. Catholics and Protestants have been having this argument for centuries. Such conversations convinced me that in fact I am inescapably an Irish Catholic, no matter where I go to church.

Quite aside from the question of who is correct about God—let's put that aside here if we can—the Reformed doctrine of predestination soon created important socio-religious problems. If God's choice is arbitrary (i.e., not based upon our morality) and already determined, then what difference does it make how we live? If everything is settled already, why not eat, drink, and be merry? What's the point of a church at all?

Perhaps today one can imagine shrugging off the question with such insouciance. That wasn't the case five hundred years ago. "Am I among the Elect?" remained a spectacularly important question, because everlasting torment was the alternative. If we are to understand our own cultural past in useful ways, we have to rustle up the imaginative power to give that question the psychological weight it had at the time. As a rule of thumb, triple the terror evoked by questions like "Am I successful?" or "Am I making it?" or "Do I have what it takes?" The meaning of "Am I saved?" was exponentially more serious yet.[36]

"How do I know if I am saved?" There were two possible answers, both of which have had very wide currency in the centuries following the Reformation. One was an inner assurance, a simple personal confidence, a feeling or intuition that one has been "born again," this time to the eternal life of the saved. As Weber observes, that option leads to an emphasis on emotions or personal piety and often to withdrawal from the world. It was somewhat more characteristic of those churches following Luther (and, later, splintered from Lutheran churches) rather than those following Calvin.

In rather more secular and contemporary ways, this answer also funds the radically individualist versions of spirituality, especially when tied to such practices as self-consciously moralistic vegetarianism or to a morally separatist emphasis on all things "natural" and "organic." ("Organic," like "kosher," is a set of agricultural practices with unquestionably solid environmental credentials, but it can also serve as an identity-defining social boundary.) Other contemporary heirs of the "inner assurance" tradition are people who find their own way spiritually by patching together bits and pieces of various religions into a quilt of their own devising. "What works for me" is their criterion for religious practice. That criterion draws its original legitimacy from the strong individualist tenor of Reformation theology—even though the original Reformers would have been horrified by it.

"Inner assurance" will never be a workable option for everyone. What about people who are less introspective, less intuitive, or more oriented to pragmatic action and visible social norms? And so, the other way to cope with the question "How do I know if I am saved?" is to live in relentless effort to conform to God's will. Because—as Luther had taught—God has called every person to a given role in society, obedience to God's will necessarily involved the greatest possible diligence in meeting the obligations of that calling. One's effort in that regard can never be said to *merit* salvation, to *earn* or to *deserve* God's approval, just as superb performance reviews won't mean anything if the plant is closed or the company is sold or downsized. On the other hand, "profligate sinners" obviously run high probabilities of finding themselves among the damned—or the unemployed.

In short, *hard work*—not just "good works"—gained moral importance as indirect evidence of one's salvation. Furthermore, prosperity was thought to follow reliably from hard work. That's naïve, but surely it's also true that prosperity seldom comes *without* hard work—especially for the small, independent entrepreneur. Ultimately, the Protestant Reformation was overwhelmingly a religious movement by the rising middle class of urban shopkeepers, artisans, and small traders. Unlike the nobility, these people earned their prosperity. In some quite paradoxical ways, the practical theology of the Reformation has visible roots in entrepreneurial experiences and attitudes—including double-entry bookkeeping and the competitive mechanisms of a free market. The strict distinction between the Elect and the Damned seems to imagine God as a celestial accountant, sorting debits and credits into separate columns. In Geneva, Calvin wanted Christians to give advance notice of their intention to receive the consecrated bread of Holy Communion. Providing such notice would allow the local clergy to do a moral version of the credit check.[37]

Max Weber argues at length that Western economic development was fuelled by a tremendously disciplined and ascetic self-denial that ultimately rested upon religious anxiety provoked by the doctrine of predestination. Economic historians rightly object that he oversimplifies the rise of capitalism, which was a very complex, slow-evolving arrangement with many and various causes. More to the point here, historians of religion rightly object that he oversimplifies the theological nuance of a deeply diverse and widespread religious movement. Weber undoubtedly simplified the theology—in effect caricaturing Calvin—but on the other hand, popular culture doesn't pay much attention to theological nuance either.

If one frees predestination from its place in complex, nuanced systematic theology, then it becomes even more powerful culturally, because it ties itself in so very neatly to all sorts of primal anxieties about self-worth and social status. As social animals, largely without biological self-defenses other than intelligent cooperation and shared vigilance, we are intensely sensitive to ranks and relationships within our own social groups. Our survival depends upon our social sensitivities. We are hardwired to react to questions like "Am I among the Elect?" And if hard work—not good works—assures us that we belong and therefore we are safe, then we will work very hard indeed.

Success as Salvation

As we consider the risks involved in limiting the hours we work or the demands of our employers, we come up against this submerged but nonetheless toxic fusion of success and salvation. We also come up against a pervasive, exceedingly dark vision of what it means *to be human.* Rational-actor theorists are the secular heirs of the innate-depravity theologians in their exceedingly low opinion of human nature. No matter what we think or how we try, all of our behavior is governed by selfishness and self-seeking. In this secular dispensation, however, there's no possibility of "grace" and no hope for "redemption"—there is simply no way at all to act generously or with genuine compassion. We are self-seekers no matter what. None of us is Elect; none of us is saved. Those who dispute this doctrine are threatened not with hell (as Milton feared) but rather with exploitation and bankruptcy at the hands of the ruthless.

Rational-actor theorists also reclaim the arbitrary God as the "invisible hand" of the market responsible for the devastating losses of those who are laid off, those who work for companies or in industries that go down in flames, those who live where wages are measured in pennies or where safety and environmental regulations don't exist, and so forth. As the workplace has become increasingly capricious in the last fifty years, as the social contract between employers and employees increasingly unravels, ordinary and reasonable anxiety about economic security can resonate to these deeper, far less conscious cultural anxieties linking financial success to ethical stature. We are left feeling that we "ought to" earn as much money as we possibly can, or that we "ought not to" make any moves that might diminish our income. Above all, we are apt to feel that our socioeconomic status says something important about who we are and about our ultimate moral worth—even though, exactly like the anxious disciples of Calvin and Luther, we know that there's a huge element of raw luck in who gets ahead and who doesn't.

Both unpredictable markets and implacable management demands might have less of a psychological hold upon us if we were purely rational and therefore able to deconstruct success as a measure of our moral worth. But none of us is purely rational in that way. Furthermore, American popular culture still exists under the shadow of Calvinism in the form of the American Dream that hard work will prove ultimately redemptive. With the hard work and self-discipline of Benjamin Franklin, we too can come into the Paradise, the Promised Land, called Wealth and Success. In thinking about all this, we should keep in mind that in eighteenth-century America, subsistence agriculture and life on the frontier demanded brutally hard work; it's not surprising that American culture found religious significance in the inescapable facts of survival under harsh conditions. Despite our easier, more comfortable lives, however, the money that follows from hard work still carries an aura of inescapably powerful cultural meaning from our national past. Both employers and advertisers exploit those powerful cultural meanings to their own ends.

And so, like Dante, we can awaken lost in the woods of middle age to find ourselves alone and besieged by the demons of pathological individualism, consumerism, and ambition.[38] As religion scholar Robert Thurman argues in his lectures on the Three Jewels of Buddhism, we find ourselves in an economy and a society based upon anger, greed, and fear.[39] These are powerfully negative feelings that we have to keep suppressed in order to function, and so we end up with a culture shaped by the anxiety of repressed hostility. As Gregg Easterbrook points out, "In the past 100 years, academic journals have published 8,166 articles on 'anger' compared with 416 on 'forgiveness'; in its latest edition, the presumably encyclopedic *Encyclopedia of Human Emotions,* a reference for clinicians, lists page after page of detrimental emotional states but has no entry for 'gratitude.' Sigmund Freud declared mental torment the normal human condition and suggested that most people's best possible outcome would be to rise from neurosis into 'ordinary unhappiness.' It's a wonder we don't all lose our minds."[40]

Whether or not we are struggling to stay sane, we end up isolated from one another. Protestantism is intensely individualist: no priest, no community, no sacred communal ritual mediates between the individual and the Almighty. Regardless of anyone's personal religious identity or heritage, there's no way to escape how this Protestant individualism funds the radically secularized individualism of contemporary American culture. In a romantic or expressive individualism, "self" or "self-realization" takes the place of God—while leaving the individual no less lonely, no less isolated from other people and from meaningful cultural forms and activities.[41] As Robert Bellah and his colleagues explain, ". . . this is a society in which the individual can only rarely and with difficulty understand himself and his activity as interrelated in morally meaningful ways with those of other, different Americans. Instead of directing cultural and individual energies toward relating the self to its larger context, the culture of manager and therapist urges a strenuous effort to make of our particular segment of a life a small world of its own."[42]

In the secular form of radical religious individualism, the individual gets to define "salvation" for himself.[43] We are to set our own goals. And yet, as Bellah astutely observes, "For most of us, it is easier to think about how to get what we want than to know exactly what we should want. There is something inescapably and by-definition arbitrary about 'the goals of a good life' if each of us is to determine those goals alone, for ourselves as individuals."[44] In the meantime, however, we know we will need money. Furthermore, as we become an increasingly mobile, fragmented society, work provides life's primary array of relationships and social interactions for a growing percentage of the population.

America's Reformation heritage, in secular form, thus contributes to the exaggerated importance of work in our lives. That might be clearer if we contrast our contemporary high-anxiety investment in our careers with an older, less romantic perspective. Work need not be the means to our redemption, whether that's defined as religious salvation or self-realization. Work can be seen as the means to a simple material end outside of itself, as Volf proposes. This external end can be a paycheck or any other utilitarian goal or obligation—like a front walk on which one can walk safely in winter, or a meal when one is hungry. The point is that work is not required to justify itself with dramatic purpose or elaborate meaning beyond the honor of doing one's duty as a responsible adult.

When expectations are that plain, limited, and straightforward, it's a lot easier to enjoy one's work to some extent or in some regards. It is a lot easier to clear one's mind and to find some small but worthy challenge that can elicit "flow." It is easier in these ways because such pleasure is not expected to equal or even to justify the physical labor or the intellectual drudgery involved. The effort is justified by its material rewards or outcomes, and by the personal satisfaction of meeting one's moral and social obligations. It doesn't matter what the obligations are. If we have the spiritually disciplined energy that is required, we can respect ourselves for doing what has to be done, and for doing so with mature, responsible care and pride. We can do so even when the task itself is, or has become, routine, or once we realize that our work is unlikely to make us rich and famous.

I think that there is a lot to be said for self-respect on the basis of a job well done—even when it is the means to an end outside itself. That was something of a discovery in my own life, I confess, perhaps because life in professional academia unduly encourages romantic notions about the ultimate significance of one's own endeavors. But Karl Marx would have disagreed with—or at least disapproved of—my midlife discovery of small but real levels of flow within simply utilitarian work (whether shoveling snow or editing medical research papers). According to Miroslav Volf, Marx maintained throughout his career that work has to be personally meaningful, because work that is primarily the means to an end outside itself is necessarily alienating.[45]

But if the meaning of work depends in that way upon the task itself, then we are trapped: only a small fraction of the work that needs to be done will ever offer rich intrinsic meaning. A lot of necessary work will always be drudgery or at least fairly tedious routine. Even highly skillful work with a lot of intrinsic meaning sooner or later comes down to a daily grind of essentially routine work demanding high levels of self-discipline and mature persistence. (After a certain point, I can attest, grading student essays becomes brutally tedious.) In his view of work, Marx was in many ways quite a romantic—although he was also rightly appalled by the loss of artisan traditions and by the soul-numbing repetitiveness of factory jobs.

But the meaning of work need not be situated exclusively within the character of the task itself. The meaning of a task can also be determined in part by our motives for doing it. For instance, work of any kind, whether plain honest drudgery or composing symphonies, helps us to establish or participate in the network of relationships through which we realize our unity with one another. Through our work we realize how much we depend upon others, how much others depend upon us, and how much honor and meaning can be found in that mutuality. Esther DeWaal, in one of her books about Celtic spirituality, explains that traditional blessings of looms were so precise that one can thereby trace the evolution of technical innovations in weaving. She wonders what it might do to our lives if we began each day by blessing our own tools—in her case, a desktop computer, its cables, its software, its miscellaneous peripheral devices, and so forth—and by blessing those people whose work in design, manufacture, supply, and support makes our own work possible.[46] I don't have an answer to her question, but neither can I forget it. Do I click Help with a grateful heart? Not very often, I confess—although I do try for a flash of real thanks when I find what I need.

In particular, I think that those of us who do enjoy intrinsically rewarding work are morally obligated to remember how very much we depend upon others whose work is out-and-out tedious. We should honor that dependency by supporting such policy changes as a genuine living wage that includes maternity or family leave and health insurance.

Stanley Hauerwas argues, on quite different grounds, that work has moral value in part because it provides an opportunity for us to be of service to one another.[47] In and through work, we discover that our lives are entwined in a web of mutual moral obligation and material interdependence within the larger human community. Our work might not be fun, but it is necessary to the common good. We need others, and we are needed in turn. There is dignity for each person inherent in that reality. Everyone matters, and any single job, no matter how prestigious or well-paid, is dwarfed by the sum of gifts from countless others in our intricately articulated economy.

Ed Wolff, a kindly Chaucerian and my freshman composition professor in 1968, had a poster in his office that took deliberate aim at the working-class insecurities of his students, overwhelmingly in the first generation of our families to attend college. As I recall, the poster depicted an array of pipes dripping water upon the mortarboard of a foolish-looking professor vaguely modeled upon Albert Einstein. Across the bottom was a line (as I recall from Santayana) that went something like this: "The society that despises its plumbers, because they work with their hands, and worships its philosophers, because they work with their minds, is headed for disaster: neither its pipes nor its philosophy will hold water." Ed's unrelenting demands and his fatherly encouragement made such an impression upon me as a young writer that I've had dreams ever since in which waterpipes morph into manuscripts rolled over a typewriter platen, and typewriter keys become pipe wrenches become pencils and back again. (Twenty-some years of writing on a computer hasn't changed this private iconography in the least . . .)

Such recognition of our interdependence generates an intensely social vision that is grounded in altruism rather than competition as the central human interaction. It is also far less anxious, less solitary, less uncertain and besieged than the degenerate secularized "Calvinism" of popular culture. It is systematically compassionate.

Think, just for a moment, about how your life would be different if you could, at every point, assume that everyone around you was not only honestly doing their very best but also deeply committed to the common good. There would still be some inescapable quantity of ordinary mistakes, let us assume, and also some inescapable level of irresponsible self-centered laziness. I'm not imagining some magic wand whereby to perfect the flawed human character. I'm merely imagining what life might be like if we could escape the pressures generated when we accept the notion that self-seeking, self-serving ruthless competition is an objective or necessary basis for human society. Cultivating a grateful heart is more than a classic spiritual discipline, after all: it is also a powerful, deeply subversive practice securely rooted in how our evolutionary survival depended upon our ability to cooperate and to tend to one another's needs.

Make a practice of looking sales clerks in the eye and offering a "thanks" you really mean, and see what a difference that makes over time. Such small subversions won't change the world, not by an inch. But even the small, regular expression of personal integrity ripples outward within the soul and beyond it in all sorts of interesting ways.

My Job, My Self

The secularized heritage of the Protestant Reformation also underlies the ways in which employment has become an ever-increasing determinant of social identity. This happens in two ways. First, our sense of self is determined by the ways in which we earn a living. Second, it is determined by the ways in which we spend what we earn. Although as a practical matter the two determinants are closely interwoven, highest status is reserved for people who score high on both measures. And yet, since there are significant social prohibitions against revealing what one earns, and since in an economy like ours we often don't understand what other people actually do for a living anyhow, high status can often be maintained by carefully managing one's appearance and lifestyle—no matter what sort of indebtedness one acquires in doing so. It's no wonder, then, that the money we earn—or at least the money we spend—can powerfully shape our sense of personal identity. If we don't have a "good job," we can certainly make it look as if we do.

It's very dangerous when such pressures remain outside of our awareness, because then we are at the mercy of pop culture. As business ethicist Al Gini argues in *My Job My Self,* "Careers and identities are inextricably tied up; indeed, they are equivalent. People are what they do, and what people do affects every aspect of who they are."[48] Gini surveys a wide array of books on careers, working, management, etc., to portray this identification as necessary and inescapable. The problem with jobs, as he sees it, is that very few jobs help us to sustain satisfactory identities. Ciulla accurately portrays that equation between work and self as wholeheartedly romantic and deeply hazardous to boot. But Gini makes a very strong case that the equation is nonetheless alive and well and quite widespread—no matter how unhappy people are with the selves their jobs generate.

As a result of the (perhaps unconscious) equation "my job, my self," the question *What do you do?* has become shorthand for "Who are you really?" in ways that the unemployed and the "underemployed" find painful—and Europeans find rude. As Herbert Marcuse argued in *One-*

Dimensional Man (1964), that's a strangely narrow concept of identity. Identity used to be established through kin, community, religious allegiances, leisure activities, and social roles that had nothing to do with employment. Identity used to depend upon one's life, not one's work. Above all, identity used to be largely *given* rather than essentially and individually *constructed*. And in being given us, it was secure. Socially determined identity proved confining for some people—but it was neither anxious nor fragile. In a fundamental way, you knew who you were, so did everyone else, and in the ordinary course of events nothing that happened could destroy your sense of yourself. Extraordinary events that *did* were the makings of great literature.

Like identity, social status is no longer given: because of our deeply Protestant cultural heritage, work has become the key determinant of social status. As Joan Williams argues in *Unbending Gender,* social status that once was largely given us is now largely self-constructed and self-defended through our employment.[49] Although racism persists, identity is no longer as profoundly dependent as once it was upon who "your people" are and how honorably you have struggled to meet your moral obligations. The American Dream promises—with its fingers crossed behind its back—that anyone can become anything. But the flip side of such grandiose romantic pretension is that anyone can be reduced to nothing at all. As a result, most of us will spend our lives either struggling to prove ourselves through our earnings and career trajectories or at some level anxious that the status we have so carefully constructed will be deconstructed by the next economic downturn or the next round of downsizing.

More darkly yet, in deeper disguise, is the threat that in our day none of us counts for anything at all just on our own, just standing here inhaling and exhaling. We have to prove ourselves. We have to "make something" of ourselves, or else we are nothing.[50] But as any psychologist will tell you, that's a hopeless task. Essential worth is an emotional given, a psychological presupposition, a metaphysical premise rooted far below consciousness. It cannot be proved, and the effort to do so is both doomed and neurotic. Embedded deep within the false pretenses of romantic individualism, then, one finds the structural anxiety and insecurity of predestination, transformed into the individualist American illusion that we are all "self-made men." When or as we become conscious of that besieged loneliness and abiding anxiety, we blame our "wounded inner children" upon the failures of our parents—when the real culprit is more likely to be the pressure of cultural history and the pretensions of radical individualism.

What If Work Does Not Define Us?

Christianity provides an alternative vision: we are creatures made by God in the image of God. Success cannot elaborate nor failure destroy the *imago Dei* within us. God loves us and through that love calls us into compassionate responsibility for one another. The biblical claim that we are *imago Dei,* that we are the "images of God," doesn't say anything about who we are specifically or as distinctive individuals. But it certainly does insist upon our innate value and our inescapable obligations to one another. These obligations constrain or should constrain exploitation, abuse, and indifference.

Furthermore, our distinctive individual identity is given both moral content and ethical framework not by small-town expectations but by the idea that we are individually known and cherished by God. All of us—not simply the Elect—are "the beloved" of God, who calls us to attain our deepest individual identity through the use of our distinctive array of gifts for the common good. That process is thoroughly entwined with our own spiritual growth in understanding who we are, who our "neighbors" are, and who this God is who calls us all into these powerful, generative relationships.

When Luther and Calvin insisted that recognizing God's free, unearned love provides our only possible escape from despair and alienation, neither of them could have foreseen the "Calvinist" desperation of "self-made men" such as Willy Loman in *Death of a Salesman.* When Luther insisted that all lines of work are holy, that all are vocations from and in God, he could not have imagined the contemporary form of the equation "my job, my self." But that is indeed what work collapses into as we lose the older, deeper, spiritually nuanced definitions of personal identity and social identity. As Stanley Hauerwas objects, in Christian terms the idea that our jobs define ourselves comes down in the end to idolatry, to the worship of false or nonexistent gods: "Our work does not need to have or contribute to some grand plan; its blessings are of a more mundane sort. Work gives us the means to survive, to be of service to others, and perhaps most of all, work gives us a way to stay busy. . . . Attributing greater significance to work risks making it demonic, as work then becomes an idolatrous activity through which we try to secure and guarantee our significance, to 'make our mark' on history."[51] The spiritual question is whether our experience of this deeper identity as the beloved of God is sufficiently powerful to overcome all the cultural pressures insisting that we are what we make of ourselves by our own efforts—and through earning money.

12

Selling Ourselves Short in a Buyer's Market

Consumerism and Self-Definition

When America set out to become a nation of "self-made men," we jettisoned—or thought we could jettison—all the traditional determinants of status and identity that used to be supplied by family, religion, community roles, etc. We did so because such a "given" or extrinsic identity could be confining, narrow-minded, or blind to talents where talents were not expected or not welcome. The one thing it wasn't, however, was insecure. Nonetheless, as Robert Bellah wryly observes, rejecting tradition became an absolutely central part of our tradition, a set of "habits of the heart" that now leave us ever-more isolated, lonely, and besieged in our efforts to remain kind, good, and decent people who have thereby some measure of integrity and honest self-respect. We have become social ascetics, denying our need for supportive companionship as if we were desert monks living in isolated caves—not lonely condominiums.

Furthermore, in rejecting traditional determinants, we find ourselves trapped within what's apt to be the narrowest, most extrinsic determinant of all: how location, talents, and prior choices intersected with the needs of some employer at the point when we were looking for employment. As economist Juliet Schor remarks, ". . . it is precisely when traditional markers of identity and position, such as birth and occupation, begin to break down that spending comes to the fore as the more powerful determinant of social status."[52] When what we inherit, broadly speaking, is such unworkable self-images as the sacrificial Angel in the House and her mate, the amoral Oaf in his Office, then no wonder we resist. But when we substitute the radically self-defined individualist for the Angel/Oaf pairing, we are trapped within an even more truncated, even more clichéd version of the absolutely rationalist, absolutely isolated, absolutely alienated Victorian male.

No ideological conviction can change the fact that human beings are social creatures. We are necessarily and inescapably liable to one another's feelings, needs, and behavior. None of us is "self-made." At best, at most, we can select the peer group or the community that matters most to us. If we refuse to make that choice deliberately, or if we fail to realize that it is indeed our choice to make, the default setting is apt to be that our identity is overdetermined by advertising and by our employers. The risks of that are considerable, given how little loyalty large corporations feel toward their employees. Furthermore, it's a setup for consumerism. We find ourselves not self-made at all, but rather defined by the market image of the clothes we wear, the car we drive, or where we live.

Schor argues at length (and with all the detail one would expect of a Harvard economist) that we are spending ever-more hours at work and ever-more money at the mall, more or less trapped between the demands of management and the blandishments of advertising. We are not trying to keep up with the neighbors, she argues, but with the discretionary purchases of those who earn far more than we do.[53] Economist Robert H. Frank calls this "luxury fever" in his book by that title: our sense of personal prosperity and well-being depends upon how much we earn relative to those to whom we compare ourselves.[54] That is why the mass-market advertising of luxury goods encourages us to compare ourselves to the fabulously wealthy.

As a result, Frank argues, even prosperous and financially secure Americans often feel impoverished.[55] Juliet Schor adeptly documents that perception: "twenty-seven percent of all households making more than $100,000 a year," she explains, "say they cannot afford to buy everything they really need. Nearly 20 percent say they spend 'nearly all their income on the basic necessities of life.'"[56] (Bear in mind, if you will, that the median income has hovered about $40,000 per year for decades; in 1998, when her book was published, households earning $100,000 or more ranked approximately in the top 5 percent of income.) Furthermore, Schor continues, "the more education a person has, *the less he or she saves.* Each additional level of education (going from a high school diploma to some college, for instance, or from a college degree to postgraduate credentials) reduces annual savings by $1448." Savings *decrease* with education despite the fact income *increases* with education.[57]

Any number of books further document the power and scope of consumerism in our society. For instance, John De Graff, David Wann, and Thomas H. Naylor call this situation "affluenza" in their book of that title: we find ourselves trapped within essentially addictive patterns of overspending.[58] Jane Hammerslough contends, quite persuasively, that we spend in these ways primarily to express feelings and emotional needs that our competitive, consumerist society otherwise silences.[59] Roger Rosenblatt assembles a fascinating array of thinkers, many of whom argue (one way and another) that this spending is largely compensation for what I have been calling the besieged and fractured modern self.[60] Robert B. Cialdini reveals the devious strategies whereby salespeople and marketers exploit these social needs to sell us stuff we do not genuinely desire.[61] There is something both decadent and desperate about the American accumulation of stuff.

On the other hand, it is also unquestionably true that median-income households are beset not only by "luxury fever" but also by objective financial difficulties. Inflation-adjusted median income has been essentially stagnant for decades, even though the inflation-adjusted costs of housing or college tuition have skyrocketed. As sociologist Teresa Sullivan and her law school colleagues argue in *The Fragile Middle Class: Americans in Debt,* the result is that median-income households have now fallen into precarious levels of indebtedness.[62] As sociologist Theda Skokpol argues in *The Missing Middle,* working-class households face even more dire economic straits.[63] The logical result of global competition for working-class work would be to reduce working-class Americans to the standard of living of their counterparts in the Third World, even while "luxury fever" and manipulative advertising combine to make people feel that they simply "have to have" cell phones, computers, Internet access, cable-TV subscriptions, designer clothes, and so forth and so on.[64]

And then consider this: as Barbara Ehrenreich demonstrates in *Nickel and Dimed: On (Not) Getting By in America,* the minimum wage is scandalously far from being a living wage—a fact that theologian and ethicist D. Stephen Long rightly condemns as "intrinsically evil."[65] The rapidly expanding economy of the late twentieth century was essentially a rapid expansion of the wealth of the very rich at the expense of the misery of the very poor, both within America and in the world generally.[66]

As each of us struggles to balance earning a living with having a life we can live with, these are the massive cultural pressures we face.

Consumption neither consoles us for what is missing from our lives nor satisfies our deepest longing to lead lives that are substantial or rich with moral significance. Consumerism transfers that ultimate moral yearning for meaning onto *stuff,* which is why "more is never enough." Ultimately, I contend, what gives meaning to our lives is not our desires but our sacrifices, not what we have but what we dare to give away or to do without. Religious faith, it seems to me, is not a "lifestyle strategy" in the sense of being a social and quasi-therapeutic undertaking. It is, rather, a profound, humbling acceptance of the immediate contingency but ultimate significance of life.

Marketplace Realities and the Time Bind

"The world is too much with us," Wordsworth complains, "late and soon/ Getting and spending, we lay waste our powers/ . . . We have given our hearts away, a sordid boon." If our earnings define us, as our culture expects, then we will bring to our employment an array of subtle vulnerabilities. These vulnerabilities set us up to be exploited and manipulated by management strategies that are based upon decades of astute psychological research.

One of the most sophisticated scholars of such manipulation is Arlie Russell Hochschild. In *The Time Bind,* she closely studied a single anonymous company dubbed "Amerco," documenting the ways in which it endeavored to generate within the workplace all of the emotional richness of personal life and committed relationships. In historical terms, this is importing from the household all the moral and psychological resonance that "separate spheres" doctrines had once attributed exclusively to "Home Sweet Home." In her earlier book, *The Managed Heart,* Hochschild had already studied the various ways in which employers demand not simply that a given task be done, but also that a given set of emotions be generated—or faked—by employees as they did their work. Amerco does much the same thing, but in a far more sophisticated, far more nuanced, perhaps far more pernicious way than the managers of airline stewardesses in the 1960s.

What makes Amerco worth close study, however, is a second managerial initiative atop this ongoing "Amerco family" rhetoric. The company decides that it is losing valuable employees because of work-life conflicts, and so it sets up an array of work-life accommodations. Hochschild arrives to study the impact of these accommodations—flex time and so forth—both upon the company and upon the personal lives of employees. Several years earlier, Hochschild had offered a widely influential study of that burden in a book she called *The Second Shift.* (The "second shift" is nonmarket work waiting to be done after the "first shift" in paid employment.) In its opening scenes, so to speak, the dramatic conflict in *The Time Bind* is between well-trained hearts and the corrosive demands of that second shift. What toll is all this taking on the "third shift" of nurturing children and maintaining intimate relationships within the household or the community?

For the first fifteen chapters of *The Time Bind,* Hochschild documents all the ways in which time for personal life was losing out to time on the job. In yet another extension of the self-denial characteristic of Western dualism, parents have become what she calls "emotional ascetics," denying their own needs to care and to be cared for.[67] That leaves them liable to all the well-managed emotional appeals of sophisticated management programs celebrating "the Amerco family." The pressure of resentful children and chaotic households made the comforts of home far less than the well-managed cheer, courtesy, orderliness, and recognition available at work.

So people worked longer hours. They did so, Hochschild argues, to deny and to escape the mayhem of their personal lives. As she explains, ". . . in the cultural contest between work and home, working parents are voting with their feet, and the workplace is winning. . . . One reason some workers feel more 'at home' at work is that they feel more appreciated and more competent there."[68] She describes the final result of ascetic capitalism: all of our psychological and physical energies are absorbed by work, and all of our needs for a life outside of work are denied.

Hochschild systematically examines the reasons why workers might not take greater advantage of flexibility options and opportunities to be home, and she finds each of these reasons insufficient. It is not the case, for instance, that parents don't take more time at home because they cannot afford to. The majority of parents don't take all the paid vacation to which they are entitled, for instance, and the best-paid parents are the least interested in such work-life accommodations as job sharing or part-time work. Workers with small children put in longer hours than workers without children.[69]

She also sharply discredits the "quality time" approach to parenthood as a fallacious attempt to transfer "the cult of efficiency" from office to home. "Instead of nine hours a day with a child, we declare ourselves capable of getting the 'same result' with one more intensely focused quality hour." Over and over again she watches children sabotage or attempt to sabotage their parents' plans: "When workers protest speedup, industrialists can replace them. But when children react against a speedup at home, parents have to deal with it. Children dawdle. They sulk. They ask for gifts. They tell their parents by action or word, 'I don't like this.' They want to be having quality time when it's a quantity time of day; they don't want quality time in the time slots parents religiously set aside for it. . . . Parents now increasingly find themselves in the role of domestic 'time and motion experts.'"[70] Ultimately, she portrays a wholesale reversal of the moral and psychological meanings defined by Victorian separate-sphere doctrine: "the valued realm of work is registering its gains in part by incorporating the best aspects of home. The devalued realm, the home, is meanwhile taking on what were once considered the most alienating attributes of work."[71]

This sounds like a stunning indictment of the Amerco parents, especially the better-educated, better-paid parents—until you read Hochschild's final chapter. Amerco downsizes. It essentially dismantles the work-life program and fires its director. Demands for longer hours and greater productivity escalate, enforced by the threat that remaining employees will soon depart along with the many who were fired initially. There are small hints all through the book that something like this would happen. Early on, Hochschild quotes the employee handbook's somber warning that time on the job is taken as the measure of one's commitment to the company. She repeatedly interviews senior managers who are convinced that long hours are necessary and an appropriate measure of a worker's performance and value to the company. She points out that "In the modern workplace . . . 'family man' has taken on negative overtones, designating a worker who isn't a serious player. The term now tacitly but powerfully calls into question a worker's masculinity."[72] If this were a novel, rather than nonfiction, these hints would be called "foreshadowing." I kept waiting for this clearly entrenched attitude to make itself felt; and in the last chapter, these expectations were satisfied. Unfortunately, Hochschild did not manage the implicit dramatic and narrative structure of her exposition with quite as much finesse as she might have.

Given how the book ends, the parents she profiled suddenly looked not so much negligent as perhaps far more sophisticated than she at reading the mixed messages posted by Amerco management. The distinction between a naïve narrator and a naïve professor is not as clearly drawn as it might have been—although of course I am asking a sociologist to have the skills of a novelist, and that's probably not fair. Nonetheless, this is a very fine and thought-provoking book. It seems to me that the parents Hochschild profiles come across as both trapped and morally floundering in a situation that would have been psychologically devastating to face squarely. It's quite well known that people accommodate to impossible situations through a variety of protective denials.

In this situation, such denials testify to another dimension of the threat Hochschild earlier called "the managed heart." If the highly educated parents of small children work longer hours than comparable employees, or deny their own emotional needs and the emotional needs of their own children, that may reflect how shrewdly they understand the threat of layoffs. Such threats are proportionally more severe for young parents than for young singles. Their anxieties—their fears of failing to provide for their children—amplify the manipulative stratagems of "family friendly" corporate image-mongers.

The "Divine Right" of Markets

Despite its flaws, *The Time Bind* recognizes the suffering of both parents and children: "there seemed to be no way out," she concludes ruefully, "—no time off for good behavior, no parole, and no possibility of a jailbreak."[73] Although Hochschild comments trenchantly on the sometimes flimsy excuses parents offered, she is equally sharp in her portrait of the intractable predicaments these parents face and the bitter frustrations of those who struggle hardest to protect the time they needed for the second shift of nonmarket work, for their families, and for their own humanity. She formulates a core issue very wisely (and the italics here are mine): "A giant *public* issue appears to us as millions of individual problems, each to be solved *privately* at home. Companies have far more power over families than families have over companies. So time demands at work come to seem implacable while those at home feel malleable."[74]

In this context, let's look again at Mona Harrington's account of the essential predicament involved (and her italics are her own): "*Without women's full-time unpaid caretaking labor, families must buy needed care in the private market, and most do not have sufficient resources to buy enough of it. Therefore, the system as a whole is undercapitalized, and the unavoidable result, on the whole, is inadequate care.*"[75] The inadequacies that Hochschild describes, the emotional asceticism that she laments, are the result of how marketplace ideology has ceded to profit-makers' undue power to thwart the common good and to force employees to sell themselves short. Economist Nancy Folbre puts it well: "employers . . . free-ride on the contributions of parents, friends, and neighbors. If they're not willing to pay, they should be kicked off the bus."[76]

Above all, Hochschild understands Crosby's claim, in *The Measure of Reality,* that "Generally speaking, nothing is more diagnostic of a society's reading of reality than its perception of time."[77] At Amerco, and by extension throughout the economy, time is by definition scarce because only what is scarce has value in a capitalist system. According to Crosby, quantification by means of mechanical clocks was a key feature of the social changes that culminated in the development of a modern worldview. If time can be counted—if as at Amerco, your manager regards your "face time" as a measure of your commitment to the company and thus your value to the organization—then under the infinite and ruthless competitiveness of a 24/7 global economy, there is no such time as "free time." Your time is never "your own" unless you can freely decide to spend some at home rather than at work. That "spending" choice, like all spending choices in a zero-sum system, comes at a cost. As Hochschild so astutely explains, "Many working parents strive mightily to counter this conception of time. They want not simply more time, but a less alienating sense of time. . . . In this alternative view, time is to relationships what shelters are to families, not capital to be invested, but a habitat in which to live. People are not time-capitalists but time-architects who structure time to protect their relationships."[78]

When Hochschild's book was first released, the newsweeklies responded with cover stories titled "The Myth of Quality Time: How We're Cheating Our Kids and What You Can Do" (*Newsweek,* May 12, 1997) or "The Lies Parents Tell About Work, Kids, Money, Day Care, and Ambition" (*U.S. News and World Report,* May 12, 1997). Other reviewers and pundits were outraged and defensive. It seemed to me that no one was paying much attention to her last chapter and its devastating account of managerial dishonesty and dangerously successful psychological manipulation. But since then, it has suddenly appeared commonplace that cutting back on work for the sake of family life can be the kiss of death for a high-power career.[79] Although a forest of consultants has sprung up overnight, offering to help companies design and implement programs to help workers to meet their familial obligations, these consultants offer largely anecdotal evidence that such programs do in fact cut employee turnover.[80] Apparently there is not yet good hard evidence that such programs serve the corporate bottom line, a fact that worries the more rigorous thinkers in the business community.

In strictly rational terms, that concern makes sense. But the need for bottom-line proof also systematically demonstrates that work-life programs are essentially concerned with corporate well-being, not employee well-being. A work-life program will have to show a profit for the company or it's apt to be dropped. And then heaven help you if senior management decides that workaholics actually do more work for the same salary.

Furthermore, competition remains extremely tight for the good jobs, the jobs demanding high educational achievement, and the jobs toward the top of an organization. As even Christopher Lasch points out, in the competitive realms of business and the professions, most jobs are "package deals" demanding long hours and single-minded commitment. Those who fail (or refuse) to meet that norm can be penalized quite severely.[81]

Losing such employees can be expensive for an organization, but they are nonetheless easily replaced. And workers who know they are easily replaced are going to be very cautious—what Ciulla calls the fear ethic. The jobs that employers do have trouble filling are at the lowest ranks, where turnover is traditionally very high anyhow and—as Hochschild documents—work-life flexibility is least likely.

I suspect that, at least in some organizations, the benefits to companies of offering work-life flexibility to higher-ranked employees may be more rhetorical than practical—more a matter of corporate image-making than anything substantial and trustworthy. "We care about your second shift" can be in-house hokum. Surely some senior management are absolutely sincere and honestly motivated to make work more humane and their company more socially responsible. But when the cost-benefit calculations of the free market also serve as a generalized social paradigm, we are inevitably cynical. As I said before, we have no major "public" grounds on which to give the common good priority over corporate profits. When the only "rational" basis for action is cost-benefit spreadsheets and quarterly profit reports, then what we have is not wise compassion but merely shrewd investment.

Stanley Hauerwas argued, in a short, comic essay on Bill Clinton, that Clinton cannot tell a lie because he says what is expedient. You can't tell a lie unless you can tell the truth, and if expedience governs every statement, then in fact you cannot tell a lie.[82] When we have trapped ourselves culturally into viewing all managerial behavior as necessarily expedient and only expedient, then honest offers of work-life accommodation will not be recognized and put to use—except by a small cohort of people who are either very brave, or very desperate, or very confident in their own intuitive assessments. Social change will come slowly indeed at this rate.

I do not for a minute dispute that cost-benefit calculation—both for employers and for employees—is how our economy works. In fact, that's the point here. If you want the benefit that is having a life, there will be a cost to bear. But given the extraordinary disparities in power between employers and employees, corporations have more than enough clout to make that cost prohibitive if they choose to. The entire culture suffers when employees sell themselves short: children, elders, communities, civic participation, the arts—social-capital formation in every way, shape, and form. Employers who make such corrosive demands are simply and profoundly immoral ("intrinsically evil," in Christian theological terms). They are denying their responsibility to the humanity of their employees—to the spark of the divine, to the *imago Dei*—when they assert that stockholder profits (and therefore CEO bonuses) must always and systematically take precedence over the human rights of those who work for the organization. Law professor Lawrence Mitchell explains and documents this situation in *Corporate Irresponsibility: America's Newest Export.*[83] In 1995 Benjamin R. Barber argued—presciently—in *Jihad vs. McWorld* that this ruthless pursuit of profits in the global economy disastrously undermines the national interest and furthermore provokes widespread anti-Americanism.[84]

As both Robert Bellah and Christopher Lasch argue, the most dangerously manipulative managerial scheme of all is how we are led to believe that "the market" or "the demands of the market" are as inexorable as the demands of gravity rather than the work of human hands, human culture, human choices made collectively and over time.[85] The sacrifices that some employers demand are not counterbalanced by a pervasive moral vision that all of us are accountable for and responsible to the well-being of everyone else. D. Stephen Long, a brilliant young ethicist and theologian, delineates in massive scholarly detail how the Christian tradition can deconstruct the pretensions that underlie this exploitation.[86]

In the Middle Ages, after all, the rights of nobility were as much of a given, as far beyond question, as the "demands of the market" are now. Then as now, those who questioned these rights were seen both as irrational and as saboteurs of social stability. But ultimately, there's not much difference between the divine right of kings and the divine right of the market—and it is still a small elite who profit, even while insisting that we pay no attention to the little man behind the screen. Ultimately, employers cannot evade responsibility for the consequences of work-demands upon employees' "private lives"—their nonmarket work and their personal relationships. Whether we call it "sin" or whether we call it "karma," choices have consequences that we cannot evade.

Unregulated capitalism, unrestrained by moral responsibility to a genuinely common good, will destroy the social capital upon which it is itself dependent. Societies based upon false notions of human nature and human interaction—upon the notion that we are innately and inescapably at odds with one another competitively, unconstrained by compassion, the common good, or our own biological sociability—will sooner or later find themselves facing the massive disorder that such a vision generates. Skyrocketing levels of dysfunction among children and adolescents—everything from Columbine to suicide rates to declining academic achievement—is evidence in the case. Anti-American sentiment in Europe also reflects, in part, resistance to the ruthlessly Americanized, decadently Calvinist "global market."

It is as if, culturewide, moral obligation has become nothing more than a lifestyle choice, and a quirky one at that. This situation endures because American culture has a most peculiar psychological investment in market work. This overinvestment is made manifest in our individualist vulnerability to how our jobs generate our selves. Worse yet, our socioeconomic status demonstrates whether or not we are among the Elect—whether we are saved or damned. Such cultural pressures hold the key to the time-bind trap holding those Amerco workers—and by extension any of us, all of us.

Conscience and the Divided Self

Hochschild's single most trenchant observation gestures—lightly but no doubt deliberately—to the enormously complicated, largely unconscious heritage of predestination at the core of the ever-anxious self-made American soul. To the extent that success defines who we are, and success depends in turn upon meeting the ever-escalating demands of employers, the cost of success is an ever-deepening of the emotional asceticism archetypally demanded of powerful males from the Roman Empire onwards. As Hochschild explains,

> Instead of trying to arrange more flexible or shorter work schedules, Amerco parents applied themselves to evading the time bind and so avoided facing it. Three strategies were common. Some developed ideas that minimized how much care a child, a partner, or they themselves "really needed." In essence, they denied the needs of family members, as they themselves became emotional ascetics. . . . They emotionally downsized life. Some time-poor Amerco parents readjusted their ideas about how to meet the family needs they did acknowledge. Instead of trying to meet these needs themselves, they paid others to do it for them and detached their own identities from acts they might previously have defined as part of being "a good parent" or "a good spouse." As with many efficient operations, they outsourced ever-larger parts of the family production process. Finally, many parents divided themselves into a real and a potential self, into the person each of them was and the person each would be "if only I had time." Often the real self had little time for care at home while the potential one was boundlessly available.[87]

It is the divided self once again, the self-annihilating Angel and the morally impoverished Drone. These two familiar characters now have even more powerful roles as conflicting parts of the self—as interior aspects of the normal adult.

One of the most pernicious forms this asceticism takes, however, is not career penalties for failing to be a "team player" but rather the ways in which parents can encourage—even demand—that other parents ignore and discount their own responses and the responses of their children. I sat dumbfounded in a parking lot one day, listening to a call-in show on the car radio. A caller to the show described her own devastating distress and her baby's distress when she began to leave the infant at a daycare center. A variety of subsequent callers repeated what the woman said her friends at work had assured her: her distress and the child's distress were to be ignored. They were without meaning, without substance or significance. Listening to herself was "unrealistic."

On a near-deafening parallel track in my mind I heard two thousand years of Western male voices similarly dismissing women's painful yearnings for education, for opportunities to read, to write, to study, to paint, to govern, to manage, to shape public health, to reform policy, to conduct research or symphony orchestras. I heard the voices of women driven literally to madness by those who insisted that such drives should naturally be denied, and by nineteenth-century male physicians who prescribed "rest cures" in which women were denied all access to books, paints, writing materials, visitors, etc. I heard Virginia Wolff on Shakespeare's "sister," on the terrible battle for a "room of one's own" and financial self-sufficiency. I heard a good friend, remembering in humiliated tears even decades later how, despite her standing as a full-time Harvard graduate student, she was denied admission to the principal Harvard University library in 1969 because she was a woman. I remembered that day with the photocopier, the phone call from a colleague expecting me of course to abort my first child because I was not yet tenured, and countless other encounters with professional hostility to the presence of women—especially women with children.

Has it come to this, that we have traded one set of blind authoritarian constraints for another? That women (especially mothers) are still ordered around by others because women are by definition incapable of mature conscience and responsible judgment? That women are still subject to constraints that ultimately deny not only our adulthood but our humanity? Let me repeat what Monroe said about altruism:

> . . . altruists see the world differently. Their behavior results from the recognition that the actor is human and therefore required to act in a certain way, and that the needy person is human and therefore entitled to certain treatment. Humanity plus need: This is the only moral reasoning, the only calculus for altruism. This is a far cry from the cost/benefit calculus which I had been trained to apply to human behavior. . . . It is this shared perception of themselves as part of an all-embracing humanity that was one common characteristic that consistently and systematically distinguishes altruists from other individuals.[88]

Those advising the distraught young mother were denying that there might be in fact a substantial and morally important reality to her needs and to her child's needs. When paying attention to pain conflicts with the demands of employment, is the pain to be set aside as necessarily insignificant? No one seemed to consider that such distress should be taken seriously, much less that a wide variety of responses and remedies to it are possible and should be considered.

At the time I didn't know that call-in shows screen callers, selecting those whose comments match what the radio host wants to hear. The callers' unanimity was probably illusory. But it was archetypal nonetheless in its demand for conformity rather than conscience, obedience rather than discernment, and above all denial rather than thoughtful self-awareness.

The alternative here is not simply and always to do whatever will keep our children from screaming. Even if we were to try, that's not possible; and if it were possible, it would be as hazardous to their development as ignoring profound distress when it does occur. Martyrs make good saints but terrible parents: studies over and over demonstrate that parents with a strong, well-bounded sense of themselves are much better parents than those who incessantly cave in to every passing demand from a child because they themselves are chronically insecure or fundamentally uncertain. Monroe's Rescuers and her other altruists were not sacrificial wimps; they were not so lacking in any sense of themselves that they surrendered their own well-being willy-nilly to the needs of anyone else. That's a point she probed and considered in rigorous detail. And what she found were strong characters who were remarkably resistant to all the pressures of popular culture.

As Germaine Greer argued so many years ago in *The Female Eunuch,* we can give from the abundance of self and of strength, and not because we lack the wherewithal to resist what others demand that we provide. In the same way, the morally complete, mature adult—not the eunuch, whether male or female—must be able to resist when others claim that generosity, compassion, and self-sacrifice are perforce illegitimate. Zero-sum calculations have gotten out of hand if we have come to presume that any self-giving arises only from exploitation. If we think that we cannot give without giving ourselves away, then getting and spending have reduced our lives to a puzzle we will never assemble.

Conclusion: Reclaiming Our Lives

One way or another—and perhaps not entirely as he expected—Karl Marx was right in arguing that the way we work comes to shape our souls and to shape our society as well. Despite separating work off into a formally amoral "public" realm of Darwinian competition, despite the grandiose claims of pathological individualism that we are exclusively self-made, self-realized characters, we remain profoundly social creatures. Work shapes our souls because we spend so much time doing it; work relationships shape our sense of self because most of us spend far more time with colleagues than we do with significant others. From Frederick Winslow Taylor's "scientific management" to the latest gurus of "spirituality in the workplace," the workplace has been managed to get the most from us for the least in return, enforced by threats of financial disaster that resonate to submerged but culturally viable threats of ultimate damnation. As more and more has been demanded of us, we have had less and less ability to sustain the traditions and the institutions whose counterpressures would help us to resist or sustain us in confrontation.

Earning a living makes it increasingly difficult to have a life. For the most vulnerable among us—for the very young—the costs of that are enormous.

PART FIVE

Decoding the Child-Care Debates

Prelude

Today's parents struggle in historically unprecedented ways both to provide for children's personal growth and simultaneously to provide for children's material needs. These two vitally important aspects of parental altruism are in conflict with one another. That conflict becomes even more difficult to the extent that financial success demands a competitive drive at odds with the compassion at the core of nurturant human relationships. Strict gender-role divisions—the men are ambitious, the women altruistic—fail to resolve the problem, because gender dualisms ultimately corrupt ambition and altruism alike. The conflict between careers and children also resonates painfully to the unworkable, neurologically inaccurate, gender-laden Western antagonisms between intellect and emotions. It's no wonder, then, that historically sophisticated women may suspect that child-care research is yet another exercise in pseudo-science essentially intended to exclude women from the *public* realm altogether. Faced with these deep-seated, sometimes unconscious tensions, ordinary parents can find it difficult to think critically and to talk openly about who should provide the stable, daily, attentive presence and physical care that young children need, how this should be provided for, and where it should take place.

At stake in the child-care controversy is a set of serious cultural issues of concern to everyone, not just parents of young children.* The relentless demands of a radical free-market economy have the capacity to destroy the social-cultural web at its origins in the socialization of children and the sustenance of community. As that happens—and I believe the process is unmistakably underway—the cultural traditions and transmissible skills that sustain social capital can be destroyed.[1] Once destroyed, such complex psychosocial networks are very difficult to re-establish, as they have learned who try to reanimate nearly dead languages or artistic traditions.

Both democracy and capitalism vitally depend upon social capital. Money is not enough. Maximizing wealth in the short term does not provide a solid foundation for the good society, just as it does not provide a solid foundation for the good life of an individual. If we can ignore the massively documented needs of children, whose needs will be respected? The answer to that question is also at stake in the child-care controversy. If the desire of parents to care for babies is massively penalized rather than respected and substantively supported, then as we age our own personal care will someday depend either upon eliciting heroic sacrifice from our families or upon ruinously expensive, profit-driven, institutionalized "care." If it is not legitimate to set limits to employers' demands because of our collective national interest in the well-being of children, then surely other vital but less-visible nonmarket human needs and activities are doomed. If an infant does not succeed as the "poster child" for our nonmarket lives, loves, and endeavors, then nothing will.

Both Joanne Ciulla and Robert Reich argue that the increasingly brutal "rationalizing" of the global marketplace has replaced the work ethic with a fear ethic.[2] But from a longer cultural-historical perspective, our economy seems not "rational" but increasingly delusional. Social scientists who have studied the predicament of parents in detail agree that the key child-care issues are structurally fundamental to the socioeconomic order. They exist at the confluence of many other social

*Researchers distinguish between "daycare" (care of a group of children by a group of adults in a place which is no one's home) and "family care" (care of one or more children by an unrelated adult, often a solitary adult, in her own home). Care by a grandmother or other relative is called "relative care" in those few places were it is discussed or tracked separately at all. Nannies, au pair, and babysitters are lumped together under various labels. The most comprehensive or umbrella term for all nonparental (or sometimes nonmaternal) care is "child care," and so that's the label I use. In the very few places were I do talk about daycare, it should be clear from context that I am referring to daycare centers.

issues. In that regard, child care is much more nearly akin to a pervasive public-health problem.

Imagine, if you will, the spectacular costs involved in building the first enclosed sewers, the first sewage-treatment plants, the first systems to assure and to distribute clean water. The gradual, bitterly contested triumph of "germ theory" in the nineteenth and early twentieth centuries probably had a greater impact upon the health of more people than any other medical advance either before or after. But at the time, the costs must have seemed enormous, the challenge to individualist sociocultural traditions insurmountable, the link between waterborne illnesses and poverty hopelessly complex. Visionary people prevailed, and we are the better for it. We need visionaries now for another apparently insuperable problem.

But until policy proposals save us from centuries of accumulated cultural tradition, we have to live in the world as it already exists. Those with young children face enormous difficulties; the rest of us have to be aware of that so that we can be quick to lend a hand (or a vote) as opportunity provides. In the next set of chapters, I want to analyze both cultural and scientific aspects of the bitter controversy over child care. I'll begin that by sketching the basic research findings from the best current child-care research, but only to set the stage. What interests me more, and what I hope will interest you as well, is how this controversy is rooted in classic Western arguments about what it means *to be human.*

What it means *to be human* is an important issue, because from it flows answers to some of those questions that awaken us in the night. Is there more to life than seeking pleasure and avoiding pain? What's behind our relationships with one another? Are we isolated, autonomous self-seekers controlled by our genes and our immediate environment, or is there some deeper bond that generates morally coherent relationships? If we trust, if we sacrifice, if we make costly commitments to moral principles and to one another, are we fools? Or are we wise? The bitterness of the child-care controversy depends far more upon deep-seated cultural arguments about questions like these than it does upon empirical research into the social skills and intellectual attainments of five-year-olds.

13

The Predicament of Parents

Every reasonable parent wants to provide both a comfortable, secure physical environment and a rich, secure personal relationship. But implicit in that perfectly ordinary set of desires is the symbolic opposition of "intellect" and "emotions" in the spiritual grammar of the West. To the extent that (consciously or not) parents buy into the classic Western priority of intellect over feelings, the rich material environment that we can buy will appear more important than the rich individual attention that we must provide personally. The rich material environment, in turn, is easily translated by advertising, a consumerist culture, etc., into the drive to live in the most prestigious neighborhoods, to enroll children in the most expensive schools, to take the most elaborate vacations, to buy the latest educational toys and software, and to sign up for the glitziest summer camps or after-school enrichment programs. It demands fortitude and resilience to turn away from all that alluring stuff and from all the sharp, sophisticated ploys used in selling it. It demands fortitude and resilience to insist that kids need not "stuff," or not simply "stuff," but also us, plain and simple, just us, playing with babies, attending to little kids, listening to teenagers. The materialism of a consumerist culture obscures the lineaments of a responsible balance between appropriately valuing the security of financial success and what it can provide (such as high-quality schools) with valuing the security we offer personally as role models, as mentors, as spiritual counselors, and, quite simply, as reliable sources of affection, affirmation, and reassurance.

The child-care controversy sits in the middle of all this perplexity, because an infant's full development is particularly dependent upon attentive, affectionate, personal interaction. Quite aside from the high level of physical care that they need, children less than three years of age need a lot of this individual attention. Lingering images of the sacrificial, Angelic mother can encourage parents to exaggerate that need, to feel that children need decades of absolutely incessant personal attention and supervision—a style of parenting that sociologist Sharon Hays calls "intensive mothering."[3] On the other hand, providing even sane and reasonable levels of individual attention is directly opposed—both literally and mythographically—to the individualist self-seeking that is (a) the presumptive moral norm of adult behavior in a capitalist free market and (b) the most reliable route to the highest levels of income. Buried in all this is a potent symbolic threat we considered toward the end of part two: culturally unsophisticated parents are apt to fear that in stepping off the fast track even for a moment they will be swept away into Angelic serfdom. Even if we don't become serfs, of course, there are well-documented opportunity costs, as we have already seen. Attentive, responsible parenting is apt to require genuine economic sacrifice. "Having a life" doesn't come easy. It never has.

When the popular press turns its attention to the problems children face, or the problems adults face dealing with other people's children, parents are commonly accused of being either irresponsible consumerist dingbats who neglect their children or else hovering neurotics grandiosely obsessed with every detail of a child's development. Both accusations float in the air of popular culture, because there has been increasing attention to the deteriorating state of the nation's children. All too often parents hear these accusations face to face as well. I certainly have! For a long time I thought that such tirades are simply a risk introverts face: one who is innately disposed to listen will sometimes get an earful. Eventually I realized that powerful cultural issues had to be at stake somewhere, because my accusers were inexplicably distraught, especially given how remote they were from my own household.

Sorting through these cultural issues is only the beginning of what parents face. Purchasing high-quality child care is difficult, because child-care providers are overwhelmingly untrained workers earning poverty-level wages. Furthermore, daycare centers are very poorly regulated, and the regulations that do exist may not be enforced rigorously. Academic studies have repeatedly demonstrated that the care provided in the vast majority of daycare centers is seriously inadequate, perhaps even dangerously so.[4] Family care—that is, care given by a nonrelative in her own home—commonly escapes both regulation and academic study as well. Finding a competent nanny is even more of a gamble.

Furthermore, quality child care is prohibitively expensive for most households. Parents who work forty hours a week with a thirty-minute commute and who place a child less than three years old in a licensed, accredited daycare center will easily spend twice as much as they would for a year's college tuition—during years when they are apt to be paying off their own college loans as well.[5] Nannies are even more expensive. Given these problems of cost and quality, many parents sacrifice deeply to meet what feminist legal theorist Joan Williams adeptly calls the cultural "norm of parental care."[6]

National data suggest that the most common form of this sacrifice is working fewer hours. According to census and Bureau of Labor data, for instance, children less than three years of age with employed mothers average only twenty-three hours a week in child care if the mother is without a high school diploma, twenty-five hours if the mother has a high school diploma, and twenty-four hours in child care if the mother has a college degree. Furthermore, according to the same data, 44 percent of mothers with children younger than one year old are not in the workforce at all. The mothers who *are* employed overwhelmingly leave their babies with family members, not with nonfamily paid caregivers: 86 percent of infants less than a year old with employed, married mothers are cared for primarily by a parent, a grandparent, or another relative.

What all these percentages add up to is this: 92 percent of the care of all children less than a year old with married parents is provided by family members, and 14.9 percent by others. (Obviously, many families use both kinds of arrangements: these figures include child care while parents go out for dinner and a movie.) Almost 75 percent of children younger than five years old are cared for primarily by their parents or other relatives.[7] As these remarkably high percentages suggest, wealthy families are not the only families who make huge adjustments so as to care personally for young children. Household income data confirm this reading of the situation: the median income of married fathers with nonemployed wives is only a little bit more than the median income of married fathers with employed wives. Evidence suggests that it's not only rich folks who are cutting back employment to care for their youngest children themselves.[8]

It is simply unconscionable to defend either the cost of quality child care or these dramatic economic sacrifices of young parents by appeal to "marketplace realities." The only "reality" involved is spectacular loss to the common good, the nation's future, and the human rights of children. The bill for such moral oblivion and irresponsible shortsightedness is apt to prove brutal indeed.

The predicament of parents is made even worse by how the pathological individualism of American culture can distort public discussion of such complex issues. If, as Robert Bellah argues, the core of individualist self-realization and self-esteem is acting in accord with one's own opinions, and one's own opinions are based exclusively upon one's utterly subjective feelings of what one desires in life, then woe to anyone who points out the hard edges of an unaccommodating reality that is largely oblivious to human desires.[9] Such a messenger is liable to attack from those who would deny the reality or the validity of any difficult or personally expensive obligation.

Western gender ideology is pernicious nonsense; the Angel in the House is a deeply pathological cultural archetype. As I see it, the challenge now is to extricate from that matrix of ideologies some insight into the legitimacy of the demand that parents be allowed to care for their own infants without spectacular economic penalty. As Sylvia Ann Hewlett and Cornel West shrewdly observe, parents are expected to behave—and overwhelmingly do behave—as stunningly irrational actors economically. I think that suggests that strict economic rationality is itself dangerously crazy.

The Data on Child Care

The most comprehensive and scientifically most rigorous research to date is underway at more than two dozen universities and research centers, funded and coordinated under the auspices of the National Institute of Child Health and Human Development (NICHD). In 1991, a diverse mix of 1200 households with children were enrolled without regard to their intentions concerning child care. Their child-care choices and the consequences of these choices are being followed in great detail to see what difference various kinds of child care make in outcomes for children. The size and design of the study will make it possible to control for many possible confounding variables, such as parental education levels, income, region, ethnicity, etc. Various professional summaries and bibliographies are available on the Web, and of course the popular media report specific research findings from time to time.[10]

The NICHD program is, for child-care questions, essentially akin to the famous long-term studies collecting health data about the citizens of Framingham, Massachusetts, or about nurses. It is unquestionably the best kind of research design for these issues, but of course any such proper long-range study takes a long time to accumulate all its data. The full fruits of this work will not be available for many years—perhaps decades as these children grow up and as researchers continue the monumental task of tabulating and analyzing millions upon millions of data points.

Although the NICHD research still has a long way to go, some trends in the data have become apparent. For instance, some psychological theories in the early and mid-twentieth century would have predicted out-and-out developmental catastrophe if babies were to be separated from their own mothers, but most children in child care do just fine. Children in higher-quality care clearly do better than children in low-quality care; very high quality care particularly helps three- and four-year-old children who are at serious risk for difficulties because of poverty (Head Start programs, for instance). On the other hand, there is some evidence that the more time children spend in child care before starting school, and especially when extensive, continuous child care begins in the first year, the more likely they are, later on, to have difficulties in their relationships with their mothers, their peers, and their teachers. (These findings hold even when socioeconomic status is taken into account.) School-readiness scores may also be adversely affected. Such problems are more likely when child care is not of high quality, but some difficulties are evident regardless of the quality of care or the sensitivity of the parent. Nonetheless, the majority of children in child care grow up to be indistinguishable from children who have similar family backgrounds but who are cared for by their own parents: family of origin matters more than child care.[11]

All this sounds just a bit equivocal to me. But that's probably inevitable. Child-care research is extraordinarily complicated because human psychosocial development is extraordinarily complex. That's why it's foolish for parents to fixate upon this research—much less upon newspaper reports about any single NICHD report. But of course we are tempted to do so: anything that looks like "hard numbers" from the "public" realm of academic research carries greater authority in the quantifying modern mind than "soft," intuitive, or qualitative assessments of realities in one's own "private" family life. In the "public arena," after all, "subjective" can be a polite synonym for "self-deceiving." And when the question at hand is whether or not a mother should traverse the magic line from "home" to "work," from "private life" to "public life," we are on a cultural minefield.

It's important to remember that the young mother faces a double bind of mythic proportions.[12] To be a "real adult," to earn her secular salvation in a consumerist society, she must maximize earnings; but to be a "good woman"—to avoid the classic Western link between the female and moral disorder—she must maintain some claim to Angelic status. It's damned if we do, ladies, and damned if we don't—unless we see through the ideological trap altogether and turn aside from "what people will say" on either side to make our own decisions in good conscience and based upon a full array of relevant facts about our own situations. Meanwhile, child-care research is massively controversial because it sits smack in the middle of this mythic double bind.

The problem here—the overwhelming problem—is that gender symbolism, "family values," and "the market" can combine to give child-care research an inappropriate prominence for individuals making decisions. Because child-care research carries that ideological and cultural burden, it provides a battleground for deeply rooted ideological conflicts about what it means *to be human.* Child-care research also elicits all our ambivalence about how American culture is increasingly dominated by getting-and-spending and by impersonally competitive market exchanges.

Obscured by all that cultural baggage is the fact that the NICHD studies, like all child-care research, are exercises in epidemiology—in the health of populations. Literally, it is "about the people," not about your kids or mine as individuals. This is public-health research, just like the testing of London wells for cholera in the mid-nineteenth century. Such studies have major implications for public policy, because even a small increase in the frequency of psychosocial problems among six-year-olds yield thousands of children with problems that might have been prevented. Such data can be used to argue for better child-care regulation, for longer and paid parental leave, and other similar changes in government policy. Epidemiology simply does not translate into unequivocal advice—much less predictions—about what any particular household ought to do. Parents need to consider a much wider range of information than just this research.[13]

By comparison: epidemiologists monitoring emergency rooms and hospital admissions know that asthmatics react badly to high ozone levels, to small-particulate air pollution, etc. *Taken in isolation* this evidence would seem to suggest that my family would be better off if we did not live in a major metropolitan area. Will people think we are bad parents for living in Chicago nonetheless? I doubt it. Because allergies and airway disease do not carry the ideological burdens of child-care research, no one has trouble understanding that as good parents we have many other things to consider as well—the quality of health care available in Chicago, for instance, in comparison to that in pristine rural areas. Or consider the fact that agriculture produces its own array of allergens. And what about the aerial spraying of crops? Or what about the fact that small towns won't have the jobs for which we are trained? It seems to me that most people understand all this without any trouble at all—and understand as well the correlative need for air pollution regulations. Air pollution sends some people to emergency rooms—but it's not *good* for anyone. Neither is the quality of care in many run-of-the-mill daycare centers good enough—especially not for infants less than a year old.

NICHD research, like emergency-room monitoring vis-à-vis air pollution, is significant primarily for questions of government policy and government regulation. And in that regard, the NICHD research comes down to some very ordinary and familiar common sense. First, as a nation we need to provide both long, paid leaves of absence for new parents and intelligent policy support for part-time work (benefits, for instance; wages proportional to those of full-time workers; a minimum wage that is a living wage). Second, child care needs to be both strictly regulated and, since quality child care costs more than college, substantially subsidized. As a nation we cannot afford to neglect children nor to do without what mothers can contribute to the GNP and to the national interest if we can keep their careers from being derailed. Third, the earlier a child goes into child care, and the longer the hours of that care, the more important it is for the care to be very high quality indeed.

Meanwhile, I think it's very sensible for parents to do everything they can to maximize postnatal leave and generally to minimize child care in the first year—especially in the first six to nine months. Census data clearly suggest that most parents are already minimizing child-care hours for their very youngest children, perhaps at great cost or risk to the future financial security of their families. Advice like this is nothing new, nothing new at all. What does it come to but "do the best you can within the constraints of your own situation"?

Furthermore, in considering the results to date of the NICHD research, one must remember that these are not controlled studies but merely observational ones. As the recent uproar over hormone replacement therapy (HRT) for women revealed, the findings of observational studies sometimes differ in important ways from those of controlled studies. But for child care, controlled studies are impossible. Furthermore, it's no easy business to measure a child's development, especially when the child is very young and what's at issue is something as subtle as self-confidence and social skills. The question is not whether infants in child care roll over or stack blocks at much later dates than other infants. The developmental issues at stake are far more subtle and therefore inherently controversial.

My guess is that most parents will sacrifice a lot for their children if they feel it's really necessary. Evolutionary pressures have probably hardwired that willingness quite securely. It is, for the same evolutionary reasons, exquisitely painful to consider risking the well-being of our children—whether that's their financial security or their psychosocial development.

And so it is deeply disappointing to besieged parents—employed parents, nonemployed parents, and all of us in between—that child-care research does not provide the absolutely certain answers for which our hearts yearn. As I said at the beginning: we are finite, mortal creatures constrained by the contingencies of space and time and cultural context. Becoming parents would have been easier if only we had also become gods. But we are not. There is no Tree of Absolute Knowledge out there, and thinking we have its fruit in our own hands is the human error primeval. No matter how large the database and how fine the statistical controls, there is no Absolute Knowledge of Child Outcomes to be had. Life is hard, and the care of very young children is one of the hardest aspects of the conflict between earning a living and having a life

When I set out to do the research behind this chapter, I was braced to discover solid evidence either that I had risked serious harm to my firstborn by putting him into forty hours per week of nonfamilial care at age nine weeks, or that, after the twins were born, I had unnecessarily compromised our financial security and economic options by pursuing the irregular career of an independent writer rather than continuing full-time on the academic fast track as an English professor. At the time, our only alternative was borrowing money to pay for a nanny—probably an RN—competent to manage three children under three years of age *and* their intimidating array of medical problems. If we could find one! This was in the early eighties, when mortgage rates were 18.5 percent. We had signed one of those mortgages on our first house days before we learned I was carrying twins. We still had huge college debts; we were without collateral other than a car too small to accommodate all five of us. During the pregnancy I had come down with mononucleosis, and I remained quite sick for some time after giving birth.

Once in a while life simply happens, and for us this was one of those moments. I confess that our choices were not shaped by diligent inquiry into the state of child-care research in 1981. I had mono, the babies had pneumonia, and I was flattened by the prospect of my ordinary sixty-hour workweek on top of all that. Daring I am; foolish I am not. It was as if the Angel of the Lord showed up in the kitchen, fixed me a cup of tea, and said, "Hey, honey, hang up your Superwoman cape! Life is short—and the diaper guy has just left this week's supply of 385 diapers in white plastic bags on the porch. Do you really want to go grade freshman composition papers?"

I did not. Within my cautious scholarly soul I found a hitherto unexpected streak of crazy Celtic wanderlust. Life at home, like a small barque set out upon the Irish Sea, beckoned irresistibly.

Soon enough I decided that life home with little kids nourished certain creative drives and interdisciplinary curiosities that had been cramped by life in high-powered literary academia. The adjustment was tough, but in reasonably short order I found myself quite happy after all. I discovered that other women home full-time with small children included some of the gutsiest, liveliest, most self-possessed people I had ever known: there was not an oppressed wimpette among them. I edited literature anthologies for a while, working around nap times or during evenings and weekends. Then I pursued accreditation from the American Medical Writers Association and went into business for myself as a freelance medical editor. After ten years of such things—which is to say past the point where every child had pneumonia at least once every winter—I found myself with time enough for serious reading and writing, so I went back to writing books of my own.

It has been a very good life, even though the person I was when the twins were born would never have chosen to do it this way, had there been any choice in the matter. But we couldn't afford the quality of child care our particular children had to have. We gambled because we had to gamble, and twenty years later all is well. Sometimes grace happens, and it seems this was one of those moments.

As all three of them headed off to college, I settled down to read child-care research—as I had not done when they were all in diapers. As I did so, my initial question shifted. *What difference does high-quality child care really make?* gave way to another question altogether: *Why is child-care research so ferociously controversial?*

That's what the next chapter will examine.

14

Parents in the Cross Fire

Disputes among Academics

Child-care research is controversial in part because the issues involved so quickly come down to sex and power: the power of intellect over emotions, the power of men over women, the power of the "public" domain of status and money over the "private" domain of relationships and morality. Mix into that mess the highly charged Western iconography of Madonna and Child, and no wonder the results are so explosive. In the spiritual grammar of the West, as we have seen, "woman" is symbolically linked to "body" and to "death" and therefore, generally speaking, to all forms of disorder. In exactly the same ways, "child" is symbolically linked to all that is "dependent" and "vulnerable" and therefore, again speaking in general, to the morally innocent. As mothers, women can participate in the moral purity of the child—that's part of "Angel in the House" ideology, as we have seen. But Victorian gender-role ideology has its exceedingly dark reverse: women can just as easily become icons of evil.[14] The idea that mothers might willfully separate from their young children—which is the premise of child care as an issue in the first place—easily evokes not only the long-abiding connection between the female and the abhorrent but also primitive fears of abandonment by what can seem like the only true love anyone has in a world of innate depravity and rationalist self-seekers. It's a hot button, a loose wire, in the Western soul.

Furthermore, the child, especially the infant child, is at the opposite extreme from the ruthlessly competitive, relentlessly self-seeking rational actor. As a result, questions about what is good for a baby, questions about what is necessary for a child to flourish, function as lightening rods attracting all the free-floating anxiety and hostility involved in that deepest of philosophic and religious questions, "What does it mean *to be human*?" When *love your neighbor as yourself* has given way to *get the most for the least* or *he who dies with the most toys wins,* then of course it will be nearly impossible to hold a sane, courteous discussion of children's needs. If all of us are self-seeking rational actors, then the common good has no standing in the "public" sphere except as the sum of individual utilities. Young children are poor contenders in such a debate, because they have no recourse to the only strategy that matters: refuse, resist, retaliate.

And so—as we shall see in this chapter—debates about "the nature of the child" come down to unresolved questions about ourselves: Are we depraved or not? Is there an *imago Dei?* What does it mean *to be human*? Can we make it through life essentially alone, as self-realizing individualists? Debates about "what children need" come down to unresolved questions about our own needs: What do *we* need to be human? In this chapter, we will be looking closely at ferocious debates within developmental psychology and within biology. My guess is that few or none of these scientists see themselves as addressing philosophical and moral questions such as "What does it mean *to be human?"* That's a "private" question, a "subjective" question, a "soft" or "humanist" question, not a "hard" and "scientific" one. But their work is nonetheless richly involved in that question. My major conclusion is small but powerful: *in the absence of major public "languages" for arguing about how we understand the meanings of our lives and the meanings of our humanity, we have displaced the debate into scientific arenas where it does not belong and cannot be resolved.* Ferocious arguments about child-care research are a proxy war and—as usual—women and children are the most numerous civilian casualties of the fighting. Child-care debates are but the newest form of the ancient Western struggle to reconcile the false oppositions that habitually shape our thinking.

The struggle is a particularly bitter one in our own day, because the post-industrial global economy is built upon a narrowly rationalist, increasingly dehumanized individualism. The contest between earning a living in that economy while still having a life in any sense of the word is epitomized in the problems of parents with young children. Turning to "hard science" for a resolution to that contest is no answer at all, as I hope to show. The answers we need are not there. In what follows, I hope to extricate the moral questions about our own humanity from within these disputes among scientists, and then, in subsequent chapters, to resituate those questions where they do belong: within ancient traditions of wise discernment and good conscience. "What does it mean *to be human?*" is a moral question, not a scientific one.

From a basis in small-but-significant research findings, the child-care controversy spreads out in what can be imagined as concentric circles. At the smallest or narrowest of these circles, the controversy is rooted in persistent misunderstanding of research data and statistical concepts.[15] (I discuss this problem briefly in Appendix Two: Statistics and Spinmeistering.) The second circle, so to speak, is angry disputes between competing academic "schools" or theories of developmental psychology. Proponents of each theory sharply critique research findings and conclusions by their rivals. I will be examining this dispute in some detail, because ultimately it gives way to the third level of controversy: the old nature-nurture debate within biology about genetic determinism.

The academic discipline of developmental psychology is bordered on one side by biology and on the other by the philosophy of consciousness.[16] These two approaches to developmental psychology can be imagined as locating themselves on either side of the cultural crevasse that we have been examining all along. The behaviorists emphasize hard data, precise observation, and scientific rationality; the attachment theorists emphasize holistic assessments and human relationships, which entails a radically different approach to what counts as "precise observation" or "scientific objectivity." Jerome Kagan (at Harvard University) and Jay Belsky (at the University of London) are eminent researchers who come from differing "schools" within the discipline; for the purposes of explanation, let each stand for his own school.

The Behaviorists

Jerome Kagan comes from the biological side of developmental psychology, where researchers focus primarily upon neurological normality and abnormality. The lineage of this "school" includes behaviorists like Ivan Pavlov (1849–1936) and B. F. Skinner (1904–1990), as well as a more contemporary array of evolutionary biologists and molecular biologists. Steven Pinker fits in here: *How the Mind Works* offers an essentially mechanistic account of psychology. So does Judith Rich Harris, whose book *The Nurture Assumption* takes a radically empiricist and mechanist route toward denying that parents influence children in the least. In *The Selfish Gene,* Ronald Dawkins takes this mechanist model to its obvious conclusion in his now-famous portrait of organisms as essentially the means whereby DNA seeks molecular immortality.

Nor is Kagan alone in examining child care from this perspective. Sandra Scarr, for instance, is an eminent behavior geneticist and at one point president of the Society for Research in Child Development. In 1987, she told the *New York Times* that before the second year, children's "brains are Jell-O and their memories akin to those of decorticate rodents." At a 1987 conference at the University of Virginia, reportedly, she maintained that by biological design, early social and intellectual development is nearly invulnerable. In an article in the *Wall Street Journal,* also in 1987, she dismissed concerns about early child care as nothing more than backlash against employed women.[17] (I emphasize the year because neuroscience developed very rapidly in the last quarter of the twentieth century: her opinions today may be different.)

I should note, albeit in passing, that the policy implications of this position are quite serious indeed. If early development is under such strict genetic control as to be essentially invulnerable, then maybe it does not matter that child-care workers are paid less than parking-lot attendants and kennel workers, or that nine states allow one caretaker per six infants.[18] (Imagine, for a moment, having solo responsibility for three sets of twins, even if you are sharing a room or two with another person who is also responsible for another six infants.) In Illinois, for instance, people who cut hair for pay must be individually trained and licensed; not so the employees of daycare centers.[19] It's not reasonable to advocate changing this situation if the quality of early care makes no lasting difference discernable even by the president of the Society for Research in Child Development.

Research into early childhood from a behaviorist perspective has traditionally involved the quantitative analysis of observable behaviors. At what age does a child roll over? How many words does he know by age two? When does she demonstrably master concepts such as *underneath, behind,* or *inside,* or the relationships among shape, volume, and number? In short, does this child have a brain that functions normally? Is this child's neurobiological development on track? This body of research carefully avoids discussing such philosophical concepts as consciousness or self.

In *The Feeling of What Happens: Body and Emotion in the Making of Consciousness,* neurologist Antonio Damasio wittily acknowledges how the tremendous power and prestige of this school came to bear upon defining consciousness itself as both a naïvely prescientific construct and as an impenetrable black box to which rigorous professional science had as yet no access. "Studying consciousness was simply not the thing to do before you made tenure," he explains, "and even after you did [make tenure] it was looked upon with suspicion. Only in recent years has consciousness become a somewhat safer topic of scientific inquiry."[20] For someone deeply schooled in and personally committed to the physical sciences and mathematics as models of "real" science, such concepts as "consciousness," "self," and "trust" are unworkably soft, entirely subjective, and conceptually undisciplined—in short, part of the nonserious, nonreliable, nonrational cultural domain archetypally associated with the feminine and the private. "In the end," Damasio remarks, "not only was emotion not rational, even studying it was probably not rational."[21] The core problem, he explains, is "the fact that consciousness is an entirely personal and private affair and that it is not amenable to the third-person observations that are commonplace in physics."[22] What can't be measured and counted, what can't be directly observed and quantified, has very little standing in the modernist scheme of things.

The Attachment Theorists

On the philosophical side of psychology, so to speak, one finds researchers who trace their intellectual ancestry one way or another back to psychodynamic theories whose contemporary history begins with Sigmund Freud (1856–1939), but whose deeper roots extend at least to the monastic tradition of spiritual counsel developed in classical antiquity and arguably back to the time of Socrates. Developmental psychologists in this tradition ask all the questions about consciousness and about the origins and development of self that the behaviorists regard as unscientific or unanswerable in any sufficiently rigorous ways. As the behaviorists ask the question "biologically normal or biologically abnormal?" the attachment researchers ask the question "happy or unhappy?" (or, more precisely I suppose, "well adjusted and high-functioning or poorly adjusted and lower-functioning?"). Major figures in this school of developmental psychology include Mary Ainsworth, Jay Belsky, John Bowlby, Stella Chess, Margaret Mahler, Mary Main, and Alan Sroufe. In *Becoming Attached: First Relationships and How They Shape Our Capacity to Love,* psychologist Robert Karen offers a detailed and critically informed history of how this school developed in the several decades following World War II.[23] By far the most outspoken figure is Jay Belsky, who changed from supporting infant child care to criticizing it based upon the accumulation of evidence from the research he and others were doing. His essay explaining this change, published in 1986 in the policy journal *Zero to Three*, set off a firestorm.[24]

According to attachment theorists, the key to normal emotional and social development is a stable, secure, trusting relationship between an infant and a primary caregiver during the infant's first two or three years. This initial psychological development, called "attachment," depends upon the sensitivity and skill of the primary caregiver's attunement to the child. Secure attachment is not simply a function of the quantity of time the adult and the child spend together: the foundational research, performed by Mary Ainsworth in Uganda and again in Baltimore, focused exclusively upon mothers who were at home with their babies full-time.

Ainsworth observed, as anyone might, that mothers' interactions with their babies reflect the whole ordinary diversity of skill, sensitivity, perceptiveness, consistency, and so forth. The question was not how much a mother held her child, for instance, but whether she held her child when it signaled its desire for some cuddling. Ainsworth demonstrated that the child's capacity for age-appropriate autonomy in the second year varied in relationship to the sensitivity with which the mother had recognized and responded to its needs early on. The way to have secure and independent children, she argued, was to provide sensitive and generous attention to infants and toddlers. (In this she differed from the famous—or infamous—behaviorist John Watson, who argued that parents should never cuddle children at all, and especially not when the child was upset. Doing so only rewarded, and thus encouraged, the child's dependency. Even B. F. Skinner argued that the young child's apparent affection for parents was based upon the parents' providing food, nothing more—hence the comment one still hears regarding a baby's cooing at its mother, "he's just in love with his lunch.")

Beginning in the 1960s, Mary Ainsworth and her followers developed an assessment tool, called the Strange Situation, that elicited evidence of this security by gently challenging a toddler's natural ambivalence about the comforts of maternal security versus the enticements of new toys and a new situation to explore.[25] Securely attached children demonstrated superior capacity both for autonomous exploration and for intimate relationship with the primary adult. The children of distant, insensitive mothers were dramatically less secure in their connection to their mothers and much less comfortable exploring independently of them. A third, intermediate group of children, deemed "insecurely attached," were in various, complex ways ambivalent both about autonomous exploring and about their relationships to their mothers, whose nurturant behavior tended to be erratic. Poorly attached and insecurely attached children together constituted about 30 percent of the original sample, a percentage that has held remarkably stable in other studies of children reared at home by their parents. (Obviously, then, secure attachment is not simply the result of full-time at-home mothering.

What matters is the skill of the mother or primary caregiver, who does not need to have any biological relationship to the child.)

Sorting Out the Issues: New Work in Neuroscience

Unlike the NICHD studies, which on the whole show only a small increase in attachment problems, child-care studies from attachment researchers have shown that 40 percent of children in child care more than twenty hours a week in the first year rank as insecurely or poorly attached—up from 30 percent in the home-care sample.[26] But subtle, wholistic assessments like the Strange Situation are inevitably open to attack by those who want to move psychology closer to the model of "real" or "hard" sciences such as molecular biology.

As it happens, however, attachment researchers now have strong corroboration for their theories from researchers outside the child-care arena altogether. Follow-up studies of children adopted from negligent Romanian orphanages confirm the essential tenets of attachment theory: the longer these children were in those orphanages (the older they were at adoption) the more likely they are to have devastating problems in relating to other people.[27] As Harvard biopsychologist Martin H. Teicher explains, researchers used to think that child abuse simply induced "software problems" that could be fixed with psychotherapy or resolute determination to "get over it." Instead, they have found that child abuse "induces a cascade of molecular and neurobiological effects that irreversibly alter neural development."[28] If an abused child develops in demonstrably abnormal ways, then it is reasonable to think that there will be some negative developmental consequences for a child whose care is inadequate even if never abusive.

Jay Belsky offers what he calls a "nice linear function" to document that fact: 85 percent of maltreated children are insecurely attached, as are 50 percent of children with clinically depressed mothers, 40 percent of children with more than twenty hours a week in child care in their first year, and 25–30 percent of children in low-risk, stable, middle-class households who had less than twenty hours a week of outside care in the first year.[29] Within epidemiology as a field of inquiry, such progressions are considered very strong evidence indeed that the Strange Situation test accurately measures some important aspect of the mother-child relationship.

Linear progressions like this are serious evidence for two reasons. Partly, the West has tended chronically to dismiss the power, the importance, and above all the skill involved in anything that is "women's work." What mothers do is merely "natural," which is why some people have advocated using unemployable welfare mothers as child-care workers: people who can't otherwise hold a job can care for children, because caring for children is a no-skill brainless task. Second, this is serious evidence because insecure toddlers grow up to have higher rates of interpersonal difficulties than one finds among children who were secure as toddlers. For some Romanian-orphanage survivors, these interpersonal difficulties are catastrophic.

One must bear in mind, of course, that every insecure toddler is not doomed to trouble, much less to catastrophic trouble: insecurity is not itself a pathological condition but rather a general indicator of how well a child is doing at a particular point in time. General indicators of well-being are useful stuff for epidemiologists. Resting heart-rates, for instance, are an important general indicator of health and physical condition: if we found that children who spend twenty hours a week or more playing violent videogames had elevated heart rates in comparison to other children, ears would perk up.

Jerome Kagan dismisses these studies of Romanian orphans because most of the adopted orphans developed normally.[30] I do not mean to suggest that he doesn't understand epidemiology. The explanation lies elsewhere. First, Kagan operates largely within all-or-nothing models of causality such as one finds in physics.[31] If A does not cause B all of the time, A is not a cause of B. If most abused but adopted orphans survived intact, then abusive orphanages (while deplorable) were not the absolute-and-exclusive *cause* of disability for other orphans. That's true as far as it goes.

But human disease and disorder are fairly seldom a matter of all-or-nothing causes. Most cigarette smokers, for instance, do not get lung cancer. Insisting upon all-or-nothing causality is part of what earlier I called "spreadsheet" thinking. All-or-nothing, like profit-or-loss, presents artificially rigid alternatives. The West chronically tends to understand a problem—any problem—in terms of falsely rigid opposites. The very real danger here is thinking that early childhood experiences will be either absolutely and entirely determinative—a position called "infant determinism"—or that early childhood experience has absolutely no permanent consequences at all unless the features of that environment prove permanent (for instance, continuing to live among people who speak the same language). But it seems to me that a parent's role in a child's development is neither all nor nothing: it's a human part, a contingent part. As Daniel Seigel wisely cautions, ". . . a balanced view enables us as parents, for example, to have a sense of responsibility for the experiences we provide without the unnecessary burden of guilt generated by the belief that our actions are solely responsible for the outcome of our children's development."[32]

Second, Kagan's dismissal of the Romanian orphan studies reflects his scientific judgment that attachment theory and the techniques used to measure attachment are simply *not* scientific.[33] Whatever happened to the psychological development of some Romanian orphans cannot be explained scientifically by the absence of loving, attentive parents, because good science simply doesn't ask about such "soft" and "subjective" and "nonquantifiable" things. The key dispute here is more about the nature of "science" than the quality of life in Romanian orphanages—which Kagan of course would never excuse.

If, at an extreme, the behaviorists regard the attachment researchers as soft-minded and radically unscientific, the attachment researchers regard the behaviorists as oblivious to the complexity of the mind. Attachment researchers contend that a serious, accurate account of the human psyche cannot possibly ignore the power of conscious and unconscious memory. Individual experience, variously mediated and modulated through memory, shapes the remarkably plastic and adaptable human consciousness into distinctive individuals who love, suffer, question, and hope in their own particular ways. Strictly physical, quantitative science is designed more for investigating the material world of things than investigating the elusive, passionate, spiritual domain of mind and soul and self. The attachment theorists are trying to be rigorous without falsely simplifying the realities they want to understand.

As I said before, this fundamental dispute within developmental psychology goes all the way back to disputes between two late Victorians: Freud and Pavlov. But in the century since then, and especially in the last couple of decades, we have developed technologies that promise eventually to supercede important aspects of this dispute. In the last couple of decades, developments in neuroscience have begun to make some extraordinary progress in closing the chasm between the mind and the brain. As that gulf narrows, developmental psychology may gradually achieve a new synthesis.

Under any circumstances, we have come to understand some of the biological processes that embody the mind. As we have done so, one of the first and most important Western dualisms has been radically discredited: the traditional opposition between reason and emotion, between intellect and feelings, has been shattered.[34] As a result, the entire relationship between "subject" and "object" is being reworked—a reworking that may open a whole new chapter in the spiritual grammar of the West.

The scope and the cultural significance of this development are simply immense. For instance, it has been determined that critical intelligence depends upon emotions as upon a sensory organ. Emotions provide two services upon which rationality depends: first, information about the survival value of an experience or a perception; second, the "key word" terms under which our experience is organized and available to recall. Rationality is thus served not by the control of emotions, much less by the subjugation of emotions, but rather by the neural capacity, probably centered in the frontal lobes, to integrate emotions both across the array of sensory modalities and over time and thus to reach executive decisions about "what is true" or "what should be done."

We have also come to understand the complexity of early neurological development in an infant. Let me sketch just a little bit of what we know about brain function, so that we can see, later on, what's at stake in questions about who cares for a baby.

The human brain is the single most complex entity in the known universe. The numbers alone are mind-boggling: the ordinary brain has something like one hundred billion neurons. That's 100,000,000,000 cells. In addition, the brain has at least twice as many glial cells (from the medieval Greek word "glia," which means "glue"). These cells seem to provide merely "architectural and administrative support services," so to speak; but the history of neurophysiology is replete with discoveries that cells or areas that seemed to be doing nothing much were in fact performing all kinds of important functions.

As cells go, neurons are stringy little things, replete with specialized structures that fray out at their ends, sometimes fairly modestly and sometimes into gorgeously elaborate "trees." Through its own sending units (called "synapses") on the frayed-out tips of these specialized structures and related receptor sites on its own cell wall, each single neuron has connections to something like 10,000 other neurons. The hundred billion neurons of the human brain thus comprise an elaborate, multidimensional web whose precise operations we are only beginning to understand as we have begun to develop technology adequate to monitor its anatomical, electrical, and biochemical signaling systems. (This technology includes functional Magnetic Resonance Imaging scans, Positron Emission Tomography scans, Computerized Axial Tomography scans, very delicate chemical assays, etc.)

As a result of this anatomical and functional complexity, the neural networks of the brain have a fabulous capacity to encode and transmit information. The number of on-off patterns of neural activity is immense, perhaps ten times ten one million times.[35] We don't have words for numbers that big. Furthermore, each neuron can fire and reset itself to fire again within 0.5 milliseconds. That works out to a potential for firing *two thousand times per second.* So that ten times ten one million times can change twelve thousand times each minute. I get a headache just thinking about it.

Children are born with an excess number of neurons but with relatively few connections among neurons, at least in comparison to the brain of an adult.[36] Even high school seniors have brains that still differ in their patterns of activity from the adult brain.[37] (This comes as no surprise to some of us.) A baby's hands, by comparison, are completely developed anatomically. Hands merely get bigger and stronger, which is why there's something so powerful about those pictures of a premature baby's perfect, miniature hand curled around a single finger of an adult man's hand. Brains are not like that, contemporary neuroscience has explained. The difference between the minimally wired infant brain and the massively interwoven adult brain depends upon experience.

Experience—especially early interpersonal experience—organizes, reorganizes, and physically modifies the brain's structure and function.[38] The way that works is described by what is called "Hebb's Axiom." Hebb's Axiom states that the more often one neuron transmits an electrochemical impulse to another, the lower the minimum size of the impulse needed to fire the next neuron successfully.[39] In particular, interactions with caregivers serve to regulate—or to deregulate—patterns of neural activity in the infant brain. These patterns of neural activity in turn regulate the biochemical expression of genes and thereby the unfolding of genetic potential. Newly activated genes then go on to direct the building of anatomical connections, the imprinting of neural circuitry, and the potential range of future development.[40]

The Social Skills of Newborns

I think the most amazing work on extremely early neurological development has to do with the complexity of early relationships. This work was pioneered by Daniel Stern, at the time a professor of psychiatry at Cornell University. Some of Stern's research used pairs of video cameras, one focused on an infant, the other on its mother, to record and then to study the interactions between them. At other times he used pacifiers hot-wired to transmit information about how hard and fast a baby is sucking (which is a measure of enthusiasm or excitement). Stern's research offers dramatic empirical evidence that the infant has extraordinary social skills and rapidly evolving capacity for relationships and for self-expression. His work provides an unprecedented account of how a child's sense of self emerges and grows over the first two years.[41]

In the first six to nine months, babies can't do much more than look around. The only muscles they have under much control are those of the face and, with some support, the neck. As a result, the relationship between an adult and a very young baby is overwhelmingly dependent upon looking at, looking away, and facial expressions. It is a rich and complex human relationship nonetheless. As such, it is dramatically subject to all the "continuous variables" that delineate the personality of the two people involved.

In *The Developing Mind: Toward a Neurobiology of Interpersonal Experience,* Daniel Siegel synthesizes the kind of work Stern is doing with what we are now learning about how brains work and how they develop. As Siegel explains, ". . . caregivers are the architects of the way in which experience influences the unfolding of genetically preprogrammed but experience-dependent brain development. Genetic potential is expressed within the setting of social experiences, which directly influence how neurons connect to one another. Human connections create neuronal connections."[42] And *that's* why it matters whether the adult is more or less sensitive. It matters whether the adult is more or less domineering, more or less willing to be engaged, more or less creative, witty, predictable, kindly, courteous, personally secure, and generally attuned to the child's moods, interests, perceptions, etc. Adults can match or "mirror" the child's feelings in ways that help the child to make the feeling fully conscious by sharing it with someone. Or adults can overrespond, underrespond, or miss the cue altogether. We do so with one another all the time, of course; but babies are far more dependent upon adults than adults are on one another.

Like Ainsworth's work in Uganda and in Baltimore, Stern's work adeptly documents the commonplace observation that some adults are much better with children than others are. His videotapes reveal that mothers vary quite a bit in the perceptive sensitivity with which they read and respond to their babies' cues.[43] Just as some babies are genuinely difficult and relatively inscrutable, some adults are fairly clueless. We all know that; we all cope with it every day. Babies have to cope with it too, despite the fact that they have spectacularly fewer resources for dealing with difficult or insensitive people. Many parents learn on the job, so to speak. In a remarkable process of adult growth and change, some parents who were at first entirely bewildered by babies soon become quite skillful. Some never do.

The sensitivity of the parent or caregiver matters quite a bit, because the brain completes its fundamental circuitry and begins to develop its millions upon millions of links among neurons through these countless small interactions with the early primary caregiver. Stanley Greenspan and T. Berry Brazelton, both of them eminent academic pediatricians, estimate that a baby's ordinary day probably includes sixteen fifteen-minute episodes of these short but powerful interactions.[44] Stanley Greenspan also insists that the sensitivity of the child's caregiver is massively influential for the development of language, social skills, intelligence, and creative problem-solving abilities.[45] In the first year or so, this developmental process also sharply influences the development of permanent anatomical connections that serve as the biological basis of such important characteristics as emotional regulation and attention span.[46]

As Daniel Siegel explains in great detail, what we call or experience as "empathy" is quite literally embodied at the neurobiological level by roughly parallel patterns of neural firing in the brain: empathy is the mechanism, so to speak, or perhaps the consequence of the process whereby interpersonal experience wires or rewires networks built in accordance with Hebb's Axiom.[47] The fussy infant develops the capacity to console himself, for instance, through the repeated consolations of a patient and caring adult. The baby learns to maintain focus upon an object as the adult empathically shares his curiosity or delight, thereby strengthening the neurological systems that supply the child's capacity to attend. Such utterly commonplace interactions provide the environmental input whereby the innately responsive human brain completes its fundamental biological maturation.

Furthermore, the child's development depends upon more than simply the perceptual and interpersonal acuity of the attentive adult. The child's development also depends upon or is shaped by the adult's own emotional issues. Such issues govern how the adult reacts to what the adult perceives about the child or about the child's behavior or reactions: Is a spilled cup of juice merely inconvenient or actively reprehensible? Are an older baby's noisy protests always ignored, always sternly chastised, always capitulated to, always negotiated? Or sometimes one, sometimes another, depending upon variables? What variables?

From his study of videotapes and hot-wired pacifiers, Stern concludes that "Through the selective use of attunement, the parent's intersubjective responsivity acts as a template to shape and create corresponding intrapsychic experiences in the child. It is in this way that the parent's desires, fears, prohibitions, and fantasies contour the psychic experience of the child."[48] The innumerable, transient episodes of day-to-day "quantity time" interaction are the process whereby caregivers influence the psychological and neurophysiological development of infants. That's undoubtedly why (or how) the primary caregiver's capacity for secure intimate relationships very powerfully correlates with the degree of self-awareness, autonomy, and confidence that the child has at age twelve to eighteen months.[49] Parents—or paid caregivers—who are personally distant, resentful, or ambivalently inconsistent in their behavior are much more likely to have toddlers who are insecure.

Other neuroendocrinologists and neuropsychologists doing very different kinds of research have documented that supportive relationships are just as important—just as physically important—for adults. Supportive, sympathetic, compassionate friends will diminish our physiological stress responses in ways that modulate levels of immune system function, lower blood pressure and heart rate, and so forth.[50] Just as intensely social babies develop a sense of themselves within relationships, so also adults maintain a sane, relaxed, resilient, flexible sense of self by and through supportive interactions with others. Compassion is a crucial element in human survival and human evolutionary success. When tradition insists that love is at the heart of us, that's not just a metaphor. It's demonstrable in brain physiology as well as blood pressure or heart rate.

And yet, none of this elaborate neuroscience suggests that it matters whether a child's primary caregiver is a biological relation. What matters is whether this person is loving, self-aware, flexible, mature, and above all genuinely pleased to take part in this complex, intimate, challenging relationship. Parents may of course feel strongly that they want to claim this primary relationship for themselves, but babies will simply fall in love with and be influenced by whoever is there to make faces and play face-games in that crucial first year of stunningly rapid neurological development. As Penelope Leach explains, "Babies fall in love with people who mother them emotionally, talking to them, cuddling them, smiling, and playing with them. . . . [a] baby doesn't just need someone who'll come and feed him when he's hungry; he needs someone to come when he needs company, someone who notices when he smiles and smiles back, who hears when he 'talks,' listens, and replies. . . . Every baby needs at least one special person to attach to—and more are better."[51]

Ultimately, no matter who is the primary caregiver, babies are influenced by personal relationships; and in a real personal relationship the personality of both partners matters. I think this is the foundation upon which we can insist both upon the human rights of parents to attend to their own infants in the first year, and furthermore the human rights of infants to their own parents for most of the time. In addition, because babies need both love and a roof overhead, this nation needs a very strictly regulated, heavily subsidized child-care system that supplies ample one-on-one attention from loving, well-trained, competent professionals who both know what they are doing and have the support they need to do it well.

Despite professional academic blood sport among biologists and psychologists, everyone does agree that the immature brain depends upon experience to complete its essential maturation. Animal studies have demonstrated that beyond any question at all. As experience and genetic heritage differ, then, brains differ. People differ. People who are anatomically and functionally normal differ within a given range, but the range is wide if your scale of measurement is finely graded, and furthermore the differences can be remarkably unpredictable. The stunning diversity of human behavior, in comparison to the available repertoire of behavior among any other species of vertebrate, testifies unequivocally to the developmental plasticity of the human brain. As organisms, we take a big risk in being born at such a radically undeveloped stage neurobiologically. The payoff is in a dramatically enhanced adaptability and in the correlative capacity of parents and other caregivers to transmit the array of beliefs and skills we call "culture."

The Battle among Biologists: Genetic Determinism

Daniel Stern's videotapes and new research into the developing brain have provided the scientific data whereby one might argue, *contra* the behaviorists, that the first three years of life are particularly important for long-term outcomes. I find the data and the arguments persuasive, but there is another layer to this dispute that we need to consider. Should genetics account for personality or for variations in personality across a normal range—as some strongly argue that it eventually will—then the psychodynamic and interpersonal account of personality development would of course collapse. With it goes the theoretical foundations of attachment-theory research into child care and child outcomes. The more heavily one emphasizes the determinative power of the genes, the less likely one is to credit the influence of parenting—much less any single stage-specific parental choice, such as whether or to what extent to place a child in child care.

As it happens, behaviorism in its contemporary form is closely allied with molecular biology, which is the foundation of molecular genetics: both endeavor to meet the classic materialist and positivist (and culturally "masculine") norms of physical observation, abstraction, and quantification. We need to understand the real, albeit limited, role of genetic inheritance before we can come fully to terms with behavioralist claims that early-childhood experiences have minimal long-term significance. What we will see is that behaviorism ultimately depends upon or at least converges with the postmodern denial of a core self. If by "myself" you mean only a transient set of illusions without moral substance or moral responsibility, then the jig is up. Completely. There's no point in worrying about child care, or for that matter about "having a life," because all such concerns are egotistical projections and pretenses.

According to biologist Richard Lewontin, the contemporary emphasis upon the power of genetic inheritance is badly mistaken. It is an extreme example of what he calls "physics envy." As he explains in patient, lucid detail in *The Triple Helix: Gene, Organism, and Environment,* biology is a very different project than physics or chemistry.[52] The physical sciences predict outcomes as accurately as they do because they can study the major causal effect of a few, single, extraordinarily powerful factors such as gravity. A living organism, by comparison, exists within a complicated nexus of very many factors, each of which considered alone has only a weak causal effect. Genetic inheritance certainly does explain why tulips are tulips and not tomatoes, or how alley cats differ both from alligators and from mountain lions. If that's the question, genes certainly do assert a powerful causal effect: even the tiny genetic differences between children and chimpanzees have major consequences.

But if we want to know "how will my infant who is in child care fifty hours a week be different *as a result of that experience* from what he or she would be otherwise?" then we are shifting the question in major ways. Specifically, we are very dramatically changing the scale whereby differences are measured. The scale that works for displaying an answer to the question "How is my cat different from my dog?" will be far too crude to display an answer to a question that is spectacularly more delicate and subtle: What—if any—are the long-term consequences for a given individual of this or that set of early experiences? The only possible answers, from Lewontin's point of view, will be very delicately delineated relative probabilities.

That is, given the complexity of human development, the only honest answer is "Well, that depends." Depends upon what? Upon that complicated nexus of very many factors, each of which considered alone has only a weak causal effect. So does child care make a difference to brain development? Of course it makes a difference, *because everything makes a difference.* There is also a difference between raising your children in Minnesota or raising them in Manhattan, bringing them up Buddhist or perhaps Presbyterian. Parents' major choices about life will always matter to their children: we are a crucial part of the child's environment.

But environment does not call the shots in some determinative way. Neither do genes. Genetic inheritance alone simply cannot explain as much as the genetic determinists claim about why and how one individual of a species differs from another. Lewontin learnedly disputes the assertion that from the genetic code one can theoretically compute the individual; he asserts that the individual does not develop by computing itself from its genes.[53] Real development, he explains, depends both upon interactions with an environment and with essentially random encounters between molecules floating about inside a cell, molecules that, when they do encounter one another, interact in some significant way.[54] The characteristics of the environment and the precise timing of those molecular encounters make for observable, demonstrable differences in the "behavior" of a cell and ultimately in the form and functioning of genetically identical individuals.

For instance, he describes a famous set of studies in which three genetically identical cuttings were taken from each of several common yarrow plants (*Achillea millefolium*). Each cutting was then rooted and grown into its own plant—three identical clones of the parent plant. (Cloning animals is remarkably difficult, but cloning plants can in some circumstances be very simple indeed. Put the cut end in water and it will grow roots.) Yarrow is a popular garden perennial; I've grown it in front of my own house. The plant has fuzzy, fragrant foliage, deeply cut leaves, and large flat flower heads several inches across made up of many extremely tiny individual flowers (hence "*millefolium*"). The usual form is a pale, somewhat lemony yellow that contrasts beautifully with the elegant, slightly grayish cast to the foliage. In the experiment, cuttings from each original plant were rooted, potted, and then grown at one of three altitudes to see what impact altitude alone would have on how the genetically identical clones would grow.

No one parent plant had clones that performed the very best at every altitude. Nor did altitude have the same impact upon all of the plants altogether, no matter which parent they had come from. For instance, the clones of the plant that did best at the highest and at the lowest altitude was among the very worst—failing to flower at all—at the moderate altitude. According to Lewontin, this array of results, technically called the "norm of reaction," is typical of what such experiments show.[55] In different environments, young plants with the exact same genetic heritage nonetheless develop into measurably different adults. Furthermore, it is extremely difficult to predict how genetically identical individuals will respond to different environments. At a practical level, and without the precise vocabulary, every serious gardener has seen this. More to the point, so has every parent of identical twins.

We can do such rigorously controlled studies on plants that mature into blossom in a few weeks. Even if it were morally possible to do that with children, it would be practically impossible. Human development is so long and socially so complex that one could never control for every relevant (or "confounding") variable but one. Furthermore, as Jerome Kagan repeatedly insists, the vast majority of children "bloom" in the sense of growing up biologically normal and at some point having children of their own.

But there is much more to human happiness than a biologically normal brain: even among those with normal brains, some are happy and some are miserable. Some are capable of intimacy, commitment, and creativity; others tend more toward being solitary, suspicious, and relatively rigid. The continuum of "normal" is enormous. Good parents want to do their best to help their children mature into genuinely flourishing adults, which demands both loving individual attention and substantial economic resources. We want more for our children, whether personally or materially, than mere survival at physiologically normal levels.

To answer such concerns, we need a scale of measurement still finer yet. In the language of statistics, we are asking not about the "dichotomous" variable normal versus abnormal but rather about what are called "continuous" variables. Dichotomous variables are pass-fail, yes-or-no questions: Did the plant bloom or not? Is this person psychologically impaired or not? Is this brain normal or not? Research into dichotomous variables quite reasonably focuses primarily upon what statisticians call "threshold conditions." That is, what is the cutoff point beyond which one finds an abnormal outcome? For instance, how long can a plant go without water before it keels over? How long must baby birds be deprived of hearing other birds sing before their own ability to sing is ruined? If you are interested in dichotomous variables and in child care, then the pass-fail, yes-or-no question takes this form: "Does competent child care hurt infants?" The answer to that question is "No!" Infants in competent child care do *not* grow up abnormal in some manner akin to baby birds deprived of hearing other birds sing.

Continuous variables, on the other hand, are the more-or-less ones: more or less cheerful, more or less resilient, more or less self-confident, more or less intelligent. Research into continuous variables tends to focus not upon the threshold conditions that separate the normal from the abnormal but rather upon the relatively broad spectrum that we regard as normal human variation. In the language of statistics, that's investigating the interval between thresholds and ceilings; it's asking "Is more better?" At the ceiling point, adding or doing "more" of something doesn't get "more" of the desired outcome; and it may, in some circumstances, be detrimental. You can, for instance, ruin a flower bed by watering it either too little or too much, just as you can warp a child either through neglect or through excessive attention. Somewhere between too much and too little, however, is the vast domain of the Aristotelian mean. Moderate moderation in most things. Researchers investigate the moderate middle by using continuous variables, which map the continuum from "iffy" to "good enough" to "better yet" to "whoa! that's plenty."

At some point many years ago, I read a magazine article about watering. As I recall, someone wired the pores on the underside of the leaves of corn plants with sensors that turned on those massive agricultural "sprinklers" whenever the pores began to close, which is a sign that the plant is becoming dry. Botanists discovered thereby that corn (a) needs more water than they had thought and (b) that ideally watered fields are far more productive per acre. The problem, of course, is that irrigation isn't free. Furthermore, sometimes the sprinklers switched on when rain was imminent. There are all kinds of financial and environmental costs associated with irrigating your farm to that extent, just as there are costs involved in making major career and economic sacrifices necessary to provide absolutely optimal individual nurture and attention to a child.

Parents would love to have a formula whereby to calculate the relative value to their children of their personal time and attention versus the value to their children of what money can provide. But we can't do to kids what we do to corn. Coping with such contingency, learning to live with such uncertainty, is innate to the human condition. It is also a central feature of the spiritual and psychological adventure of becoming a mature compassionate adult, whether or not one is a parent. Furthermore, subtle, wholistic research that tries to address such issues—that is, research into continuous variables among such highly various creatures as human beings—is liable to attack from behaviorally based researchers who (a) prefer yes-or-no dichotomous variables, (b) refuse to examine variables that are difficult or impossible to observe in a direct, quantifiable, material way, and (c) attribute all variation within normal limits to variations in genetic endowment.

Jerome Kagan, for instance, tends to be a genetic determinist in his biology and a behaviorist in his psychology, repeatedly emphasizing the essentially quite sturdy and uniform ways in which human development unfolds.[56] That's an unquestionably legitimate level at which to study the human organism. But Kagan is sharply dismissive of any level of causality other than the necessary and sufficient quantifiable cause; his ideal model for psychology is molecular biology, a field which, like chemistry proper, explains quite a lot by reference to a relatively few, strongly acting factors.[57]

A double dose of Kagan's scorn is reserved for developmental psychologists who *are* interested in contingent, contributing factors and who *do* try to measure realities that cannot be directly observed and counted. In a variety of ways, he characterizes them as sentimental, irrational, magical thinkers who refuse to face the facts, who allow their own emotional needs to interfere with clear observation, and who cling to the last, irrational shreds of a religious perspective upon experience.[58] Those who emphasize the lasting importance of how we care for an infant in the first few years, he explains, are like those who clung to a geocentric worldview in the face of Gallileo and Kepler.[59] They are refusing to face the "hard" facts.

Such vitriol is reciprocated. Writing in the *New York Review of Books*, for instance, Richard Lewontin offers the following observation about genetic determinism: "Richard Dawkins's claim that the genes 'create us, body and mind' seemed to be the hyperbolic excess of a vulgar understanding in 1976, but it is now the unexamined consensus of intellectual consciousness propagated by journalists and scientists alike."[60] As the chairman of psychology at Harvard has remarked, disputes among psychologists have become a "blood sport."[61] More sobering yet is Stephen J. Gould's lament: "I've been in this business (of academia) for nearly a quarter century now and nothing depresses me more than the rampant, seemingly inveterate mischaracterization that lies at the core of nearly every academic debate."[62] I should point out that Richard Lewontin and Jerome Kagan are professors at Harvard, Ronald Dawkins at Oxford, Jay Belsky at the University of London. When experts of such stature disagree so sharply—when academic dispute deteriorates into "blood sport"—ordinary parents reading newspaper accounts of child-care research can be caught in the cross fire. This is what makes the Mommy Wars so very dangerous: relatively few parents know the issues or the technical vocabulary well enough to recognize polemical misrepresentations when they occur.

Reclaiming the Question: The Concept of Memory

Few of us can argue with these eminent psychologists and biologists on their own turf. But ordinary parents certainly will have important commonsense opinions about the fundamental philosophic issues that stand behind the issues I have been describing, and that's what I want to look at next. For instance, as I said, behaviorists classically regard consciousness itself as a nonscientific concept, at best a black box into which rigorous science cannot inquire. It's one thing, I propose, simply to disregard the human experience of self-awareness as one goes about investigating other aspects of human psychology. But for a variety of subtle reasons, the behaviorist position on child care also involves a correlative dismissal of human memory and, ultimately, a sharply curtailed understanding of self or identity. These are issues upon which many ordinary adults will have reasonable opinions: a Ph.D. is not required.

The first thing to notice, then, is that the concept of memory is spectacularly important in the child-care debates. In *Three Seductive Ideas* Jerome Kagan clearly formulates a claim he makes other places as well, a claim that I've seen repeated by many nonscience writers. (The italics here are mine.) "Some of the psychological products of the first two years might be preserved, *but only if the environment sustained the behavior, not because the original reaction was destined to remain stable.* . . . If an adult has impairing symptoms, it is more reasonable to attribute them to the continuous influence of an adverse environment than to conclude that the symptoms represent the untouched traces of early neglect."[63] Consider that for a moment. Current troubles reflect current and sustained environment, not personal history. Not memory.

Whatever you are doing now, feeling now, however you are reacting right now to my argument or to the world around you, the causal agency resides either in your genes or in the outer world itself. The causal agency is not within your consciousness itself, not within your memories, and not within the feelings, experiences, opinions, and interpretive habits that constitute memory, reflection upon memory, and the consequences of memory extended over time. This dispute about memory, often deeply submerged, plays a key role in popular discussions of child care, because implicit in the behaviorist/determinist account is the promise or the hope that an early child-care situation cannot possibly have a lasting impact upon behavior, feelings, or meanings. Child care cannot have lasting consequences because the child does not remain in that environment forever.

In short, behaviorists and genetic determinists attribute the persistent "parts" of personality to genetics, and everything else to the immediate (and therefore potentially transient) impact of environment. Judith Rich Harris, quite predictably, takes this position to such an extreme that its fallacy is self-evident: "If your parents made you feel worthless, those feelings of worthlessness are associated with the social contexts in which your parents did that to you. The feelings of worthlessness will be associated with outside-the-home contexts only if the people you encountered outside your home also made you feel like that."[64] Her formulation transparently encodes an essentially behaviorist account of classical conditioning as the basic relationship between an individual and his or her social setting.

There is, quite the contrary, massive evidence that people early in life develop persistent, extremely powerful interpretive paradigms that they carry with them, so to speak, into every environment and across time. As an array of evidence attests, these paradigms are not indelible nor are they carved in genetic stone, but neither are they as transient as the behaviorist model of stimulus-response conditioning seems to suggest. For instance, in *The Seven Sins of Memory: How the Mind Forgets and Remembers,* Daniel Schacter (chairman of the psychology department at Harvard) explains both the neurobiological persistence and the survival value of memories for important experiences—especially painful experiences.[65] Neurologists have documented how stress influences the infant's developing brain.[66] Western literature repeatedly depicts the ways in which we are both haunted and blessed by memory. Dan McAdams affirms the power of memory when he explains the link between personal identity and the stories a person tells about his or her own past.[67] What's true for the individual is true of us collectively as well: culture and the transmission of culture depend upon human memory enshrined within narrative snippets and storytelling of all kinds. Behaviorism coupled with genetic determinism denies all this. It dismisses such beliefs as sentimentality and as naïve, "prescientific" illusion.

Reclaiming the Question: The Reality of "Self"

Ultimately, I contend, the behaviorist/determinist account reflects (or at least plays into) the commonplace postmodern denial of a persistent identity or a core self.[68] If one reduces the self to its responses to a surrounding environment, then the self is no more "real" than foam on a wave momentarily cresting on the surface of the sea. That is an ancient philosophic position. It is, I suspect, one among the very small number of essential premises or fundamental presuppositions that inform critical thinking from its deepest origins. In various sophisticated forms, for instance, the denial of individual identity seems to be centrally important in Eastern thought.

Western thought, on the other hand, has more often insisted upon the reality and the significance of each individual person. Western individualism has massive origins in the Christian tradition, but beginning in the Renaissance it began to develop its distinctively modern form. In its modern form, Western individualism has brought about both democracy and a slow, progressive shuttering of communal social forms necessary for human flourishing. There is no doubt that individualism has by now gotten out of hand in some fairly serious ways. One response to that extremism has been an equal and opposite insistence by Western thinkers that our core sense of self is simply an egotistical illusion.

What is meant by the phrase "egotistical illusion" is nonetheless quite different in Eastern and Western thought. In the West, denial of the reality of the self is part of what James C. Edwards calls "normal nihilism."[69] Nietzsche, for instance, famously celebrates the individual strong enough to face this illusion and to insist upon his own egotism nonetheless. In the East, the denial of individual identity is one aspect of ancient spiritual and philosophical traditions that are not at all nihilist in the contemporary Western sense of that word. Translating between Eastern and Western traditions in metaphysics is a very dicey business indeed, but generally speaking when Eastern thinkers talk about the nonexistence of the individual self, what they are getting at is what Westerners describe as the ways in which the self-centered ego generates essentially grandiose illusions, illusions that spiritual practice seeks to dismantle. Nietzsche argues, in effect, that if egotistical illusions are all we have, then let's go for it. But the premise of spiritual practice, East and West alike, is that we can get past egotistical illusion to another realm, another realm that different traditions understand in very different ways.[70] The philosophical and moral question in dispute here is whether utterly persuasive egotistical illusions are all that we have.

At this point, my own argument comes full circle. Here we are again facing the same question with which I began: Are we essentially and exclusively self-seeking competitors? Is everyone out for himself and for himself alone? Or is there a spark of the *imago Dei* in everyone? Christian spiritual disciplines and practices have convinced me that this spark is inescapably real. (I also realize that different people, trained in the spiritual disciplines of different traditions or approaching the question within secular intellectual disciplines, will have different descriptions of what lies "beyond" egotistical illusion. Those differences are important; so is the fundamental accord that nihilism is simple-minded and egotistical.) Because there is this spark of the Holy One in each of us, Christian tradition as I read it teaches that what we sacrifice for others is not necessarily and exclusively a bottom-line loss for us individually if we understand what we are doing in what Buddhists would call "enlightened" ways. Compassion is *never* a net loss.

Compassionate generosity is not necessarily a bottom-line loss because the universe is not, at its heart, a zero-sum spreadsheet. What we give to others can return to us multiplied and transformed, because as we give from the heart we encounter the loving-kindness of God. Our good hearts draw on the cosmic energy that is the heart of God—and the encounter with God is always a blessing, no matter how we name or understand that encounter.

In straight psychological terms, compassion involves the problem of intimacy. Can we be closely related to others without loss of self? Are psychological boundaries secure enough to allow for a long-term give and take in which no one keeps score? The needs of children are needs that we all have, all of our lives, for compassionate, generative relationships with one another. Whether you face a babe in arms or an uncle with Alzheimer's, a neighbor with a dead battery or a neighborhood with no life of its own, the needs around you are ultimately your own needs as well. We are all in this together, despite all the ways in which deep-rooted strands in American popular culture tell us "look out for #1." Having a life in any worthy sense of the word demands courage, sacrifice, and commitment. None of that is easy, and none of it's cheap.

All of it is priceless.

Conclusion: Compassion and Parenthood

As I suppose every experienced parent knows full well and firsthand, some parents are passionately and intelligently committed to their children's well-being, deeply and creatively involved in their children's lives and perceptions, and both generous and appropriate in their self-sacrifice. Within this group there is some range of interpersonal skill or observational finesse, but if we can distinguish for the moment between quality of performance and depth of intent, their intent is quite clear. Some parents, on the other hand, are clueless, careless, self-absorbed, and distant—except when they are crossed, at which point they become hostile and rigidly authoritarian. Laurence Steinberg estimates that this second group is about 30 percent of the parents of teenagers, and he correlates that style of parenting with significant trouble among the kids.[71]

In both groups there are households where both parents work full-time, and there are households where one parent or both parents significantly recalculated the number of hours devoted to employment. Like any observant parent, I have seen firsthand that the negligent will neglect their children in order to play tennis just as easily as they will to earn money; the engaged will be engaged despite the psychological and economic cost of nonconformity to a self-centered and consumerist culture.

Engagement, not employment, is the crucial issue. How much employment is consistent with how much engagement? There is no calculus that can tell us. Not everything that counts can be quantified in ways that generate reliable advice from total strangers. What I can say is this: the example parents set will always matter. The balance we establish between earning a living and having a life will always have an impact on our children. Once there is a roof overhead and food on the table, little in life matters more than whether we have time and energy to share our lives with our children, with our families, with our friends and neighbors. If the sum of market work and nonmarket work leaves us numb with exhaustion night after night, that will count in the long run. If we don't make the choices necessary to have a life worth living, we marginalize ourselves in the long term from the lives of everyone else—including our children.

To have a life worth living requires that we stand back from the complex, subterranean pressures exerted by how we think about gender roles, about family values, and about the marketplace. It requires that we recognize and face down the hidden persuaders and buried metaphors in Western thought that keep trying to divide our lives into unworkable oppositions and foolish contraries. Everyone who has written in detail about that process agrees that isolated individuals are nearly helpless. We are complexly social and deeply situated in our own times and places. Those connections can be for evil, or they can be for good, but they are inescapable. Economists talk about reference groups, sociologists talk about positive communities, ethicists talk about communities of practice, believers East and West talk about spiritual community. However you want to label the need, it arises from the fact that we are not isolated clumps of DNA blindly competing against other clumps of DNA. We are human, which is neither a fiction nor a birthright but an ethical achievement.[72]

How, then, shall we live? What does it mean in our cultural context to make and to sustain a commitment to *having a life?* Sustained intimate relationships—with babies or with friends and neighbors—demand time, energy, and at times sacrifice. Those who assert a need for and a human right to have such relationships run into the massive controversy that this chapter has delineated, even when the commitments in question are to infants less than a year old. What about the rest of us? The needs of babies can indeed serve as the "poster child" for needs that all of us have, all of our lives, for lively, mutual, caring relationships with one another.

That's a spiritual need, and behind it stands a complex religious reality. As theologian Christine Gudorf argues so gracefully, love is always intended to generate mutuality, because the capacity for a loving relationship is itself a good which we hope the beloved will in turn achieve. Love that does not ultimately intend mutuality—love that is literally self-sacrificing—is manipulative, pathological, and sterile. But there is an extraordinary religious mystery at the depths of our ability to give to others, deeply and profoundly to give to others, without giving our souls away in an evil, self-destructive parody of love. In Christian thought, that is the mystery to which the Resurrection attests.[73] The empirical sciences of neurobiology and developmental psychology cannot attest one way or another to the reality of such mysteries.

What's at stake in the child-care debates, then, is whether we need "hard evidence" to prove the depths of our need to love and to be loved, which is to say our abiding, inexplicable, profound need to be compassionate not merely competitive, to serve and not merely to succeed. Behind the question, "Do infants need to be cared for mostly by their own parents?" is a deeper question that cuts to the heart of contemporary culture: "Do any of us need a life?" As we have seen, census data clearly demonstrate that most parents just about turn handsprings to keep their youngest children mostly in their own care or the care of another family member, commonly a grandparent. But even in junior high, children still need a lot of attention. Gymnastics is not a good long-term model of family life.

Until such times as politicians and policy wonks devise a new and better world, we have to live in this one. If we can't escape the time bind with the skill of Houdini, if we can't balance and leap and twist through our overscheduled weeks with the skill of an Olympic gymnast, how are we to survive? That's the next and final issue I want to engage: ancient methods of morally and spiritually mature decision-making amidst heartbreakingly difficult situations.

Part Six

Survival and Integrity

Defining Our Choices, Living Our Lives

Prelude

As Henry David Thoreau famously lamented, "the mass of men lead lives of quiet desperation."[1] That was in 1854, but his claim still rings true: our ruthlessly competitive society is shaped far more by desperation than by compassion. But how, then, shall we live? That's the central question of Western ethics. How shall we live? Consumerism proclaims that more is never enough, but wisdom traditions East and West insist that the good life cannot be based upon getting and spending. Net worth does not take the measure of our lives, nor does the trajectory of our careers. What we want, what we need to escape the quiet desperation of a consumerist society, is to center our lives upon intelligent, compassionate responsibility for one another and for the common good. That's an extraordinarily difficult and complicated challenge. Nonetheless, despite our violent, troubled times and because of them, despite our secular society and because of it, many people are struggling with the classic moral question, *How shall I live?* That's not a question one can answer at the mall or in consultation with a stockbroker.

Our lives are shaped by how we cope with what I call "defining choices." When we face important decisions, the choices we make eventually shape our identity. We define choices that define us in turn, such that in deciding *what to do* at key points in our lives we are also deciding important aspects of *who to become.* That's a rudimentary sort of existentialism, I suppose, but as the years go by and I watch how my choices and my friends' choices spin out over time, I've become reasonably convinced that the process of defining choices serves also to define us in fairly significant ways. All of us are shaped by the morally important, morally significant choices we have made over the years. And we are fooling ourselves if we think that these are individual decisions, untouched by cultural context and the network of human relationships into which our lives are woven. Human beings are densely, biologically social creatures.

Defining choices appear whenever we face genuine options that will shape our lives at their deepest levels. Often, all too often, the most difficult, most important of these defining choices are between competing goods. Relatively few of us actively struggle to decide whether to earn our pay or to rob a bank, whether to negotiate with or to murder a difficult colleague. For most of us, the difficult choices, the life-defining choices, are the choices we have to make among competing aspects or visions of the good. When push comes to shove, which priorities fall toward the bottom of the list? When desires conflict, should choices be strictly rational and absolutely consistent, or should we agree with Ralph Waldo Emerson that "a foolish consistency is the hobgoblin of little minds"? When consequences are genuinely hard to foresee, should choices be safely conventional or should we take a chance? Where do we turn to find the strength and the wisdom that life demands? Whom do we trust, for whom do we care, for what will we sacrifice? Gradually, over time, what gives a life meaning is how we cope or what we choose at moments like these. There is no life without sacrifice; there is no sanity without functional levels of trust and its reciprocal, care. *Trust in what?* and *Care for whom?* are the only choices we have.

The choices we make about market work, nonmarket work, and human relationships are pre-eminent in this domain of morally defining choices, because the issues involved are complicated by our cultural moment and historical heritage. The interlocked ideologies of gender, marketplace, and family values depend upon a set of false presuppositions and unworkable claims about what it means *to be human* and about how we relate to one another as intensely, necessarily social creatures. Today as in Thoreau's day, too many of us lead lives of quiet desperation. Too many of us suffer what he described as "a stereotyped but unconscious despair," because over and over again we face false alternatives masquerading as the "reasonable" and "professional" realities to which any "mature" person is expected to adapt.

As I have tried to argue all along, the most dangerous of these false assumptions is the idea that compassion is for chumps and victims. The most dangerously false foundation of today's chronic, low-grade anxiety and depression is the feeling that people are inevitably and necessarily out for themselves, and hence the "mature" and "reasonable" life must be based upon chronic, low-grade hostility and abiding suspicion. As Jesus of Nazareth is said to have said, "Judge not, and you will not be judged; condemn not, and you will not be condemned; forgive, and you will be forgiven; give, and it will be given to you; good measure, pressed down, shaken together, running over, will be put into your lap. For the measure you give will be the measure you get back" (Luke 6:38). That's not an ontological claim that life is always fair. The Jews have never been known for that sort of foolish optimism. Jesus' assertion is both simple and sophisticated: grasping, self-centered hostility will never generate peace of mind. A life blessed by abundance and by love can only be grounded in the courage to love abundantly and to live generously.

The issue I want to examine in these concluding chapters is whether—and if so, how?—it is possible to make the morally responsible, spiritually liberating decisions necessary to manage work-life issues in our own lives. How do we—or can we?—make decisions in ways that will help us to center our lives upon compassionate wisdom, not the addictive get-and-spend competitions of consumerism?

15

The Question of Conscience

Each of us makes do with a given array of talents, experience, character traits, social obstacles, and so forth. Whatever the particular variables, each of us has a life within which some possibilities exist and some possibilities do not exist. Sometimes we can make fundamental changes to enlarge these options, but only within certain limits. Contrary to American mythology, for instance, we cannot "be anything we want when we grow up." According to tests I once took, for instance, I simply do not have what it takes for a career in entrepreneurial business. If I tried for the proverbial corner office, I'd more likely end up in a padded cell. On the other hand, the life that I do lead would undoubtedly drive some other people crazy. Within the real but limited array of choices open before each of us, we are morally obligated to choose as well or as wisely as we possibly can.

When I say that we are morally obligated to choose wisely and deliberately, I am assuming we do have some glimpse of what "well" or "wisely" actually mean in our own lives. I am assuming that there is such a thing as "conscience," and furthermore that we need both to refine this capacity and to heed its voice. That's a dicey claim these days. Radical skeptics—advocates of what James C. Edwards calls "normal nihilism"—would throw such claims out of court from the very beginning. In this chapter I want to acknowledge and to answer some of their objections. If it would never have crossed your mind to think that conscience is merely an oppressive illusion, feel free to skip ahead to page 225. Those who are interested, on the other hand, should be forewarned that I won't be tangling with the fabulous philosophical complexities of the issues. I want simply to explain the grounds on which an intelligent person might continue to believe (a) that there is a genuine or morally solid difference between right and wrong and (b) that we have ways to figure out what the difference is, even though none of these ways is absolute, hard, objective, infallible, and so forth.

Deconstructing Conscience

Let me begin by ceding an important point to the skeptics. Our individual understanding of the good to be sought and the evil to be avoided in our own lives is no simple matter. When we try to think about complicated moral obligations, when we try to cope with life's most important defining choices, we are almost always doing something fabulously more complex than simply applying a general rule (do not steal) to a particular circumstance ("Wow, what a nice PDA . . . !"). The more carefully we watch our own minds at work doing nuanced thinking about complicated problems, the easier it will be to recognize the ways in which our own sense of priorities and obligations has been built up over time. Several things contribute to this process. First, our own experience of life. Second, the networks of relationships within which we have lived. Third, the history behind those human networks—family history, regional history, national history, cultural history, and so forth, all of it merging and swirling, mostly at subconscious levels.

At the highest possible levels of abstraction, no doubt there are statements of moral norms to which the vast majority of people (and religious traditions) will consent: do not kill, do not steal, and so forth. To some limited extent, I agree that applying moral principles can be simply a problem in critical thinking: careful definitions, rigorous logic, thorough observation, and so forth. But when one good conflicts with another good, when one obligation conflicts with another obligation, our moral choices are far more complicated than looking up the answer in a rule book. In these complicated situations, our thinking is deeply influenced by the ethical traditions within which we have developed into morally mature adults. As social creatures, we have no choice but to "live in community" in this regard. The only choice we have is to select among communities that constitute themselves around different sets of priorities.

The default setting, especially in our fragmented, mobile society, is the community of consumers. At the everyday level of popular culture, we are all earners and spenders. All of us are barraged everywhere and at all times by advertising. Most of us live in cities, towns, and suburbs centered upon shopping malls and organized around commerce. If we yearn for something better than that in living our lives, then we inevitably turn to friends and to the settings where friendships develop. We turn to the wisdom we inherit from the past.

No wonder, then, that "spirituality" and "religion" are by a considerable measure the fastest-growing segment of the adult trade-book market. Traditional mainline Christian denominations are rapidly losing both active members and sociopolitical prestige, but "religion" far more widely defined is flourishing. As religion-sociologists Rodney Stark and Roger Finke demonstrate in some detail, there are no empirical grounds for the "secularization" thesis that faith is psychologically primitive and that religion, like the Marxist state, is historically doomed to wither away.[2] Some sense of "the holy" appears to be a steadfast part of human culture over time; and so, inevitably, it plays or can play some part in the most serious questions.

Nonetheless, contemporary nihilism—radical skepticism in any of its many forms—commonly describes religion and spirituality as necessarily false or at best meaningless. That's the first claim I want to examine. Richard Posner, for instance: "That the Nazis killed millions of defenseless citizens is a fact; its truth is independent of what anyone believes. That the Nazis' actions were morally wrong is a value judgment. It depends upon beliefs that cannot be proved true or false."[3] Posner's claim depends in turn upon his criteria for "proof," criteria that I find quite shallow.[4]

The wrongness of murder is not simply deduced from adequately established philosophical premises. It is immediately grounded in visceral and limbic recognitions. It is based upon a minimally sane capacity to see through another's eyes and to feel through another's skin. Only sociopaths are without this quality of fundamental empathy. The moral status of torture and of murder rests upon gratuitous human agony, not upon criteria for philosophical proof. Posner's disembodied position reflects a radical form of the familiar Western habit of privileging the abstract and intellectual over the visceral and embodied.

The general principle is this: radical skeptics contend that if the ends or purposes of life cannot be rigorously defined and scientifically demonstrated, *then they don't exist.* Similarly, if the objective principles of morality cannot be rigorously defined and scientifically demonstrated, *then they don't exist either.* If we cannot rigorously, rationally, objectively define the good and deduce from it the objective ends or logical purposes our lives should serve, then life has neither meaning nor purpose. The inner experiences we attribute to conscience are then (supposedly) an illusion. Such nihilist arguments derive from the claim that a God whose existence cannot be logically or scientifically demonstrated must perforce be an illusion.

At worst, such thinkers appear to argue that they can absolutely and unequivocally prove that there is no such thing as absolute, unequivocal proof. But if all truth claims are nothing more than social constructs, then we have to consider the possibility that "all truth claims are nothing more than social constructs" is itself a social construct. Other people, differently situated, might still continue to think that there actually is a difference between right and wrong.

At best, however, these radical claims are merely old wisdom in a new guise: as the ancient Greeks understood full well, to be human is to be contingent, frail, and mortal. Totalitarianism of any kind is both false and dangerous; absolutist thinkers usually succumb to hubris, and sooner or later they blindly self-destruct. Although radical skepticism easily turns into a totalitarianism all its own, there are other ways in which its "deconstructive" strategies are righting a dangerous cultural imbalance, a hazardous tilt toward the hard, "male," rationalist, objective, quantifiable absolute. It is wise to be very skeptical about any kind of absolutist claim; where radical skeptics go wrong, it seems to me, is in carrying their skepticism too far. Skepticism itself can become an absolutist claim—and a particularly destructive one.

How does this relate to the question of whether "conscience" names something real? Christian theologians and nihilists alike agree that there can be no rigorously successful "proof of God." But nihilists then go on to claim that all we have left (to borrow some famous vocabulary from Nietzsche) are self-devaluing values asserted by our own strong will-to-power. Radical skepticism insists that our choices and our decisions are merely self-assertions. Our moral judgments have no objective validity. We cannot honestly say that something is good or true or beautiful—all we have is our own willingness to make assertions. What Christian traditions see as the ineluctable accountability and moral autonomy of conscience, radical skeptics see as the will-to-power, accountable to nothing.

But the will-to-power is not so much genuinely autonomous as massively, inhumanly isolated. The Nietzschean individual is besieged on all sides by others similarly asserting themselves—as if we are buyers and sellers of a free-market "morality," or as if we are like lions competing for a limited supply of wildebeests on the Serengeti. If the marketplace is the established church of our day, then normal nihilism and rational-actor theory are its orthodox theology, and radical skeptics function as its clergy.

I have three commonsense responses to this array of nihilistic claims. First, in moral questions the demand for rational proof is both naïve and literal-minded. The demand is literal-minded because the arts of living are differently based than the physics of objects in motion. There is more to morality than logic can encompass. The demand is naïve because spiritual enlightenment, broadly defined, cannot be forced upon someone by any variety of strong argument or conclusive evidence. As Voltaire quipped, "Doubt is not a pleasant condition, but certainty is an absurd one."[5] Despair over the absence of certainty is more absurd yet, and nihilism is the philosophical form of despair.

Second, I contend that commonplace radical skepticism is both psychologically and morally intolerable when we have to make decisions with serious, perhaps dire consequences in our own lives *no matter what*. We do not live in a world of infinite resources. Everyone understands that. We do not live in a world where we have infinite time or infinite opportunity to pursue all that we deem worthwhile. Everyone understands that as well, ever more clearly as decades tick by. In the world as it is, the meanings of our lives are determined not by the stuff that we own but by the sacrifices we are willing to make. When sacrifice and suffering are inescapable, mere "personal opinion" is an insufficient basis for decision making. We need—we inevitably seek—not only to be "personally authentic" but also to be morally right insofar as we can discern what is the right thing to do in our own situations. We want not only to survive the practical demands of life in our times but also to maintain our own personal integrity.

When good conflicts with good in some genuinely serious situation, then the insouciance of normal nihilism stands revealed not as philosophical sophistication but as the oblivion of the privileged whose resources shelter them from the hard edges of unforgiving reality and painful choices. To opt merely for the will-to-power—literally to deny the reality of anything that cannot be systematically, rationally demonstrated to our scholarly satisfaction—is to deny moral responsibility for the suffering we cause or fail to prevent in and through the choices that we make in our own real and individual lives. As Nietzsche himself said, "The weak and the failures shall perish: the first principle of *our* love of man. And they shall be given every possible assistance."[6] That's about as far from spiritually enlightened compassion as I can imagine.

My third response to radical skepticism is this: the claim that we cannot accurately distinguish between right and wrong flies in the face of ordinary social experience, where we do observe that people sometimes make stupid or evil decisions, and sometimes wise or courageous ones, *and in general we can indeed tell one from the other.* We do so immediately, viscerally, intuitively, pragmatically, on the basis of our social and spiritual formation, and not by rigorous deductions from remotely abstract first principles. Is it wrong for a priest to rape a six-year-old boy? Is it wrong for a CFO to restructure a corporation as a Ponzi scheme? Is lynching wrong? Burning crosses? The presence of difficult or ambiguous cases does not call into question our general ability to distinguish between good and evil. Despite the variability and fallibility of human judgment, the assumption that ordinary people can distinguish between right and wrong is the basis of American democracy and our entire system of law. To conclude that human judgment is worthless because it is fallible and subjective is to invite the most egregious evil and transparent irresponsibility. Our capacity to recognize the good is not context-free nor is it theoretically rigorous, but neither is it entirely an illusion. People who are radically without any sense of right and wrong are judged mentally ill and categorized as sociopaths.

Radical skeptics also make a couple of psychological or psychotherapeutic arguments against the idea of conscience, and I want to respond to these as well. They contend that "the good" is nothing more than systems devised by authorities to serve themselves. I would never deny that power corrupts, but I would just as confidently assert that experience teaches—and furthermore that through community, through tradition, and through sustained, ancient spiritual practices we can learn from the experiences of others. To refuse tradition across the board because some in the past were knaves is merely to make ourselves far more liable to the knaves around us now: those who refuse to study history are condemned to repeat it.

No doubt the most common deconstruction of conscience, however, is the therapeutic argument that guilt is a neurotic symptom. The potential for guilt to be neurotic is like the potential for power to corrupt: none but a fool would deny it. But we are selling ourselves short—we are failing in due regard of our own humanity—if we reduce the demands of conscience to nothing more than the unconscious internalizing of oppressive, exploitative social norms.[7] The deeper reaches of Christian teaching fully recognize that the malformed conscience will generate a scrupulous, self-punitive self-denial.[8] Contemporary theologians argue eloquently that exploitative authorities have too often tried to enhance their own power by demanding pathological self-sacrifice from the powerless.[9] Yet the inner voice which says "I ought to do thus" or "I ought not to do thus" can also be the voice of a good heart, the voice of a highly integrated self that recognizes both its moral freedom and its responsibility to seek the good and to avoid evil.

The question is discernment: How do we distinguish between the authentic voice of conscience and the neurotic voice of exploitative social systems?[10] But before we get to that question, I want to look a little more carefully at "conscience" as an idea.

Moral Norms and the Deliberate Life

None of us can escape moral responsibility for the specific choices that shape our lives. If the atrocities of the twentieth century taught us nothing else, they taught us that we cannot defend our decisions by saying either that we were only doing what we were told was right (or "professional" or "reasonable" or "realistic") or that we were only doing what everyone else was doing as well. After Auschwitz and all too many other horrors, we have lost whatever innocence might have excused "just going along." In *Moral Freedom,* Alan Wolfe thoroughly documents our reluctance to articulate critical judgment upon how other people lead their lives. Gertrude Himmelfarb, among others, reads that reluctance as a loss of moral standards, as a corrosive "demoralization" of society.[11] To some extent I suppose it is: Philip Rieff argues persuasively that moral constraints have largely lost credibility with the nation's intellectual and cultural elite.[12] But we misunderstand the reluctance that Wolfe documents unless we realize that it is also rooted in our common moral horror at what can go wrong when corrupt and authoritarian social norms overrule individual ethical discernment and the moral autonomy of genuine conscience. The Roman Catholic bishops in this country have demonstrated that hazard no less clearly than Enron, WorldCom, or Arthur Anderson.

In midcentury horror at abused authority—at both Stalin and Hitler—perhaps the culture rebounded into a diffidence about asserting moral norms in general. But no one can look at twentieth-century history or at contemporary affairs and then claim that moral norms don't exist or don't matter. If thoughtful people speak diffidently at times, that is because history convinces us that each person has to remain inescapably responsible for applying moral norms to his or her own situation. The conflict between the obviously good and the obviously evil is simple, at least in the abstract. But real life is never abstract and seldom simple, especially for those caught in the midst of it. And so, each person is accountable for figuring out what to do in life's usual predicament, which is one good conflicting with another. Each person is accountable for recognizing what is the greater good to be achieved, even at personal cost.

In that crucial endeavor we would be foolish to ignore the accumulated wealth of wisdom traditions, the eldest of which are deeply embodied within religious and philosophic traditions worldwide. As Linda Hogan explains so clearly, "[conscience is] the individual's personal and self-conscious integration of collective moral wisdom with her/his own learned insight."[13] But collective moral wisdom is inevitably lodged within fallible human organizations. The only defense against dysfunctional organizations or self-serving leaders is many ordinary people, each of whom is morally "awake" and deeply rooted in a tradition of wise thinking about the moral complexity of the good life. In what follows I will be exploring and explaining Christian traditions in some detail, because this is the only rich, ancient tradition in which I am literate—not literate in a merely cerebral sense, but the deeper literacy that comes from a lifetime of allegiance, engagement, and practice.

To face life's defining choices consciously, to make such choices courageously and honestly, is to live *deliberately* rather than passively. Thoreau's explanation of the term is a classic bit of the American literary heritage:

> I know of no more encouraging fact than the unquestionable ability of man to elevate his life by a conscious endeavor. It is something to be able to paint a particular picture, or to carve a statue, and so to make a few objects beautiful; but it is far more glorious to carve and paint the very atmosphere and medium through which we look, which morally we can do. To affect the quality of the day, that is the highest of arts. . . . I went to the woods because I wished to live deliberately, to front only the essential facts of life, and see if I could not learn what it had to teach, and not, when I came to die, discover that I had not lived. I did not wish to live what was not life, living is so dear; nor did I wish to practise resignation, unless it was quite necessary.[14]

Moving to someplace like Walden is not an option for most of us. Neither is telecommuting via wireless Internet from the Oregon wilderness. We have to lead deliberate lives right where we are.

But I don't think that matters. Having a life worth living is something anyone can do, anywhere at all: deliberation does not demand solitary retreat to the woods. One can endeavor to live wisely even here in the suburbs with a tan minivan, a mortgage payment, and people who count on us not to turn away when they turn to us for help.

My argument is this: To live a good life is to live in good conscience, which is to say we must lay claim to moral responsibility for our lives. We must accept the ways in which we are accountable to moral norms that are essentially independent of our own convenience, gratification, desires, fears, and vanities. At various points we have to look up from the mundane details of our own daily lives honestly to consider the consequences of our decisions, both large and small. As years go by, the thoughtful person does this spontaneously and repeatedly. We do so prospectively, retrospectively, and when like Dante we awaken in the middle of life, lost in the middle of dark trackless woods and besieged by radical individualism, consumerism, and ambition.

As we live alert to what threatens our physical survival, we must live alert to what threatens our personal integrity. We must live alert to the incessant cultural pressures implicitly discrediting the priorities, communities, and traditions that help us to identify and to sustain the deepest sources of compassion, integrity, and meaning. The good life necessarily involves an honest effort to seek the good and an honest effort to avoid evil—to whatever extent we can figure out exactly what that means in our own lives. To figure it out, we have to pay attention. In classic spiritual terms, we have to "awaken" and by diligent effort to stay awake. Thoreau again: "To be awake is to be alive. I have never yet met a man who was quite awake. How could I have looked him in the face?"[15]

If we do not endeavor to define our defining choices carefully, then we risk the fate that Thoreau feared: to discover, at the end of life, that we never actually lived. At the end of life, we may discover that we earned a living and spent it but never had for ourselves something whole and substantial that we could point to and say, *this has been my life.* What generates that fundamental sense of integrity, I contend, is how consciously and deliberately we have defined the major choices that shape our lives by shaping our most costly commitments to what we cherish most deeply. The growing popularity of biography and autobiography in the last two hundred years—and acutely so in recent decades—testifies eloquently to the psychological and moral reality of our desire to lead meaningful lives based upon crucially defining choices. One of the ways in which we develop and exercise that desire is by watching how other people's choices turn out—and how their decisions shape their sense of who they most truly are. Both fiction and biography serve that purpose. So do the narratives embedded within religious traditions.

As I see it, there are two major issues called to the fore by my claims about defining choices. First, What is conscience? Second, How do we go about making a conscientious effort to recognize and to follow the dictates of conscience? In the remainder of this chapter, I will very briefly review the classic Christian teachings on the nature of conscience. I will also sketch my own position, derived from the poet and theologian Samuel Taylor Coleridge, that conscience is among the richest and most important functions of the creative imagination. The next (and final) chapter will offer an account of discernment, which is the ancient moral art of decision making and problem solving. If we are to live deliberately, we must understand how to deliberate, how to define the choices that define our lives. That will not render us infallible or even happy, but it will certainly help to awaken us to the lives we are leading or trying to lead. And that's plenty.

The Moral Autonomy of Conscience: A Christian Account

According to classic Christian teaching, we have not only the capacity but also the moral obligation to recognize, to desire, and by our choices to seek the good. We are motivated just as deeply to avoid evil. As a result of these capacities and obligations, the conscience operates with moral autonomy. That is, to disobey one's own conscience is always wrong. To be human is to be fallible, of course, and so conscience may be mistaken. But that does not change our primary obligation to conduct our lives in accordance with the dictates of conscience. We must, therefore, extend the domain of conscientious behavior to include the quest for knowledge of what we should know in order to seek the good and to avoid evil: there is such a thing as morally culpable ignorance.

It is morally culpable ignorance, for instance, when executives choose not to know about the conditions of workers in factories in the Third World, or when politicians choose not to know about fund-raising activities that border upon extortion or influence peddling. Culpable ignorance happens closer to home as well, as when teachers ignore how students bait one another, or parents fail to keep track of their children, or neighbors and colleagues remain willfully oblivious of one another's needs. Among our central moral obligations is the obligation to pay attention, to stay awake, to notice what ought to be noticed, and to ask the questions that need to be asked.

Furthermore, claims about the autonomy of conscience cannot be collapsed into pathological individualism. The Christian individual remains deeply accountable to something outside the self—accountable to the common good and to God as both the origin and the culmination of all that is good. Like believers in many traditions, the Christian is also accountable to the community of all those who seek the good within the same framework—habitually offering and asking for accounts of the critical processes informing life's choices and decisions, and habitually engaging the shared tradition in all of its dimensions, including prayer, study, and worship. (Over time, of course, or repeatedly, this communal dimension of conscience has generated authoritarian claims that would collapse moral responsibility into nothing more than mindless obedience to duly consecrated religious authorities.[16] I'll get back to that in a minute.)

Within Christian tradition, some attribute this way of explaining moral responsibility to Augustine of Hippo (354–430 C.E.). More commonly, it is attributed to Thomas Aquinas (1225–1274). Under any circumstances, the roots of the idea extend all the way back to the epistles of Paul, and back beyond Paul to Hebrew scriptural teachings about living with a good heart or a clean heart.[17] Its foundation is not empirical social science concerning human behavior, nor philosophical demonstrations of how we attain the truth, but rather the primary religious claim that we are made in the image of God. In theological language, this claim is a "revealed truth." That is, it is not an observation, nor a theory, nor a human claim. It is a given. Such realities can only be perceived by those who undertake sustained and attentive spiritual practice. One can learn to see the spark of God in everyone, just as one might with practice learn to hear chord progressions in music, or to recognize the interplay of colors in a garden or a painting.

My father could do it, for instance, and he was not a book-reading man. I remember traipsing after him as he ran errands on Saturdays, at an age when I was about eye-level with countertops. I could not hear or did not think to listen to whatever verbal exchanges were taking place. But I remember noticing the change in the faces of all the store clerks, how their shoulders would relax, their eyes brighten, how they would smile—as if my father spread something warm around him everywhere he went. It was years before I understood. He looked people in the eye. He always said "please" and "thank you," "hello" and "good-bye"—and he always meant it. He never took anyone for granted, nor was anyone ever invisible.

The spark of the Sacred is not "in" us as a cup is in a cabinet, or a microchip in an answering machine. "Within" is a metaphor. What the metaphor emphasizes is that "something of the Holy" is deeply seated within us, or perhaps that this spark of the Holy is integral to our sense of self at its deepest, most important levels. By this "light," and despite the tremendous complexities of our lives, we can recognize the good that is available within our own situations. Through this spark of the Holy within us, we are reliably moved to seek that good even though we remain existentially free to resist and to choose evil instead.

This recognition or desire is understood as a profound religious mystery—something inescapably true and yet beyond mere secular rationalist demonstration. No matter how often we choose evil, short of brain damage our capacity to see and to choose the good is never entirely or permanently extinguished because we are durably created in the image of God, who is love.[18] In theological shorthand, this capacity is sustained by divine grace, not by willpower and not by analytical intelligence. The drive for the good, like the Holy within us, is a given. It is a gift—and we all get it. It comes with being human. (It may come with being other kinds of creatures as well.) This sturdy optimism about human nature is the foundation of Aquinas's famous dictum that to act against conscience is always wrong.[19]

Let me repeat: this optimism is based neither in social science nor in rationalist philosophy. Nor is it a "proof of God." It is a consequence of God, whose reality cannot be trapped within the nets of human intellect and then analytically displayed. This vision of God and of what it means *to be human* can be illumined—not demonstrated—only through sustained, carefully guided spiritual practice solidly situated within religious tradition. The vision itself is not a propositional claim but a way of life.

By analogy, one can only come to know what it is to dance by learning to dance. Dance critics and dance theorists have their place in the larger scheme of things, but the essence of dance is established by dancing, not by arguments about dance. Similarly, the "validity" or "value" of dance is established by dancing and not by arguments about dance. So too, the truth about God depends upon the religious experience of millions of people over thousands of years, not the debates of theologians. Theologians, like dance critics, certainly have their place in the larger scheme of things. But faith—the human experience of the Holy One—remains a way of life, not a set of propositions to which one might agree or refuse to agree. Coleridge's explanation of this point is justly famous: ". . . religion, as both the cornerstone and the keystone of morality, must have a *moral* origin; so far at least, that the evidence of its doctrines could not, like the truths of abstract science, be wholly independent of the will. It were therefore to be expected, that its *fundamental* truth would be such as MIGHT be denied. . . ."[20] As Stanley Hauerwas bluntly asserts, "if you could 'prove' the existence of God, if you had evidence that something like a god must of necessity exist, then you would have evidence that the God that the Jews and Christians worship does not exist."[21]

Needless to say, the morally autonomous individual is plainly a threat to the absolute authority of the public institutions of both church and state. There have always been ferocious theological arguments within Christian tradition about the autonomy of conscience (and about the appropriate theoretical grounds and boundaries of that autonomy). And there have always been religious leaders claiming one variety or another of absolute authority and complete practical control. What we see today, in many ways, is pathological individualism facing up to pathological authority. Isolated individuals, refusing to listen to anyone, confront totalitarian religiosity that also refuses to listen to anyone. But if we set aside both, we can perhaps see far enough back into the tradition to recognize these older, richer, more subtle resources.

Conscience, Faith, and Imagination

How does conscience help us with the question, *How shall I live?* Conscience is, among other things, a kind of faith in ourselves as good people seeking the good. Both faith and conscience are among the fundamental activities of human imagination in its ordinary, universal operation within the human soul. (Although highly creative activity of any kind—in the arts or elsewhere—demands a more developed power of imagination and a more conscious ability to engage that power, there is a fundamental creative and imaginative capacity in all of us. It's a human universal.[22]) Imagination funds or supports the operations of conscience because imagination synthesizes thinking and feeling. Imagination both perceives and generates the essential unity of consciousness that chronic Western dualism keeps splitting into antagonistic pairs. The rational and the emotional, the self-preserving and the self-sacrificing, the competent, well-bounded self and the self intimately related to others—none of these are truly opposed within the sane, mature, well-developed adult. But we certainly get trapped into thinking that they are, because our ordinary habits of problem solving and critical thinking are so powerfully influenced by false oppositions and dualist habits that comprise our Western cultural heritage.

More broadly yet, imagination synthesizes universals and particulars. As it does so, or when it does so, imagination both perceives and creates all kinds of patterns or relationships, including relationships among ideas and relationships among people. As a result, imagination is the premier human capacity not only to cope with paradox but also to live with (and within) the highest levels of spiritual mystery. Some of these mysteries underlie the operation of conscience. For instance, how can we connect universal truths—"love your neighbor as yourself"—with the particular details and conflicts of our own lives? More complexly yet, how can we look at our own particular situations and see within them the universal issues that spiritual writers describe? How can we look at our lives and see what's at stake in the choices we make? How can we be who we most truly are, how can we keep faith with the image of God within us, and yet still remain within committed relationships that sometimes demand self-sacrifice?[23]

When we see and care about the good at stake in some particular choice in our own lives, we are witness to our own imaginative capacity manifest as conscience—as the quest for the good. If we see conscience in this way—as essentially a creative activity—then we can also see that conscience cannot be collapsed either into radical obedience to authority or into nothing more than the isolated, nihilist pursuit of immediate personal desire. Authoritarianism versus egotism is the kind of mindless, destructive, depressing opposition that imagination overcomes.

Imagination also mediates between the rational and the intuitive. Guy Claxson calls these opposites Hare Brain and Tortoise Mind, and those are very handy metaphors for fundamental operations of our minds. Hare Brain works fast, on the whole. It is conscious, deliberate, logical problem-solving. Tortoise Mind is slower: it is indirect, intuitive, visceral, unconscious and subconscious insight. Claxson offers an entertaining array of empiricist psychological studies demonstrating that we know much more than we are conscious of knowing. He argues persuasively that we make far better decisions when we give ourselves time to collect and to process all this subterranean information and then to synthesize it with Hare Brained logic. We need to stop and mull awhile if we are to allow imagination to do this kind of work.

Claxson is particularly interested in a variety of densely creative thinking that we commonly call "wisdom." My point is that what makes Hare Brain and Tortoise Mind work together inside our heads is the power traditionally called "imagination." In the following account, notice all the opposites that have to be balanced and the patterns that have to be recognized if we are to make wise decisions about our own lives.

> Wisdom has been defined as "good judgment in hard cases." Hard cases are complex and ambiguous situations in which conventional or egocentric thinking only results in heightened polarisation, antagonism, and impasse. In hard cases personal values may conflict: [for instance] . . . to choose adventure is to jeopardise security. . . . Hard cases are those where important decisions have to be made on the basis of insufficient data; where what is relevant and what is irrelevant are not clearly demarcated; where meanings and interpretations of actions and motives are unclear and conjectural; where small details may contain vital clues; where the costs and benefits, the long-term consequences, may be difficult to discern; where many variables interact in intricate ways. The conditions in which wisdom is needed, in other words, are precisely those in which the slow ways of knowing come into their own. To be wise is to possess a broad and well-developed repertoire of ways of knowing, and to be able to deploy them appropriately. To be able to think clearly and logically is a constituent of wisdom, but it is not enough on its own. One needs to be able to soak up experience of complex domains—such as human relationships—through one's pores, and to extract the subtle, contingent patterns that are within it. And to do that one needs to be able to attend to a whole range of situ-

> ations patiently and without comprehension; to resist the temptation to foreclose on what experience may have to teach.[24]

Work-life problems constitute an array of "hard situations" from beginning to end. Logic alone, for instance, cannot get anyone past the mere probabilities of epidemiology that animate the child-care debates. Logic alone cannot get us past the economic forecasts influencing our employment prospects, or the statistics on divorce and poverty rates for households headed by single mothers. When we add uncertainties to uncertainties, uncontrolled variables to other uncontrolled variables, then logic collapses, public discussion devolves into bitter controversy, and parents feel haunted no matter what they do. So does everyone with a life to live, with people to love, with needs and with responsibilities that go beyond the survival needs met by earning a living. Ultimately, then, Aristotle is probably right: wisdom is good judgment not only in hard cases but in any situation where we face reasonable alternatives.

Fortunately, logic is not our only intellectual resource, although in our day it may be the only resource that most people are trained to use in any rigorous way. That is why so many people are turning to spiritual practices of many kinds, to spiritual practices that seek to develop far more flexible and powerful tools than rationality per se. Pre-eminent among them, although seldom named as such, are the fundamental moral operations of imagination. The liturgies, rituals, music, visual arts, symbolic writings, and ancient mind-body practices of religion all serve to strengthen and to develop the human creative and perceptive ability that I am calling imagination.

In its capacity to synthesize hard facts or universal principles with the depths of our elusive intuitive abilities and insights, imagination finds the patterns and the meanings which necessarily underlie a decision made in good conscience. The operations of conscience generate self-authenticating, deeply persuasive outcomes, just as the best creative work also persuades us. There is a moment of "aha," and such insight, once attained, feels self-evident. That feeling is something more than mere confidence or relief. Both in Christian accounts of conscience and in poetic accounts of imagination, the emotional consequences of imagination are technically called "joy."

Such joy is not merely "happiness" or "satisfaction," much less "self-realization." "Joy" is the traditional name of what we are feeling when we encounter the consistency between our inner lives and our outer lives. It is the human response to the momentary glimpse of the fundamental harmony between self and universe. Once in a while, just once in a while, for a brief out-of-focus moment, the world can feel beautiful and meaningful and beneficent. For a moment we find ourselves at peace with ourselves, with all of humanity, and with everything that is real.

Some people explain away such moments as nothing more than a brief oversupply of brain endorphins or the brief harmonic firing of brain cells. But such moments are more commonly recognized as religious experiences, experiences which Coleridge—a major theologian and a major poet as well—unequivocally attributes to imagination. Such joy arises from the overcoming of all that fractures us into opposition—into opposition with ourselves, into opposition with one another, or into alienation from the Holy. Holiness, in this sense, is also wholeness—the greatest possible integration of the complexities and the depths within each of us.

Joy (in this sense) is what we are after as we make the defining choices that life requires of us. Such joy—what the Gospel of John calls "the peace that passes human understanding"—is the activity of imagination made manifest in decision-making as the work of conscience. Imagination reconciles the Hare Brain supply of collective moral insight with the Tortoise Mind array of deeply complex personal experience and insight. When it works, and it certainly does work, we may not be happy. Our problems will not be solved, nor our bills paid, nor our conflicting obligations reduced to a simple, limited, one-dimensional list of things to do. But we will have begun to live deliberately; we will have stopped living lives of quiet desperation and unconscious despair.

There's a poem in the Book of Isaiah that I've always loved (chapter 55). It seems to me to describe what I'm after in trying to get past zero-sum competitiveness and preoccupation with how much money I'm earning or what sort of status I have in the eyes of everyone else. In this poem, God is speaking, calling us away from the crazy pressures of a consumerist culture:

> Ho, every one who thirsts, come to the waters;
> and he who has no money, come, buy and eat!
> Come, buy wine and milk without money and without price.
> Why do you spend your money for that which is not bread,
> and your labor for that which does not satisfy?
> Hearken diligently unto me, and eat what is good,
> and delight yourselves in fatness.
> Incline your ear, and come to me;
> hear, that your soul may live . . .
> For my thoughts are not your thoughts,
> neither are your ways my ways, says the Lord.
> For as the heavens are higher than the earth,
> so are my ways higher than your ways
> and my thoughts than your thoughts. . . .

For you shall go out in joy,
  and be led forth in peace;
the mountains and the hills before you shall break into singing
  and all the trees of the field shall clap their hands.
Instead of the thorn shall come up the cypress;
  instead of the brier shall come up the myrtle[.]

The key line in this poem is "Hearken diligently to me, and eat what is good." At that point in the poem, we can see that the images of thirst and hunger, the images of eating and drinking, are all metaphors for spiritual yearning. Consumerism is nothing new, after all. Excessive accumulation of stuff, excessive desire for status, excessive indulgence of egotistical and sensual appetites—these are ancient temptations. That's why "temperance" is one of the classic moral virtues (the others are justice, fortitude, and prudence). What we are promised—what good conscience offers—is the chance to "go out in joy and be led forth in peace." We can watch the thorns of our lives morph into blossoming shrubs.

This is visionary poetry, of course; this is not "what happens." This is what it feels like. We are standing here in the landscape of the psyche, not in our own backyards—which will continue to produce their annual crop of dandelions, crabgrass, and mosquitoes. But if we work toward living in good conscience, then we are indeed laboring for that which satisfies. Or that's the teaching. It's not a counsel for cowards; but as Thoreau argues, our lives are at stake one way or another.

Conscience is also made manifest in our drive to account for ourselves to ourselves and thence to others. The integrity of these narratives—their moral coherence and completeness—reveals the depth or extent of our own moral integrity. Conscience is evident in the personal integrity with which we choose to make the choices we make or we want to do what we want to do. We come upon our own wholeheartedness in the intellectually honest, heartfelt conviction that *this is the good* at least as far as we can see. In short, if we are to face and morally to survive the wrenching conflict between earning a living and having a life in our day, we need to make our most defining choices *in good conscience.*

But please keep in mind that to decide *in good conscience* is not necessarily to decide for all time. Good conscience is not an infallible form of knowledge. We may be wrong, and if we discover that's the case, then in continued good conscience we can change course. Or even if we were right to begin with, the particular situation that we face can change. Once again, in continued good conscience, we can change course. As Rosemary Radford Reuther explains, ". . . freedom of conscience, thought, and speech is not a rejection of the existence of truth, but it assumes that truth cannot be finally and fully known. It can only be approximated. The way to best approximate truth is to allow all voices to be heard."[25] The discernment process encourages us to hear all the many voices in our own heads—voices of personal experience, of rational analysis, of cultural history and social context—and to remain attentive to this inner debate.

When we act or decide carefully and in good conscience, we can be confident and at peace without becoming trapped in defensiveness, rigidity, and the insecure refusal to consider new evidence as it appears. All we have to do is to surrender the grandiose, easily deconstructed claim that we possess an absolute, timeless, unchanging truth as opposed to our own honest insight into what appears to be the right choice, right here, right now, in our own lives, as far as we can see and with the best help we can find.

No matter what, alas, we are not in complete control of outcomes, and so we cannot claim entire responsibility for outcomes, both good and bad. We are nonetheless responsible for a thoroughgoing effort to act in accord with the good as we see it—and to make a solid, responsible effort to see that good as clearly as we are humanly able. The Christian name for that thoroughgoing effort is "discernment." That's what I want to explore next.

16

The Arts of Moral Discernment

Discernment is the traditional name for the complicated process of making choices or decisions based upon the moral imperatives of one's own conscience in reasonable dialogue with both spiritual guides and subject-matter experts. Discernment differs from ordinary decision making in two ways. First, discernment is attuned to the morally good rather than simply to the expedient, the profitable, or the solidly conventional. We are trying to figure out what course of action is morally best, not what's easiest, most profitable, or least likely to get people talking about us critically.

Second—and far more subtle—we are working under the assumption that "the good" is not something we can recognize or achieve simply through careful logic. There is a huge modernist tradition, most famously argued by Immanuel Kant (1724–1804), claiming that "the good" is a rational norm universally available to anyone who looks for it carefully. That reduces conscience to logical problem-solving. Scholars of various sorts have demonstrated that Kant's position doesn't hold water: there's no one self-evident premise from which we can deduce our obligations in a tidy linear way.

But in the great simmering stew that is culture, ideas don't go away just because they have been formally disproved. It's easy to think that morality is mostly a matter of logic, because logic certainly does have a big role to play. Discernment, as a process and a tradition, takes logic into account quite rigorously, but just as rigorously it sets us up to use our other mental faculties as well.

Let's begin with an overview of the discernment process.

Ignatian Discernment: An Overview

The most influential formulation of how discernment works is by Ignatius of Loyola (1491–1556). Unlike his contemporary John Calvin, but like the medieval scholastic theologian Thomas Aquinas, Ignatius had enormous confidence in our ability to see and actively to seek the good. Ignatius also understood that accurate discernment depends upon our ability to cope wisely with the psychological and cultural pressures we face. His advice clearly reveals how very complicated it is, in real terms, to seek the good in our own lives.

Ignatius outlines a seven-step process of considerable elegance: I suspect that self-help books on making decisions are still simply rearranging and relabeling his process. Despite superficial or procedural similarities, however, the difference between discernment and secular decision-making is enormous. The difference, as we shall see, is that the discernment process explicitly includes or involves mindful meditation and attentive awareness to one's own relationship to God.

In brief, the process of Ignatian discernment laid out in his *Spiritual Exercises* goes like this.[26] In step one, the person prays for or centers consciousness around disinterestedness or nonattachment: we are to seek the good—not simply what at first we may think we want, what would be least controversial, most convenient, or whatever. In step two, we have to collect and evaluate for ourselves all information we can think of that is relevant to the situation at hand. Some of that is apt to be facts and figures of a plainly quantitative kind. What does something cost, what does a job pay, or what's the cost of living in that town? But in complicated situations, there's more to cope with than such facts. There is also the context that makes a given fact important, whether objectively important or simply important to us personally.

My accounts of the interlocked ideologies of gender, "private" life or "family values," and the marketplace are among the resources that fit in here. To what extent, if any, do these three historical or cultural pressures impinge upon your own thinking? Do any facts or issues show up that resonate to these traditions? These three ideologies—and others as well—help to shape the cultural context within which we live; cultural context in turn powerfully shapes how people think and how people behave.

Nonetheless, for any given individual that comes down to a specific set of pressure points, some of them far more sensitive than others. And so, this step in the discernment process asks both about cultural pressures and about one's own sensitivities to them. For instance, I grew up in a family with many strong women, in a neighborhood richly supplied with competent, confident women of acknowledged local authority. I was sent to a girls' high school that had only one man on the faculty—a part-time dance teacher. The school took an unequivocally aggressive stance advocating public leadership and professional achievement for all of us.

When I was fourteen, two young nuns argued ferociously both with me and with one another about whether I should be a biologist or a literary critic. Maybe one day I would marry—no one spoke of that one way or another—but nothing could mitigate my moral responsibility before God for the talents given me. "Of those to whom much is given," the much-feared principal kept reminding me, "much is demanded." It was many years before I recognized that she was adapting a line from Scripture to be gender-neutral. I was a skinny, shy, bookish kid: these nuns terrified me. And yet they also told me, in effect, that I had talents that mattered.

Such personal cultural contexts, so early established, easily outweighed the more distant heritage of Western misogyny. Arguments about the inherent superiority of the "masculine" weighed no more heavily upon me than equally ancient arguments that the earth is flat and the stars orbit around it. I certainly ran into my share of misogynists later on, of course. But the strong women of my childhood also equipped me to recognize misogynists as primitives, as barbarians, as Flatlanders clinging to an ancient but foolish misunderstanding.

I have a far more complicated response, however, to the notion that professional success somehow testifies to my inherent moral worth—that "success" is morally demanded of me. At least for me, the work-around for that particular hot button is quite densely theological. The terrifying principal, for instance, was quoting Scripture. The demands were presented to me as God's demands, which left open the possibility of asking myself whether hotshot success is God's demand or rather the demand of my own sturdy ego or the popular culture surrounding me.

All such things will sort out differently for different people, but step two of the discernment process is sorting it out. All of us have to figure out the hot buttons and the work-arounds generated by our own personal experience. That usually means applying an adult's judgment to childhood memories and to naïvely unexamined assumptions.

Step three is double-checking step two by talking to people. We need to verify our evaluations of the facts with folks who have a trustworthy knowledge of our own characters, personal history, general situation, and so forth. People who know us may see our vulnerabilities far more clearly than we do ourselves. When I have a decision to make, I have lunch with shrewd and kindly friends who will listen objectively, see clearly into my own blind spots, and cheerfully point out the moments when someone or some situation has its thumb on my hot buttons. Like anyone else, I suppose, I have some friends who are particularly adept at this. In Irish spiritual tradition, they are called *anam cara*—soul friends. We all need them. And we all need to listen to them, especially when we don't want to. Such conversations are step three in the discernment process.

Step four is prayer. In and around all this research and consultation, we should take time to pray over each "fact" as it is identified, considered, and discussed with others. Dennis Billy and James Keating do a very nice job of explaining the mutuality of prayer and good conscience underlying this advice. They begin by quoting *The Philokalia,* an ancient spiritual resource from the Eastern Orthodox tradition:

> "A good conscience is found through prayer, and pure prayer through conscience. Each by nature needs the other." This observation, from *The Philokalia,* an anthology of spiritual texts from Eastern Orthodoxy, reminds us of the close, reciprocal relationship that spirituality and morality can share in the daily lives of believing Christians. Holiness and goodness are not unrelated spheres of human experience, but two sides of the same existential coin. Prayer helps conscience by opening it up to the divine and enabling it to discern more clearly the good to be done and the evil to be avoided in the daily circumstances of life. Conscience, in turn, helps prayer by providing the moral starting point from which a person sets out . . .[27]

When we "pray about" or "pray over" some fact relevant to the decision we are making, we are not only "asking" conscience to consider its significance but also opening conscience itself to a clearer, more intelligent, more nuanced, spiritually more sophisticated perception than we might have had heretofore. As Billy and Keating contend, goodness and holiness are reciprocal; and as Guy Claxson argues on other grounds, wisdom takes time. The best thinking—and praying—is done at Tortoise Mind speed.

Let me explain how such prayer works, or how it might be imagined, or at least what it feels like in my own experience. Each fact, each bit of advice, is brought into the presence of God and held there in the sustained, silent, attentive, nonpossessive openness that is common to meditation practice across many traditions. I think of it this way: Buddhist teachings elegantly describe sitting on the banks of the stream of consciousness, watching what flows past but without chasing any particular thought. When I am praying about or meditating upon some particular element in a decision I am trying to make, it feels to me as if that fact or element is "sitting beside me" on the banks of the stream of consciousness and in the presence of God. I am not staring at the fact; I'm not trying to disassemble its parts. I am simply aware of the fact, aware of the stream of consciousness flowing past, aware of the unseen presence of God, and aware of my own in-breath and out-breath. I am mindful of all of it and fixated upon none of it.

Of course, what "comes to mind" in such situations will reflect the impossibly complex array of neural networks and unconscious memories that comprise my experience over a lifetime. It will also reflect the depths of my own spiritual identity or character and all the ways in which that identity or character has developed within a particular historical situation—in my case, a fiesty, urban, Midwest, working-class Irish Catholicism layered on top of traditional Celtic spirituality that was complemented in the 1960s and early 1970s by theological education from radical nuns and liberal Jesuits. Arching over all of that is the English literary tradition. The voices are many, and that is all to the good. The dangerous voices are those we don't stop to hear. I sit breathing in, breathing out, letting tidbits of this treasure bob to the surface and float past.

But what surfaces is not to be lost or ignored altogether. In the Ignatian (and Christian) tradition of prayerful meditation, I am to note any patterns or repetitions in what flows past, and to reflect further on that another time—commonly after yet more conversation with an *anam cara* or other good friend. After Freud, of course, we all understand what's involved in doing so. Spiritual directors, like their heirs the psychotherapists, can be very helpful in recognizing these patterns, interpreting them shrewdly, or situating them within the inherited wisdom of the tradition. Some traditions of spiritual direction assign passages from various sacred writings as "streamside companions" for further prayerful meditation upon the issues which slowly emerge within the stream of consciousness. Guides to spiritual practice in the Christian tradition sometimes include thematically organized lists of passages one might use in this way. In the same way, good friends sometimes suggest books we should read or movies we should see: these too "take a turn" sitting beside us on the banks of the stream of consciousness.

Ignatian discernment acknowledges the ways in which "facts" are not always or not exclusively as "objective" or as beyond question as they may have seemed at first. The meaning of a fact or an argument is not complete until its bearing upon one's own situation has been prayerfully discerned in this way. Above all, discernment helps to protect us from selling ourselves short. We are selling ourselves short if we ignore our own responsibilities for our lives and our choices by deferring heedlessly to pop culture, contemporary social norms, or even bullies in our own life (past or present). Discernment helps us to remain alert to anything that might pressure us to act in opposition to our own good conscience.

As the discernment process develops, these four steps—a prayerful, centering resolve to maintain nonattachment, getting the facts, consulting about them, praying over them—are repeated as often as necessary. Facts have a way of leading to other facts; conversations sometimes lead to new facts; prayer often triggers the search for other facts or the need for further conversation. It all circles around until new things stop showing up. Then one begins to move to closure. Step five can be any of a variety of techniques for getting closure. For instance, a list might be made of reasons for and against every reasonable option. Making a list is one of several ways that Ignatius suggests may help us to elicit a conclusion from the process to this point. Other suggestions include imagining what the consequences might feel like ten or twenty or fifty years down the road. (Once again, it's clear that the discernment tradition continues to fund our ordinary, secular, self-help decision-making advice, which offers any number of such exercises.) The point of closure exercises is (a) to help the person to make a tentative decision about what action to take and (b) to integrate insofar as possible the rational and the intuitive or prayerful take upon all the factual dimensions of the decision at hand.

In Christian theological terms, these closure exercises are also an effort to find or to see God incarnate within the mundane details of our own predicaments and to feel God's love drawing us more in one direction than another—to feel the intimations of "joy."

Step six is marvelously creative—even a bit quirky. We should, for a set period of time, live with the possibility of acting upon one of the discarded or least-favorite options. Imagine—seriously picture yourself—doing what you think you really do *not* want to do. In a mundane but regular way, pay careful attention to the feelings that surface. This step clearly invites the recognition that what we have discarded is what, in fact, we most deeply desire to do. It is a guard against impulsive decisions and what real estate agents call "buyer's remorse." It is a recognition that Hare Brain and Tortoise Mind sometimes sharply differ, and when that happens Hare Brain is apt to triumph.

This step in the process also reflects the Christian self-understanding that Christianity is profoundly countercultural. We need time and spiritual support if we are to make decisions that are both personally authentic and yet contrary to "what people expect." Because our culture is once again amidst stunningly rapid social change—as it was in Ignatius's time, shortly after the invention of the printing press—we are once again quite aware of how easily our lives are dictated by social norms rather than by our deepest, highest self reflecting upon its own immediate context. When the times are changing so swiftly, this step in the process of discernment is likely to be quite fruitful.

Step seven is the mirror image of step six: we should, for the same set period of time, live with the possibility of doing what we want to do. Then see how this feels. "I want a day job!" I've often thought. "I want to get up, get dressed, and get out of the house like everybody else does. I want to leave the house when I go to work, and I do *not* want to work alone! I want a paycheck once a month, month after month!" But if I force myself to spend a few days resolutely imagining what a day job would feel like, I inevitably settle back into being a writer. I no longer remember who taught me to do this or where—but I had a long and rich education in Catholic schools amidst all the ferment of Vatican II. Suffice it to say that I was both amused and startled to discover Ignatius's account of the technique.

Imagining ourselves into a decision is powerful stuff because it can generate such confident resolve. Calm and confident resolve is potentially quite subversive. It's also deeply satisfying, especially when life proves difficult and unexpected, as life so often does. Careful discernment is insurance against the ordinary temptation to see only what we want to see about a given situation.

Steps six and seven together *should* elicit both confident resolve and a sort of psychological relief. There should be some glimpse of the joy involved in doing and being what is deeply and personally right. If not, the whole process should be repeated. Resolve again to practice nonattachment. Recollect and reconsider every fact, consult with both subject-matter experts and personal friends, pray over each aspect of the decision in turn, make lists, etc. Under any circumstances, enduring and important decisions should not be made in haste, nor under the pressure of life changes, emergencies, grief, and so forth.

It certainly would be nice if life always allowed that! Decisions have to be made these days a little faster than they did in the sixteenth century or in Greek antiquity, where the Western tradition of spiritual exercises ultimately originated.[28] Nonetheless, stalling even for a day or two—at least "sleeping on it"—can be very wise. And when the issue is initiating a change rather than responding to a change, often one does have time for a careful discernment.

Neuroscience and Discernment

In its slow, deliberate pace and in its highly intentional waiting for whole-soul certainty, the classical discernment process is obviously replete with opportunities for Tortoise Mind thinking. Neurologist Antonio Damasio might more literally describe discernment as the gathering into conscious awareness of widely scattered but profoundly important emotional and existential associations based upon the reactivation over time of neuronal networks "keyed" to the major issues involved. Stanley Greenspan argues even more strongly than either Claxson or Damasio that emotions operate essentially as a sense organ, a level of perception upon which critical intelligence is radically dependent—and a level of perception to which the discernment process directs particular attention. His evidence directly supports the idea that conscience—and, with conscience, the moral imagination—transcends all the ways in which the modern self is divided against itself. His account also explains in more detail what we are actually doing as we attempt to decide something in good conscience. What exactly is this wholehearted confidence or joy that we are seeking?

In *The Growth of the Mind and the Endangered Origins of Intelligence,* Greenspan explains that from the first days of life, every sensation has an affective correlate: whatever we are feeling physically, we are also feeling emotionally.[29] As a result of the ways in which physical sensations are always paired with emotional responses (consciously or not, of course), everything we experience or learn is "filed away" under a cross-referenced system of sensory data and affective data. As it happens, however, the affective data provides the key to retrieving relevant information in the future, because the affective "data-search" capacity is fabulously faster. It is also more subtle or more nuanced than objective sensory memory and formal intellectual reconstruction. He explains:

> . . . any sort of creative thought or problem solving follows an emotional pathway. An individual must first decide which of the myriad physical and emotional sensations that constantly bombard each of us or the innumerable ideas stored in our minds are relevant to the issue at hand. The only way a person can make this decision—the only way he can determine which ideas and features to emphasize and which to ignore—is to consult his own catalogue of physical and emotional experience. The emotions that organize it create categories from which to select[,] from the compiled memories and intuitions[,] the information that bears on a given issue.[30]

One of the principal features of schizophrenia, for instance, is a biological inability to focus attention in this very fundamental way upon the pertinent aspects of a given situation. The selective or retrieval operations of emotional and physical feeling generate not only normal consciousness (of the sort that schizophrenics lack), but also the high-level pattern-finding that is or that generates both deeply imaginative critical thinking and creativity of all sorts.

Greenspan contends that our ability to manage high-level abstract concepts—"justice," for instance—depends upon our ability to synthesize the emotions held in common by a vast array of ordinary physical and social experiences. Emotions function in this way because emotions exist or operate across a wide and subtle range. Consider, for instance, the ways in which anger, frustration, and jealousy can variously combine or fade across a continuum into one another.

Antonio Damasio in effect supports that claim in *Descartes' Error*, where he describes a very bright, highly functioning professional who suffered damage to his frontal lobes as the result of a tumor. The man's intelligence was perfectly intact, but he seemed without visceral emotional responses to the world around him. He was also without conscious emotional responses even to the tragedies of his own life. As a result of this loss of emotional life, he was unable to deploy his intelligence in any practical way. He was unable to guide his choices by the "survival value" of the options before him—and thus he could not hold a job, manage his own personal and financial affairs, or live independently. Nonetheless, he continued to score at very high levels on all the pen-and-paper ordinary neurological assays of intelligence. Those tests evaluate one's ability to think, not to make and implement good decisions or actually solve problems in life. Only life tests living skills, and this man's life had become a hopeless shambles.[31]

The "endangered origins of intelligence" about which Greenspan principally argues is the growing impersonality of contemporary culture. Cognitive development not only in children but also among adults, all through life, depends upon the warm interpersonal interactions that feed our souls. Without a steady diet of compassion, it seems, without compassion offered and compassion received, critical intelligence itself fails to develop and to sustain its most sophisticated skills. Child care is only one example of how our culture has become increasingly impersonal. We are also far more mobile, which is to say we don't know our neighbors nor do we have deep, nourishing roots in our own communities. We deal with ATM machines, not bank clerks; we buy on the Web, not in stores; even in stores or banks or the neighborhood post office we do not know the clerks by name, and their parents, siblings, cousins, etc. in all the traditional small-town ways. We move through our social worlds anonymously, and even at work the incessant patterns of mergers and downsizing and so forth can make personal relationships fragile and distant if not suspicious or even hostile. Such trends are a threat to the continued development of adult intellectual skills at this highly creative level, Greenspan argues: our collective creativity is progressively impoverished by the lack of pleasant, genuinely personal, ordinary day-to-day interactions with one another. When we work so hard that we have little time and less energy for pointless, playful, affectionate interactions with others—at home or at work—then our capacity for creative problem solving will be progressively diminished.

This kind of neuroscience research obviously supports some of those management-organized exercises in "team building." It also supports the commonsense wisdom that exhausted, frazzled, anxious people will have trouble making good decisions or solving problems creatively. Much of what sustains the work-life crisis, perhaps, is that too many people are so overextended and stressed out that they simply cannot think straight. Greenspan in effect argues that "can't think straight" is not a metaphor but a fairly literal account of the neurobiological consequences of life in America at this point. Discernment, then, is a way to get our heads on straight. It is a way to stop, take stock, and come face to face with the wholeness and the integrity of who we most truly are, both as unique individuals in highly particular circumstances and as individual incarnations of the Holy One.

Among the most puzzling yet familiar facts that Greenspan's dual coding explains is why computers are so remarkably incompetent at the kind of pattern recognition and fuzzy logic that underlie the highest levels of critical thinking and problem solving. At tasks like these, four-year-olds outperform even the fanciest machines. If creative or critical thinking were a variety of logical computation based on like/unlike mental bookkeeping, computers should outperform humans just as computers out-compute us. But they don't, they can't, because data is merely data for a machine, some patterns of ones and zeros, opens and shuts, plusses and minuses.

It's no surprise that exceedingly ancient advice about slow, prayerful discernment now has support from empirical research in psychology and neuroscience. That conjunction cautions us, however, to respect the complexity of what we are trying to do. It offers fine defense against those who glance at our lives from outside and offer facile advice, or those who blithely insist that "it's obvious" what we should do in some circumstance that we face. Solving problems in life is not as straightforward as summing a column in a spreadsheet: life is not a two-click undertaking. Good conscience is a spectacularly nuanced, deeply creative human capacity.

It is also a deeply spiritual process. How or whether God plays the role in this process that tradition attributes to God is a question of faith, not fact: faith is among the most defining of all defining choices that anyone faces. As Coleridge quietly observes, the foundations of religion are necessarily "such as might be denied." Given the complexity of both brains and minds, there is no way to rule on that question objectively. But resolving work-life conflicts in any of their myriad particular forms will inevitably engage the spiritual depths of every single one of us as we struggle to engage both the promises and the demands of genuinely compassionate lives.

The Core of a Decision: Consolation and Desolation

I want to return to a question I raised earlier. How do we distinguish between inherited wisdom and inherited error? What rises from the depths of Tortoise Mind neural networks can be either. What feels authentic can be authentic, or it can be nothing more than the internalizing of flotsam and jetsam from the cultural and personal currents around us. If I am thinking about cutting back on my work hours and thereby compromising my career, am I giving in to the Mother Almighty Syndrome—the idea that to be a woman is to care for everyone and anyone within reach, no matter what? Or am I standing up to consumerist pressures that claim "more is never enough" and "you are what you earn"? Am I abandoning my deepest talents and refusing my moral responsibility to them? Or am I clearing space in my life not only to care for others but also to care for myself—to create time and energy in my life to nurture parts of my identity that my job pushes to the margins? No one can answer such questions for anyone else. Furthermore, any one person's answers to such questions will keep evolving over time. These are not questions we can answer once and for all and then lock the answers away in some psychic bank vault.

The ancient world did not have our conceptual language for talking about the unconscious, but there is ample evidence that they knew the realities involved. In particular, the ancient spiritual guides understood the danger of what we would call "internalizing" screwball stuff from the surrounding culture. That's why Christian traditions assume that a particular exercise in decision-making takes place within disciplined, familiar habits of prayer. Such spiritual practices, sustained in a community and over a lifetime, help the believer to distinguish what is truly God's presence within consciousness from what is merely the incursion of one's own unconscious or culturally determined "stuff."

Ignatius and the monastic traditions funding his thought refer to this sorting process as "the discernment of spirits"—good spirits drawing us to the good, evil spirits drawing us to the evil. Such personification can seem quaint. If we take it literally, it can seem schizophrenic. But simply as a metaphor for internal experience, it has an uncanny emotional accuracy. What surfaces from the unconscious, what Tortoise Mind comes up with, can feel as if its origin is outside us. What it is "outside" of, literally, is verbal consciousness. That doesn't mean it's not real in the sense of originating in our own empirical experience. The memory is simply not wired in ways that let us trace back consciously to the originating event. In particular, our own urges or desires, especially at the most primal levels, can feel as if they have origins "outside" of us. It is no small matter to distinguish accurately between our own darkly egotistical urges or fears and our glimpses of the genuine, objective, universal abiding presence of the Sacred drawing us to itself.

The history of religion testifies to how easily people can attribute to God their own worst urges: we are easily deceived by the complex power of our own unconscious needs and submerged memories. Yet it is easier to make what Jung called the "shadow side" conscious—and thus more amenable to control—if we can at the same time maintain a certain distance from the angry or primal urges that may surface. Such distancing is facilitated by traditions which metaphorically personify and thus externalize the origins of feelings as the promptings of the "evil one" or what *Star Wars* called "the dark side."

Ignatius contends that we can most accurately distinguish between "good spirits" and "evil spirits"—we can most accurately come to see what is the good in our own situations—by attending to our own feelings of consolation and desolation. What is good ultimately consoles us, even when it is somehow costly or difficult in the short run. Although this is perhaps simplifying, consolation is a lot like secular "authenticity" but with one enormous difference: what genuinely consoles is objectively the good; the good consoles in this way because it resonates to the spark of divinity indelibly present within each one of us. What genuinely desolates us—that which leaves us feeling depressed, lost, hopeless, worthless, angry, confused, incompetent, etc.—is for the very same reason antithetical to the good, the godly, and the wise.

Steps six and seven in Ignatian discernment—stopping to imagine oneself actually implementing one or another course of action—are particularly intended to invite feelings of consolation and of desolation in a global way. Imagining ourselves making one decision or another gets us past feeling depressed about this particular fact or consoled by that particular conversation. Steps six and seven are designed to elicit wholehearted responses that reconstitute the divided self into a moral whole. Such broadly generalized feelings of consolation and desolation can be very powerful: they can be dangerously exhilarating, or overwhelmingly painful. And so, tradition advises, we need someone to talk to who can help us to sort through the difference between what is authentic and what is internalized rubbish leaking toxins into our soul.

Ideally that "someone" is formally and rigorously trained in doing this—whether as a psychotherapist or as a spiritual director.[32] Often this person is simply a friend. As I have watched this informal seeking and giving of advice among my friends over the years, I have been pleased to see how often people wisely insist upon a point that Ignatius also urges: beware of implementing any decision that feels terribly urgent. Beware of feeling compelled. Be suspicious of near-panicky needs. Such urges are spiritually dark. What is spiritually light or spiritually enlightened is relaxed and composed; it is at ease; it is—and has—grace. What is wise always feels like a release from anxiety and compulsion, even when the decision itself involves loss, sacrifice, or the messy management of complicated details. Healthy discernment gets us to a still center from which we can act with the serenity, confidence, and freedom from inner compulsion that is the hallmark of actions undertaken in good conscience.

Once again, the theological presupposition at the core of the method is the conviction that deep within us is the image of God, a spark of the sacred residing far prior to distinctions among analytical intelligence, intuitive imagination, visceral realities, commonsense survival instincts, and so forth. We need carefully to attend to all the input available from all these human faculties, tradition teaches, because they are the gifts of God; but at some point we need also prayerfully to attend to a moral bottom line. What truly is the right thing to do in this situation? The best way to recognize what is the good to be sought or the evil to be avoided, Ignatius argues, is to plan a decision and then wait before implementing it. Before we do anything, we should imagine taking action and then watch to see whether we feel consoled or desolated. Consolation and desolation are our best guides to distinguishing between the authentically wise and the powerful but stupid or exploitative.

There is an extraordinary optimism at the heart of these teachings about discernment, and there is an extraordinary realism as well. Life is hard. The easy solutions are not always the best solutions. Above all, we can err by attending both too much and too little in any direction you can name. We can care too much or too little or in the wrong way about our own needs or about the needs of others. We can care too much, too little, or in the wrong way about the opinions of experts or the opinions of our friends. Honestly to seek the good in our own lives demands that we take the time and the energy to sit in silent, attentive, nonpossessive openness and observe our own deepest yearnings in confidence that we are indeed made in God's image, innately attuned to the good, the true, and the beautiful.

Many human traditions name and know this rudimentary but holy and hopeful fact about what it means *to be human*. How we *name* the light of God within us seems to me far less important than the depths of our efforts to live by that light. Wisdom can be reached by many spiritual paths—but none of them are easy, none of them free, and all of them have unique gifts or insights to offer those who undertake serious spiritual formation. What I have described here is the only path I know firsthand.

The Rational Actor and the Religious Believer

Careful discernment helps us to be wise when we face life's defining choices: whom to trust, for whom to care, and for what to sacrifice. Discernment helps us to live deliberately in sober recognition that life is hard and sacrifice is inescapable. Our only choice is to sacrifice wisely and intentionally, rather than blindly and passively. I'm not simply arguing that sacrifice is necessary for the good life or as a means of escape from lives of quiet desperation. If my point were that simple, rational-actor theory would still be right: smart sacrifice is an investment with a payoff (the good life). My position is much more complicated than that—or perhaps far more simple.

Rational-actor theory is ultimately grounded in the zero-sum spreadsheet model of reality in which whatever I give to you counts as a loss for me. My dispute is with that rationalist zero-sum spreadsheet model of reality, which is why my argument is also essentially religious. I believe that we are all held together (*religio* means "bound together") by our common origin in God's creative love. We can center our lives around the reality of that love. We can learn to see the *imago Dei* in ourselves and in everyone else—in our clients and our children alike, our neighbors and our customers and the sweatshop child who made our shoes. Until we do so, we are apt to remain trapped in the rational-actor spreadsheet cosmos. We are apt to remain boxed into our little cell on that spreadsheet, thinking that the sum of all we are and have can be calculated by adding up credits and debits, profits and losses.

To escape the life of quiet desperation, we have to unlock those spreadsheet cells and walk away. Thoreau, who had been reading Eastern thought, used metaphors of "light" and "awakening" for that process of unlocking. Christians point to Jesus, whom the Gospel of John introduces as the light of the world, a light that the darkness cannot comprehend. *Comprehendere:* to grasp with the hands. Light cannot be grasped as gold can be grasped. Furthermore, this light does not make any intellectual sense at all to those who dwell in the darkness. But in the words of Isaiah, Jesus came to set captives free.

Free, that is, from the prison of thinking that our portfolios, our résumés, or our adjusted gross income take the measure of our lives. If we are made in the image of God, our lives have no measure: we partake in the infinity and the immortality of God. Jesus' resurrection attests to that as well. He lost his life to the imperial powers of his day, and he had a life of incomparable power and significance, a life that extended past the doorway of death to show all of us that life is eternal. We all partake of the Infinite. Some have eyes but see not, Jesus cautioned, ears but hear not. He who has eyes to see, let him see.

I'm convinced that one learns to see the light—one begins to see the lock in the cell door and the key to that lock—not by memorizing Christian creeds, studying catechisms, or reading the sad history of how often Christians have failed to shed any light at all upon a suffering world. Neither does one learn to play tennis or the violin by reading rule books, theory, or history. One begins to see the light by beginning to pray. Books about prayer are somewhat helpful, but only as books about violin playing might be helpful to a violinist. The practice of prayer, like the practice of violin-playing, is understood, preserved, and transmitted only through a fragile, more or less continuous community of people who have learned and taught, learned and taught, for centuries on end.

Let me caution you: these people can be hard to find. The local congregation of the bureaucratic, institutionalized church can have a visible chorus of violin players, or it can be held captive by a consumerist culture and the powers of getting and spending. Such congregations can preach little more than "I'm okay, you're okay, don't rock the boat," all of it encased in pseudoscriptural platitudes. But with patience and persistence, even in those congregations one may eventually hear people playing violins. It's not easy. None of this is easy. (American Buddhists have the good sense to begin with beginners by teaching the techniques of meditation practice, not the massive complexity of Buddhist history and belief. You are not told to begin with believing in the Buddha.)

It's perfectly obvious that people can make good decisions without religious practice. That's not the issue here. What is at issue is whether the discernment process can be secularized. Will it still generate "gladness and singleness of heart" in someone who does not believe that the sustaining love of God flows in and through the very currents of human consciousness? I don't know. Many voices in the tradition say that discernment depends upon religious faith, but surely the matter is open to debate. God's love flows through us, after all, whether or not we realize that it does so. Consciousness encompasses only a bare fraction of what is going on in our minds: even the highest levels of critical thinking and creativity are still massively dependent upon unconscious processes. Intellectuals of a certain kind are prone to overrating self-conscious intellectual positions and allegiances. They think too much of thinking.

It seems to me that the goal of discernment goes beyond seeking a solid, self-aware, sophisticated decision. Obviously it can achieve that much, at least ideally. But consciously or not, one who seeks discernment is also seeking God. And those who seek God are apt to encounter God, no matter how they have been taught to name that experience. The God that I have found thereby is deeply incarnate within and deeply consoling of human suffering—and not particularly invested in human orthodoxies, labels, rules, and regulations. Nor does the God I have encountered much resemble the Old Man in the Sky depicted on the Sistine Chapel ceiling.

My concern is this: for those who cannot imagine even for a moment that such spiritual realities might somehow be possible, then the discernment process may bog down in suffering and uncertainty. It may circle endlessly in the second-guessing and what-if scenarios that it is both designed to elicit and designed to bring to spiritual closure.

But maybe that fear is entirely misplaced. If pushed, I am inclined to trust that honestly seeking to do the good and to avoid evil will be successful because God is remarkably indifferent to the limits we set upon what beliefs we find credible and what beliefs we consider outlandish, psychologically primitive, or philosophically naïve. God—as I have experienced God—is entirely unpredictable and elusively subtle. God is entirely outside our human and cerebral theorizing about what counts and what doesn't count as religion. The wind blows where it will.

Prayer, it is said, is our response to God's efforts to reach us. Centered, meditative attentiveness may begin in a deliberate act of the will; but as it deepens and expands, deliberateness gives way to the spontaneous activity of imagination drawing all of the human soul into graceful equipoise, like a dancer who leaps and extends and for an infinite moment rests in midair. At that point, meditation opens our awareness to an ongoing, sustaining, loving-kindness made manifest within consciousness, within the mind's swirling currents of confusion, fear, and opinionated, judgmental grousing.[33] Prayer is an intentional, often traditional set of practices intended gradually and carefully to shut down our sustained, often unconscious, sometimes terrified resistance to recognizing this presence within and around us. Prayer is also a hazardous business, it is said, because shutting down our resistance to God is apt to entail shutting down some parts of the defenses which keep unconscious repressed material securely repressed. Every meditation tradition recognizes that danger. But the hazard is lessened when we are guided by a spiritual teacher and when we heed the traditional moral teachings and ritual-liturgical practices built upon centuries of critically informed experience with prayer, with discernment, and with the dangerous incursions of unconscious material. That's why so many people are now turning to monasteries and to convents—the traditional residence of such teachers and repositories of such wisdom.[34]

Well-trained spiritual directors can be very difficult to find even for those reasonably networked within Christian churches, although slowly that situation is improving. But there are plenty of books, and with a certain courageous persistence, one finds soul friends in unexpected places. Even for regular "churchgoers," the life of faith is substantially comprised of ad-lib relationships and serendipitous connections.

I think that most people—inside and outside of congregations—do begin essentially on their own, reading and sampling and finding what works, learning how to listen for the small hints dropped in ordinary conversation that someone else is also seeking greater spiritual depths. The effort to pray—the willingness to gamble with new ways of thinking about how we think about our lives—can be a way to discover for oneself whether or not there is anything real named by the word "God." Wherever you go, there you are, observes Buddhist meditation teacher Jon Kabat-Zinn.[35] There God is also, I would add. So be alert. The stream of consciousness carries "trace elements" washed into our minds from the holy mountains of the Most High.

Conclusion

To Seek the Discerning Heart

Midwinter. Midday in a storefront Thai place. A man and a woman, both middle-aged.

My glass noodles were congealing and I didn't know what to do. Hungry, determined, I struggled with the rubbery mass, longing for a knife and fork rather than chopsticks. Lunches with editors are always like this, I groused to myself. Something inedible happens.

I should have known better than to arrive actually hungry. It's a plot, a devious tradition. The minute a writer's eating slows for any reason, the editor unleashes such a swift and relentless stream of questions that the writer never gets another mouthful. That's the real origin of "starving artist" traditions. When I was on a book tour once, a shrewd media escort cautioned me, prior to a dinner interview, to order soup if I expected to eat anything at all.

"Just swallow," she advised. "You don't have to chew soup. Didn't they tell you that in New York?"

This particular editor, from a national newsweekly, was clearly a master of his trade: he had suggested lunch at this noodle place, which offered no soups at all.

"What about your own work-life problems?" he asked. "If you could do it over, what would you do differently yourself?"

My answer was half-spoken before I realized what I was saying, which was something like this: "I'd worry less. I drove myself nuts, thinking that I was managing badly, thinking that there was some ideal way to cope with this, something I just had not figured out yet. There's not. All we can do is the best we can do, and that's what I was already doing. I just thought it should be easier. And it would have been a lot easier if I had just known how hard it always is, hard for everyone, no matter what."

I ground to a halt, verbally lost between the easy and the hard. He put down his chopsticks and squinted at me as editors do.

I didn't know how much more I could say, how much more I should say. Should I talk about God and imagination and the spiritual quest for alternatives to leading a life of quiet desperation? Or was he merely hunting for hidden motives, for unconscious presuppositions? Maybe he was simply making preliminary small talk with a writer: when in doubt, ask us about the next book.

Stop thinking so much! I told myself sternly: you will drive yourself crazy doing this! So I met his gaze steadily for a few heartbeats, watching him watch me, waiting for a clue. He smiled slightly and nodded and changed the subject. Editors can be an inscrutable lot.

By this point my noodles were completely cold and inaccessible to chopsticks. Lunch was a loss, at least as far as eating goes. So if he had pursued the question further, I might have said something like this: life is indeed hard, but that's not our fault; and it's not something we can fix by becoming better managers. Life is not a management problem. I think I thought it was, but I was wrong.

Furthermore, although the truth may set us free, it will not necessarily protect us from pain. Pain is an intransigent part of what makes life hard. It is not a sign of failure, but neither is it proof of integrity. We cannot escape suffering, which is to say we cannot escape uncertainty or at times perhaps despair. The most we can hope for is hope itself—not optimism, which can be foolish stuff, but hope, which is the courage to love. Love, we are told, is the greatest virtue. Hope will end when all is consummated and there is no contingency before us. Courage—faith—will end when there are no more decisions to make, no more chances to take, no more risks to be run. But love abides.

To find a life we can live with, to do more than earn a living and spend it, we must above all discover the good within us which is love, a good manifest as compassionate love for one another and as resolute determination to meet the full range of our human obligations. No one else can find that for us, because it is in the seeking that we find it. Only by rising above our fear and our pain do we recognize who we are.

In making the choices that make us who we are, in defining the choices that define us in turn, we come face to face over and over again with a single, stubborn, central fact: innately we recognize and desire the good, seeking it in our own lives however blindly, however imperfectly, and despite all obstacles. Only a fool will try to do that all alone, but only a bigger fool yet will presume that experts or authorities can spare us the slow work of moral discernment. To have a life worth living, we have to ask ourselves the hard questions: Whom do I trust? For whom do I care? For what will I sacrifice? Such questions reveal the trajectory of love. They lay bare the foundations of meaning and integrity; they illuminate the deepest, most elusive spiritual mysteries inhabiting the human heart. The good life depends upon our laying claim to these deep, mysterious reaches of our own compassionate souls.

Appendix *One*

Wait Here for Rescue

As Stephanie Coontz contends in *The Way We Never Were: American Families and the Nostalgia Trap,* we need policies that appeal to the best that is in us.[1] Surely that is the case! Sociologists have risen to that challenge: the intellectual landscape is littered with policy proposals designed to alleviate the conflict between earning a living and having a life. All of these proposals, however, are subject to the simple but profound question of cost: if we did not enact major social legislation when the federal budget was running a fabulous surplus, there's little reason to expect major initiatives when we face even more fabulous deficits. But cost is not the only problem. In what follows I want very briefly to sketch the cultural obstacles that I see to salvation by policy proposal.

The most common form of policy proposal argues, in effect, *We Should Be Sweden.* Like Sweden, America should have cradle-to-grave social insurance against all the slings and arrows of outrageous fortune. The most sweeping proposals are those called the "full commodification model." That is, somehow or other taxes should subsidize the cost of either purchasing care for dependent family members or paying willing relatives to stay home to provide this care themselves.

The Swedish model has much to commend it, but it's not easily exportable—especially not to a ruggedly individualist, richly diverse, exponentially larger nation. Furthermore, the business pages regularly blame European economic stagnation on the kinds of high taxes and close regulation that the social-democratic model requires. That claim is based upon a central tenet of free-market thinking—essentially, a major theological principle in America's state religion: *competition is good.* Anything that limits competition or lessens competitiveness is anathema. Because social responsibility and responsibility to the common good or the national interest lessens the competitiveness of a global corporation, we must not force profit-seekers to be responsible socially. Such a failure to protect our common good or our own national interest in effect testifies to the progressive loss of the implicit social contract between our nation and the corporations who do business here. But as Benjamin Barber demonstrates in *Jihad vs. McWorld,* the process is unmistakably underway. Those who want to import the Swedish model are naïve, but so was George W. Bush naïve in his oft-repeated campaign claim that the purpose of national government is to create a climate favorable to business.[2]

Repent and Be Saved, others insist. Mothers should be more motherly, fathers more fatherly, parents more parental, marriages more stable. Neighbors should be more neighborly, citizens should be more civic-minded, church folks should be more communal, and so forth and so on. These critics have seen the enemy, and he is us: irresponsible, self-centered, lazy, frivolous, promiscuous, indifferent. The underlying problem is understood to be a radical self-expressive individualism that renounces any impediment to self-gratification or self-realization.

There's no denying that all kinds of human relationships get in the way of self-gratification—relationships not only with children but also with marital partners, parents, siblings, friends who count on us, and so forth. Being human is messy and inconvenient at times, particularly for the relentlessly ambitious or the relentlessly self-indulgent. Nor is there anything wrong with programs and policies to stabilize marriage, to encourage parents to pay more attention to their children, or to support community-wide mutual care and responsibility.

But ultimately, that's a lot like teaching nursing skills to help families cope with waterborne diseases when the problem is contamination of the community well. Although some children, elders, or frail lonely neighbors are neglected because the relevant adults are incompetent idiots who might be taught or forced to shape up, many more are neglected because so many responsible adults are overwhelmed by problems whose solution lies far outside their control. Anyone who tries both for love and for work is up against the sociopathology of our times.

There Oughtta Be A Law, claim theorists of jurisprudence. The litigiousness of American society is manifest in this issue as in every other. Joan Williams, in *Unbending Gender: Why Work and Family Conflict and What to Do About It,* sets her considerable skills as a feminist theorist of jurisprudence to work in devising a stunning array of potential lawsuits as the answer to this mess.[3] Her goal is to insure that businesses do not sweep aside wholesale those individuals who work fewer hours because their children are young, their parents are old, their spouses are sick, their neighbors need help navigating difficult governmental or medical systems, etc., etc., etc. She wants to insure that such individuals will be promoted and paid in rational proportion to their actual contribution to an organization. The work such people have done should not be measured against the norm of productivity set by self-centered, ruthlessly ambitious, socially isolated workaholics. She contends that lawsuits are the way to halt the tendency to define "ideal worker" as someone who has no moral responsibilities, no social bonds, and no ordinary household chores.

If promotion decisions were as strictly rational as she imagines, that might make sense. But as Guy Claxson argues in *Hare Brain, Tortoise Mind,* decision-making at the very highest levels always and necessarily includes tremendously important intuitive and deeply subconscious or even unconscious components.[4] Furthermore, it doesn't take much to imagine the response of Elinor Burkett, author of *Baby Boon: How Family-Friendly America Cheats the Childless.*[5] Burkett applies a straightforwardly rationalist zero-sum bookkeeping mentality to the whole problem of "family friendly" policies. She quite reasonably concludes (given her premises) that whatever is given to parents is necessarily taken away from those who are not parents. By extension, then, any accommodation offered to people with disabled parents, ailing spouses, or needy neighbors or siblings is taken away from those whose help is not needed by (or at least not offered to) anyone at all. What's ahead on this front is yet another long siege of futile conflicts based on modernist or Enlightenment premises that don't hold water in the first place: human social reality is simply not the rationalist machine that such thinkers imagine.

Rework Working. By far the most common demand, however, is that work must be restructured. No doubt some employers, like some parents, are oblivious, self-centered, irresponsible, exploitative, etc. But once again the enormous scope of the problems involved strongly suggests that the issue is not only individual failure but also large structural problems. As Charles Lindblom explains in considerable detail, the market system is a complex of mutual adjustments in which there is no single central authority but rather many, widely diffused, roughly equivalent sources of influence.[6] As Nancy Folbre contends, "Competitors can't always afford to be nice."[7] Individual managers or entrepreneurs may have fairly limited ability to restructure work in more humane and socially responsible ways. The structure of work is not determined by fiat of employers but rather by economic and market pressures, including the employment choices made by those whose skills are particularly in demand. It may prove impossibly difficult to legislate changes in the way work is organized in a free society—much less in a global economy. I agree with those who would contend that companies who want to do business in the United States will have to be morally responsible to the social fabric just as they are (at least in theory) required to be morally responsible to the landscape. But "the social fabric" is a cultural construct: it is neither measured nor adjusted with the empirical simplicity of checking for pollutants in rivers and wells—not that environmental science is a simple matter in and of itself!

All of these policy proposals variously rearrange or reimagine the same basic set of ideas: substantive child-care regulation and funding, paid maternity leave, before- and after-school programs, health insurance and other benefits for part-time workers, leave allowances for family illnesses or conferences with teachers and caregivers, massively increased tax deductions for children and dependent adults, shorter workweeks, more flexible workplaces, and, crucially, a minimum wage for full-time workers that is truly a living wage (along with penalties of some sort for keeping disproportionate numbers of workers at the part-time level).[8] I have shelves full of these books whose concluding chapter demands that the world should change, that the world should become a better place than the world is right now. For my twenty-some years as a mom, I've been nodding and agreeing with all these articulate social scientists and policy experts and all their elegant statistics demonstrating that changes are needed.

But very little has changed. And life goes on regardless. When my children were small, unlicensed, unregulated child care would have cost more than 100 percent of my take-home pay as an assistant professor at a Big Ten research university. Now they are all in college. Life is like this for all of us: none of us can put our responsibilities on hold until the world is changed by some mix of social scientists, policy experts, and politicians. We have to find our own best solutions to bad situations without waiting for Washington to discover and act upon the rudimentary mathematics of household finance among those of us who work for a living.

And so this is not a book *about* policy, because at this point any policy recommendation has a devastating subtext: *wait here for rescue*. That's a counsel of passivity. In our cultural moment, such passivity is a counsel of despair. Real parents simply cannot wait for the rosy-fingered dawn of policy changes. Neither can those who need to care for an elderly parent or a sick friend, or those who feel morally accountable to duties, roles, and talents that exist outside the domain in which they find themselves earning a living. No matter what the future brings to this country, none of these proposals will work their way into legislation and social practice soon enough to help the current crop of children, dependent adults, elderly folks, single people with broken legs, or anyone who wants to live a compassionate, generous life in variously committed relationships with a whole array of other people. For the foreseeable future, responsible and caring adults still have to cope with work-life conflicts essentially on their own.

And so, rather than concoct yet another pie-in-the-sky policy proposal, in this book I want to offer what the early monastic tradition would call an "aid to discernment." My goal is to facilitate historically informed critical thinking about the decisions and pressures that individuals face as part of the commonplace struggle to maintain a sane and fruitful balance between material and nonmaterial needs in a socioeconomic system wildly skewed toward predatory capitalism, get-and-spend consumerism, and career anxiety.

Appendix *Two*

Statistics and Spinmeistering

Here is a handy list of concepts to keep in mind as you try to evaluate the importance of any given report of research into child care. The practical significance of any given research finding can be exaggerated by ignoring, misunderstanding, or spinmeistering upon concepts like these.

1. *Persistence.* Will the observed differences continue? Will higher verbal scores at age three or age five translate into higher SAT verbal scores? How much higher? Persistence operates in the other direction as well. Will a stormier year in kindergarten lead to a stormier adolescence? Troubled adolescents can get themselves into much more serious troubles than obstreperous five-year-olds. But maybe none of these differences will persist at all, or maybe they will persist for such a small fraction of children that it is no longer clear, statistically speaking, that child care made a difference one way or another. Child care vs. home care is only one variable in what is a very long and massively complex developmental process.

Obviously if one assumes that there will be strong persistence, one can write a much flashier news account with a much more dramatic headline. Picture the video possibilities: two toddlers fighting over a toy, then cut to scenes of murder in a high school hallway.

2. *Amplitude.* Amplitude is closely related to persistence. Amplitude is something like compounding interest: small initial differences in interest rates, for instance, compounded over decades, add up to enormous

differences in long-term financial cost or financial return. Those useful tables showing the consequences of different thirty-year mortgage rates demonstrate this effect quite vividly. And so, small initial differences in verbal skills or social skills might play out into large differences over time. But maybe they won't. Maybe the differences will not "compound." We simply have to wait to see. Once again, however, popular accounts can leave the impression that of course the differences will compound at a fabulously dangerous rate.

3. *Generalizability.* That's an unwieldy word naming an important concept. If some children suffer demonstrable difficulties at an early point developmentally, then does that mean that most children will suffer some degree of difficulty at some point later on? This is the "canary in the coal mine" argument. Perhaps these problems threaten everyone in some important way, even though, at this early stage, the problems are visible only in particularly vulnerable children. Maybe children whose development is disrupted in some way by child care serve as warnings to the whole community that something is happening that is bad for everyone, whether or not we have the technology to document that precisely. Or maybe not. Maybe the children who are currently having difficulties will simply outgrow them, and all will be well. Any "older parent" has watched anxiously as some kid has struggled through some very difficult stage, only to emerge successfully, with nothing more to show for the struggle than parents with somewhat greyer hair and more deeply lined faces.

By comparison: in response to high levels of air pollution, asthmatics may begin to wheeze or to cough and to become short of breath. That's why on some days there are warnings on the TV and radio that people with pulmonary problems should stay indoors—warnings that some of us have learned we must heed. Those with less sensitive airways will not react so quickly or so visibly, but there is good epidemiological evidence that high levels of air pollution are dangerous for everybody. All things being equal, of course parents (and everyone else) would rather live where there are minimal levels of air pollution.

Unfortunately, all things are never equal in that simple, abstract, theoretical way. There is simply no way to eliminate all known risk factors for negative outcomes. There's nothing anyone can do to rescue themselves from the slings and arrows of outrageous fortune or the random vicissitudes of the human condition. As I said before, becoming a parent would have been so much easier if I'd become a god at the same point! But that's not how the system works. I'm just a mom.

There's another aspect of "generalizability" that needs to be understood. Maybe the cohort of kids in child care contains just slightly more than a truly random sample of certain kinds of kids or certain kinds of parents. Researchers cannot assign genetically identical babies to different experimental groups, as they can set genetically identical rats into this cage or that one. Especially when statistical correlations are small to begin with, questions like this are very important. That makes for a very lively research environment for scholars who are fascinated by trying to tease apart such complex problems. But it makes for great confusion and anxiety among ordinary parents waiting on the sidelines. And waiting. And waiting. And wondering when policies will change to ease the conflict between providing for children and nurturing them appropriately. As I said at the very beginning, while I was waiting my children grew up and left for college. And we still don't know.

4. *Random Sample.* A random sample is not one assembled without any particular plan—as in, "select a card at random." A scientifically "random" sample is planned and supervised with excruciating care to avoid every possible way in which the study cohort might be biased by including too many of one group or too few of another.

If you are studying people, that's a remarkably difficult, expensive, and sophisticated undertaking. And yet writers carelessly bandy around references to their "research" or their "research findings" when all they did was interview some group of people without the least effort to assemble a proper "random sample," much less to follow the highly developed science of question writing, questionnaire design, and data analysis. It is remarkably difficult to word questions properly, or to design a research project in such a way as to generate meaningful data that can be statistically analyzed. Interviewing a nonrandom sample using a nonstandardized format is gossip, not research.

The written account of such conversations can be more or less interesting, of course. It can satisfy a certain natural curiosity about other people's lives. An essay or a book doesn't have to be rigorous science to be thought provoking. But such helpful journalistic exercises in back-fence neighborliness do not support the kinds of sweeping, absolutist conclusions one so commonly finds in the small but incessant stream of "motherhood" books.

5. *Risk Factor.* A risk factor is not a cause. In particular, a risk factor is not a necessary and sufficient cause in the way that an overnight temperature of five degrees below zero *causes* a puddle of snowmelt on the sidewalk to refreeze into a dark, slick hazard. A risk factor is some thing or some event which is *associated with* increased probability of a particular outcome. A risk factor is a clue, not a cause.

During the Black Plague, for instance, people believed that plague might be caused by "bad air." They pinned flowers to their clothes—nosegays—to protect themselves with the pleasant fragrance, a tradition memorialized in the children's chant, "Ring Around the Rosy." We understand now that the plague was carried not by smells but (at least initially) by fleas upon rats that populated foul-smelling garbage dumps. Similarly, "night air" was often thought to cause disease. We now know that a variety of illnesses are carried not by night air but by mosquitoes who are more active at dusk. Mosquitoes breed in standing water, of course, and standing water often smells foul, and so in medieval thought there was an overlap between "bad air" and "night air" as threats to health.

Our finer perception of causality doesn't change the fact that our ancestors were correctly observing risk factors. Risk factors speak more to correlation than causality, but when correlation is strong it is worth attending to—especially when exact causality is difficult to determine or dependent upon the interaction of many different contributing factors. As we will see, the biology of development, especially human brain development, is shaped much much less by simple necessary-and-sufficient causes than it is by the interweaving of perhaps innumerable contributing factors, each of which exerts a weak causal effect. As a result, there is scientific importance to documented evidence that A is a "risk factor" for B, or that A is "associated with a higher incidence of" B. These are vitally important, unquestionably valid concepts, but their meaning within any particular research report is extremely precise and very delicately dependent upon many technical details of the research design and the statistical analysis.

The problem for parents, however, is that news reports of this research seldom explain the necessary details. How were participants in the study selected or identified to be participants? What measurements were taken, and how, and by whom? What sort of controls were used, and which potentially confounding factors were controlled for? How were confounding factors controlled for? In short, the concept "risk factor" can operate as an invitation to spinmeistering and polemics, quite aside from the simple distortions and misunderstandings generated by reporters with insufficient education in statistics, in epidemiology, and in research design—or sometimes with axes of their own to grind.

One simple example: much has been made in the popular press of a study correlating the education of parents with how many words they spoke to their child in a given hour.[1] College-educated parents spoke an average of something like 2200 words; working-class parents more like 600. That's an important issue because the amount of language actually addressed to a baby correlates highly with its verbal development, and it's an issue for highly educated parents hiring minimally educated women to care for their children.

But I'm suspicious of these findings. As any writer knows, 2000 words is about ten pages, double-spaced. Properly delivered, a ten-page lecture takes me at least twenty minutes to deliver—and even at my best I tend to speak too quickly! Properly delivered, by a well-trained actress perhaps, 2000 words would take a solid half hour. And that's a monologue. So parents who are speaking 2000 words an hour to their children must be engaging a solid hour of particularly intensive verbal play. As an *average* that seems wildly unlikely, if for no other reason than the fact that young children very seldom manage to sustain that sort of attention span for anything.

I've seen reports of that study over and over again—but none of them ever indicated how the recordings were made. Where were the recordings made? Did the parents know they were being recorded? Did they know why they were being recorded? Was there a researcher or research assistant in the room listening? Did anyone take into account—and if so, how—the fact that parents might be more relaxed and therefore more talkative to their babies in various settings? That highly educated parents might exaggerate their behavior if they knew they were being watched and their words recorded, or that working-class parents might be inhibited by the presence of a Ph.D. candidate with a microphone?

I hope that all this was taken into account. Maybe it was. My point is that all the popular press reports of this research omitted these absolutely crucial details. Nor are we told how old the babies were, or whether all the babies were the same age, or whether all the babies were firstborn, or none of them were, or whether there was a mix. Or how the parents scored on tests of introversion and extroversion, not simply education and income. In short, reports of this research score, as journalism, no better than reports of a murder that doesn't say who, or where, or when.

Furthermore, such apparently mindless word-counting suggests the ongoing prevalence of a rage for quantification, as if on the assumption that whatever we can quantify has to be meaningful. But consider, just for a moment, the differences between these two pairs of exchanges between parent and child:

A. child: Where are my shoes?
   adult: By the back door.
B. child: Why are people mean?
   adult: Because they are afraid.

Both exchanges involve the same number of words. They are numerically equal. But they are certainly not equivalently important for the development of the child.

In short, this oft-bandied bit of research, as usually reported, means absolutely nothing. Do differences in a caregiver's verbal skills or verbal engagement with a child make a difference for the language development of a baby? Quite possibly they do. Does this study, *as usually reported*, give parents useful information about how social class has a bearing on that issue? No.

6. *Significant.* As a risk factor is not a necessary-and-sufficient cause, as "random" does not mean "at random" but rather "selected with excruciatingly rigorous efforts at objectivity," so also "significant" need not mean "important." Once again: "significant" is a highly technical term in statistics. It doesn't necessarily mean "likely," much less "important." A number is "significant" if it measures or identifies an entity that can be distinguished from what would happen by chance.

Consider this example: at certain times, people who live in the northern reaches of the northern hemisphere may be statistically more likely to have a meteor land on their roof. Imagine a headline: "Chicagoans Run Significant Risk of Meteor Attack." That may be a true statement, statistically speaking, but it would not be true that the risk of meteors on the roof is an important risk, or that it is likely to happen, or that if you live in Chicago you need to do something immediately. There is a difference, in short, between *statistical* significance and what physicians call *clinical* significance.

Without such careful distinctions and a reasonable array of information about experimental design, there is simply no way to estimate the validity, relevance, and practical importance of experimental results. Nonetheless, partial and often garbled reports about "significant differences" haunt parents and achieve an immortality of their own in the footnotes of popular books. As Christina Hoff Sommers illustrates in another context, the 24/7 information environment means that misinformation spreads and imbeds itself with the uncanny speed of a malicious computer virus.[2]

7. *Relative Risk and Absolute Risk.* Closely related to the concept of "significance" is the crucial, often-neglected distinction between relative risk and absolute risk. For instance, in the recent flurry of news about the hazards of hormone replacement therapy (HRT) for women, it was widely reported that women on HRT faced a 22 percent greater risk of heart disease. That does not mean that 22 percent of women on HRT will get heart disease! Rather, 3 percent of women receiving a placebo developed heart disease during the years of the study, and 3.7 percent of women on HRT did so. Although the *relative* risk is substantial, the *absolute* risk is small—and smaller yet I'm sure if one does not already have other risk factors for heart disease, risk factors such as high cholesterol, high blood pressure, family history, obesity, lack of exercise, etc. Risk factors matter most when they pile up like that. So if you are trim, your numbers are great, there's no family history, and you run two miles every morning, then if hot flashes have become incapacitating one could

reasonably say that the figures for heart disease among women on HRT lack clinical significance. It's still a judgment call, but adulthood is full of judgment calls. Life comes with no guarantees about anything.

Look at it this way: if the risk of a given outcome changes from 30 percent to 90 percent, the outcome is three times as likely. It is also three times as likely if the change is from 1 percent to 3 percent. Both sets of numbers represent the same relative risk, but 90 percent is a huge absolute risk. So when the *New York Times* reports that children who were in thirty hours per week of child care prior to the age of nine months are three times as likely to be aggressive with their peers, that's a statement of relative risk.[3] It's also the basis for a catchy headline on the evening news. But one needs to know the absolute risk to know whether or not to be concerned about this study, particularly given the difficulties of getting observers to agree about what counts as inappropriately aggressive behavior among five-year-olds. (It was an increase from 6 percent to 17 percent.)

All these technical terms can be given ominous or exaggerated importance by reporters who are either careless or poorly educated. In cutting the terms down to size, I hope I have not left you with the impression that child-care research is all meaningless academic babble, professors fighting with one another about how many angels are dancing on the head of a pin. It's incredibly important work, because global free-market capitalism is interfering with childrearing practices that go all the way back in evolutionary time. Young children have always been cared for by close kin, even though the boundaries of who counts as "kin" are not necessarily settled only through blood inheritance. But when work—when the means to material survival—moved out of the household, the West set off on a monumental experiment in early childhood development.

We need to keep track of that experiment. Spinmeistering, politicizing, and flame-thrower rhetoric unduly complicates the cultural context in which this research is both funded and assimilated. That's a disaster. It seems to me the best response is for the rest of us to learn a bit of the relevant conceptual language so that we can listen to the news or read the paper without falling prey.

Notes

Part One: What Does It Profit? *Wanting More from Life Than a Paycheck*

1. Anne Tyler, "Still Just Writing," *The Writer on Her Work,* vol. 1, ed. Janet Sternburg (New York: Norton, 1980), pp. 3–16.

Chapter 1. How Competition Has Replaced Compassion in American Culture

2. Sallie McFague, *Life Abundant: Rethinking Theology and Economy for a Planet in Peril* (Minneapolis: Augsburg Fortress, 2001). See also Harvey Cox, "The Market as God," *Atlantic Monthly* (March 1999), rpt. in *The Best Christian Writing 2000,* ed. John Wilson (San Francisco: HarperSanFrancisco, 2000), pp. 79–91.

3. William Blake, *The Marriage of Heaven and Hell,* plate 7. Cf. "the fool sees not the same tree that a wise man sees," also plate 7, and "if others had not been foolish, we should be so," plate 9.

4. It is undeniably important that full-time nurturing generates less social status for the adult involved than a full-time, fast-track career, but social status does not translate directly into human and moral significance. We will return—repeatedly—to the differentials in status and in sociopolitical power between these two tasks.

5. "Domestic Demographics: 1970 and 1998," Bureau of the Census and the National Center for Health Statistics, cited in Andrew Hacker, "The Case Against Kids," *New York Review of Books* (30 November 2000), p. 14.

6. *Expenditures on Children by Families,* Center for Nutrition Policy and Promotion, U.S. Department of Agriculture, March 2000, cited in Andrew Hacker, "The Case Against Kids," *New York Review of Books* (30 November 2000), p. 16.

7. Laurence Steinberg, Ph.D., B. Bradford Brown, Ph.D., and Sandford M. Dornbusch, Ph.D., *Beyond the Classroom: Why School Reform Has Failed and What Parents Need To Do* (New York: Touchstone Books/Simon & Schuster, 1996), especially chapters 6 and 7.

8. Arlie Russell Hochschild, *The Time Bind: When Work Becomes Home and Home Becomes Work* (New York: Holt, 1997).

9. Lester Thurow, "62 Cents to the Dollar: The Earnings Gap Doesn't Go Away," *Working Mother* (October 1984), p. 42; cited in Kathleen Hall Jamieson, *Beyond the Double Bind: Women and Leadership* (New York and Oxford: Oxford University Press, 1995), p. 64, p. 224 n. 48.

10. Kathleen Hall Jamieson, *Beyond the Double Bind: Women and Leadership* (New York and Oxford: Oxford University Press, 1995), p. 64.

11. *Statistical Abstracts of the United States: 2001* (Washington, D.C.: U.S. Census Bureau, 2001), table 675, p. 440.

12. Ann Crittenden, *The Price of Motherhood: Why the Most Important Job in the World Is the Least Valued* (New York: Metropolitan/Holt, 2001), p. 88 and p. 286, n. 2. Crittenden also points out that a woman's contribution to her family does not "count" in the GNP nor toward her own Social Security earnings.

13. Crittenden, *The Price of Motherhood,* p. 95, and p. 288, n. 20, which cites Jane Waldfogel, "Understanding the 'Family Gap' in Pay for Women with Children, *Journal of Economic Perspectives,* vol. 12, no. 1 (winter 1998): 137–156; and Waldfogel, "The Family Gap for Young Women in the United States and Britain," *Journal of Labor Economics,* vol. 11 (1998): 505–519.

14. Sylvia Ann Hewlett and Cornel West offer an impressive list of policy failures relative to families. See *The War Against Parents: What We Can Do for America's Beleaguered Moms and Dads* (Boston: Houghton Mifflin, 1998), chapter 4.

15. Joanne B. Ciulla, *The Working Life: The Promise and Betrayal of Modern Work* (New York: Times/Random, 2000), chapter 9.

16. Mona Harrington, *Care and Equality: Inventing a New Family Politics* (New York: Routledge, 2000), p. 26.

17. On how this nation has become inimical to its own children—and thus to its own future—see Hewlett and West, *The War Against Parents,* chapters 4 and 5; David Popenoe, *Life Without Father: Compelling New Evidence That Fatherhood and Marriage Are Indispensable for the Good of Children and Society* (New York: Martin Kessler Books/Free Press, 1996), p. 14; Penelope Leach, *Children First: What Our Society Must Do—And Is Not Doing—For Our Children Today* (New York: Knopf, 1994), p. xiii; and Stephanie Coontz, *The Way We Never Were: American Families and the Nostalgia Trap* (New York: Basic, 1992), p. 215. Instances could be multiplied almost indefinitely. James Garbarino offers advice to parents on coping with this situation in *Raising Children in a Socially Toxic Environment* (San Francisco: Jossey-Bass, 1985).

18. This is Nancy Folbre's table-of-contents summary of chapter 8 of *The Invisible Heart: Economics and Family Values* (New York: New Press, 2001), p. ix.

19. Charles E. Lindblom, *The Market System: What It Is, How It Works, and What to Make of It* (New Haven: Yale University Press, 2001), p. 4, pp. 27–28.

20. Philip Rieff, *The Triumph of the Therapeutic: Uses of Faith After Freud* (Chicago: University of Chicago Press, 1966, 1987), p. 52, p. 71.

21. Harrington, *Care and Equality,* pp. 37–38.

22. Hewlett and West, *The War Against Parents,* p. 124.

23. Nel Noddings, *Starting at Home: Caring and Social Policy* (Berkeley and Los Angeles: University of California Press, 2002), pp. 72–73. Noddings offers an analysis of care that is essentially akin to older political and philosophical analyses of human rights. Analyses of rights tend inherently toward individualism; her analysis of care yields a highly relational vision of human society.

Chapter 2. Compassion, Altruism, and the Common Good

24. Daniel Goleman, *Emotional Intelligence* (New York: Bantam, 1995).

25. See Hans Küng and Karl-Joseph Kuschel, *A Global Ethic: The Declaration of the Parliament of the World's Religions* (New York: Continuum, 1994); *Parabola*, vol. 28, no. 1 (spring 2003)—the whole issue is devoted to compassion; and Patrick Glynn's comments in *God, The Evidence: The Reconciliation of Faith and Reason in a Postsecular World* (Rocklin, Ca.: Forum/Prima, 1997), p. 169.

26. *Hamlet*, II. ii, 300ff.

27. Robert Fuller, *Spiritual But Not Religious: Understanding Unchurched America* (Oxford and New York: Oxford University Press, 2001), pp. 98–99. See also Catherine A. Brekus, "America's Mythical Religious Past" on the website "Sightings" 12 October 2000, published by the Martin Marty Center at the University of Chicago Divinity School (http://www.marty-center.uchicago.edu). The essay is posted at www.divinity.uchicago.edu/sightings/archive_2000/sightings_101200.html. Brekus points out that colonial Americans argued ferociously about what constitutes authentic Christianity. Furthermore, most of the original colonies had "established" churches and denied freedom of worship to members of other Christian denominations. America's diverse and contentious religious past was much more like the present than most people realize. Furthermore, as Peter Steinfels argues, "secular" arguments can be just as absolutist as "religious" arguments: all arguments depend upon premises, and most people neither recognize nor are willing to question the premises they take for granted (see Steinfels's "Beliefs" column in the *New York Times* (12 May 2001), p. A17.

28. Phyllis Tickle explains our situation quite adeptly: "The most remarkable characteristic of all this looking and spiritual striving, at least from a professional religionist's point of view, is not that it is going on, but that it is going on with almost no sectarian or even tradition-oriented guidance. The average [spiritual] seeker in America today is being shepherded to a large extent by commercially published books" (*God Talk in America* [New York: Crossroad, 1997], p. 33).

29. Other traditions within Christianity begin the story in another way—by emphasizing our sinful alienation from God. The "first fact" in this telling is not the spark of the sacred within each of us, but the utter and hopeless loss of this primordial gift through an original, freely chosen option for evil.

30. Marcus Borg, *Jesus, A New Vision: Spirit, Culture, and the Life of Discipleship* (San Francisco: HarperSanFrancisco, 1991), p. 192.

31. What I say here about virtue is roughly paraphrased from Stanley Hauerwas, *Sanctify Them in the Truth: Holiness Exemplified* (Nashville: Abingdon, 1998), pp. 112–113. See also Alasdair MacIntyre, *After Virtue: A Study in Moral Theology*, 2nd ed. (Notre Dame, Ind.: University of Notre Dame Press, 1984) and Stanley Hauerwas and Charles Pinches, *Christians Among the Virtues: Theological*

Conversations with Ancient and Modern Ethics (Notre Dame, Ind.: University of Notre Dame Press, 1997).

32. John Drury, *Painting the Word: Christian Pictures and their Meanings* (New Haven and London: Yale University Press, in association with National Gallery Publications Limited, 2000), p. 153, p. 147.

33. Thomas Aquinas, *Summa Theologiae,* 1A, 2AE 2:2 and 3:1–2, cited from *St. Thomas Aquinas: Summa Theologiae, A Concise Translation,* ed. and trans. Timothy McDermott (Allen, Tex.: Christian Classics, 1989), pp. 175, 176.

34. On the relationship between Buddhist and Christian theology, see His Holiness the Dalai Lama, *The Good Heart: A Buddhist Perspective on the Teachings of Jesus,* trans. Geshe Thupten Jinpa, ed. Robert Kiely (Boston: Wisdom, 1996) and Laurence Freeman OSB, *Jesus: The Teacher Within* (New York and London: Continuum, 2000). Dom Freeman is the Dalai Lama's interlocutor in *The Good Heart.* There is of course a huge literature on this issue, but these are reliable and sophisticated starting points. It is sometimes said that Buddhism differs from Christianity in that it is not organized around or in response to a deity. Highly elite or intellectual levels of Buddhism do without a deity; but as a culturally general religion, Buddhism has quite an array of such figures. And, on the other hand, there are highly placed Christian theologians who also—as far as I can tell—dispense with the deity. Paul Tillich comes to mind; so does the Episcopal bishop John Spong, who has popularized a version of Tillich's theology. Much of the appropriation of Buddhism within the Christian West seems to me to have derived from the influence of Tillich and those who stand in turn behind Tillich's as his own theological sources. See also note 25, above.

35. Hauerwas, *Sanctify Them in the Truth,* p. 214: "Our task [as theologians] is very simple: to show the difference that God makes about matters that matter."

36. Dean Sluyter, *The Zen Commandments: Ten Suggestions for a Life of Inner Freedom* (New York: Tarcher/Putnam, 2001). Sluyter errs, it seems to me, when he insists that it doesn't matter what anyone believes. There is a profoundly complex and logically necessary doctrinal basis within Buddhism for his connection between the nothingness of everything and the remaining fact of our moral responsibility for our behavior. If you don't believe that there is a connection between the two, you are left with the nothingness of everything as a perfectly good reason to eat, drink, and be merry. What religion provides, ultimately, is an explanation of the nonempirical, noncausal but nonetheless necessary connection between virtuous behavior and human happiness. We are not virtuous in order to become happy, but that which elicits virtuous behavior will also alleviate and console most human suffering if we refuse to seize particular actions or activities as means to this end. Such paradoxes are far better conveyed by poets and storytellers, who dwell at the heart of every religious tradition.

37. Peter Berger explains this quite adeptly: "Social order, when it functions well, envelopes the individual in a web of habits and meanings that are experienced as self-evidently real. . . . Despite this semblance of solidity, social order is always vulnerable to disruptions. . . . The sacred is one such intrusion. The comic is another" (*Redeeming Laughter: The Comic Dimension of Human Experience* [New York: Walker de Gruyter, 1977]). Yet another is the newborn infant, I suggest: as every new parent discovers, the world B.B. (Before Baby)

can look stunningly different from the world A.B. (After Baby). The "way things are" is neither the way things have always been (history teaches us that) nor the way things have to be. I think that learning to laugh at ourselves is nothing less than crucial. A little wit, a little theology, a little cultural history, and a little frontline experience at parenthood combine into a potent set of tools for asking good questions that disrupt the desperate, driven, "given" reality that life is little more than compete, consume, and die. Other Berger titles well worth exploring are *A Rumor of Angels: Modern Society and the Rediscovery of the Supernatural*, 2nd ed. (New York: Doubleday, 1990), and, with Thomas Luckmann, *The Social Construction of Reality: A Treatise in the Sociology of Knowledge* (Garden City, N.Y.: Doubleday, 1967).

38. I particularly admire Alasdair MacIntyre's explanation of what's wrong with utilitarianism. It's a very important issue, because utilitarianism is the closest that rational-actor theory can come to proposing an intelligible basis for politics and social policy. See *After Virtue: A Study in Moral Theology,* 2nd ed. (Notre Dame, Ind.: University of Notre Dame Press, 1984), pp. 62–71.

39. Sallie McFague, *Life Abundant: Rethinking Theology and Economy for a Planet in Peril* (Minneapolis: Augsburg Fortress, 2001). See also Harvey Cox, "The Market as God," *Atlantic Monthly* (March 1999), rpt. in *The Best Christian Writing 2000,* ed. John Wilson (San Francisco: HarperSanFrancisco, 2000), pp. 79–91.

40. The book is *Dance Lessons: Moving to the Rhythm of a Crazy God* (Harrisburg, Pa.: Morehouse, 1999). The publisher reissued the book a year later in paperback as *Motherhood in the Balance: Children, Career, God, and Me.*

41. Kristen Renwick Monroe, *The Heart of Altruism: Perceptions of a Common Humanity* (Princeton: Princeton University Press, 1996), p. 137. Monroe is by no means alone in challenging rational-actor theory. Jane Allyn Piliavin and Hong-Wen Chang contend that "theory and data now being advanced are more compatible with the view that true altruism—acting with the goal of benefitting another—does exist and is a part of human nature." See "Altruism: A Review of Recent Theory and Research," *Annual Review of Sociology,* vol. 16 (1990): 27–65. See also Shelley E. Taylor, *The Tending Instinct: How Nurturing Is Essential for Who We Are and How We Live* (New York: Times/Holt, 2002).

42. In his book *Treatise on the Family* (enlarged edition, [Cambridge, Mass.: Harvard University Press, 1991]), Nobel laureate Gary Becker explains that "altruists receive psychic income in place of money income—they consume as they sell their products and services—and they can survive as well as money-income maximizers if they do not try to consume too much" (p. 209). One way or another, however, we are always seeking to maximize our "utility function" whether with money income or "psychic income." If I do something nice for you, my ultimate motive is making myself feel better somehow—enhancing my own "psychic income." I'm sure that's an accurate way to describe some human interactions. The question at issue is whether or not it is dangerously reductive to insist that all human behavior is motivated exclusively by self-interest of one kind or another. The cynicism of rational-actor theorists is sometimes as bracing and clear-minded as the postmodern hermeneutics of suspicion, which of course it resembles closely. But in the long run or at a plainly empirical

level, rational-actor theories may not explain as much as they seem to at first. Becker's account of whether a husband will move in order to take a better-paying job if his wife will have to take a poorer-paying job is a case in point. As one who has never been particularly adept in mathematics, I very much enjoyed slowly parsing the formula Becker offers—until I began to wonder where it took into account and calculated all the variables in a two-career move that involve questions other than income. As it happens, on the afternoon when I sat reading Becker's book, the windchill was well below zero; my face had been painfully frozen by the time I walked from the parking lot to the library. I gazed out the library window at the snowy, windswept winter landscape, thinking that my own husband—who simply loathes weather like this—would surely calculate in the climate wherever the new job was located. In fact, I slowly realized, there are many factors that shrewd people will consider. I did not see how any one formula could hold them all—or what predictive value it would have if it could, given the near impossibility of accurately quantifying all these elusive variables. A mathematical representation of the two-career job move might not be much more than a visual metaphor for what anybody knows is a spectacularly complicated situation. For a very famous and rather more sophisticated critique of rational-actor theories, see Donald P. Green and Ian Shapiro, *Pathologies of Rational Choice Theory: A Critique of Applications in Political Science* (New Haven: Yale University Press, 1994). Jonathan Cohn recounts the controversy in a long, very interesting article, "Irrational Exuberance," *New Republic* (25 October 1999), pp. 25ff. The Royal Swedish Academy of Science explanatory press release when it awarded Becker the Nobel Prize in economics can be found at www.nobel.se/economics/laureates/1992/press.html.

43. For a short, elegant account of these developments, see Bruce Bower, "Return of the Group," *Science News* 148 (18 November 1995): 328–330. For a longer, more deeply historical account, see Frank Sulloway, "Darwinian Virtues," a review of Matt Ridley, *The Origin of Virtue: Human Instincts and the Evolution of Cooperation,* in the *New York Review of Books* (8 April 1998), pp. 34–40.

44. Shelley E. Taylor, *The Tending Instinct: How Nurturing Is Essential for Who We Are and How We Live* (New York: Times/Holt, 2002), p. 3 and chapter 1 generally.

45. Esther Sternberg, M.D., describes how this works in *The Balance Within: The Science Connecting Health and Emotions* (New York: Freeman, 2000).

46. On Gary Becker, see above, note 42.

47. Monroe, *The Heart of Altruism,* p. 92.

48. Monroe differs, in short, from those who ground altruism in feelings rather than principles or ideas. See, for example, Carol Gilligan, *In a Different Voice: Psychological Theory and Women's Development* (Cambridge, Mass.: Harvard University Press, 1982) or Nell Noddings, *Caring: A Feminine Approach to Ethics and Moral Education* (Berkeley: University of California Press, 1984). Monroe bases her conclusions upon interviews with both men and women altruists; on the whole, gender differences and developmental psychology are outside the question she addresses, which is whether the rational-actor theorists are correct that altruism can always be deconstructed into self-interest.

49. Monroe, *The Heart of Altruism,* p. 86.

50. Monroe, *The Heart of Altruism,* p. 145.

51. Marilyn Robinson, "Hearing Silence: Western Myth Reconsidered," in *The True Subject: Writers on Life and Craft,* ed. Kurt Brown (St. Paul, Minn.: Graywolf, 1993), p. 150.

Part Two: The Angel and the Oaf: *How the Self Divided against Itself and Everybody Lost*

1. Mona Harrington, *Care and Equality: Inventing a New Family Politics* (New York: Routledge, 2000), p. 31.

2. Nancy Folbre, *The Invisible Heart: Economics and Family Values* (New York: Free Press, 2001), p. xi.

Chapter 3. How Did We Get into This Mess?

3. James C. Edwards, *The Plain Sense of Things: The Fate of Religion in an Age of Normal Nihilism* (University Park: Pennsylvania State University Press, 1997), pp. 7–8.

4. Feminist theologians commonly contend that regarding God as "father" can serve to deconstruct the sociopolitical power of literal fathers. Part of this argument is pointing out how deeply Jesus himself critiqued the clan-based structures of social power in his own day. Nonetheless—and as feminist theologians also point out—endlessly and exclusively talking about God in masculine terms has an impact upon how everyone thinks about men and about masculinity.

5. This phrase appears in one of the versions of the concluding prayer of the major Sunday worship service in the Episcopal *Book of Common Prayer* (New York: Church Hymnal, 1979), p. 365. Consider as well how the Gospel of John recounts a set of promises that Jesus offers shortly before he is arrested: "Peace I leave with you, my peace I give unto you: not as the world giveth, give I unto you. Let not your heart be troubled, neither let it be afraid" (John 14:27, KJV). In *God: A Biography,* Jack Miles contends that the Hebrew deity is quite remarkably at odds with himself; because Christians are called to the imitation of God, the *imitatio Dei,* we tend naturally to see ourselves as at odds with ourselves as well ([New York: Knopf, 1995], pp. 22–24).

6. John Milton, *Paradise Lost,* book IX, line 1183; book XI, line 168.

7. See, for instance, John Wijngaards, *The Ordination of Women in the Catholic Church: Unmasking a Cuckoo's Egg Tradition* (New York: Continuum, 2001), pp. 48–55. It's a marvelously accessible book, replete with references to websites where primary documents can be reviewed—but I do wish it had an index! As late as the nineteenth century, Wijngaards explains, official Roman Catholic church law ("canon" law) asserted that women are not made in the image of God (p. 86, p. 193 n. 5). Peter Brown, *The Body and Society: Men, Women, and Sexual Renunciation in Early Christianity* (New York: Columbia University Press, 1988) thoroughly documents the fact that where Christianity was most influenced by Roman culture it was also most actively hostile to sexuality of any kind—a bias that always translates into hostility toward women. In what was to become the

territories of Eastern Orthodox Christianity, holiness did not require hostility to all things sensual. Roman traditions also did not penetrate to Ireland, where traditional Celtic Christianity was far more affirming of women, women's full humanity, and the value of the physical world.

8. Rosemary Radford Ruether, "Christian Understandings of Human Nature and Gender," in *Religion, Feminism, and the Family,* ed. Anne Carr and Mary Stewart Van Leeuwen, *The Family, Religion, and Culture,* gen. ed. Don S. Browning and Ian S. Evison (Louisville, Ky.: Westminster John Knox, 1996), p. 96. Her essay offers a sharp, engaging, critical history of Western constructions of gender identity; Christian doctrines are of course densely woven into that construction.

9. Psalm 33:16–17, Revised Standard Version. The King James Version of verse 17a is marvelous: "A horse is a vain thing for safety."

10. Psalm 20:7, King James Version.

11. This point is made by Jack Miles, *Christ: A Crisis in the Life of God* (New York: Knopf, 2002), a book which explores at length the theological implications and developments consequent upon the perception that God promises military victory.

12. Those who wish to pursue the matter further might consult Rodney Starke, *One True God: Historical Consequences of Monotheism* (Princeton: Princeton University Press, 2002).

13. The Romans were much more concerned with the control of anger than the control of erotic energy: see Brown, *The Body and Society,* pp. 1–12. The Roman male was expected to be firm but kind or compassionate with loyal members of his staff and his household: obviously no society can function for long without some formal emphasis on teaching and sustaining the interpersonal skills upon which the higher levels of social functioning depend. Brown also explores at considerable length the difference between North African Christians and those of the Eastern empire in their attitudes toward the body and toward the erotic.

14. Brown's *The Body and Society* has a whole chapter on Origen—a colorful, complicated, and important figure by any measure. For more on the view of women within Christianity as the religion assimilated to the Roman Empire, see Wijngaards, *The Ordination of Women in the Catholic Church*.

15. For a useful, accessible, and in fact entertaining account of Stoicism, see John Dominick Crossan, *The Historical Jesus: The Life of a Mediterranean Jewish Peasant* (San Francisco: HarperSanFrancisco, 1991), pp. 72–88. The opposite response was also available, of course: orgiastic cults and, for the more philosophically inclined, Epicureanism. Crossan describes these as well.

16. Brown, *The Body and Society.* See chapter 1 in general. These numbers are cited on page 6.

17. Brown, *The Body and Society,* p. 6 (and n. 3), citing John Chrysostom (C.E. 345?–407) for the phrase "grazed thin by death." In our own day, fertility rates are dramatically different from one country to the next. Amartya Sen, Nobel laureate in economics (1998) and Master of Trinity College, Cambridge, has argued that both fertility rates and childhood mortality decline as female literacy and employment opportunity increase. A quick survey of the relevant statistics

can be found in his essay, "Population and Gender Equity," *Nation* (24–31 July 2000) and a much longer, more detailed account of the issues in *Development as Freedom* (New York: Random, 1999).

18. This point is argued and documented at length by neuropsychologist Shelley E. Taylor in *The Tending Instinct: How Nurturing Is Essential To Who We Are and How We Live* (New York: Times/Holt, 2002). See also Shelley E. Taylor, Laura Cousino Kleim, Brian P. Lewis, Tara L. Grunewald, Regan A. R. Grurung, and John A. Updegraff, "Biobehavioral Responses to Stress in Females: Tend-and-Befriend not Fight-or-Flight," *Psychological Review*, vol. 107, no. 3 (2000): 411–429.

19. Rosemary Radford Ruether, *Christianity and the Making of the Modern Family* (Boston: Beacon, 2000), pp. 60–66.

20. Reuther, *Christianity and the Making of the Modern Family*, p. 62 (Aristotle), p. 78 (Adam and Eve).

Chapter 4. Can We Blame the Victorians?

21. "Intrinsic evil" is theological code for that which is inexcusably wrong under any circumstances. D. Stephen Long discusses economics from an historically informed theological perspective in *Divine Economy: Theology and the Market* (London and New York: Routledge, 2000).

22. Stanley Hauerwas, *Sanctify Them in the Truth: Holiness Exemplified* (Nashville: Abingdon, 1998), pp. 130–131.

23. Stephanie Coontz, *The Way We Never Were: American Families and the Nostalgia Trap* (New York: Basic, 1992), p. 44.

24. Rosemary Radford Reuther offers a short, astute summary of this shift in "Christian Understanding of Human Nature and Gender," *Religion, Feminism, and the Family*, ed. Anne Carr and Mary Stewart Van Leeuwen, *The Family, Religion, and Culture*, gen. ed. Don S. Browning and Ian S. Evison (Louisville, Ky.: Westminster John Knox, 1996), pp. 95–110. As she explains, "Patriarchal anthropology was based on the assumption that the (free, ruling-class) male was not just an individual but a corporate person who exercised 'headship' over a 'body' of persons: women, children, and servants. Women were credited with legal autonomy only when this concept of the family as the base of rights was replaced with an individualism in which each adult was considered to be autonomous. This liberal individualism thus abstracted men and women from their social context as isolated 'atoms,' each motivated by its own self-interest. . . . Feminist anthropology must thus reject both the patriarchal family, where only the patriarch is fully a person, and liberal individualism, where all are assumed to be autonomous persons but isolated from relationships, in order to envision new families in a new society where individuation and community can be interrelated" (p. 108). Coontz's claim—which Reuther would never dispute—is that despite these changes in legal status, women remain culturally situated in an inferior place to the extent that women are regarded as uniquely caring *and therefore* deficient in personal autonomy and competitiveness. My point is that radical individualism portrays compassion itself as a character flaw or deficiency regardless of the gender of the compassionate person.

25. Nancy Folbre makes this point in *The Invisible Heart,* p. xiii. Smith's first book, for instance, was called *The Theory of the Moral Sentiments.*

26. A fine short account of the cult of sensibility is G. J. Barker-Benfield, "Sensibility" in *An Oxford Companion to the Romantic Age: British Culture 1776–1832,* gen. ed. Iain McCalman (Oxford: Oxford University Press, 1999), pp. 102–113. Immanuel Kant, of course, was also hard at work situating the origins of morality within the subjective—although in strictly rational, not emotive ways. I realize that it's hard to imagine anyone further from the cult of sensibility norms than the Sage of Königsberg, but the difference is more in how subjectivity is defined or understood—not in the movement toward individualism itself.

27. Cf. Philippians 4:8.

28. John R. Gillis, *A World of Their Own Making: Myth, Ritual, and the Quest for Family Values* (Cambridge, Mass.: Harvard University Press, 1985), pp. 71–73.

29. Kathleen Hall Jamieson, *Beyond the Double Bind: Women and Leadership* (New York and Oxford: Oxford University Press, 1995), p. 16. On the origin of the double bind in Western habits of dualist oppositions, see p. 5.

30. Christopher Lasch's summary of Wollstonecraft's position is superb: "In the eighteenth and nineteenth centuries, early feminists and antifeminists had attacked the view that women, through fashionable education, should dedicate themselves to a life of leisure and ornamentation. Both Hannah More and Mary Wollstonecraft, for instance, warned that mimicry of aristocratic ways rendered middle-class women unfit for their real obligations, discouraged self-sufficiency, and led to unproductive behavior. In the long run, however, their emphasis on virtue, serious work, and responsibility lost out to a kind of neopaternalism according to which women (and men too) depended upon the assistance of specially trained professionals for the conduct of everyday life. . . . The ability to take seriously and to fulfill individual responsibility in the process of living a productive life was the foundation stone for the attack on patriarchy, whether launched by feminists or antifeminists. The inability to do so is a source and sign of continued inequality or worse" (*Women and the Common Life: Love, Marriage, and Feminism,* ed. Elisabeth Lasch-Quinn [New York: Norton, 1997], pp. 88–89.

Chapter 5. Why Gender Dualism Leaves Us All Half-Crazy

31. Gillis, *A World of Their Own Making,* pp. 124–125.

32. William Julius Wilson, *The Truly Disadvantaged: The Inner City, the Underclass, and Public Policy* (Chicago: University of Chicago Press, 1987), pp. 81–90, cited in Kristin Luker, *Dubious Conceptions: The Politics of Teenage Pregnancy* (Cambridge, Mass.: Harvard University Press, 1996), pp. 166–169 and p. 257 n. 128.

33. David Popenoe documents this at length in *Life Without Father: Compelling New Evidence That Fatherhood and Marriage Are Indispensable for the Good of Children and Society* (New York: Martin Keller/Free Press, 1996): "In my many years as a functioning social scientist, I know of few other bodies of evidence whose weight leans so much in one direction as does the evidence about family structure: on the whole, two parents—a father and a mother—are better for the

child than one parent" (pp. 8–9). Later he comments, "Economic difficulties, such as the loss of the father's income following a divorce, ultimately account for a considerable portion of the negative social and behavior outcomes found among children living in single-parent families. . . . By the best recent social science estimates, however, economic status accounts for no more than half of the negative social and behavioral outcomes of growing up in a single-parent family. . . . The evidence pouring in is powerful that father absence is an independent causative factor of major proportions in these negative outcomes. And these negative outcomes, it turns out, are remarkably large and pervasive" (pp. 55–56). For instance, controlling for family configuration erases the statistical relationship between race and crime and between low income and crime. See also Gertrude Himmelfarb, *One Nation, Two Cultures* (New York: Knopf, 1999), pp. 47–48: "Young men who have grown up in homes without fathers are twice as probable (and those with stepfathers three times as probable) to end up in jail as those who come from two-parent families (keeping constant such other factors as race, income, parents' education, and urban residence). Or (refuting the familiar racial stereotype) the school drop-out rate for white children living with a single parent is substantially higher (28%) than that of black children living with two parents (17%)" (pp. 47–48). On race as a variable in outcomes, see Popenoe, *Life Without Father*: "Up to now, at least, the characteristics of black families in America have anticipated the characteristics of white families by several decades" (p. 26; cf. p. 34). For instance, 22% of black children were living with only one parent in 1960; in 1990, 20% of white children were doing so. In an update of their magisterial *The Social Organization of Sexuality: Sexual Practices in the United States* (Chicago and London: University of Chicago Press, 1994), Edward O. Laumann and Robert T. Michael report that the best predictor of whether a teen is likely to abstain from sex is now whether her parents remain married to one another (cited by Peter Gorner, "Study ties family status to abortions," *Chicago Tribune* [25 January 2001], p. 1A). The most likely predictors used to be a middle-class mother and a Roman Catholic upbringing (ibid.). Adolescent sexuality is a remarkably complex topic: one should also consult Kristin Luker, *Dubious Conceptions: The Politics of Teenage Pregnancy* (Cambridge, Mass.: Harvard University Press, 1996).

34. Roughly 25% of fathers with employed wives care for their own preschool children while the mother works. See "My Daddy Takes Care of Me! Fathers as Care Providers" Current Population Reports #P70–59 (Washington, D.C.: Census Bureau, September 1997), table 1, p. 2. This report can be accessed online at www.census.gov by clicking "Publications" and then finding the title in the list that appears. Jennifer Ehrle, Gina Adams, and Kathryn Tout report similar numbers based upon a more limited data set provided by the National Survey of America's Families in "Who's Caring For Our Youngest Children? Child Care Patterns of Infants and Toddlers," Occasional Paper Number 42 (Washington, D.C.: The Urban Institute, January 2001). They find that for children under the age of three whose married mothers are employed, while the mothers work the fathers care for 30% of children less than one year old, and for 25% of children between one year and three years of age (figure 2, p. 5). When the mother has a college degree, fathers care for 30% of children under the age of three (figure

5, p. 8). Because men seldom marry women with more education than they have themselves, the evidence here suggests that college-educated fathers take a more active role in the care of their young children than other fathers do. In wondering how this works out in particular households, one should keep in mind that children less than three years old with employed mothers average only 23–25 hours of child care per week, depending upon the education of the mother (p. 9). Fathers and "other relatives" together care for 65% of children less than a year old whose mothers are employed and roughly 50% of such children between ages one and three (figure 2, p. 5). This report can be accessed online at www.urban.org or through the National Child Care Information Center, www.nccic.org, by clicking "Selected Resource Lists," then "Infants and Toddlers," then looking for the title in an alphabetized list.

35. Popenoe, *Life Without Father,* p. 149.

36. Bruce Naughton, "Living with Less Power," *Newsweek* (12 June 2000), pp. 56–58.

37. Ann Crittenden, *The Price of Motherhood: Why the Most Important Job in the World Is the Least Valued* (New York: Metropolitan/Holt, 2001).

38. Joan Williams, *Unbending Gender: Why Family and Work Conflict and What To Do About It* (New York: Oxford University Press, 2000), pp. 166–167. See also Christina Hoff Sommers, *Who Stole Feminism? How Women Have Betrayed Women* (New York: Touchstone/Simon & Schuster, 1994), pp. 229–230 and 258–259. Sommers explains—and quite sharply critiques—the philosophical basis upon which gender feminists berate the "false consciousness" of women who stay home to care for their own children themselves.

39. Carol Gilligan, *In A Different Voice: Psychological Theory and Women's Development* (Cambridge, Mass.: Harvard University Press, 1982). Gilligan makes several empirical claims about gender differences in ethical thinking; it is commonly noted by social scientists that subsequent researchers have been unable to duplicate her statistical findings. Christina Hoff Sommers investigates the issue at some length in *Who Stole Feminism?,* pp. 151–154; Dan P. McAdams notes the failure to reproduce the evidence of empirical differences but acknowledges both the utility and the significance of the essential distinction between kinds of moral reasoning in *The Stories We Live By: Personal Myths and the Making of the Self* (New York: Guilford Press, 1993), pp. 88–89. Christopher Lasch offers a very thought-provoking critique of Gilligan's presuppositions, a critique made the more important by how influential her work and her presuppositions have become. See *Women and the Common Life: Love, Marriage, and Feminism,* ed. Elisabeth Lasch-Quinn (New York: Norton, 1997), chapter 6. The history and consequences of patriarchy have of course been studied and debated at length in the last century or so. Classic starting places are Gerda Lerner, *The Creation of Patriarchy* (London: Oxford University Press, 1986) and *The Creation of Feminist Consciousness: From the Middle Ages to Eighteen-Seventy* (London: Oxford University Press, 1993) and Sister Prudence Allen, R.S.M., *The Concept of Woman,* vol. 1, *The Aristotelian Revolution, 750 B.C.–A.D. 1250* (Canada, 1985, rpt. Grand Rapids, Mich.: Eerdmans, 1997) and *The Concept of Woman,* vol. 2, *The Early Humanist Reformation, 1250–1500* (Grand Rapids, Mich.: Eerdmans, 2002). Allen traces the evolution in thought from seeing women as necessarily

inferior to seeing women as complementary to men. Complementarity doctrines are of course fully compatible with functional or sociopolitical inferiority. Claiming complementarity rather than equivalence between males and females often founders upon practical implications for the division of power. More recent work in neuroendocrinology supports the claim that women's biological response to stress is both different from men's and specifically designed to elicit "tend and befriend" behavior. That's an interesting (and potentially hazardous) version of complementarity, although it certainly can be managed in ways that argue for women's skill at leadership and fundamental managerial expertise. Under any circumstances, differences in the physiology of stress response do not require that women will think or talk about ethical issues in some distinctive way. See Shelley E. Taylor, *The Tending Instinct*. See also Shelley E. Taylor, Laura Cousino Kleim, Brian P. Lewis, Tara L. Grunewald, Regan A. R. Grurung, and John A. Updegraff, "Biobehavioral Responses to Stress in Females: Tend-and-Befriend not Fight-or-Flight," *Psychological Review,* vol. 107, no. 3 (2000): 411–429.

40. Susan Chira, *A Mother's Place: Taking the Debate About Working Mothers Beyond Guilt and Blame* (New York: HarperCollins, 1998). On self-immolation, see p. 262; on self-annihilation, p. 8; on mother's needs not counting, pp. 46–47; on failure to have a sense of self, p. 34, pp. 22–23.

41. Chira, *A Mother's Place,* p. 254.

42. Chira, *A Mother's Place,* pp. 22–23.

43. Chira, *A Mother's Place,* p. 262.

44. Chira, *A Mother's Place,* pp. 86–87.

45. This point is explored in wise detail by Christine E. Gudorf, "Parenting, Mutual Love, and Sacrifice," in *Women's Consciousness, Women's Conscience: A Reader in Feminist Ethics,* ed. Barbara Milkert Andolsen, Christine E. Gudorf, and Mary Pellauer (San Francisco: Harper & Row, 1985), pp. 175–192. Although one strand of Christian thought has insisted that "self-sacrificial" love is the Christian ideal, enforcing this standard in particular for women, Gudorf skillfully argues the theological error of that claim. The proper theological model is not self-immolation but rather mutuality: over time and with maturity, the child comes to love as the parents love. Meanwhile, of course, love is patient, love is kind, and love puts up with plenty—without giving the soul away, a sordid boon. Martyrs may make good saints, but they are terrible parents.

46. Joan K. Peters, *When Mothers Work: Loving Our Children Without Sacrificing Our Selves* (Reading, Mass.: Addison-Wesley, 1997), p. 90.

47. Peters, *When Mothers Work,* pp. 217–218.

48. Al Gini, *My Job My Self: Work and the Creation of the Modern Individual* (New York: Routledge, 2000).

49. Peters, *When Mothers Work,* pp. 84–89.

50. Peters, *When Mothers Work,* p. 72.

51. Peters, *When Mothers Work,* p. 75.

52. Bonnie J. Miller-McLemore lucidly outlines the ethical, theological, and psychological shortcomings of this expectation in "Family and Work: Can Anyone 'Have It All?'" in *Religion, Feminism, and the Family,* ed. Anne Carr and Mary Stewart Van Leeuwen, *The Family, Religion, and Culture,* gen. ed. Don S. Browning and Ian S. Evison (Louisville, Ky.: Westminster John Knox, 1996),

pp. 275–293. She contends that "behind the middle-class struggle over 'having it all' lies a fundamental religious question about the nature of the generative life" (p. 282). She contends that the primary challenge of becoming adult in our culture is facing down the psychological fragmentation or loss of self caused by overextending ourselves to the point of exhaustion. Trying to be everything and do everything erodes the healthy psychological boundaries of a coherent self (pp. 289–290). Jane Smiley covers much the same territory from a very different angle: there is a lot about motherhood that we fail to understand clearly because so few literary works have been published by women who are also mothers and who therefore understand firsthand the moral complexity of good mothering. See "Can Mothers Think?" in *The True Subject: Writers on Life and Craft,* ed. Kurt Brown (St. Paul, Minn.: Graywolf Press, 1993), pp. 3–15. "It means something," she argues, "if mothers never speak in a literary voice, and if their sense of themselves as mothers and their view of those around them is not a commonplace of our written culture. It means, for one thing, that everyone in the culture is allowed, or even encouraged, to project all their conflicting fantasies, wishes, and fears onto the concept of motherhood, and onto their individual mothers and wives, which in turn creates of motherhood an ever-changing kaleidoscope of unrealistic and often conflicting aspirations and roles. . . . And the failure of literature to include mothers means that the delicate negotiations between responsibilities to self and to others, as represented by children and husband, but also by social networks of friends and co-workers, is never modeled for the culture at large. . . . Successful motherhood is a unique form of responsibility-taking, rooted in an understanding of competing demands, compromise, nurture, making the best of things, weighing often competing limitations, in order to arrive at a realistic mode of survival. . . . Can a culture exist without such a strong model of responsible, realistic care?" (pp. 7–9). In the absence of that model, we are left with the self-immolating Angel in the House and her absentee-parent partner, the Victorian Oaf in the Office. Smiley's essay ends with a celebration of novelists and story-writers who are also mothers: the literary situation she laments has changed rapidly in the last half-century.

53. Lasch, *Women and the Common Life,* p. 116.

54. Peters, *When Mothers Work,* p. 203.

55. See Chira, *A Mother's Place,* pp. 121–123 and Peters, *When Mothers Work,* pp. 161–166. It is a commonplace story.

56. Robert Karen details the research on this topic in *Becoming Attached: Unfolding the Mystery of the Infant-Mother Bond and Its Impact on Later Life* (New York: Warner, 1994). Some centrally important research originally had to do with the impact upon young children of hospital policies forbidding or limiting visits by parents during a child's hospitalization. Sharon Hays appears to know nothing of this very famous work when, in *The Cultural Contradictions of Motherhood* (New Haven: Yale University Press, 1996), she begins with a particularly critical account of a mother who insists on staying with her hospitalized child. On the other hand, John Bowlby was going overboard, I think, when he (famously) insisted that mothers should never be separated from children. Karen discusses Bowlby at length as well. We will get back to this in part five.

Part Three: Home Sweet Home: *How "Family Values" Fail Us*

Chapter 6. Making It Official: *Why Morality and Compassion Don't Belong in Public*

1. John R. Gillis, *A World of Their Own Making: Myth, Ritual, and the Search for Family Values* (Cambridge, Mass.: Harvard University Press, 1966), pp. 176–177.

2. Philip Rieff, *The Triumph of the Therapeutic: Uses of Faith After Freud* (1966; rpt. Chicago: University of Chicago Press, 1987), pp. 52–53. Sylvia Ann Hewlett offers a good short summary of the same cultural developments in *When the Bough Breaks: The Cost of Neglecting Our Children* (New York: Basic, 1991), pp. 104–107. See also Christopher Lasch, *The Culture of Narcissism: American Life in an Age of Diminishing Expectations* (New York: Norton, 1979), pp. 11–13: "The decline of institutionalized authority in an ostensibly permissive society does not, however, lead to a 'decline of the superego' in individuals. It encourages instead the development of a harsh, punitive superego . . . The struggle to maintain psychic equilibrium in a society that demands submission to the rules of social intercourse but refuses to ground those rules in a code of moral conduct encourages a form of self-absorption that has little in common with the primary narcissism of the imperial self. The egomaniacal, experience-devouring self regresses into a grandiose, narcissistic, infantile, empty self." Once again, I think, a novelist does the best job of articulating the key issue. Here is Marilyn Robinson: "The one thing true about any myth is that among those who are its host population it has the status of belief—not consciously held opinion, but settled assumption, with a penumbra of related assumption spreading away on every side. There is nothing harder than to know what it is we assume. . . . What are we? Why are we here? What is being asked of us? A central myth of ours, if it were rendered as narrative, would sound like this: One is born and in passage through childhood suffers some grave harm. Subsequent good fortune is meaningless because of this injury, while subsequent misfortune is highly significant as the consequence of this injury. The work of one's life is to discover and name the harm one has suffered. . . . It is a myth that allows us to keep ourselves before our eyes as the first claimant, in extreme cases the only claimant, upon our pity and indulgence. This entails indifference to certain values celebrated in older myth, for example, dignity, self-possession, magnanimity, compassion, loyalty, humor, courage, selflessness, reverence expressed as gratitude for one's experience of the goodness of life, reverence expressed as awe in the face of the pain and mystery of life. I suppose it is obvious that I consider this a mean little myth, far worse than most it presumes to displace. Try to imagine it translated into statuary or painted on temple walls, or illuminating its texts. Again, it is a myth of origins that establishes the human personality as small and victimized, fixed in childhood unless—and here is the paradox, I suppose—one recovers one's childhood. In this world of sorrow . . . we ourselves are the children with whom we are compassionate. . . . Our myth disqualifies literal and virtual parents, not only by assuming that they in essential ways have failed, but also by dismissing them as appropriate models of adulthood.

It devalues adulthood as an attainment, as a work of character or imagination, and makes it merely conditional upon the circumstances of childhood. . . . We don't want to have parents, and we don't want to be parents" ("Hearing Silence: Western Myth Reconsidered," in *The True Subject: Writers on Life and Craft,* ed. Kurt Brown [St. Paul, Minn.: Graywolf Press, 1993], pp. 148–149).

3. Robert Bellah et al., *Habits of the Heart: Individualism and Commitment in American Life* (New York: Harper & Row, 1985), p. 83.

4. *New York Times* (10 February 2002), Section 4, p. 1 and p. 6.

5. Christopher Lasch, *Haven in a Heartless World: The Family Besieged* (1977, rpt. New York: Norton, 1995), pp. 168–169.

6. John Gillis, *A World of Their Own Making,* chapter 2 generally, especially pp. 26–27. See also pp. 156–157.

7. Robert Putnam, *Bowling Alone: The Collapse and Revival of American Community* (New York: Simon & Schuster, 2000). Christine Leigh Heyrman describes much deeper roots to this tendency in *Southern Cross: The Beginnings of the Bible Belt* (New York: Knopf, 1997). She describes how evangelical Christians actively opposed the frivolity of merely entertaining social gatherings that, in Heyrman's words, "turned strangers into neighbors" (p. 18). In our day, the pressure to prove our salvation through our success also turns us aside from these communal pastimes. We will return to the social consequences of secularized Reformed theology in part four.

8. Stephanie Coontz, *The Way We Never Were: American Families and the Nostalgia Trap* (New York: Basic, 1992), p. 22.

9. I particularly admire Alasdair MacIntyre's explanation of why utilitarianism does not work. See *After Virtue: A Study in Moral Theology,* 2nd ed. (Notre Dame, Ind.: University of Notre Dame Press, 1984), pp. 62–68.

10. Lasch, *Haven in a Heartless World,* pp. 4, 12–13, 23–24, 123. See also Diane Johnson's review of eight "parenting" books in "My Blue Heaven," *New York Review of Books* (16 July 1998), pp. 15–20.

11. Rosalind C. Barnett and Caryl Rivers, *He Works, She Works: How Two-Income Families Are Happier, Healthier, and Better Off* (San Francisco: Harper-SanFrancisco, 1996), p. 109.

12. This research is cited in Daniel Goleman, *Emotional Intelligence* (New York: Bantam, 1995), p. 86, pp. 88–89. See also Susan C. Vaugh, M.D., *Half Empty, Half Full: Understanding the Psychological Roots of Optimism* (New York: Harcourt, 2000). Vaughn contends that optimists do better on any measure you wish to take, thereby confounding those who think that the basis of optimism is an illusion or at least a failure of hard-headed realism.

13. See note 7, above.

14. Penelope Leach, *Children First: What Our Society Must Do—And Is Not Doing—For Our Children Today* (New York: Knopf, 1997), p. xv.

15. Lasch, *Haven in a Heartless World,* p. xxiv.

Chapter 7. What Counts Is What Counts—And Nothing Else Does

16. Thus Nobel laureate economist Gary S. Becker: ". . . [parents'] utility is raised when their children are better off. Altruistic parents are willing to

contribute to the cost of investing in their children's human capital, but their contribution is limited by the recognition that greater spending on children means less spending on themselves. Therefore, even altruistic parents may under-invest in children in the sense that the equilibrium rate of return on children's human capital exceeds the rate on assets owned by the parents" (*A Treatise on the Family,* enlarged edition [Cambridge, Mass.: Harvard University Press, 1991], p. 5). Elaborate mathematical statements summarize this in an equation; a concerned parent might plug into that equation the expected rate of return on the assets against which the child is competing for investment. He also offers complicated mathematical statements about how each spouse maximizes utility within a marriage while taking the other spouse into account at least in some regards.

17. Alfred W. Crosby, *The Measure of Reality: Quantification and Western Society, 1250–1600* (Cambridge, Mass.: Cambridge University Press, 1997), pp. 237–239, p. 56.

18. Crosby, *The Measure of Reality,* p. 17.

19. Crosby, *The Measure of Reality,* pp. 40–46. The *Oxford English Dictionary* offers nine pages and sixteen separate meanings of the verb "to count."

20. Barbara Tuchman, *A Distant Mirror: The Calamitous Fourteenth Century* (New York: Ballantine, 1978). See also "Hazards on the Way to the Middle Ages," *Atlantic Monthly* (December 1975), pp. 72–78.

21. Crosby, *The Measure of Reality,* pp. 227–228. On the concept "zero," see Charles Seife, *Zero: The Biography of a Dangerous Idea* (New York: Penguin, 2000).

22. Crosby, *The Measure of Reality,* pp. 220–221.

23. Crosby, *The Measure of Reality,* p. 71.

24. Joel Kaye, *Economy and Nature in the Fourteenth Century: Money, Market Exchange, and the Emergence of Scientific Thought* (Cambridge: Cambridge University Press, 1998), p. 2.

25. Stephen Toulmin, *Return to Reason* (Cambridge, Mass.: Harvard University Press, 2002).

Chapter 8. Home Sweet Home as Sacred Center

26. Marilyn Robinson, "Hearing Silence: Western Myth Reconsidered," in *The True Subject: Writers on Life and Craft,* ed. Kurt Brown (St. Paul, Minn.: Graywolf Press, 1993), p. 136. Robinson argues that the prevailing myth of our time is the often futile effort to overcome our dysfunctional families, a myth she depicts as hopelessly small-minded and narcissistic. Her explanation is quoted above, note 2.

27. Robert Frost, "The Death of the Hired Man" in *The Poetry of Robert Frost,* ed. Edward Connery Latham (New York: Holt, Rinehart and Winston, 1969), p. 38.

28. Stephanie Coontz, *The Way We Never Were: American Families and the Nostalgia Trap* (New York: Basic, 1992); Gillis, *A World of Their Own Making.* I should add to the list Lasch, *Haven in a Heartless World,* and Sylvia Ann Hewlett and Cornell West, *The War Against Parents: What We Can Do For America's*

Beleaguered Moms and Dads (Boston: Houghton Mifflin, 1998). All these books are both engaging and rich in social-science specifics. I am grateful for the scrupulous research they provide.

29. D. W. Winnicott, *Home Is Where We Start From,* ed. Claire Winnicott, Ray Shepherd, and Madeleine Davis (New York: Norton, 1986), pp. 190–193.

30. Mircea Eliade, *The Sacred and the Profane: The Nature of Religion,* trans. Willard R. Trask, Bollingen Series XLVI (Princeton: Princeton University Press, 1954), pp. 20–21.

31. Witold Rybczynski, *Home: A Short History of an Idea* (New York: Viking, 1986), pp. 1–13.

32. This is among the major claims by Stanley Hauerwas and William H. Willimon, *Resident Aliens: A Provocative Christian Assessment of Culture and Ministry for People Who Know that Something Is Wrong* (Nashville: Abingdon, 1989).

Chapter 9. Having a Soul That's Not For Sale

33. James C. Edwards, *The Plain Sense of Things: The Fate of Religion in an Age of Normal Nihilism* (University Park: Pennsylvania State University Press, 1997), pp. 46–47.

34. ". . . if we could have the kind of evidence of God the evidentialist desires, then we would have evidence that the God Christians worship does not exist" (Stanley Hauerwas, *With the Grain of the Universe: The Church's Witness and Natural Theology* [Grand Rapids, Mich.: Brazos, 2001], p. 29. Or as Hauerwas explains at a later point, God is not "available to anyone, without moral transformation and spiritual guidance . . . because some propositions are evident only to the wise. That is why in matters of our knowledge of God and our knowledge of God's law, we need training from one another" (p. 36). Sages in every tradition I have studied have been saying this for millennia: true wisdom is an art passed from person to person in an endless work of teaching and learning. That's not "anti-intellectual." It's the natural of spiritual realities. See also *Parabola,* vol. 14, no. 2 (May 1989). The issue, titled "Tradition and Transmission," describes how this recognition is explained and enacted within a variety of religions. On the need for this teaching to happen face-to-face, see *Parabola,* vol. 18, no. 3 (fall 1992). The title of this issue is "The Oral Tradition."

35. Alan Wolfe, *One Nation After All: What Middle-Class Americans Really Think About God, Family, Racism, Welfare, Immigration, Homosexuality, Work, the Right, the Left, and Each Other* (New York: Viking, 1998), and *Moral Freedom: The Impossible Idea That Defines the Way We Live Now* (New York: Norton, 2001). See also Alasdair MacIntyre's famous and witty account of how we have lost the capacity to talk coherently about virtue, in the opening pages of *After Virtue: A Study in Moral Theology,* 2nd ed. (Notre Dame, Ind.: University of Notre Dame Press, 1984).

36. Edwards, *The Plain Sense of Things,* pp. 23–27.

37. Edwards, *The Plain Sense of Things,* p. ix.

38. Edwards, *The Plain Sense of Things,* pp. 53–54.

39. Hewlett, *When the Bough Breaks,* pp. 26–27.

40. David Popenoe, *Life Without Father: Compelling New Evidence that Fatherhood and Marriage Are Indispensable for the Good of Children and Society* (New York: Martin Kessler/Free Press, 1996), p. 9.

41. Rowan Williams, *Lost Icons: Reflections on Cultural Bereavement* (London: T & T Clark, 2000).

42. Dan McAdams, *The Stories We Live By: Personal Myths and the Making of the Self* (New York: Guilford, 1993), pp. 120–121.

43. James A. Holstein and Jaber F. Gubrium, *The Self We Live By: Narrative Identity in a Postmodern World* (New York and Oxford: Oxford University Press, 2000), pp. 60–61. The word "multiphrenia" was coined by Kenneth Gergen to name the psychological consequences of how we are bombarded with information and demands for our attention; they discuss Gergen's claim in some detail. See also Sven Birkerts, "Fractured Being," *Hungry Mind Review* (winter 1998–1999), pp. 11–12 and 24.

44. McAdams, *The Stories We Live By,* p. 122. Like other major religions, Christianity provides at least an outline or plot structure for such a narrative of personal identity, as evident for instance in Bunyan's *Pilgrim's Progress* or Dante's *La Commedia.* Robert W. Jenson explains how this works in "How the World Lost Its Story," in *The New Religious Humanists,* ed. Gregory Wolfe (New York: Free Press, 1997), pp. 135–149. Daniel Siegel, M.D., contends that storytelling is also the means by which people influence one another's neural organization (*The Developing Mind: Toward a Neurobiology of Interpersonal Experience* [New York: Guilford Press, 1999], p. 62.

45. Bonnie J. Miller-McLemore, "Family and Work: Can Anyone 'Have It All?'" in *Religion, Feminism, and the Family,* ed. Anne Carr and Mary Stewart Van Leeuwen (Louisville, Ky.: Westminster John Knox, 1996), pp. 275–293.

46. Hewlett, *When the Bough Breaks,* pp. 104–106.

47. Philip Rieff, *The Triumph of the Therapeutic: Uses of Faith After Freud* (Chicago: University of Chicago Press, 1966, 1987). Cultural pressures that deter us from commitment have been traced by many writers over the years. See, for instance, Leach, *Children First,* Hewlett and West, *The War Against Parents,* and Barbara Dafoe Whitehead, *The Divorce Culture* (New York: Knopf, 1997).

48. Lasch, *Haven in a Heartless World,* pp. 23–24.

49. Stanley Hauerwas, *Sanctify Them in the Truth: Holiness Exemplified* (Nashville: Abingdon, 1998), p. 38.

50. Edwards, *The Plain Sense of Things,* pp. 46–47.

51. Samuel Taylor Coleridge, *Biographia Literaria* (1817), ed. J. Shawcross, 2 vols. (London: Oxford University Press, 1907), vol. 1, chap. 10: "I became convinced that religion, as both the corner-stone and the key-stone of morality, must have a *moral* origin; so far at least, that the evidence of its doctrines could not, like the truths of abstract science, be wholly independent of the will. It were therefore to be expected, that its *fundamental* truth would be such as MIGHT be denied; though only by the fool, and even by the fool from the madness of the *heart* alone" (p. 135). Or later, volume 1, chapter 12: "They and they only can acquire the philosophic imagination, the sacred power of self-intuition, who within themselves can interpret and understand the symbol, that the wings of the air-slyph are forming within the skin of the caterpillar; those only, who feel

in their own spirits the same instinct, which impels the chrysalis of the horned fly to leave room in its involucrum for antennae yet to come. . . . In short, all the organs of sense are framed for a corresponding world of sense; and we have it. All the origins of spirit are framed for a correspondent world of spirit: though the latter organs are not developed in all alike. But they exist in all, and their first appearance discloses itself in the *moral* being" (p. 167).

52. Robert Bellah et al., *The Good Society* (New York: Knopf, 1991).

Part Four: Secular Salvation and the Divine Right of Markets: *He Who Dies with the Most Toys Wins*

1. Christopher Lasch, *Haven in a Heartless World: The Family Besieged* (1977, rpt. New York: Norton, 1995), p. xvii.

Chapter 10. What's Work?

2. Miroslav Volf, *Work in the Spirit: Toward a Theology of Work* (London and New York: Oxford University Press, 1991), pp. 10–11.

3. Joan Williams, *Unbending Gender: Why Family and Work Conflict and What To Do About It* (London and New York: Oxford University Press, 2000).

4. Williams, *Unbending Gender.* This fact is evident throughout her book, but certainly clearest in chapter five, "How Domesticity's Gender Wars Take on Elements of Class and Race Conflict." She cautions, "To avoid class as well as gender wars, feminist proposals need to maintain a tone of respect for domesticity" (p. 157; cf. other references to a "tone of respect" on p. 156, p. 168). I would urge a higher standard yet: academic theorists in these areas should acquire and offer genuine respect, not merely a "tone of respect," for the choices and priorities held by other women. Williams makes the same error in her earlier discussion of false consciousness: "The most common existing language speaks of individuals making bad choices due to false consciousness. The drawbacks of this approach include its judgmental tone and the implication that some of us escape the social structures that, to a greater or lesser extent, create all of us" (p. 38). It seems to me that the problem here goes far beyond "tone."

5. Williams, *Unbending Gender,* particularly chapter 5.

6. Thus Gary Becker, for instance: "Altruistic parents are willing to contribute to the cost of investing in their children's human capital, but their contribution is limited by the recognition that greater spending on children means less spending on themselves. Therefore, even altruistic parents may under-invest in the sense that the equilibrium rate of return on children's human capital exceeds the rate on assets owned by the parents" (*A Treatise on the Family,* enlarged edition [Cambridge, Mass.: Harvard University Press, 1991], p. 5).

7. Mihaly Csikszentmihalyi, *Finding Flow: The Psychology of Engagement with Everyday Life* (New York: Basic, 1997), p. 117.

8. Marlane van Hall, "The Zen of Housework," in *Sacred Dimensions of Women's Experience,* ed. Elizabeth Dodson Gray (Wellesley: Roundtable, 1988), p. 149, p. 151.

9. Csikszentmihalyi, *Finding Flow,* pp. 110–112.

10. Catherine M. Wallace, *For Fidelity: How Intimacy and Commitment Enrich Our Lives* (New York: Knopf, 1998), p. 67.

11. Robert D. Putnam, *Bowling Alone: The Collapse and Revival of American Community* (New York: Simon & Schuster, 2000).

12. Robert H. Frank, *Luxury Fever: Money and Happiness in an Era of Excess* (Princeton: Princeton University Press, 1999), pp. 159–160. *Luxury Fever* was also published by Free Press/Simon & Schuster, with a different subtitle: "Why Money Fails to Satisfy in an Era of Excess." Robert Frank is Godwin Smith Professor of Economics, Ethics, and Public Policy at Cornell.

13. Frank, *Luxury Fever,* pp. 8–9, pp. 148–158.

14. Frank, *Luxury Fever,* pp. 175–187 and chapter 6, "Gains that Endure," pp. 75–93.

15. Joanne B. Ciulla, *The Working Life: The Promise and Betrayal of Modern Work* (New York: Times/Random, 2000), pp. 190–191. For a quick survey of the issue, see Bonnie Miller Rubin, "Jumping Off the Fast Track," *Chicago Tribune Magazine* (22 January 1995), pp. 10–15. As she points out, "In an expanding economy, hitching one's identity to a career may have made some sense, but when the pie is shrinking, it's a recipe for disaster. A 30-year-old man in 1949 could expect to see real earnings rise by 63% by the time he turned 40; the same man in 1973 would see his income decline by 1% by his 40th birthday, making Baby Boomers the first American generation to be less successful than their fathers at the same age." Another good source on these issues is Jeremy Rifkin, *The End of Work* (New York: Putnam, 1995).

16. Ciulla, *The Working Life,* pp. 106–107.

17. Ciulla, *The Working Life,* on HEW study see pp. 117–119; on Studs Terkel, p. 119. Don't miss her short but thought-provoking discussion of what's involved in the employment choices people make, pp. 16–21.

18. Ciulla, *The Working Life,* p. 108, p. 109. I have silently corrected a minor copyediting error in the second sentence.

19. Robert B. Reich, *The Future of Success* (New York: Knopf, 2001). See also Mary Williams Walsh, "Luring the Best in an Unsettled Time," *New York Times* (30 January 2001), p. E1: "In its day, the pact [between employers and employees] could reinforce itself for a lifetime, for the higher one climbed in a company, the greater the rewards and the stronger the incentive to stick around and try for more. Eight million layoffs later, the old understanding is dead. . . . Companies are now searching urgently for new ways to foster old-fashioned loyalty and commitment."

20. On pre-emptive layoffs, see David Leonhardt, "The Wave of Layoffs: Is It Bound To Get Bigger?" *New York Times* (30 January 2001), p. E1.

21. Ciulla, *The Working Life,* p. 162.

22. Ciulla, *The Working Life,* p. 222.

23. Ciulla, *The Working Life,* p. 230. See also Robert B. Cialdini, Ph.D., *Influence: The Psychology of Persuasion,* rev. ed. (New York: Quill/Morrow, 1993).

24. Elizabeth McKenna, *When Work Doesn't Work Anymore: Women, Work, and Identity* (New York: Delacorte, 1997).

Chapter 11. The History of Our Dilemma

25. Max Weber, *The Protestant Ethic and the Spirit of Capitalism,* trans. Talcott Parsons (Los Angeles: Roxbury, 1998).

26. Ciulla, *The Working Life,* pp. 54–55.

27. On the term "monastic capitalism": Life inside an actual monastery is humanely attentive to our need for human relationships and for creative leisure, as for instance the Rule of Benedict makes clear.

28. Luther expected people to stay put in the social class and family trade into which they were born, but his idea was later used to justify social mobility. Nonetheless, Luther's original position shows up in those who criticize employed women for rejecting their "sacred duty" to care for children and to perform nonmarket work around the household generally.

29. A fine short account of the interweaving of politics, theology, and excommunication is Richard E. Rubenstein's *When Jesus Became God: The Epic Fight over Christ's Divinity in the Last Days of Rome* (New York: Harcourt Brace, 1999). That pattern is also fully evident in any good history of the high Middle Ages and the rise of nationalism.

30. Barbara W. Tuchman, *A Distant Mirror: The Calamitous 14th Century* (New York: Ballantine, 1978).

31. On the distinction between the good heart and the controlling ego, see *Parabola,* vol. 27, no. 1 (spring 2002). The entire issue is addressed to this distinction.

32. The doctrine of predestination is derived from John Calvin, but it is not central to his thought; it became prominent after his death principally through the work of Theodorus Beza, who took over leadership in Geneva after Calvin's death. See Karen Armstrong, *A History of God: The 4000-Year Quest of Judaism, Christianity, and Islam* (New York: Ballantine, 1993), pp. 282–283; see also William J. Bouwsma, *John Calvin: A Sixteenth-Century Portrait* (London and New York: Oxford University Press, 1988), pp. 35–36, pp. 172–173.

33. For what we do have, see *Pelagius: Life and Letters,* ed. B. R. Rees, two volumes bound as one (New York: Boydell, 1991). Don't miss Hilaire Belloc's "The Drinking Song of Pelagius," in vol. 2, Appendix IV, pp. 143–144.

34. Robert Barron, *Thomas Aquinas, Spiritual Master,* A Spiritual Legacy Book, gen. ed. John Farina (New York: Crossroad, 1996), p. 156.

35. Relevant excerpts from the Westminster Confession of 1647—and Milton's famous comment about it—are provided by Max Weber in *The Protestant Ethic and the Spirit of Capitalism,* pp. 98–101. The Westminster Confession can be found among the historical documents in the Presbyterian *Book of Order.*

36. Once again, I'd direct the curious to Christine Leigh Heyrman, *Southern Cross: The Beginnings of the Bible Belt* (New York: Knopf, 1997). She cites from a fascinating array of primary documents—letters, journals, etc.—that bring this issue to life in quite engaging ways.

37. Bouwsma, *John Calvin,* pp. 218–219.

38. Or, in the properly medieval terms Dante used, pride, lust, and avarice. Three heraldic beasts, icons of these vices, attack Dante's first-person narrator in the opening pages of his epic, *The Divine Comedy.*

39. Robert A. F. Thurman, *Buddhism,* three videotapes (New York: Mystic Fire Video, 1999). Robert Thurman has also written many books, but the tapes are particularly engaging for how extemporaneously Thurman moves back and forth between lively, concrete analogies and quite sophisticated theological argument and explication. American-born, American-educated advocates of Buddhism sometimes insist that Buddhism is without deities and without doctrine as well. Like His Holiness the Dalai Lama's book *The Good Heart: A Buddhist Perspective on the Teachings of Jesus* (Boston: Wisdom Publications, 1996), Thurman's work goes a long way toward dispelling that misunderstanding. As sociologist Rodney Starke and Roger Finke explain, the Buddhism of "a small intellectual elite" may do without gods of any kind, but "popular Buddhism is particularly rich in supernatural beings" (*Acts of Faith: Explaining the Human Side of Religion* [Princeton: Princeton University Press, 1996], p. 90). As Starke and Finke also point out, some Christian theologians do not believe in a deity either. Paul Tillich is probably the most eminent of these.

40. "Psychology Discovers Happiness: I'm OK, You're OK," *New Republic* (5 March 2001), pp. 20–23.

41. American liberal Protestant theologians have, at times, explicitly endorsed this shift, essentially by arguing that what is meant by "God" is the higher or the deeper or the essential "Self" rather than, in more traditional terms, the Creator of all, ultimately unknowable except quite indirectly and entirely transcendent to human consciousness at any level. See, for instance, Paul Tillich, *The Courage to Be* (1952, rpt. New Haven: Nota Bene editions of Yale University Press, 2000). It is a massively influential book, finely argued and beautifully articulate; but from a much older Christian perspective ("orthodox" not "reformed"), Tillich is also astoundingly wrong-headed. Karen Armstrong, in *A History of God,* recounts the history of Western monotheism from within this identification of "God" with the "true self." One does not have to believe in the Mean Old Man in the Sky god, in the arbitrary, magic-working, projection-of-human-control-needs god, to question the liberal-Protestant individualist collapse of the philosophic distinction between the human and the transcendent sacred. In short, I am at heart a profoundly Irish Catholic, despite what Rome or its cardinals would say of me if anyone asked. The deeper reaches of Celtic Christianity never much worried about Rome or its imperial pretensions; neither do I. My Protestant friends tell me that makes me a Protestant after all. My Jewish friends also insist that at heart I'm a Jew, a claim that I take as the most serious compliment they know how to offer. But in the kingdom of God there are no franchises and no factions: at last we do succeed in seeing one another as echoes in the finite of the infinite creative and self-creative Holy One. Thereby will we discover that we are finite only in part, that death is not an end but a transition into something we can only imagine.

42. Robert M. Bellah et al., *Habits of the Heart: Individualism and Commitment in American Life* (Berkeley: University of California Press, 1985; rpt. New York: Harper & Row, 1986), p. 50.

43. Dan McAdams explains this adeptly: "In order to find meaning, . . . we must consciously and seriously consider the possibility that nothing is meaningful, that all of life is random and without purpose. We must reject society's pat

answers to questions of meaning, lest we find ourselves living hypocritically and in 'bad faith.' Meaning must come from within ourselves and through our own actions. With each thought, word, and deed, we define the self. We must never forget the possibility of nothingness and meaninglessness lurking behind every action and thought. If we forget the possibility that our lives are meaningless, then they will indeed become meaningless. But if we make it our 'fundamental project' in life to create, redeem, and sanctify ourselves and our world, then we will find meaning and we will become like God. A person does not have to believe, with Sartre, that God is dead in order to find his words convincing. . . . Whether we are Christians, Jews, Muslims, agnostics, or 'other,' we are each alone responsible to engage in the heroic battle for meanings, waged on a precipice above the void" (*The Stories We Live By,* p. 165). McAdams seems not to realize that his account is as fully a cosmological myth as anything to be found in the Bible or in other foundational Scriptures and religious traditions. Replace "bad faith" with "sin," the battle with angst for the battle with evil, and creating meaning with attaining redemption: the parallels are exact. Secularize radical Protestantism, and what results is the liberal myth: we are to create, redeem, and sanctify ourselves and our world, thereby becoming like God. The problem here is that meaning that comes exclusively "from within ourselves" is indistinguishable from the egocentric narcissism that wisdom traditions regard as the central spiritual trap humans face. This sort of cosmic individualism also leaves the individual radically isolated and therefore especially prey to the sophisticated manipulations of advertising and a consumerist culture.

44. Bellah et al., *Habits of the Heart,* p. 21.

45. Volf, *Work in the Spirit,* p. 57.

46. Esther De Waal, *The Celtic Way of Prayer: The Recovery of the Religious Imagination* (New York: Doubleday, 1997), chapter 5.

47. Stanley Hauerwas, *In Good Company: The Church as Polis* (Notre Dame, Ind.: University of Notre Dame Press, 1995), p. 115, p. 117.

48. Al Gini, *My Job My Self: Work and the Creation of the Modern Individual* (New York: Routledge, 2000), p. 5.

49. Williams, *Unbending Gender,* pp. 34–37, p. 159.

50. Wendell Berry makes this point quite eloquently in his novel, *Jayber Crow* (Washington, D.C.: Counterpoint, 2000). Jayber Crow, his first-person narrator, observes that people attend the university in an effort to "make something" of themselves—which presupposes, he muses, that they were nothing at all otherwise.

51. Hauerwas, *In Good Company,* p. 115.

Chapter 12. Selling Ourselves Short in a Buyer's Market

52. Juliet B. Schor, *The Overspent American: Upscaling, Downshifting, and the New Consumer* (New York: Basic, 1998), p. 59.

53. Schor, *The Overspent American,* pp. 3–4, p. 10, p. 21.

54. Robert H. Frank, *Luxury Fever: Why Money Fails To Satisfy in an Era of Excess* (New York: Free Press, 1999). See also sociologist Alan Wolfe's review essay of half a dozen books on this topic: "Undialectical Materialism," *New Republic* (23 October 2000), pp. 29–35.

55. Robert H. Frank, "Why Living in a Rich Society Makes Us Feel Poor," *New York Times Magazine* (15 October 2000), pp. 62–64.

56. Schor, *The Overspent American,* p. 6.

57. Schor, *The Overspent American,* p. 76. Jennifer Cheeseman Day and Eric C. Newburger, "The Big Payoff: Educational Attainment and Synthetical Estimates of Work-Life Earnings" #P23–210 (Washington, D.C.: U.S. Census Bureau, July 2002). This report can be reached online at www.census.gov by clicking "Publications" and looking through an alphabetical list of titles.

58. John De Graff, David Wann, and Thomas H. Naylor, *Affluenza: The All-Consuming Epidemic* (San Francisco: Berrett-Koehler, 2001).

59. Jane Hammerslough, *Dematerializing: Taming the Power of Possessions* (Cambridge, Mass.: Perseus, 2001).

60. *Consuming Desires: Consumption, Culture, and the Pursuit of Happiness,* ed. Roger Rosenblatt (Washington, D.C.: Island Press; Covelo, Ca.: Shearwater, 1999).

61. Robert B. Cialdini, Ph.D., *Influence: The Psychology of Persuasion* (New York: Morrow, 1993). The techniques he describes are also standard fare in management programs designed to trap people into putting the needs of employers ahead of any other need or duty in their lives.

62. Teresa A. Sullivan, Elizabeth Warren, and Jay Lawrence Westbrook, *The Fragile Middle Class: Americans in Debt* (New Haven:Yale University Press, 2000). For a quick survey of this indebtedness, consult Daniel McGinn, "Maxed Out" *Newsweek* (27 August 2001), pp. 34–40. For instance, "By the end of 2000, the average cardholder had $8123 in credit-card debt" (p. 37). All through the booming 1990s, home equity plummeted and late mortgage payments increased.

63. Theda Skokpol, *The Missing Middle: Working Families and the Future of American Social Policy* (New York: Norton, 2000).

64. Consider, for instance, that a baseball-cap maker in Derby, New York, pays his workers $10–$12 an hour although cap producers in China pay fifteen to twenty cents an hour: Steven Greenhouse, "Cap Maker Is Assailed By Colleges," *New York Times* (21 August 2001), p. A15.

65. Barbara Ehrenreich: *Nickel and Dimed: On (Not) Getting By in America* (New York: Metropolitan, 2001); D. Stephen Long, *Divine Economy: Theology and the Market* (London and New York: Routledge, 2000), pp. 229, 237–238, 256. "Intrinsically evil" is theological code for utterly, indefensibly immoral. In her review of Kenneth L. Kumser, *The Homeless in American History* (New York: Oxford University Press, 2001), Ehrenreich observes, "ours is a society that routinely generates destitution—and then, perversely, relieves its conscience by vilifying the destitute" (*New York Times Book Review* [20 January 2002], p. 9). According to census data, child poverty rates in 2000 were higher than they were in 1979 (Don Terry, "U.S. Child Poverty Rate Fell as Economy Grew, But Is Above 1979 Level," *New York Times* [11 August 2000], p. A10).

66. See, for instance, George Soros, *On Globalization* (New York: Public Affairs, 2001), reviewed by Joseph E. Stiglitz, "A Fair Deal for the World," *New York Review of Books* (23 May 2002), pp. 24–28 and also reviewed by John Cassidy, "Master of Disaster," *New Yorker* (15 July 2002), pp. 82–86. Another important source is Joseph E. Stiglitz, *Globalization and Its Discontents* (New York:

Norton, 2002), reviewed by Benjamin M. Friedman, "Globalization: Stiglitz's Case," *New York Review of Books* (15 August 2002), pp. 48–51. See also Felix Rohatyn, "The Betrayal of Capitalism," *New York Review of Books* (28 February 2002), pp. 6–8. This is a stunning collection of men with unquestionable expertise in global economic affairs and government, all arguing that the global economy is being manipulated to the unconscionable advantage of already-wealthy nations. Benjamin R. Barber brilliantly describes the cultural and political consequences in *Jihad vs. McWorld: How Captitalism and Tribalism Are Reshaping the World* (New York: Ballantine, 1995, 1996).

67. Arlie Russell Hochschild, *The Time Bind: When Work Becomes Home and Home Becomes Work* (New York: Metropolitan/Holt, 1997), pp. 220–221.

68. Hochschild, *The Time Bind,* pp. 199–200.

69. Hochschild, *The Time Bind,* pp. 27–28.

70. Hochschild, *The Time Bind,* pp. 50–52.

71. Hochschild, *The Time Bind,* pp. 198–200.

72. Hochschild, *The Time Bind,* p. 132.

73. Hochschild, *The Time Bind,* p. 243.

74. Hochschild, *The Time Bind,* pp. 191–192.

75. Mona Harrington, *Care and Equality: Inventing A New Family Politics* (New York: Routledge, 2000), p. 31.

76. Nancy Folbre, *The Invisible Heart: Economics and Family Values* (New York: New Press, 2001), p. ix. This is part of her table-of-contents summary of her eighth chapter.

77. Alfred W. Crosby, *The Measure of Reality: Quantification and Western Society 1250–1600* (Cambridge and New York: Cambridge University Press, 1997), p. 160. On what's wrong with our sense of time, see Dorothy C. Bass, *Receiving the Day: Christian Practices for Opening the Gift of Time* (San Fancisco: Jossey-Bass, 2000) and Gary Eberle, *Sacred Time and the Search for Meaning* (Boston: Shambhala, 2003).

78. Hochschild, *The Time Bind,* pp. 51–52. See also Joel Kaye, *Economy and Nature in the Fourteenth Century: Money, Market Exchange, and the Emergence of Scientific Thought* (Cambridge: Cambridge University Press, 1998). Kaye argues that the development of cash and clocks engendered an entirely new understanding of time. In short, time becomes money, which is to say that life and time are no longer understood as gifts freely given by a generous, creative God.

79. Suzanne Braun Levine explores this issue at length in *Father Courage: What Happens When Men Put Family First* (New York: Harcourt, 2000); see especially p. 65.

80. See, for instance, James A. Levine and Todd L. Pittinsky, *Working Fathers: New Strategies for Balancing Work and Family* (Reading, Mass.: Addison Wesley, 1997).

81. Christopher Lasch, *Women and the Common Life: Love, Marriage, and Feminism,* ed. Elisabeth Lasch-Quinn (New York: Norton, 1997), p. 119.

82. Stanley Hauerwas, in "Why Clinton Is Incapable of Lying: A Christian Analysis," in *Judgment Day at the White House,* ed. Gabriel Fackre (Grand Rapids, Mich.: Eerdmans, 1999), pp. 28–31.

83. Benjamin R. Barber, *Jihad vs. McWorld: How Globalism and Tribalism Are Reshaping the World* (New York: Ballantine, 1995, 1996). Barber holds an endowed chair in political science at Rutgers.

84. Lawrence Mitchell, *Corporate Irresponsibility: America's Newest Export* (New Haven: Yale University Press, 2001).

85. Lasch, *Haven in a Heartless World,* p. 7, pp. 23–24. Robert Bellah et al., *The Good Society* (New York: Knopf, 1991), pp. 84–85, cf. p. 292.

86. D. Stephen Long, *Divine Economy: Theology and the Market* (London and New York: Routledge, 2000).

87. Hochschild, *The Time Bind,* pp. 220–221.

88. Kristen Renwick Monroe, *The Heart of Altruism: Perceptions of a Common Humanity* (Princeton: Princeton University Press, 1996), pp. 212–213.

Part Five: Decoding the Child-Care Debates

1. On the loss of traditions sustaining community and civic participation, see Robert D. Putnam, *Bowling Alone: The Collapse and Revival of American Community* (New York: Simon & Schuster, 2000).

2. Joanne B. Ciulla, *The Working Life: The Promise and Betrayal of Modern Work* (New York: Times/Random, 2000); Robert Reich, *The Future of Success* (New York: Knopf, 2001). Ciulla holds the Coston Family Chair in Leadership and Ethics at the Jepson School of Leadership Studies at the University of Richmond; Reich is Maurice B. Hexter Professor of Social and Economic Policy at Brandeis University's Heller Graduate School. He has served in three national administrations, most recently as Secretary of Labor under Bill Clinton.

Chapter 13. The Predicament of Parents

3. Sharon Hays, *The Cultural Contradictions of Motherhood* (New Haven: Yale University Press, 1996). Hays assumes that such obsessive attentiveness—the Angel in the House gone manic—is the only available cultural model of active, engaged mothering.

4. A major four-state review of 400 profit and nonprofit daycare centers found that only 8% of infant classrooms and 24% of preschool classrooms were rated as good or excellent in quality. Ten percent of preschool programs and 40% of infant programs were rated as poor in quality (Suzanne Helburn et al., "Cost, Quality & Child Outcomes in Child Care Centers Study" [Denver: Economics Department, University of Colorado-Denver, 1995]). The research report itself is available directly from the University of Colorado Department of Economics (http://econ.cudenver.edu/home/research_reports.htm). The figures I cite come from one of the many scholarly summaries of these findings on university websites: the National Center for Early Development and Learning at the University of North Carolina (www.fgp.unc.edu/~ncedl/PDFs/fact1_1.pdf). A longer discussion with an excellent bibliography of various daycare center studies is also available from the folks at the University of North Carolina. See www.unc.edu/~ncedl/PDFs/brief1.pdf.

A broader array of relevant information on this crucial issue is available through the National Childcare Information Center (www.nccic.org), a project of the Administration for Children and Families within the U.S. Department of Health and Human Services. They maintain a website with hotlinks to research papers and organizations concerned about a variety of topics. From the home page, click "site map" then "Selected Resource Lists," then "Early Childhood Workforce." For a better understanding of the situation of child-care workers, clearly the most important and most prestigious of these organizations is the Center for the Child Care Workforce (www.ccw.org). According to their report "Current Data on Child Care Salaries and Benefits in the United States" [Washington, D.C.: Center for the Child Care Workforce, March 2002] child care "suffers a higher concentration of poverty-level jobs than almost any other occupation in the United States." According to Bureau of Labor statistics they present, "only 18 occupations report having lower mean wages than child care workers. Those who earn higher wagers than child care workers include service station attendants, tree trimmers, crossing guards, and bicycle repairers" (p. 4). According to Bureau of Labor 2000 statistics, the median hourly wage for a child-care worker is $7.43 per hour. The median hourly wage of preschool teachers is only $8.56 (by comparison, 78 percent of education workers earn an average wage above $20 per hour [p. 5]). Despite the importance to the child of a stable relationship with a caregiver, such low wages lead to annual job turnover rates of 30–40% (p. 3). This report can also be accessed directly from www.ccw.org; it includes data about median child-care provider hourly wages and turnover rates on a state-by-state basis.

Other professional groups also track the child-care workforce. According to a report of the National Academy of Sciences, in 1988 the average salary of child-care teachers with some college education was $9,293 per year; women with the same education in the general civilian workforce earned more than twice as much ($19,369 per year). And yet, daycare research consistently finds a strong relationship between staff wages and the quality of care provided (*From Neurons to Neighborhoods: The Science of Early Childhood Development,* ed. Jack P. Shonkoff and Deborah A. Phillips [Washington, D.C.: National Academy Press, 2000], p. 317; search www.nap.edu for title to read this report online in PDF format). This same National Academy of Sciences report also points out that "Virtually every systematic effort to characterize the quality of child care in the United States has found that about 10 to 20 percent of arrangements fall below thresholds of even adequate care . . . regardless of the type of care being examined. . . . Even the NICHD Study of Early Childcare, which provides a more favorable portrait of child care quality than do other studies, reported that one in four infant caregivers were moderately insensitive . . . and 19 percent were moderately or highly detached" (p. 320). Furthermore, the Consumer Product Safety Commission found "pervasive health and safety violations" (p. 320). On these violations, *From Neurons to Neighborhoods* cites the following sources: Consumer Product Safety Commission, *Safety Hazards in Child Care Settings* (Washington, D.C.: U.S. Consumer Products Safety Commission, 1999) and Office of the Inspector General, *Nationwide Review of Health and Safety Standards at Child Care Facilities* (Washington, D.C.: U.S. Department of Health and Human Services, 1994).

5. A whole array of links to major studies of child-care cost can be found through www.nccic.org by clicking "frequently asked questions" and searching for "child-care cost." According to census data, average cost of child care for 45 hours a week is $7897 per year ($3.51 per hour). If the door-to-door commute is an hour each way, cost rises to $8775. Preschool care (ages three to five) is a bit cheaper ($2.63 per hour), although of course children have to be out of diapers. Preschool averages $5917 per year with a half-hour commute, or $6,575 with an hour commute. These data are from Kristin Smith, *Who's Minding the Kids? Spring 1997,* Current Population Reports, P70–86 (Washington, D.C.: U.S. Census Bureau, July 2002), table 7, page 15. This report is available in PDF format at www.census.gov—click "Subjects A-Z" and then select "child care data" under "C." It's also available through a hotlink at the National Child Care Information Center of the U.S. Department of Health and Human Services (www.nccic.org, click "publications" and find the title in an A-Z list) and from the National Academy Press of the National Academy of Sciences (www.nap.edu, search on title).

Furthermore, these are the average costs of actual daycare centers and preschools, many of which offer a poor to mediocre quality of care (see note 4, above). According to a National Academy of Sciences report, high quality care is much more expensive (*From Neurons to Neighborhoods: The Science of Early Childhood Development,* ed. Jack P. Shonkoff and Deborah A. Phillips [Washington, D.C.: National Academy Press, 2000], p. 321; search www.nap.edu for title to read this report online in PDF format). For instance, 90 percent of Air Force daycare centers are accredited, and in these centers actual costs per child per hour come to $3.86. (In a for-profit daycare center, of course, the hourly costs charged to parents would be higher.) For a 45-hour week, that's $8,685 per year; at 50 hours per week, $9,650. For the sake of comparison, I can attest that in the fall of 1998 full-time in-state undergraduate tuition for my son in the College of Engineering at the University of Illinois, Urbana-Champaign, was slightly more than half as expensive as 45 hours of child care for a child less than three: in 1998, college tuition was $3984; average daycare center child care in 1998, as I said above, cost $7897 but licensed, accredited child care cost at least $8685. His college tuition was 85 percent of what I paid for forty hours per week of unlicensed child care eighteen years earlier ($4690). As I recall, my annual take-home salary as an assistant professor of English at Northwestern University (Evanston, Illinois) was between $13,000 and $15,000—and we were still paying down our own college loans. It should also be kept in mind that child care costs much more in cities than it does in rural areas—where, however, child care can be very hard to find at all. Child care also costs dramatically more in some regions than others, and it costs more per hour for less than a regular 40-hour week.

6. "We need to open a debate on how much parental care children truly need given the trade-offs between providing money and providing care. A good place to start is with the consensus that children are not best served if both parents are away from home eleven hours a day. This means that the jobs that require fifty-hour workweeks are designed in a way that conflicts with the norm of parental care. Beyond the fifty-hour week, little consensus exists about how

much childcare is delegable." Joan Williams, *Unbending Gender: Why Family and Work Conflict and What To Do About It* (Oxford and New York: Oxford University Press, 2000), p. 53; see also pp. 52–54 on norm of parental care. "How much childcare is delegable" obviously depends on both the age of the child and the quality of substitute care that is available. In the absence of government regulation and support of child care, high quality care will depend upon either good luck or a very high income—or both. For a sharp, intelligent argument that it is in the interest of businesses to accommodate to parents when their children are young, see Felice Swartz, "Management Women and the New Facts of Life," *Harvard Business Review* (January-February 1989), pp. 65–76. This is the infamous "Mommy track" essay that provoked an uproar among elite women insisting that they could in fact do everything all at once all on their own. Young parents with fewer delusions of grandeur will find this essay a useful resource.

7. For average hours a week in child care, see Jennifer Ehrle, Gina Adams, and Kathryn Tout, "Who's Caring for Our Youngest Children? Child Care Patterns of Infants and Toddlers," Occasional Paper Number 42 (Washington, D.C.: Urban Institute, January 2001, www.urban.org), p. 9. For child care provided by father and other relatives, see figure 2, p. 5. These authors cite scholarly sources for their claims. For figures regarding care of children less than five, see www.familyandhome.org/media/facts.htm, citing Lynne M. Caspar, *Who's Minding Our Preschoolers?* P70–53 (Washington, D.C.: 1996).

Other sources documenting the percentage of children cared for by their own families are as follows. For child-care arrangements of employed mothers, see Kristin Smith, *Who's Minding the Kids? Child Care Arrangements: Spring 1997,* Current Population Reports P70–86 (Washington, D.C.: U.S. Census Bureau, July 2002), table 2, page 4. This report can be accessed online in PDF format at www.census.gov by clicking "Subjects A-Z" and selecting "child care data" under "C." For percentages of mothers in the workforce by age of child, see Bureau of Labor statistics cited by Deborah Phillips and Gina Adams, "Child Care and Our Youngest Children, *The Future of Children,* vol. 11, no. 1 (spring/summer 2001), figure 1, p. 36. This essay can be accessed online at www.futureofchildren.org or through a hotlink at www.nccic.org by clicking "Online Library" then searching under "Infant and Toddler Childcare" in a drop-down menu, then reading through an alphabetical list of titles.

Another source of relevant information is the National Survey of America's Families, a project of the Urban Institute which surveys a representative sample of roughly 2,500 households. This research finds that, among mothers with children less than age three, women with a college degree are half as likely to rely upon relatives for child care than women with a high school diploma. (Only 12% of women, nationwide, have a college degree.) See Jennifer Ehrle, Gina Adams, and Kathryn Tout, *Who's Caring for Our Youngest Children? Child Care Patterns of Infants and Toddlers*, Occasional Paper Number 42 (Washington, D.C.: Urban Institute, 2001), figure 2, page 5, and table A5, page 23. This report can be accessed online at www.urban.org or through hotlinks at www.nccic.org.

It should also be noted that a person is counted as being "in the workforce" if he or she can report working for pay as little as one hour in the preceding two weeks. When my children were very young, I counted as "in the workforce" because I was working freelance a dozen hours a week while the children were napping, or after they went to bed, or on weekends. When our three- or four-year-old children went to preschool for a few hours a few mornings a week, that counted as "daycare." Many years later, for several years running I did not count as "in the workforce" although I was putting in fifty hours a week writing a book for which I had not yet received an advance on royalties. Social reality is always more complicated than even the maze of tables and charts assembled by the wizard number-crunchers at the Census Bureau and the Bureau of Labor.

8. See the comprehensive discussion of income and child-care issues provided by the organization Family and Home on their website, familyandhome.org. From the opening screen, click "Defy the Stereotypes" to find the table of contents to an essay, "At-Home Mothers Defy the Stereotypes: Setting the Record Straight" (revised December 1999). The table of contents is a set of hotlinks; one can get directly to the whole essay by clicking on point I: "six important facts about at-home parenting." According to 1997 Census Bureau figures, the median annual income of fathers with employed wives and children under eighteen is $37,116; the median annual income of fathers with nonemployed wives and children under eighteen is nearly identical: $35,713. Nonemployed mothers are not exclusively the rich wives of high-income professionals. Deborah Fallows makes much the same point: "Women married to men whose earnings place them in the bottom fifth of the income distribution are more likely to work than women married to men in the upper fifth—but only slightly more than those in the middle. It seems that although economics certainly plays an important role in women's decisions to work, money is by no means the only or always the most important factor. Many families decide that the costs of one income, which are mainly financial, are easier to bear than the emotional costs of trying to earn two" (*A Mother's Work* [Boston: Houghton-Mifflin, 1985], pp. 143–144). For instance, in a married-couple household with children less than eighteen and a mother not in the workforce, in 2001 the father's median income is $45,541. For the sake of comparison, the median income of men of any age with a college degree is $47,325. Fathers with children less than eighteen are of course younger men; the median salary of *all* men with college degrees will be higher than the average income of young fathers because the median of *all* men includes the greater earnings of older men at the peak of their careers. The median *household* income of a family of three is $43,275. Median income figures can be found in *Statistical Abstracts of the United States: 2001* (Washington, D.C.: U.S. Census Bureau, 2001), table 674, p. 439, and table 675, p. 440, and in Deborah Phillips and Gina Adams, "Child Care and Our Youngest Children, *The Future of Children*, vol. 11, no. 1 (spring/summer 2001), figure 1, p. 46. This essay can be accessed online at www.futureofchildren.org or through a hotlink at www.nccic.org by clicking "Online Library" then searching under "Infant and Toddler Childcare" in a drop-down menu, then reading through an alphabetical list of titles.

9. Robert M. Bellah et al., *Habits of the Heart: Individualism and Commitment in American Life* (Berkeley: University of California Press, 1985, rpt. New York: Harper & Row, 1986), p. 21, pp. 47–48. For a quick review of the history of child care, setting the policy issues into an astute sociopolitical context, see

Elizabeth Lasch-Quinn's review essay, "Mothers and Markets," *New Republic* (6 March 2000), pp. 37–42.

10. Excellent Internet sources include several sites that understand "child care" to mean "the care of children" not "substitute care." They include hotlinks both to other, similar websites and to documents on a wide variety of topics. My favorite is the National Child Care Information Center (www.nccic.org). It's a function of the U.S. Department of Health and Human Services, and it offers an intelligently select array of very high-quality sources. The National Network for Child Care (www.nncc.org) includes more links overall. Some of these are to such stuff as press releases, but there are gems nonetheless—and it's an excellent gateway to other organizations. Major bibliographies of NICHD child-care findings are available directly from the National Institutes of Child Health and Human Development (www.nichd.nih.gov/about/od/secc/pubs.htm). As of August 2002, it offered a list of fifty-one published papers, eight papers awaiting publication, and forty-five presentations made at academic conferences but not yet submitted for publication. Another, apparently related site offers scholarly abstracts for at least some of these articles (http://secc.rti.org/abstracts.cfm). In addition there is a dated although interesting website describing the NICHD child-care studies and summarizing their findings as of spring 1998 (www.nichd.nih.gov/publications/pubs/early_child_care.htm). This document is also available from a hotlink under the list of publications available at nccic.org.

11. For instance, three-year-olds whose mothers did not work before they were nine months old scored at the 50th percentile on school readiness; children the same age whose mothers were employed more than thirty hours a week scored at the 44th percentile. At age three, all of these children were from average home environments and in average-quality child care. But as we have seen, "average-quality" child care is probably inadequate. Such studies are very important for policy specialists who want to argue for the regulation of child-care providers and centers, but for ordinary parents it doesn't mean much beyond the all-too-familiar caution about the hazards of "average-quality" child care. See Tamar Lewin, "Study Links Working Mothers to Slower Learning," *New York Times* (17 July 2002), p. A11. The research report was published in *Child Development* (17 July 2002). Still other child-care children are three times as likely (17% vs. 6%) to have elevated scores for aggressive behavior once they reach school age, in comparison to children who had more contact with their own mothers (Sheryl Gayl Stolberg, "Researchers Find a Link Between Behavioral Problems and Time in Child Care," *New York Times* national edition [19 April 2001], p. A18). In interviews, the lead researchers explained that these elevated scores for aggressive behavior were independent of such key variables as type or quality of child care, the sex of the child, the family's income, and the mother's own skill at mothering. But chasing after individual research reports is a recipe for insanity for parents who do not have Ph.D.s in developmental psychology. The number and scope of research reports is enormous. A far better source is nonpolemical professional summaries, which are not always easy to find. One sane, balanced, articulate summary is by Deborah Phillips, chair of psychology at Georgetown, and Gina Adams, senior research associate and director of child-care research at The Urban Institute, "Child Care and Our Youngest Children,

The Future of Children, vol. 11, no. 1 (spring/summer 2001): 35–51. The paper is available online at www.futureofchildren.org and via hotlinks from a variety of places. The easiest of these is nccic.org. Click "online library," search in the drop-down menu under "infant & toddler child care" and then look for the title. Another excellent source, this time from the National Academy of Sciences, is "Growing Up in Childcare," a chapter in *From Neurons to Neighborhoods: The Science of Early Childhood Development,* ed. Jack P. Shonkoff and Deborah A. Phillips [Washington, D.C.: National Academy Press, 2000), pp. 297–327. To read this report online in PDF format, go to www.nap.edu and search for the title. Those with a more scholarly bent might consult a long, very technical summary of child-care research by Jay Belsky, "Emanuel Miller Lecture: Developmental Risks (Still) Associated with Early Child Care," *Journal of Child Psychology and Psychiatry and Allied Disciplines,* vol. 42, no. 7 (2001): 845–859. If you do not have access to a university library with a subscription (or a community library with good interlibrary-loan partners), go to www.journals.cambridge.org, click "take the tour," then click "browse journals," then select "alphabetically," then find the journal name. From there one gets to a list of back issues, and thence to the table of contents for this issue, and to news that the article can be purchased for $15. The article is not particularly readable, but it may be worth $15 to convince yourself of how fabulously complicated child-care research is no matter what—there are an amazing number of relevant variables that have to be controlled for somehow. Appreciating that fact alone provides some level of immunity against spinmeistering and sweeping statements in the popular press. In general, the more sweeping the media claim about "what scientists have found" about child care, the less likely it is to be valid. See also note 24, below, in which this essay is cited verbatim. See also note 10, above, for other sources. See also www.walgreens.com to order aspirin.

12. On other varieties of the double bind women face as a result of gender ideologies, don't miss Kathleen Hall Jamieson's brilliant study, *Beyond the Double Bind: Women and Leadership* (New York and Oxford: Oxford University Press, 1995). As a scholar, Jamieson was outraged by the misrepresentations of Susan Faludi's book *Backlash: The Undeclared War Against American Women* (New York: Crown, 1991). Jamieson adeptly describes both the troubles we face and—*contra* Faludi—the very real progress we have made in overcoming the gender ideology endemic to Western thought. *Beyond the Double Bind* is a great book to give twenty-something daughters—or to place high on your reading list if you are that age yourself!

13. I came upon a couple of excellent lists of questions that parents should consider. Such lists can be daunting but nonetheless very useful as parents try to navigate this terrain and to communicate intelligently with one another. Take a look, then, at Harriet Lerner, Ph.D., *The Mother Dance: How Children Change Your Life: Seldom-Heard Wisdom, Stories, and Healing Advice* (New York: HarperCollins, 1998), p. 13, p. 21. Her questions are most useful for people considering getting pregnant or adopting a child. Parents already facing a child might consult Penelope Leach, *Your Growing Child: From Babyhood Through Adolescence* (New York: Knopf, 1996), pp. 697–706.

Chapter 14. Parents in the Cross Fire: *Disputes among Academics*

14. If this claim seems to you even a bit overstated, take a close look at Bram Dijkstra's two books on nineteenth- and early-twentieth-century images of women in Western art and culture: *Idols of Perversity: Fantasies of Feminine Evil in Fin-de-Siècle Culture* (Oxford and New York: Oxford University Press, 1986) and *Evil Sisters: The Threat of Female Sexuality and the Cult of Manhood* (New York: Knopf, 1996). Some pictures are worth innumerable words.

15. For instance, Susan H. Greenberg and Karen Springen report that "when faced with the choice about where to send their kids, more parents are choosing daycare than any other option, including relatives or family care in a neighbor's home" (*Newsweek* [16 October 2000], pp. 61–62). Later in the same paragraph, they cite the National Survey of America's Families that 32% of parents have their children in daycare centers. That is, the overwhelming majority of parents (68%) are *not* choosing daycare centers. Furthermore, a pie chart later in the article shows that 47% of employed mothers leave their children either in the care of their husbands or in the care of other relatives (p. 62). All that one can honestly say is that parents who have their children cared for outside their own families more often use daycare centers (32%) than either neighbors (16%) or nannies (6%). (The article included a picture of Louise Woodward, a nanny convicted of manslaughter in the shaking death of a child left in her care.) Only in the very last paragraph do the authors point out that "only a small percentage of [daycare] centers qualify as 'high quality.'" If the authors had checked a little further on this issue, they would have discovered that the overwhelming majority of preschoolers with employed mothers are cared for primarily either by their parents, their grandparents, or other relatives. Other newspaper articles offer incomplete and therefore misleading explanations of census data. For instance, Tamar Lewin is correct, strictly speaking, in her article "Now a Majority: Families with Two Parents That Work" (*New York Times* [24 October 2000], p. A14) when she points out that 59% of women with babies younger than a year old were employed in 1998. What she does not explain, however—and what she may not understand—is that government statisticians in the Department of Labor count someone as employed if she worked for pay for as little as one hour in two weeks or one week per year or fifteen hours per year in unpaid work in a family business. Note that fifteen hours per year works out to 1.25 hours per month. (For Department of Labor definitions and a host of other relevant facts, see the homepage of Family and Home, www.familyandhome.org. On the homepage, click "Defy the Stereotypes" which gets you to an outline of information their researchers have collected. Department of Labor definitions are found as a hotlink under point 4a.) Rosalind Barnett and Caryl Rivers begin a discussion of these issues by asserting that only 3% of families have mothers who are not in the workforce; their footnote says only "US Census figures, 1990" (*He Works, She Works: How Two-Income Families Are Happier, Healthier, and Better Off* [San Francisco: HarperSanFrancisco, 1996], p. 3). I can only imagine that the claim is a typographical error, but such errors are not trivial—especially not in the opening pages of a book that presents itself as government-supported scholarly research (see p. vii). Given that claim to scholarship, the footnote they provide

is also seriously inadequate: "US Census figures, 1990" covers a huge array of data and analyses of data both by Census Bureau specialists and by specialists employed within related government bureaus such as Labor or Agriculture. On the next page, Barnett and Rivers reproduce a census chart showing that roughly 23% of families with children are "traditional" couples, which itself contradicts their claim that only 3% of families with children have mothers at home. This time the documentation is complete, but the fact remains that the only way to get to a percentage like that is to ignore the distinction between full- and part-time maternal employment and above all to ignore the differences between families with babies or toddlers and families with teenagers. Nowhere do they indicate how broadly the Census Bureau defines both "in the workforce" and "families with children." Doing so would blunt their claim that two-career households are a cultural norm every household should emulate in order to be, as their subtitle has it, "happier, healthier, and better off."

16. John R. Searle offers a good short survey of the philosophy of consciousness in his review essay framing a review of David J. Chalmers, *The Conscious Mind: In Search of a Fundamental Theory*. Searle's essay is "Consciousness and the Philosophers," *New York Review of Books* (6 March 1997), pp. 43–50. See also Chalmer's letter in reply to the review and Searle's response to it in the issue of 15 May 1997, pp. 60–61. For a readable, focused history of child development as a field, see Penelope Leach, *Babyhood,* 2nd ed. (New York: Knopf, 1997), pp. 121–133.

17. Both of these statements are quoted by Robert Karen: *Becoming Attached: Unfolding the Mystery of the Infant-Mother Bond and Its Impact on Later Life* (New York: Warner, 1994), p. 325, nn. 33 and 34.

18. On what some states allow as adult:child ratios, see Robert Karen, *Becoming Attached,* p. 334; see also note 4, above, on comparative wages of daycare workers.

19. See www.aces.uiuc.edu/~CCRSCare/IllinoisChildCareQuality.htm.

20. Antonio Damasio, *The Feeling of What Happens: Body and Emotion in the Making of Consciousness* (New York: Harcourt, 1999), p. 7.

21. Damasio, *The Feeling of What Happens,* p. 39.

22. Damasio, *The Feeling of What Happens,* p. 82. Neither does Damasio claim that the study of consciousness is the be-all and end-all of psychology: ". . . solving the mystery of consciousness is not the same as solving all the mysteries of the mind. Consciousness is an indispensable ingredient of the creative human mind, but it is not all of human mind and, as I see it, it is not the summit of mental complexity either. The biological tricks that cause consciousness have powerful consequences, but I see consciousness as an intermediary rather than as the culmination of biological development. Ethics and the law, science and technology, the work of the muses and the milk of human kindness, those are my chosen summits for biological development. Surely, we would have none of that without the wonders of consciousness at the source of each new achievement. Still, consciousness is a sunrise, not the midday sun, and a sunset even less. Understanding consciousness says little or nothing about the origins of the universe, the meaning of life, or the likely destiny of both" (p. 28).

23. Robert Karen, *Becoming Attached: Unfolding the Mystery of the Infant-Mother Bond and Its Impact on Later Life* (New York: Warner, 1994), pp. 322–328. See also Penelope Leach's fine short summary of research into early development in *Babyhood,* 2nd ed. (New York: Knopf, 1997), pp. 121–133. Her summary of "current" research is by now quite dated, but her history of the field is excellent and not available elsewhere as succinctly. Her position on child care is cautious, moderate, intelligently balanced, and above all convinced that the crucial variables are the quality of care and the skill with which the adults involved understand and adapt to the particular details of their own situation. Daniel J. Siegel includes an excellent short bibliography on this topic in *The Developing Mind: Toward A Neurobiology of Interpersonal Experience* (New York: Guilford Press, 1999).

24. Jay Belsky, "Infant Day Care: A Cause for Concern?" *Zero to Three,* vol. 6, no. 5 (September 1986), pp. 1–7. Robert Karen situates this particular controversy in the larger setting of Belsky's career. See *Becoming Attached,* pp. 317–337. See also Sylvia Ann Hewlett, *When the Bough Breaks,* p. 95. This is what Belsky said in this famous essay (the italics are his own): "The point of this essay, and my reason for writing it, is not to argue that infant daycare invariably or necessarily results in an anxious-avoidant attachment and, thereby, increased risk for patterns of social development that most would regard as undesirable, but rather to raise this seemingly real possibility by organizing the available data in such terms. I cannot state strongly enough that there is sufficient evidence to lead a judicious scientist to doubt this line of reasoning; by the same token, however, there is *more than enough* evidence to lead the same judicious individual to seriously entertain it and refrain from explaining away and thus dismissing findings that may be ideologically disconcerting. Anyone who has kept abreast of the evolution of my own thinking can attest to the fact that I have not been a consistent, ideologically-driven critic of nonmaternal care, whether experienced in the first year of life or thereafter. Having struggled to maintain an open mind with respect to the data base, so that the evidence could speak for itself, I know how difficult a task this is" (p. 7). See also Belsky's own most recent summary of research findings, "Emanuel Miller Lecture: Developmental Risks (Still) Associated with Early Child Care," *Journal of Child Psychology,* vol. 42, no. 7 (2001): 845–859. Belsky's abstract—the very short summary found at the beginning of scholarly research reports—summarizes his major claim: "Evidence indicating that early, extensive, and continuous nonmaternal care is associated with less harmonious parent-child relations and elevated levels of aggression and noncompliance suggests that concerns raised about early and extensive child care 15 years ago remain valid and that alternative explanations of Belsky's originally controversial conclusion do not account for seemingly adverse effects of routine nonmaternal care that continue to be reported in the literature." In the "conclusion" section of the essay itself he says, "No longer is it tenable for developmental scholars and child-care advocates to deride the notion that early and extensive nonmaternal care of the kind available in most communities poses risks for young children and perhaps the larger society as well. . . . How, then, to evaluate and think about early child-care and its effects upon child development in the new millennium? The first important lesson,

somehow lost in the child-care wars . . . [is that] family factors and processes are typically more predictive of child functioning than child-care factors and processes. In other words, it appears that family matters more to children's developmental well-being than child care . . . though this result may be as much (if not more) a function of shared genes as pure environmental effects. This does not mean, however, that child-care does not matter to children's psychological and behavioral development" (p. 855, column 2). Belsky's personal website is http://www.psyc.bbk.ac.uk/people/academic/belsky_j/. It includes his substantial list of scholarly publications.

Any talk at all about "nonmaternal care" particularly enrages some feminists, because it seems to suggest that fathers are inferior at parenting. Given the theoretical foundations of attachment theory, however, research bias actually works in the other direction. By lumping fathers and grandparents into the same category as nannies and workers in daycare centers, the impact of nonmaternal care should be diluted, not enhanced. If nonmaternal care is associated with problems *even when the set of nonmaternal-care kids include those cared for by fathers and grandparents,* then maybe something serious is going on. For the purposes of experimental statistical design, however, it is remarkably easier to ask whether or not a child is cared for by its own mother, and then variously ignore or control for the difference in quality of care that mothers themselves provide. Census Bureau data suggest that roughly 25% of fathers take care of their own children while their wives are employed; 20% of fathers are the primary caregiver—that is, children spend more time with their fathers than with their mothers or with other caregivers. Evidence also suggests that the percentage of active fathers varies by region and by the state of the national economy: when the national economy is in a slump, relatively more fathers take more active roles in the lives of their children. See Lynn M. Casper, "My Daddy Takes Care of Me! Fathers as Care Providers" Report P70–59 (Washington, D.C.: Census Bureau Current Population Report, September 1997). This report can be accessed in PDF format online from the opening screen of www.census.gov by clicking the "publications" hotlink. On the next screen, click "publication subject index," and then "child care/support," and then read through a list of reports by report number (P70–59). David Popenoe argues that child well-being, particularly as measured through adolescence and young adulthood, is strongly associated with actively involved fathers; well-being negatively correlates with father absence. See David Popenoe, *Life Without Father: Compelling New Evidence That Fatherhood and Marriage Are Indispensable for the Good of Children and Society* (New York: Martin Kessler/Free Press, 1996).

25. See Karen, *Becoming Attached,* chapter 11, "The Strange Situation."

26. Karen, *Becoming Attached,* pp. 328–329.

27. T. G. O'Connor, M. Rutter, and the English and Romanian Adoptees Study Team, "Attachment Disorder Behavior Following Early Severe Deprivation: Extension and Longitudinal Follow-Up," *Journal of the American Academy of Child and Adolescent Psychiatry,* vol. 39 (June 2000): 703. This research is nicely summarized and discussed in "Attachment Disorder Draws Closer Look," *Science News,* vol. 157, no. 22 (27 May 2000): 343.

28. Martin Teicher, "Scars that Won't Heal: The Neurobiology of Child Abuse," *Scientific American* (March 2002), pp. 68–75.

29. Karen, *Becoming Attached,* pp. 328–329. See also J. Belsky and J. Cassidy, "Attachment: Theory and Evidence," in *Developmental Principles and Clinical Issues in Psychology and Psychiatry,* ed. M. Rutter, D. Hay, and S. Baron-Cohen (Oxford: Blackwell, 1995), cited in Karen's bibliography.

30. Jerome Kagan, *Three Seductive Ideas* (Cambridge, Mass.: Harvard University Press, 1998), p. 108.

31. Kagan, *Three Seductive Ideas,* pp. 105–107.

32. Siegel, *The Developing Mind,* p. xi.

33. Kagan, *Three Seductive Ideas,* pp. 98–105.

34. See, for instance, Antonio Damasio, *The Feeling of What Happens* and *Descartes' Error: Emotion, Reason, and the Human Brain* (New York: HarperCollins, 1994, rpt. 2000); Stanley Greenspan, *The Growth of the Mind;* Daniel Siegel, *The Developing Mind*; and *From Neurons to Neighborhoods: The Science of Early Childhood Development,* ed. Jack P. Shonkoff and Deborah A. Phillips [Washington, D.C.: National Academy Press, 2000).

35. All of these numbers are from Siegel, *The Developing Mind,* p. 13. A more accessible source for this information, however, is Mark William Dubin, *How the Brain Works* (Malden, Mass.: Blackwell, 2002). Anyone educated primarily in the humanities, wishing to pursue the issues raised in this chapter, would be well advised to read through Dubin lightly and then keep it at hand for reference.

36. Siegel, *The Developing Mind,* p. 25.

37. See, for instance, Daniel Weinberger, "A Brain Too Young for Good Judgment," *New York Times* (10 March 2001), p. A27. See also a Public Broadcasting Service special on the question: http://www.pbs.org/wgbh/pages/frontline/shows/teenbrain/. For a review of research on the issue, see H. T. Chugani, "A Critical Period of Brain Development. Studies of Glucose Utilization with PET," *Preventive Medicine,* vol. 27, no. 2 (March-April 1998): 184–188.

38. Siegel, *The Developing Mind,* p. x.

39. Siegel, *The Developing Mind,* p. 26.

40. Siegel, *The Developing Mind,* pp. 13–14.

41. Daniel Stern, *The Interpersonal World of the Infant: A View from Psychoanalysis and Developmental Psychology* (New York: Basic, 1985), p. 38ff. For a sketch of the major stages of infant development according to Stern, see p. 11 and following. Stern also has written a couple of popular books attempting to present his research in ways accessible to ordinary parents, but to my sensibilities his angle of address to women is quite condescending in a very dated way. Although this book is slow going for nonspecialists, it is by far the most useful source for this important research.

42. Siegel, *The Developing Mind,* p. 85.

43. Stern, *The Interpersonal World of the Infant,* pp. 192–200. See also Karen, *Becoming Attached,* pp. 346–357.

44. T. Berry Brazelton, M.D., and Stanley Greenspan, M.D., *The Irreducible Needs of Children: What Every Child Must Have to Grow, Learn, and Flourish* (Cambridge, Mass.: Perseus, 2000), p. 12.

45. Greenspan, *The Growth of the Mind and the Endangered Origins of Intelligence,* makes this argument generally.

46. Siegel, *The Developing Mind,* p. 4, p. 70.

47. Siegel, *The Developing Mind,* pp. 69–71.

48. Stern, *The Interpersonal World of the Infant,* p. 208; see also pp. 208–210.

49. The Adult Attachment Inventory is explained by Siegel, *The Developing Mind,* pp. 77–83 and pp. 89–92, and by Karen, *Becoming Attached,* pp. 363–369. It seems to me logical that low-scoring adults may be slightly overrepresented in the cohort of parents putting their infants into child care, or that the children of such parents may have disproportionate difficulty coping with child care. If so, "child-care data" will be distorted. But sorting the data with that quality of epidemiological filter will be difficult at best—perhaps impossible or at least impossibly expensive. This is a classic instance of the kind of statistical problem posed by the limits we place upon human experimentation with babies. I was explaining all this one day to a Ph.D. engineer with a young daughter, and she erupted: "This is all variables! It's nothing *but* variables! How can anyone draw conclusions from *variables?"* This is why I have always found my close friends among science-and-technology types: they can so often cut to the heart of a matter.

50. Esther M. Sternberg, M.D., *The Balance Within: The Science Connecting Health and Emotions* (New York: Freeman, 2000); Shelley E. Taylor, *The Tending Instinct: How Nurturing Is Essential To Who We Are and How We Live* (New York: Holt, 2002).

51. Penelope Leach, *Your Baby and Child,* 3rd ed. (New York: Knopf, 1998), p. 144.

52. Richard Lewontin, *The Triple Helix: Gene, Organism, Environment* (Cambridge, Mass.: Harvard University Press, 2000), chapter 3, esp. pp. 93–99.

53. Richard Lewontin, *It Ain't Necessarily So: The Dream of the Human Genome and Other Illusions* (New York: New York Review Books, 2000), chapter 5, especially p. 147ff.

54. Lewontin, *The Triple Helix,* p. 17.

55. Lewontin, *The Triple Helix,* pp. 20–28.

56. Jerome Kagan, *Three Seductive Ideas* (Cambridge, Mass.: Harvard University Press, 1998), p. 109.

57. Kagan, *Three Seductive Ideas,* p. 118.

58. Kagan, *Three Seductive Ideas,* on sentimentality, pp. 94–96; irrationality, pp. 84–86; *The Nature of the Child* (New York: Basic, 1984), on magical thinking, p. 73; on projecting, pp. 84–85, p. 56.

59. Kagan, *Three Seductive Ideas,* p. 147.

60. Lewontin, *It Ain't Necessarily So,* p. 193.

61. Daniel Schacter, *Seven Sins of Memory: How the Mind Forgets and Remembers* (Boston and New York: Houghton Mifflin, 2001), p. 196.

62. Stephen J. Gould, "Men of the Third-Third Division," *Natural History,* vol. 90 (1990): 13–24. Cited by Jay Belsky, "Emanuel Miller Lecture: Developmental Risks (Still) Associated with Early Child Care," *Journal of Child Psychology and Psychiatry and Allied Disciplines,* vol. 42, no. 7 (2001): 845–859.

63. Kagan, *Three Seductive Ideas,* pp. 128–129.

64. Judith Rich Harris, *The Nurture Assumption: Why Children Turn Out the Way They Do* (New York: Free Press, 1998), p. 73. See also Howard Gardner's review of *The Nurture Assumption,* "Do Parents Count?" *New York Review of Books* (5 November 1998), pp. 19–22, and Sharon Begley "The Parent Trap," *Newsweek* (7 September 1998), pp. 52–59.

65. Schacter, *Seven Sins of Memory,* on remembering painful events, pp. 164–165; on the neurobiology of remembering, especially remembering painful events, pp. 178–183; on the survival or evolutionary value of such memories, pp. 201–202.

66. The research literature on this topic is immense. See, for instance, C. A. Nelson and L. J. Carver, "The effects of stress and trauma on brain and memory: a view from developmental cognitive neuroscience," *Development and Psychopathology,* vol. 10, no. 4 (fall 1998): 793–809; M. R. Gunnar, "Quality of early care and buffering of neuroendocrine stress reactions: potential effects on the developing human brain," *Preventive Medicine,* vol. 27, no. 2 (March-April 1998): 208–211.

67. Dan P. McAdams, *The Stories We Live By: Personal Myths and the Making of the Self* (New York: Guilford, 1993).

68. For a wonderful account of how philosophically sophisticated sociologists have coped and theorized and responded to the problem of "self," see James A. Holstein and Jaber F. Gubrium, *The Self We Live By: Narrative Identity in a Postmodern World* (Oxford and New York: Oxford University Press, 2000). The concept "self" dissolves away under all the same arguments as those used to deny the possibility that we have or can have accurate knowledge of any reality outside of consciousness.

69. James C. Edwards, *The Plain Sense of Things: The Fate of Religion in an Age of Normal Nihilism* (University Park: Pennsylvania State University Press, 1997), discussed above, part three.

70. Intellectually serious East-West spiritual dialogue is very difficult to follow if you are not both educated and personally experienced in one tradition or the other. Here are three good starting places. His Holiness the Dalai Lama, *The Good Heart: A Buddhist Perspective on the Teachings of Jesus,* trans. Geshe Thupten Jimpa, ed. Robert Kiely (Boston: Wisdom, 1996). The Dalai Lama's interlocutor is a Benedictine monk, Dom Laurence Freeman OSB, who is described as "spiritual head of the World Community for Christian Meditation." I also recommend Laurence Freeman's own book, *Jesus: The Teacher Within* (New York and London: Continuum, 2000). Easier than either of these but very wise in its own way is Thich Nhat Hahn, *Living Buddha, Living Christ* (New York: Riverhead, 1995). Hahn's interpretation of Christianity is very clearly situated within Buddhism, but on the whole I find that easier to cope with and on some key issues less inaccurate than the interpretation of Christianity offered by literal-minded Christian fundamentalists. See also Elaine Pagels, *The Gnostic Gospels* (1979, rpt. New York: Vintage, 1989).

71. Laurence Steinberg, *Beyond the Classroom: Why School Reform Has Failed and What Parents Need to Do* (New York: Touchstone/Simon & Schuster, 1996), pp. 118–121. Notice that the percentage of disengaged parents that he finds matches the percentage of insecurely attached children that attachment

researchers find in the general population of children cared for at home by their parents in the first year.

72. Robert Inchausti, *The Ignorant Perfection of Ordinary People* (Albany: State University of New York Press, 1991), p. 12: ". . . our humanity is neither a fiction nor a birthright but an ethical accomplishment."

73. Christine Gudorf, "Parenting, Mutual Love, and Sacrifice," in *Religion, Feminism, and the Family,* ed. Anne Carr and Mary Stewart Van Leeuwen (Louisville, Ky.: Westminster John Knox, 1996), pp. 294–309.

Part 6: Survival and Integrity: *Defining Our Choices, Living Our Lives*

1. Henry David Thoreau, *Walden and Civil Disobedience,* ed. Owen Thomas, A Norton Critical Edition (New York: Norton, 1966), p. 5.

Chapter 15. The Question of Conscience

2. Roger Stark and Roger Finke, *Acts of Faith: Explaining the Human Side of Religion* (Berkeley: University of California Press, 2000), pp. 57–79.

3. *The Problematics of Moral and Legal Theory*, cited in *Context,* vol. 34, no. 8 (15 April 2002), p. 2. For more on Posner's relativism, see Gertrude Himmelfarb's essay in *Commentary* (February 2002).

4. On standards of proof or veracity in argument, see Stephen Toulmin, *Return to Reason* (Cambridge, Mass.: Harvard University Press, 2001). The "error of all rationalist philosophy," according to Toulmin, "[is] assuming that ethical theory and moral practice alike must be grounded in principles whose relevance is timeless and universal" (p. 134).

5. Voltaire, Letter to Frederick the Great, 6 April 1767.

6. *The AntiChrist,* no. 51 in *The Portable Nietzsche,* selected and translated by Walter Kaufman (New York: Penguin, 1959), p. 634.

7. Philip Rieff, *The Triumph of the Therapeutic: Uses of Faith After Freud* (Chicago: University of Chicago Press, 1979): ". . . in the classical tradition of social theory, the sense of well-being of the individual was dependent on his full, participant membership in a community. The other traditional theory, also powerful and by now equally venerable, was that men must free themselves from binding attachments to communal purposes in order to express more freely their individualities. A third view entered at this point: that there is no positive community now within which the individual can merge himself therapeutically" (p. 71). A "positive community" is one that "guarantees some kind of salvation to the individual by virtue of his membership and participation in that community" (p. 52).

8. Ignatius's own account of this is quietly charming: "In the case of persons who are earnestly purging away their sins, and who are progressing from good to better in the service of God our Lord . . . it is characteristic of the evil spirit to cause gnawing anxiety, to sadden, and to set up obstacles" (*Ignatius of Loyola: Spiritual Exercises and Selected Works,* ed. George E. Ganss, S.J., *The Classics of Western Spirituality,* gen. ed. Bernard McGinn [New York: Paulist, 1991], p. 201, which is *The Spiritual Exercises,* section 315. Roberta Bondi beautifully

explains relevant issues in *Memories of God: Theological Reflections on a Life* (Nashville: Abingdon, 1995).

9. See, for instance, L. William Countryman, *Living on the Border of the Holy: Renewing the Priesthood of All* (Harrisburg, Pa.: Morehouse, 1999), p. 54.

10. Writing in the *New York Times* (12 May 2001, p. A17), Peter Steinfels neatly describes how the common culture ordinarily distinguishes between religious convictions and secular convictions. Religious convictions, supposedly, are either revealed or radically authoritarian in their presentation and interpretation; secular convictions are based upon arguments, data, etc., and are thus open to change, compromise, and so forth. In fact, of course, even the most strictly secular arguments still have their foundation in assumptions, prior suppositions, etc. Every argument does. And anyone who reads seriously in religious tradition finds not monolithic consensus but ferocious debate.

11. Alan Wolfe, *Moral Freedom: The Impossible Idea That Defines the Way We Live Now* (New York: Norton, 2001); Gertrude Himmelfarb, *The De-Moralization of Society: From Victorian Virtues to Modern Values* (New York: Knopf, 1995) and *One Nation, Two Cultures* (New York: Knopf, 1999).

12. Philip Rieff: "The death of a culture begins when its normative institutions fail to communicate ideals in ways that remain inwardly compelling, first of all to the cultural elites themselves. . . . In what does the self now try to find salvation, if not in the breaking of corporate [communal] identities and in an acute suspicion of all normative institutions?" *The Triumph of the Therapeutic*, pp. 18–19.

13. Linda Hogan, *Confronting the Truth: Conscience in the Catholic Tradition* (New York: Paulist, 2000), p. 15.

14. Thoreau, *Walden and Civil Disobedience,* ed. Owen Thomas, p. 61.

15. Thoreau, *Walden and Civil Disobedience,* ed. Owen Thomas, p. 61.

16. In short form, the authoritarian argument goes like this: *Life is complex and so it is difficult to recognize the good. Furthermore, some people are dumb, some people are lazy, some people are careless, and everyone is fallible. Surely, then, we are all better off allowing committees of the legal, scholarly, and/or ecclesial authorities to figure out the good for us. Our duty is to obey them rather than struggling endlessly to recognize and to remain cognizant of the good as it is manifest in our own lives.* Such authoritarian claims explain the Roman Catholic concern to avoid "scandal" that might discredit the ecclesial hierarchy and to avoid any public debate, even among professional theologians speaking principally to one another, that might "confuse" the laity. On the other hand, the authoritarian turn of Roman Catholicism since the declaration of papal infallibility in the mid-nineteenth century is sharply disputed within Catholicism itself; one such group, Call To Action, organizes large annual conventions. There is an excellent short discussion of conscience and ecclesial authority in Philip S. Kaufman, *Why You Can Disagree and Remain a Faithful Catholic,* rev. ed. (New York: Crossroad, 1998). The theologically sophisticated will have already recognized that my approach to ethics is relatively more "Catholic" than "Protestant" in my sacramental view of life, in my deployment of theological resources, and in my emphasis upon community. On the other hand, I am more "Protestant" than "Catholic" in my straightforward presumption that the individual is centrally responsible for clear,

analytically sophisticated thinking about moral issues: virtue is not equivalent to obeying the bishops. The most powerful influence, I suspect, is Celtic tradition: neither Rome nor the Reformation had much impact on that little island beyond an island beyond the western edge of the known world.

17. Hogan, *Confronting the Truth,* p. 12. Aquinas argued that the truly universal aspects of the good are massively abstract (*Summa Theologiae,* Ia, IIae, 94a:1–4, as translated in *Summa Theologiae: A Concise Translation,* ed. Timothy McDermott [Allen, Tex.: Christian Classics, 1989], pp. 286–288). Such abstract principles are remote from the messy particularity of human lives, which are best governed by the good hearts of those whose lives are at stake. "No one can willfully turn away from happiness," Aquinas argues, "for man wants happiness by nature. So no one seeing God for what he is can willfully turn his back on God. Plainly then, since Adam sinned, he had not seen God for what he is" (*Summa Theologiae,* Ia, 94a:1, edition cited above, p. 145). Aquinas's relative confidence in the natural human yearning for God and for the good nonetheless gave way to huge, elaborate "casebooks" in which Catholic priests could look up "expert opinion" on any issue. The word "casuistry" now means specious or deliberately misleading logical argument, but the term derives from "casus" meaning "case." "Applied ethics"—in business, medicine, law, etc.—is still often taught by "case studies." "Casuistry" is merely the older term for a case-studies approach.

18. Hogan, *Confronting the Truth,* p. 77.

19. Hogan, *Confronting the Truth,* pp. 81–83.

20. Samuel Taylor Coleridge, *Biographia Literaria, or Biographical Sketches of My Literary Life and Opinions,* vol. 1, ed. J. Shawcross (London: Oxford University Press, 1907), p. 135.

21. Stanley Hauerwas, "Connections Created and Contingent: Aquinas, Preller, Wittgenstein, and Hopkins" (unpublished paper). Hauerwas says he is quoting himself in *With the Grain of the Universe: The Church's Witness and Natural Theology* (Grand Rapids, Mich.: Brazos, 2001), p. 15. That passage says the same thing in more technical language.

22. This portrait of imagination is derived from Samuel Taylor Coleridge, poet and theologian both. I have written about the religious dimension of Coleridge's concept of imagination at various times. For instance, *The Design of 'Biographia Literaria'* (London: George Allen & Unwin, 1983), or "Faith and Fiction: Literature as Revelation," *Anglican Theological Review,* vol. 78, no. 3 (summer 1996): 382–403, or "Storytelling, Doctrine, and Spiritual Formation" *Anglican Theological Review,* vol. 81, no. 1 (winter 1999): 39–60.

23. I have written at some length about how it is possible to reconcile personal authenticity with ongoing commitment to a relationship. See *For Fidelity: How Intimacy and Commitment Enrich Our Lives* (New York: Knopf, 1998).

24. Guy Claxson, *Hare Brain, Tortoise Mind: How Intelligence Increases When You Think Less* (Great Britain: Fourth Estate, 1997; rpt. Hopewell, N.Y.: Ecco, 1999), pp. 191–192.

25. Rosemary Radford Reuther is an eminent feminist historian and Roman Catholic theologian. This passage is from "*Mandatum* threatens covenant of respect," *National Catholic Reporter* (27 April 2001), p. 17.

Chapter 16. The Arts of Moral Discernment

26. Frank Rogers Jr. offers a superb short overview of discernment in his essay "Discernment" in *Practicing Our Faith,* ed. Dorothy C. Bass (San Francisco: Jossey-Bass, 1997). Don't miss his suggestions for further reading, under "References," pp. 210–211. William Spohn delicately explores the psychodynamic and moral complexity of how discernment and self-image are woven into the narrative bases of identity in "The Reasoning Heart: An American Approach to Christian Discernment" in *The Reasoning Heart: Toward a North American Theology,* ed. Frank M. Oppenheim, S.J. (Washington, D.C.: Georgetown University Press, 1986), pp. 51–76. It's a superb piece, and I particularly recommend it for readers who are not familiar with (or not particularly comfortable with) the languages of Christian theology. Bill generously recommended two other books to me, to be read (he said) in this order—a bit of advice I cheerfully share. First, William A. Barry, S.J., *Paying Attention to God: Discernment in Prayer* (Notre Dame, Ind.: Ave Maria, 1990) and then David Lonsdale, S.J., *Listening to the Music of the Spirit: The Art of Discernment* (Notre Dame, Ind.: Ave Maria, 1992). These are both small, practical books; for longer, more comprehensive treatment, see David Lonsdale, *Eyes to See, Ears to Hear: An Introduction to Ignatian Spirituality,* Traditions of Christian Spirituality Series, gen. ed., Philip Sheldrake (Maryknoll, N.Y.: Orbis, 2000). I like the clarity with which Lonsdale explains, "it is a fundamental tenet of an Ignatian spirituality that God is to be met in all circumstances of life" (p. 145). He also offers a chapter-long biography of Ignatius. Those who like primary documents might take a look at sections 169–189 and 313–316 of Ignatius's *Spiritual Exercises.* They can be found in *Ignatius of Loyola: Spiritual Exercises and Selected Works,* ed. George E. Ganss, S.J., The Classics of Western Spirituality (New York: Paulist, 1991). Carelessly popular accounts of discernment at times give the impression that the spiritual seeker is merely trying to guess an assignment or a decision that God has made but cannot or will not reveal to the believer in some easier way. "What am I to do" can seem to mean nothing more than "what is the docile, obedient response required of me here?" There can be no doubt that sometimes discernment has in fact been understood in exactly that way. And sometimes the label "discernment" is used by individuals wishing to claim divine authority for their own opinion in a contested matter. Such excesses to one side or another are humanly inevitable. The fact remains that true discernment is a highly sophisticated spiritual and meditative practice within Christian tradition.

27. Dennis J. Billy, C.Ss.R., and James Keating, *Conscience and Prayer: The Spirit of Catholic Moral Theology* (Collegeville, Minn.: Liturgical Press, 2001), p. 4. Billy and Keating cite *The Philokalia: The Complete Text,* trans. G. E. H. Palmer, Philip Sherrard, and Kallistos Ware, vol. 1 (Boston: Faber and Faber, 1979), p. 123.

28. The Greek philosophic origin of spiritual practice is argued at length—and quite persuasively—by Pierre Hadot, *Philosophy as a Way of Life,* ed. Arnold I. Davidson, trans. Michael Chase (Malden, Maine: Blackwell, 1995). See especially chapter 3, "Spiritual Exercises" and chapter 4, "Ancient Spiritual Exercises and 'Christian Philosophy.'" Hadot contends that philosophy lost its identity as a way

of life as Christianity appropriated its teachings and methods, reducing "philosophy" to the task of providing systematic and conceptual tools for theology.

29. Stanley Greenspan, with Beryl Benderly, *The Growth of the Mind and the Endangered Origins of Intelligence* (Reading, Mass.: Addison-Wesley, 1997), p. 18.

30. Greenspan, *The Growth of the Mind*, p. 25.

31. Antonio Damasio, *Descartes' Error: Emotion, Reason, and the Human Brain* (New York: Putnam, 1994), pp. 34–51. For more on the neurobiological foundations of decision-making, see Elkhonon Goldberg, *The Executive Brain: Frontal Lobes and the Civilized Mind* (Oxford and New York: Oxford University Press, 2001). I'd advise skipping both chapter 4 (an inept attempt to introduce neuroanatomy and neurophysiology to amateurs) and chapter 5 (which engages highly technical disputes with other experts). The rest, however, is fascinating and entertaining in equal measure.

32. The most comprehensive history of spiritual direction is Kenneth Leech, *Soul Friend: The Practice of Christian Spirituality* (San Francisco: Harper & Row, 1977). Gerald May distinguishes between spiritual direction and psychotherapy in *Care of Mind, Care of Spirit: A Psychiatrist Explores Spiritual Direction* (1982, rpt. San Francisco: HarperSanFrancisco, 1992). Among the raft of books on this topic, I have always cherished a small, gentle, friendly book by Margaret Guenther, *Holy Listening: The Art of Spiritual Direction* (Boston: Cowley, 1994).

33. Buddhist tradition is particularly good at describing the mayhem wrought by our incessant judgmental grousing-to-ourselves. See, for instance, His Holiness the Dalai Lama and Howard C. Cutler, M.D., *The Art of Happiness: A Handbook for Living* (New York: Riverhead, 1998); Sharon Salzberg, *LovingKindness: The Revolutionary Art of Happiness* (Boston: Shambhala, 1995); and Ron Leifer, M.D., *The Happiness Project: Transforming the Three Poisons that Cause the Suffering We Inflict Upon Ourselves and Others* (Ithaca: Snow Lion, 1997).

34. Eddie Ensley, *Visions: The Soul's Path to the Sacred* (Chicago: Loyola, 2000) is particularly good on the psychological hazards that can be involved, although I think his warnings should have appeared much earlier in the book—see pp. 247–262.

35. Jon Kabat-Zinn, *Wherever You Go There You Are: Mindfulness Meditation in Everyday Life* (New York: Hyperion, 1994). I think it's the best single book on praying that I have ever read—although he never uses the word and scrupulously avoids theological talk in any tradition whatsoever.

Appendix One: Wait Here for Rescue

1. Stephanie Coontz, *The Way We Never Were: American Families and the Nostalgia Trap* (New York: Basic, 1992), p. 22.

2. See, for instance, Edmund L. Andrews, "Optimism Recedes as Europe Faces Long-Term Issues," *New York Times* (14 June 2001), p. W.1. Faced with such pressure, as *New York Times* reporter Warren Hoge explains, Swedish traditions are being questioned by at least some within Sweden itself. For instance, income taxes "take 59 percent of the pay of people earning as little as $30,000 a year and oblige employers to pay up to 41 percent of employee remuneration

into social security and pension plans" ([10 August 1998], p. A1). Furthermore, welfare programs across the board consume 46% of Sweden's gross national product (ibid.). But we don't have to go as far as Sweden to remedy or at least limit the dangerous excesses of the global economy. See Benjamin Barber, *Jihad vs. McWorld: How Globalism and Tribalism Are Reshaping the World* (New York: Ballantine, 1995, 1996). See also above, part four, note 66.

3. John Williams, *Unbending Gender: Why Work and Family Conflict and What To Do about It.* (New York: Oxford University Press, 2000).

4. Guy Claxson, *Hare Brain, Tortoise Mind: How Intelligence Increases When You Think Less* (Hopewell, N.J.: Ecco, 1997).

5. Elinor Burkett, *Baby Boon: How Family-Friendly America Cheats the Childless* (New York: Simon & Schuster, 1999).

6. Charles Lindblom, *The Market System: What It Is, How It Works, and What to Make of It* (New Haven and London: Yale University Press, 2001).

7. Nancy Folbre, *The Invisible Heart: Economics and Family Values* (New York: New Press, 2001), p. vii.

8. On the minimum wage as a moral issue, see D. Stephen Long, *Divine Economy: Theology and the Market,* Radical Orthodoxy (London and New York: Routledge, 2000).

Appendix Two: Statistics and Spinmeistering

1. One such report is Sharon Brownlee, "Baby Talk," *U.S. News and World Report* (15 June 1998), pp. 48–55.

2. Christina Hoff Sommers, *Who Stole Feminism?: How Women Have Betrayed Women* (New York: Touchstone/Simon & Schuster, 1994).

3. Sheryl Gay Stolberg, "Researchers Find a Link Between Behavioral Problems and Time in Child Care," *New York Times* (19 April 2001), p. A18.